The Films of Woody Allen

Critical Essays

Edited by
Charles L. P. Silet

The Scarecrow Press, Inc.
Lanham, Maryland • Toronto • Oxford
2006

SCARECROW PRESS, INC.

Published in the United States of America
by Scarecrow Press, Inc.
A wholly owned subsidiary of
The Rowman & Littlefield Publishing Group, Inc.
4501 Forbes Boulevard, Suite 200, Lanham, Maryland 20706
www.scarecrowpress.com

PO Box 317
Oxford
OX2 9RU, UK

British Library Cataloguing in Publication Information Available

Library of Congress Cataloging-in-Publication Data

The films of Woody Allen : critical essays / edited by Charles L. P. Silet.
p.   cm.
Includes bibliographical references and index.
ISBN-13: 978-0-8108-5736-0 (hardcover : alk. paper)
ISBN-13: 978-0-8108-5737-7 (pbk. : alk. paper)
ISBN-10: 0-8108-5736-7 (hardcover : alk. paper)
ISBN-10: 0-8108-5737-5 (pbk. : alk. paper)
1. Allen, Woody—Criticism and interpretation.   I. Silet, Charles L. P.
PN1998.3.A45F55   2006
791.43092—dc22   2005035706

Contents

Acknowledgments

One of the pleasures of editing a book is that it provides an opportunity to recognize all of those who have offered the editor support through the years. I wish to thank the following individuals for their generous help in preparing this project: Elizabeth Beck, former director of the Honors Program, Iowa State University, for much needed funding; Charles Kostelnick, chair, Department of English, Iowa State University, for his many kindnesses; and Sheryl Kamps, who as always worked on the manuscript with patience and skill.

I would also like to thank the editors at Scarecrow Press of the Rowman & Littlefield Publishing Group who have aided in the preparation of this book in many ways, especially Stephen Ryan for his patience.

Thanks are also due to the many students in the honors seminars I have taught on Woody Allen. Their insights and responses to the readings I assigned helped immeasurably in guiding my choices for this collection.

As always the largest acknowledgment goes to my wife Kay, who has supported me intellectually and emotionally for the past thirty years.

Finally, I wish to express my gratitude to those authors and editors who so generously gave me permission to reprint their work in this collection.

Sanford Pinsker, "Woody Allen's Lovable Anxious *Schlemiels*," *Studies in American Humor* 5, no. 2–3 (Summer and Fall 1986): 177–89. Reprinted by permission of the author.

Leonard Quart, "Woody Allen's New York," *Cineaste* 19, no. 2–3 (1992): 16–19. Reprinted by permission of the editor.

Celestino Deleyto, "The Narrator and the Narrative: The Evolution of Woody Allen's Film Comedies," *Film Criticism* 19, no. 2 (Winter 1994–95): 40–54. Reprinted by permission of the editor.

Gary Commins, "Woody Allen's Theological Imagination," *Theology*

Today 44 (July 1987): 235–49. ©1987 *Theology Today*. Reprinted with permission of the publisher.

Christopher Morris, "Woody Allen's Comic Irony," *Literature/Film Quarterly* 15, no. 3 (1987): 173–80. Reprinted with permission of *Literature/Film Quarterly*, © Salisbury University, Salisbury, MD 21801.

Mark E. Bleiweiss, "Self-Deprecation and the Jewish Humor of Woody Allen," *Jewish Spectator* (Winter 1989): 25–34. Reprinted by permission of the author.

Maurice Yacowar, "Beyond Parody: Woody Allen and the 80s," *Post Script* 6, no. 2 (Winter 1987): 29–42. Reprinted by permission of the author and the editor of *Post Script*.

Wes D. Gehring, "Woody Allen and Fantasy: *Play It Again, Sam*," *Forum* (Ball State University) 28, no. 3 (Summer 1987): 25–34. Reprinted by permission of the editor.

Ronald D. LeBlanc, "*Love and Death* and Food: Woody Allen's Comic Use of Gastronomy," *Literature/Film Quarterly* 17, no. 1 (1989): 18–26. Reprinted with permission of *Literature/Film Quarterly*, © Salisbury University, Salisbury, MD 21801.

Devin Brown, "Powerful Man Gets Pretty Woman: Style Switching in *Annie Hall*," *The SECOL Review* 16, no. 2 (Fall 1992): 115–31. Reprinted by permission of the editor of *The Southern Journal of Linguistics*.

Thomas Schatz, "*Annie Hall* and the Issue of Modernism," *Literature/Film Quarterly* 10, no. 3 (1982): 180–87. Reprinted with permission of *Literature/Film Quarterly*, © Salisbury University, Salisbury, MD 21801.

Bert Cardullo, "Autumn *Interiors*, or the Ladies Eve: Woody Allen's Bergman Complex," *The North Dakota Review* 69, no. 1 (Winter 2002): 124–36. Reprinted by permission of the author.

Christopher J. Knight, "Woody Allen's *Manhattan* and the Ethicity of Narrative," *Film Criticism* 13, no. 1 (Fall 1988): 63–72. Reprinted by permission of the editor.

Louis Giannetti, "*Ciao*, Woody," *Western Humanities Review* 35, no. 2 (Summer 1981): 157–61. Reprinted by permission of the editor.

Paul Lewis, "Painful Laughter: The Collapse of Humor in Woody Allen's *Stardust Memories*," in *Studies in American Jewish Literature*, no. 5, ed. Daniel Walden (Albany, NY: State University of New York Press, 1986), 141–50. Permission granted by *Studies in American Jewish Literature* published by the University of Nebraska Press.

Iris Bruce, "Mysterious Illnesses of Human Commodities in Woody Allen and Franz Kafka," *Studies in 20th Century Literature* 22, no. 1 (Winter 1998): 173–203. Reprinted by permission of the author and editor.

Robert Stam and Ella Shohat, "*Zelig* and Contemporary Theory: Meditation on the Chameleon Text," *Enclitic* 9, no. 7–8 (1981): 176–93. Reprinted by permission of the authors.

Peter J. Bailey, "Woody's Mild Irish Rose: *Broadway Danny Rose*," in *The Reluctant Film Art of Woody Allen* by Peter J. Bailey (Louisville: University Press of Kentucky, 2001), 101–10. © University Press of Kentucky. Reprinted by permission of the University Press of Kentucky.

Michael Dunne, "*Stardust Memories* and *The Purple Rose of Cairo*, and the Tradition of Metafiction," *Film Criticism* 12, no. 1 (Fall 1987): 19–27. Reprinted by permission of the editor.

Diane Snow, "Woody Allen's *Interiors*: The Dark Side of *Hannah and Her Sisters*," *Encyclia* 64 (1987): 44–54. Reprinted by permission of the editor.

Maurice Yacowar, "The Religion of *Radio Days*," *Journal of Popular Film and Television* 16, no. 2 (Summer 1988): 80–86. Reprinted with permission of the Helen Dwight Reid Educational Foundation. Published by Heldref Publications, 1319 Eighteenth St. NW, Washington, DC 20036-1802. Copyright © 1988.

Maria del Mar Asensio Arostegui, "Hlenka Regained: Irony and Ambiguity in the Narrator of Woody Allen's *Another Woman*," *Miscelanea* 15 (1994): 1–14. Reprinted by permission of the editor.

Mark W. Roche, "Justice and the Withdrawal of God in Woody Allen's *Crimes and Misdemeanors*," *The Journal of Value Inquiry* 29, no. 4 (December 1995): 547–63. Reprinted with kind permission from Springer Science and Business Media.

Paul Nathanson, "Between Time and Eternity: Theological Notes on *Shadows and Fog*," in *Representing Religion in World Cinema: Filmmaking, Mythmaking, Culture Making*, ed. S. Brent Plate, 89–103 (New York: Palgrave Macmillan, 2003). Reproduced by permission of Palgrave Macmillan.

Introduction

The Films of Woody Allen: Critical Essays brings together a collection of scholarly articles on the cinema of Woody Allen. Some are general and examine various themes and issues raised by Allen's films, and some are specific, focusing on one or two of his more significant films. Among the themes examined in the general essays are Allen's connection to his Jewish background, both religious and cultural, his love affair with New York City, and his relation to various strains of humor, both specifically American film humor and more broadly the use of such traditional comic tropes as irony and parody. These essays were written not only by film scholars but also by authors from a variety of professional backgrounds. The essays on individual films were largely self-chosen because film critics have examined most exhaustively Allen's films from the 1980s, the period many feel is the most significant of Allen's career. However, there are some essays on Allen's films from the 1970s and the 1990s as well, including *Love and Death*, *Annie Hall*, *Interiors*, *Manhattan*, and *Shadows and Fog*.

The rationale for such a collection is twofold. The films of Woody Allen have generated a substantial interest among film scholars and professionals who have written extensively about them from a variety of cultural, aesthetic, and theoretical perspectives. The impetus behind this book is to present a selection of these critical articles that have never before been collected together; many of them were originally published in now hard-to-locate sources and some were selected from journals not usually associated with film studies. The result is an anthology of articles that presents an overview of the central issues raised by Allen's films and a close examination of some fourteen individual films in which can be found the working out of these larger themes and issues. *The Films of Woody Allen: Critical Essays* therefore presents a broad-ranging inquiry into the film art of one of America's most innovative and productive modern cinema directors.

Allen Stewart Konigsberg was born December 1, 1935, to Martin and Nettie Konigsberg, both first-generation Americans. Allen's grandparents were all Yiddish-speaking immigrants. His sister, Letty, was born in 1943. Although the Konigsbergs moved often during their son's early years, they remained primarily in Brooklyn. Two of the most vivid memories of his youth include his first visit to Manhattan and seeing his first movie, *Snow White and the Seven Dwarfs*, Walt Disney's groundbreaking first-of-its-kind feature-length animated film. Obviously, both experiences had a lasting influence.

Allen began school in 1940 at Public School 99 in Brooklyn, where he received all of his formal schooling, finally graduating from Midwood High School in 1953. Of his experiences in school he has been uniformly dismissive and has declared that he generally hated most of the experiences. By his final years in high school Allen was already moving into the adult world of entertainment by writing jokes and short quips and sending them to various newspaper columnists. In 1952 his first published joke appeared in Earl Wilson's column. Even before he graduated from Midwood he was hired to ghostwrite comic material for celebrities, and he changed his name to Woody Allen for professional reasons.

After graduation Allen enrolled in a movie production class at New York University that he failed for lack of interest. He also enrolled and then dropped out of a class at City College of New York. Clearly, formal education held little interest for him. Although his university career was short and undistinguished, his career as a comedy writer took off. He was signed by the William Morris Agency and began making good money continuing to write skits and material for a number of show business celebrities. In 1955 Allen moved to Hollywood to write for the *Colgate Comedy Hour* as part of the NBC Writer's Development program. In Hollywood he met Danny Simon, brother of the playwright Neil Simon, who became his mentor and helped him to develop his comedy writing. In the spring of 1956 Allen moved back to New York. During the rest of the 1950s Allen expanded his writing career by writing for television and creating nightclub routines for others.

In 1961 Allen branched out with his own performance routines in nightclubs and on the college and university circuit. He also began appearing on various television shows, which enhanced his visibility as a performer. Two years later Allen got his first break in films by writing and playing a part in Clive Donner's *What's New Pussycat?* which had an all-star cast and became a box office hit establishing his bankability in films. The 1960s were a hectic time for Allen. In 1965 his first play, *Don't Drink the Water*, opened on Broadway, he appeared frequently on television, and he contributed comic pieces to the *New Yorker*. His work in film continued with an appearance in John Huston's *Casino Royale* (1967), a James Bond spoof, his redubbing and reediting of a Japanese spy film that he released as *What's Up, Tiger Lily?* (1966), and his directorial debut with the feature movie *Take the Money and Run* (1969).

By the time Allen directed his second film, *Bananas* (1971), his career as a comic actor and director seemed assured, and the series of films he authored and directed during the 1970s—*Everything You Always Wanted to Know about Sex (But Were Afraid to Ask)* (1972), *Sleeper* (1973), *Love and Death* (1975), and *Annie Hall* (1977)—confirmed his place as a director to watch in American cinema. *Annie Hall*'s reception both at the box office and at the Academy Awards also upwardly shifted Allen's reputation. The film was nominated for four Academy Awards; it won an Oscar for Best Picture and Allen won for Best Director and for Best Original Screenplay. The film's costumes for Diane Keaton's Annie Hall even started a clothing trend.

With the release of *Interiors* in 1978, Allen signaled his intention to break out of the world of comic film and into a more serious one, one that would allow him to experiment with the techniques of filmmaking he had observed from the European art film tradition. Although *Interiors* contained familiar Allen character types and themes, it was not a comedy and did not include the by-then-familiar Allen comic persona. Critics and public alike were caught off balance by the film's seriousness. Allen, however, persisted in the face of negative reactions, turning out noncomic films like *September* (1987) and *Another Woman* (1988) and films like *Alice* (1990) and *Bullets Over Broadway* (1994) in which he did not appear. The break from the nuttier earlier films allowed Allen to experiment in ways he might not have otherwise tried. And the results were such seriocomic masterpieces as *Hannah and Her Sisters* (1986) and *Crimes and Misdemeanors* (1989).

Since the 1970s Woody Allen has maintained a steady output of films as a writer, director, and actor, with one film in release, one in production, and one in the writing or planning stage in any single year. And over the years he has remained remarkably innovative, shooting in black and white—*Zelig* (1983), *Broadway Danny Rose* (1984), *Shadows and Fog* (1992), and *Celebrity* (1998)—making period as well as contemporary movies—*A Midsummer Night's Sex Comedy* (1982), *The Purple Rose of Cairo* (1985), *Radio Days* (1987), and *The Curse of the Jade Scorpion* (2001)—and in general taking risks—the Greek chorus in *Mighty Aphrodite* (1995), a musical in *Everyone Says I Love You* (1996), the newsreel look of *Zelig*, the levitated mother in "Oedipus Wrecks" from anthology film *New York Stories* (1989), and the dual-narrative perspective of *Melinda and Melinda* (2005). His films continue to attract talented and well-known actors, and they have garnered a considerable number of Oscars and Oscar nominations for his own efforts and for those who work in them.

Woody Allen remains one of contemporary cinema's most prolific and interesting directors. The degree of control he exercises over his films has been highly unusual in corporate-driven industry, and his films' financing has given him a freedom to play with the medium in ways almost unheard of in the world of commercial film. He is not part of the Hollywood set and remains resolutely a New Yorker, living and working in the city that has featured so prominently in so many of his movies. Approve or disapprove of him personally, agree or disagree with his approach to film, the movies of Woody Allen are always worth a look. What more can one say for a director?

Chronology

1935	Born Allen Stewart Konigsberg on December 1 in Brooklyn, New York, to Martin and Nettie Konigsberg, the first of two children. A sister, Letty Aronson, was born in 1943.
1940	Begins grade school at Brooklyn Public School 99.
1941	Visits Manhattan for the first time with his father. Moves frequently with his family.
1949–1953	Attends Midwood High School in Brooklyn. His first published joke appears in Earl Wilson's column in 1952. Before graduating, seventeen-year-old Allen is hired to ghostwrite jokes for Sammy Kaye, Guy Lombardo, and Arthur Murray.
1953	Enrolls briefly at New York University and City College of New York, fails film class in movie production at NYU and drops out of CCNY. Signs with the William Morris Agency and writes comedy skits for Pat Boone, Buddy Hackett, Peter Lind Hayes, and Herb Shriner.
	Works on *Colgate Comedy Hour* in Hollywood as part of NBC Writer's Development Program. Meets Danny Simon, brother of Neil, who becomes his mentor.
1956–1958	Marries Harlene Rosen on March 15, 1956. Leaves Hollywood and returns to New York, writing nightclub routines for a number of celebrities. Works summers at Taminent, where he makes show business contacts.
1958	Begins ongoing relationship with Jack Rollins and Charles Joffe after leaving the William Morris Agency. Writes for Sid Caesar's *Chevy Show*.
1961	Starts nightclub career at Duplex in Greenwich Village, and for

the next few years tours the club circuit and college campuses as a stand-up comic. Appears on television as a frequent guest and host of *The Tonight Show*.

1962   Divorces from Harlene Rosen.

1965   Inaugurates his film career when he writes and appears in *What's New Pussycat?* Marries Louise Lasser, who will appear in two of his films. *What's New Pussycat?* is box office hit and makes his name in the movie business.

1966   Dubs *What's Up, Tiger Lily? Don't Drink the Water*, his first play, opens on Broadway. Contributes pieces to *New Yorker*, some fifty of which will appear between 1966 and 1980. Appears frequently on television.

1967   Appears in *Casino Royale*.

1968   Opens second play, *Play It Again, Sam*, on Broadway.

1969   Directs first film, *Take the Money and Run*, which he also writes and stars in. *Don't Drink the Water* appears as a film. Signs with United Artists. Divorces Louise Lasser.

1971   Directs second film, *Bananas*. Publishes first collection of prose, *Getting Even*. Lives with Diane Keaton, who will appear in seven of his films.

1972   Films *Play It Again, Sam*, directed by Herbert Ross, starring Allen. *Everything You Always Wanted to Know about Sex (But Were Afraid to Ask)* released.

1973   *Sleeper* released.

1975   *Love and Death* released. Publishes second collection of prose, *Without Feathers*.

1976   Appears in *The Front* directed by Martin Ritt. A cartoon, "Inside Woody Allen," is syndicated in newspapers and runs until 1984.

1977   *Annie Hall* released.

1978   *Interiors* released; Allen's first noncomic film, which he writes and directs but does not appear in. Appointed to directorate of Vivian Beaumont Theater at Lincoln Center. Allen nominated for Academy Award for Best Director and for Best Original Screenplay for *Annie Hall*. The film is nominated for Best Picture. *Annie Hall* wins four Academy Awards. Allen wins for Best Director and for Best Original Screenplay.

1979   *Manhattan* released. Nominated for Academy Award for Best Director and for Best Original Screenplay for *Interiors*.

1980   *Stardust Memories* released. Third collection of prose, *Side Effects*, published. Begins long relationship with Mia Farrow, who will appear in eleven of his films. Signs with Orion Pictures. Nominated for Academy Award for Best Original Screenplay for *Manhattan*.

1981   Opens play *The Floating Lightbulb*.

1982   *A Midsummer Night's Sex Comedy* released.

1983   *Zelig* released.

1984   *Broadway Danny Rose* released.

1985   *The Purple Rose of Cairo* released. Nominated for Academy Award for Best Director for *Broadway Danny Rose*.

1986   *Hannah and Her Sisters* released. Nominated for Academy Award for Best Original Screenplay for *The Purple Rose of Cairo*.

1987   *Radio Days* and *September* both released. Nominated for Academy Award for Best Director and for Best Original Screenplay for *Hannah and Her Sisters*. The film is nominated for Best Film. Wins for Best Original Screenplay.

1988   *Another Woman* released. Nominated for Academy Award Best Original Screenplay for *Radio Days*.

1989   "Oedipus Wrecks" segment of *New York Stories* and *Crimes and Misdemeanors* both released.

1990   *Alice* released. Nominated for Academy Award for Best Director and for Best Original Screenplay for *Crimes and Misdemeanors*.

1991   Nominated for Academy Award for Best Original Screenplay for *Alice*.

1992   *Shadows and Fog* and *Husbands and Wives* both released. Breakup with Mia Farrow.

1993   *Manhattan Murder Mystery* released. Nominated for Academy Award for Best Original Screenplay for *Husbands and Wives*. Loses nasty court battle with Mia Farrow over custody of three children.

1994   *Bullets Over Broadway* and *Don't Drink the Water* (television film) both released.

1995   *Mighty Aphrodite* released. Nominated for Academy Award for Best Director and for Best Original Screenplay for *Bullets Over Broadway*.

1996   *Everyone Says I Love You* released. Nominated for Academy Award for Best Original Screenplay for *Mighty Aphrodite*.

1997   *Deconstructing Harry* released. Marries Soon-Yi Previn on December 22.

1998   *Celebrity* released. Nominated for Academy Award for Best Original Screenplay for *Deconstructing Harry*.

2000   *Small-Time Crooks* released.

2001   *The Curse of the Jade Scorpion* released.

2002   *Hollywood Ending* released. Makes first appearance at the
            Oscar celebration in Hollywood and attends the Cannes Film
            Festival to receive Palm of Palms award for lifetime achievement.
2003   *Anything Else* released.
2005   *Melinda and Melinda* and *Match Point* both released.

1

Woody Allen's Lovable Anxious Schlemiels

Sanford Pinsker

Woody Allen's anxious, bespectacled *punin* has become something of a national icon: he is the "beautiful loser" par excellence, the man whose urban, end-of-the-century anxieties mirror—albeit, in exaggeration—our own. To be sure, his persona is hardly as sui generis as many of his more adoring fans suppose; scholars need not break a sweat to establish Allen's lineage to the Little Man of Robert Benchley, to Charlie Chaplin's Little Tramp, indeed, to a host of precursors from the pages of the *New Yorker* magazine. Modern humor depends on trouble, and Allen suffers not only all the indignities that come with a weakling's ninety-eight-pound body but also those he conjures up in his doom-riddled mind.

No doubt a part of the Allen persona we meet on the silver screen was formed in the noisy, yoo-hooing world of his Brooklyn childhood. His memories—even if one gives comic exaggeration its due—are filled with people who shouted rather than talked, who ended their sentences with exclamation points, and who could do neither without waving their hands. Such a world—by degrees combative and warm, ebullient and anxious—tends to divide itself between those who reach over others for a ketchup bottle and those who end up getting knocked off their luncheonette stools.

But that much said, Allen's persona adds up to something more than the usual formulation of yet another modern humorist with trouble dripping from his sleeve; for one thing, his tsuris has a metaphysical dimension Allen insists upon (even at times belabors) and that we recognize like a thumbprint. At one point a philosophical Allen argues that "the universe is merely a

1

fleeting idea in God's mind—a pretty uncomfortable thought, particularly if you've just made a down payment on a house"; at another he wonders if we "can actually 'know' the universe? My God, it's hard enough finding your way around Chinatown." Allen, in short, characteristically muses in juxta-positions. The result is a prose style in which airy ideas and gritty urban details are forced to share floor space in the same paragraph, and often on opposing sides of a semicolon.

Mark Shechner argues that Allen's persona has always been awash in "high-school existentialism"—that is, longer on posture and predictable subject (as Shechner enumerates them, "God is dead; life has no meaning; man is a lonely speck in a vast, impersonal void") than on hard, sustained thought.[1] Perhaps so, but there is, I would suggest, a difference between tak-ing Allen's comedy seriously and taking it solemnly. Shechner, to his credit, recognizes the essential difference between the persona a comic both creates and needs and the biographical self who may have given it impetus:

> Every comic needs some theatrical self [in Allen's case, the schlemiel as sexual loser-cum-narcissist] to be not only his trademark, but his muse, the inventor of the jokes he tells. The comedian plays host to his other self which lives off him as much as he lives off it, and unless he collapses into his persona entirely, he is by profession a case of split personality. Allen the comic, we are led to understand, is by no means the same man as Allen the clarinetist; and such a self-division, it appears, is something of a professional standard. It is not only for purposes of ethnic whitewashing that nearly all Jewish comedians perform under stage names. So dependent is the comic on his other self that he comes to seek shelter under it, and asking any comedian to step out from behind the mask is a little like asking Harpo Marx to speak.

By contrast, Allan Bloom, author of *The Closing of the American Mind*, not only fails to see any distinctions between Allen the persona and Allen the personality but also insists that both of them measure up to his own high intellectual standards. Bloom, of course, has made something of a specialty of the jeremiad, and it is hardly surprising he should see dangers to serious-ness everywhere in our lack of critical standards, in our worship of a mushy-headed relativism, in our vulgarized notions of nihilism. Indeed, if Bloom is even half right, our national fiber hasn't been in such bad shape since the days when Jonathan Edwards conjured up the image of us as Sinners in the Hands of an Angry God. One sees sure signs of our national decay, Bloom argues, in the sheer number of colleges and universities racing to establish women's studies programs, in the rock music that teenagers blast through their Walkmans, and in such unlikely places as the films of Woody Allen.

Allan Bloom means to bash them all, but it is his attack on the Allen known as Woody that speaks most directly to our culture's mixed feelings about comedy, at least as they are articulated by its "intellectuals." According to Bloom,

> Woody Allen's comedy [i.e., *Zelig*] is nothing but a set of variations on the theme of the man who does not have a real "self" or "identity," and who feels superior to the inauthentically self-satisfied people because he is conscious of his situation and at the same time inferior to them because they are "adjusted."[2]

In short, Allen makes us feel comfortable with our nihilism, and for this sin Bloom can offer book lists but no forgiveness: "Woody Allen really has nothing to tell us about inner-directedness. Nor does David Reisman [in *The Lonely Crowd*] nor, going further back, does Erik Fromm. One has to get to Heidegger to learn something serious about the grim facts of what inner-directedness might really mean."

Reading such testy, strident judgments, one begins to suspect that the Allan with the problem is Bloom rather than Woody. What *The Closing of the American Mind* demonstrates when it blathers on about a film like *Zelig* is precisely what H. L. Mencken once defined as the puritan temper—namely, a deep suspicion that somebody, somewhere is having a good time.[3] It has been with us, in one form or another, from the days when Thomas Morton established his Maypole at Merry Mount in 1628 (only to have Governor John Endicott transmogrify it, in Hawthorne's version of the tale, into a whipping post) to *Animal House* and the latest round of efforts to exile fraternities from college campuses.

Unfortunately, Bloom is not the only one who thinks of Allen as a philosopher rather than as an entertainer. In *Annie Hall*, the boorish young professor of film studies (now it would be know as semiotics) holds forth on Marshall McLuhan while Allen's protagonist does a slow burn. Such show-offs know everything about the medium of cinema except what makes people love it. Unable to contain his indignation any longer, he calls the scholar's bluff, only to have McLuhan himself appear from behind a cardboard cutout and wholeheartedly agree. There may not be many victories for the Alvy Singer who wins and then loses Annie Hall, who has worried, and continues to worry, about life's assorted troubles, but this is surely one of them.

Indeed, Allen has been "getting even" with brainy, professorial types since the days when he published his *New Yorker* sketches collected as *Getting Even* (1971). Sometimes the cracks take the form of memorable quips, like the one in *Manhattan* (1979) about the possibility of *Commentary* and *Dissent* merging into a new journal for New York intellectuals to be called *Dysentery*. And of course, there is *Stardust Memories* (1980)—a sustained exercise in biting the hands that have fed him, whether they belong to Allen's overly adoring fans, his reviewers, or those who subject his work to intense scholarly critical scrutiny.

Not long ago I was struck by the painstaking rigor a scholar has brought to bear on Mark Twain's reading habits. Apparently, this professor has assembled enough evidence to prove what every serious reader of Twain already knew—namely, that Twain owned and read and, yes, *underlined text* in large numbers of books and that he perpetrated the mythos of the rustic, homespun spinner of tall tales and dispenser of lowfalutin wisdom so as not to put off any segment of the population with the ready cash to buy one of his books or to crowd into one of his lectures. My hunch is that this scholar could demonstrate quite the opposite point about Woody Allen—namely, that he reads dust jackets and reviews, rather than Real Books, and that he perpetrates the mythos of a sensitive New York egghead so he will remain the darling of those who also make it a point to keep up with our culture by reading the *New York Review of Books*.

But this much said, let me hasten to add that, while I don't count Allen among our philosophers or significant social critics, I do think that his genius for parody and the systematic care and feeding he has given to his schlemielish persona are important additions to our cultural scene. Most humorists begin as counterpunchers—that is, as those who keep their eyes and ears fixed on the elements of the mainstream most susceptible to comic exaggeration. Parody, in short, allows one to prop his or her work against what is already known, what is already there. Franklin, Twain, Benchley—each started as a parodist, which is to say, as a ventriloquist with a difference. So, too, did the Allan Stewart Konigsberg who had mailed his jokes to newspaper columnists, worked for ad agencies, and paid his first showbiz dues writing material for other comics.

The difference, of course, is that when Konigsberg transmogrified himself into a *New Yorker* humorist named Woody Allen he labored under the long shadows cast by predecessors such as Benchley, Thurber, and S. J. Perelman. Consider, for example, this paragraph from "A Look at Organized Crime":

> In 1921, Thomas (The Butcher) Covello and Ciro (The Tailor) Santucci attempted to organize disparate ethnic groups of the underworld and thus take over Chicago. This was foiled when Albert (The Logical Positivist) Corillo assassinated Kid Lipsky by locking him in a closet and sucking all the air out through a straw.

On its most important, most recognizable level, Allen's fun is at the expense of what had been a popular television show—*The Untouchables*—and the spate of books about the Mob it inspired; on other fronts, he cannot quite resist the impulse to juxtapose nicknames we expect with ones we don't. But there is also the Allen who knows the traditions of American humor as intimately as he knows the trendy stuff of popular culture. In this case, the story of Kid Lipsky's comic rubout is lifted from the *New Yorker*'s pages rather than from the TV screen, and those who knew Allen from his days as a Greenwich Village comic may well have missed the allusion as well as part of Allen's humorous point. By way of illustration, I offer the following:

> Then there was Aunt Sarah Shoaf, who never went to bed at night without the fear that a burglar was going to get in and blow chloroform under her door through a tube. To avert this calamity—for she was in greater dread of anesthetics than of losing her household goods—she always piled her money, silverware, and other valuables in a neat stack just outside her bedroom, with a note reading: "This is all I have. Please take it and do not use your chloroform, as this is all I have."

Aunt Sarah Shoaf is, of course, one of the lovable eccentrics who made James Thurber's childhood in Columbus, Ohio, so ripe for the *New Yorker*'s picking. Granted, Allen dusts off Thurber's material, gives it an appropriately urban—which is to say, "hip"—twist, but the essential archetype had been around for a long, long time. As Thurber himself once put it, for the person beating his or her brains out trying to write a two-thousand-word comic sketch, there was always "the suspicion that a piece he has been working on for two long days was done much better and probably more quickly by Robert Benchley in 1924."[4]

Like Benchley, like Thurber, like Perelman, Allen cannot recount his complicated griefs without making them seem comic. But that said, Allen also has certain advantages that they lacked. He plays, in short, to a hipper house, one that Allen himself describes as belonging to those "born after Nietzsche's edict that 'God is dead,' but before the hit recording [by the Beatles] 'I Wanna Hold Your Hand.'" Moreover, Allen broke in his version of the sad-sack-as-schlemiel at a cultural moment when ethnicity was becoming a box-office plus rather than the marginal minus it had always been considered. If radio tended to obliterate regional dialects, homogenizing our speech until the diction of CBS announcers became the American equivalent of the Queen's English, then movies (and later, television) turned a country of small towns into a nation of urban states.

Granted, the process I'm alluding to happened so slowly, so subtly, that it defies precise dating. Nor is the greater receptiveness and more hospitable climate that resulted limited to Woody Allen. If one thinks of, say, Henry Roth, what cluster of events occasioned the 1964 revival, and the subsequent popularity, of *Call It Sleep* (1934), his lyrical novel about growing up amid the squalor and the terrors of New York's immigrant Lower East Side? One would *like* to give the obvious answer—namely, that it's a first-rate book that had been unfairly ignored—but accounting for popular taste is more complicated. Often, timing counts for at least as much as talent. Without a different literary context that now included the work of Saul Bellow, Bernard Malamud, and another Roth named Philip; without a cultural moment in which you didn't have to be Jewish to enjoy Levy's rye bread or to know a few Yiddish words; without, in short, the 1960s as they were. Henry Roth's novel might have continued its long, uninterrupted sleep. Similarly, after Benchley and even after Chaplin's comedies, films as aggressively ethnic as *Annie Hall* (1977), *Manhattan* (1979), or *Broadway Danny Rose* (1984) would have been impossible in the 1930s.

Roughly the same cultural changes affected what a stand-up comic could, or could not, do behind a mike. Lenny Bruce is usually mentioned in this connection. His daring—some would say sacrificial—campaign on behalf of liberating language from the unspoken taboos that made four-letter words a nightclub no-no, and of addressing formerly forbidden subjects (not only sex but also race and religion) is, of course, part of the 1960s story. But so too is Woody Allen. His public therapy sessions (conducted, for the most part, in Greenwich Village nightclubs) cast Allen as the analysand and the audience as his analyst. The result—as the comedy albums he recorded during the early 1960s attest—was very funny stuff indeed, and Allen mined the best gags for subsequent *New Yorker* sketches and films.

As the Allen persona would proudly "boast," he was weaker, more troubled, and infinitely more sensitive than anybody in the house. Given the age and its anxieties, if Woody Allen hadn't bumbled along with his brand of urban Jewish neurosis, his thick eyeglasses, his sad face, somebody else would surely have invented him. The era of the borscht belt gag (e.g., "I spent a thousand dollars to have my nose fixed, and now my brain won't work" [*bup bup bup*]) was over. That world—which Allen resurrects as the chorus of older comics who hang around the Carnegie Deli swapping stories about characters like Broadway Danny Rose—may have cracked up Aunt Sadie, but not her nephews. By contrast, Allen's characteristic shrugs and quivers, his obsessive worries and pervasive guilts, his hesitant pauses and equally tentative voice, were just right for the *Playboy* crowd. To them Allen could confess, "I don't believe in an afterlife, although I plan to bring a change of underwear." Or he would offer his remembrances of neuroses past: "When we played softball, I'd steal second, then feel guilty and go back." As one critic of the Village scene during those days recalls it, "The futzing around Allen did onstage was the gestalt of a comedic antihero . . . true neurotica."[5]

Very soon, however, Allen's onstage futzing became the trademark of his on-screen persona. He projected aspects of himself as weakling, as klutz, and most often, as schlemiel. Consider, for example, *Take the Money and Run* (1969), in which the story of Virgil Starkwell contains all three. As a parody of both the documentary (with its efforts to "explain," via sociopsychology, how a criminal like Starkwell comes into being) and the prison film—with its tough cons and daring, stylized escapes—Allen proves himself a resourceful enough counterpuncher to last through the film's eighty-five minutes.

But gags alone—even very good ones—will not a feature film make. What gives *Take the Money and Run* its durability is certain moments of what can only be called comic genius. It is, after all, one thing to hear the documentary's "narrator" (Jackson Beck) tell us in sonorous voice-over that Virgil Starkwell grew up in tough circumstances, bullied by older, stronger toughs, and then see a pint-sized version of the bespectacled Allen watch, helpless, as they break his glasses and smash the remains into bits; and quite another to hear the testimony of Virgil's first cello teacher—the low-key but exasperated Mr. Turgson. As he tells his reminiscences to the camera, we learn that Virgil loved the cello, indeed, that he stole money to pay for lessons, but we also find out that, in Mr. Turgson's words, he "had no conception of the instrument. He *blew* into it."

However (the voice-over informs us), if Virgil did not become a great cello player, he at least became proficient enough to join a local band. At this point, Allen moves beyond mere futzing to a piece of brilliant screen business: a marching band makes its way down the street with everything in apple-pie order—drum major, assorted brass, the whole Sousa entourage—when suddenly we see Allen sawing away on his cello and frantically trying to keep pace with other members of the band by moving a chair and then sitting down to crank out a few bars. Like Chaplin before him, Allen knows how to translate a funny premise into physical humor. Granted, parodic energy accounts for some of the success (e.g., the dry, slightly off narrative tone that sets the scene), but what makes the scene really work is Virgil's capacity to build in his own defeats. Here, in short, is the schlemiel in one of his most traditional incarnations—namely, as the man who unwittingly sets comic disaster into motion.

In other sections of *Take the Money and Run*, Allen is content to play Virgil as the klutz—for example, as a would-be pool hustler who (predictably enough) ruins the felt, misses his shots, and ends up shelling out money or as a would-be sneak thief who gets his hand caught in the gum ball machine. Virgil, in short, has all the earmarks of the typical Allen loser; he is too frail, too isolated, too alienated, and of course, too sensitive to make it here. Even the army rejects him when he identifies an ink blot as "two elephants making love to a men's glee club."

Not surprisingly, Virgil is equally inept as a criminal, but less because he is klutzy than because he is an inveterate schlemiel. Those who remember Willie Sutton (the man who once explained that he robbed banks because "that's where the money was" and who once escaped from prison by fashioning a gun out of a soap bar) take a special pleasure in the scene in which Virgil reenacts Sutton's bust out. There is Virgil in his cell, patiently carving a gun from a bar of soap and then applying black shoe polish for the realistic finishing touch. It can't miss—and indeed, for a while it doesn't. Virgil takes several guards hostage and makes his way into the Big Yard—only to be caught in a sudden shower that reduces his "pistol" to a handful of soap bubbles. Build in possibilities for disaster, and disaster will surely overtake you—this is the essential message of tragedy and also of Allen's most representative comedy. As Shechner points out, Allen has been "a closet tragedian all along" and

> the air of cosmic befuddlement that now colors his thought was there from the first. He has taken to telling interviewers, "My real obsessions are religious," and "Death is the big obsession behind all I've done," and "The metaphor for life is a concentration camp, do believe that." This last, he told *Time* magazine after *Manhattan* was released, was a line he had cut from that film but intended to use in his next. And despite efforts on Allen's part to keep *Manhattan* from drowning, as *Interiors* did, in too metaphysical a view of the modern condition, the void sneaks inexorably in. So, when Isaac Davis (Allen) and Mary (Diane Keaton) take refuge from a storm in Hayden Planetarium and conduct a flirtatious tête-à-tête amid lunar and nebular skyscapes, Allen, as director, is not just having fun with his sets, he's also reminding us that "We're lost out there in the stars."

Given the concerted movement *away* from metaphysical angst in *Hannah and Her Sisters* (1986)—a film that finally insists that the comic beauties of a Marx brothers' film like *Duck Soup* have a right to be, without introspection, without brooding, without metaphysical whining—Shechner might want to amend his original assessment, but I think that his general sense of Allen is on target. Even the scene from *Take the Money and Run* where Virgil botches a bank robbery because of poor penmanship (the teller has difficulty reading his note, insisting that it says "I have a *gub*") has a downside that is both tragic and, if you will, "metaphysical." To be sure, that Virgil creates so much trouble for himself ("*Act* natural" comes out looking like "Act natural") is the stuff that schlemiels are made of. But poor Virgil is also caught in a world—as are we all—in which one of the vice presidents must countersign a holdup note before tellers are authorized to give out cash, and where discussions and decisions are increasingly made by committee. As Allen escalates the scene's pacing, Virgil finds himself awash in what literary theoreticians call "reader response"—each with an opinion and each with something like a vote. Moreover, bureaucracy exerts a power—at least over the timid—that far outstrips that of the criminal. His gun reduced to a "gub," Allen's protagonist watches helplessly as he is gradually reduced to the state of childhood (where neatness counts and teachers know how to deal with the sloppy) and the police at last arrive.

One could argue that Virgil is in the wrong business, that he simply doesn't have either sufficient talent or sufficient calling to be a thief. The same thing, interestingly enough, could be said of Broadway Danny Rose's equally fatal attraction to marginal entertainers. As an agent Danny Rose has collected a veritable menagerie of bizarre acts: a one-armed juggler, a one-legged tap dancer, a women who belts out eerie tunes by waving her hand over glasses filled with water. Nonetheless, Broadway Danny Rose believes in his clients, cares for them in ways that go well beyond the call of duty, and of course pitches them whenever and wherever he can. This despite the fact that those who *do* make it abandon him without so much as a by-your-leave, despite the fact that he is a marginal man in what can only be described as a marginal business.

As the kibitzers in the Carnegie Deli (including such actual veterans of the borscht belt circuit such as Jackie Gayle, Corbett Monica, and Will Jordon) conjure up both Broadway Danny Rose and the bygone age of showbiz he represents, the focus narrows to what happened when Lou Canova (Nick Apollo Forte), a saloon singer in the Sinatra mold, began his comeback, fueled by the rerelease of his one authentic 1950s hit, the nostalgia craze, and Broadway Danny Rose's willing, but ineffectual, direction.

In *Broadway Danny Rose*, Canova gives us one version that *All For Love* can take in the contemporary world (Canova pursues the wonderfully tawdry Tina Vitale [played to comic perfection by Mia Farrow] as Broadway Danny Rose chases after him, tsk-tsking all the way), but in most of Allen's films the role of erstwhile lover is reserved for Allen himself. Generally speaking, the earlier films are manned by sexual bumblers, by little boys in grown-up clothing, by those who strike us as longer on boast than on performance. Virgil Starkwell is a typical case. He may insist (as Allen himself did during his days as a stand-up) that the proper answer to the question, "Is sex dirty?" can only be, "It is . . . if you're doing it right," but the gap between quip and condition is so great that even calling it an incongruity doesn't quite do it justice.

Much the same thing is true of, say, the Fielding Mellish (Woody Allen) of *Bananas* (1971) although, this time, the making of the Allen schlemiel *is* more developed, more sustained. Mellish is more than a timid products tester mauled by an exercising contraption for busy executives called Excusizer (shades of Chaplin's losing battle with machines in *Modern Times*), he is also a portrait of a Brooklyn intellectual as a sexual-political loser, the man whose fortunes rise and fall in volatile San Marcos (a banana republic that produces more revolutionaries than tropical fruit) and whose wedding night is covered—by none other than Howard Cosell himself—on *Wide World of Sports*. If the plotline of *Bananas* is, shall we say, loose, it allows plenty of room for Allen's spontaneous energy.

By contrast, when his films moved beyond the limitations of mere parody (e.g., *Sleeper* [the sci-fi flick]; *Love and Death* [the Russian novel]; *Every-*

thing You Always Wanted to Know about Sex (But Were Afraid to Ask) [the Dr. David Reuben best seller]). Allen's filmmaking became increasingly reflexive, that is, focused as much on the medium as on the message. Granted, the Allen persona remained in occupancy, still nervous, still a loser, still every bit the schlemiel, but there were also subtle wrinkles added to his by-now recognizable features. For example, one traditional synonym for *schlemiel* was *cuckold*, but in a film like *Play It Again, Sam* (largely concerned with how a film buff and inveterate sad sack is finally able to transfer *Casablanca*'s images into action), it is Allan Felix (Woody Allen) who cuckolds the worldly Dick Christie (Tony Roberts). And in *Annie Hall*, the tale's bittersweet unfolding depends as much upon Alvy Singer's lovability as upon his loserhood. As Irving Howe points out, the humor of schlemielhood can take savage turns (as it does in the routines of Lenny Bruce) or tender ones. Not surprisingly, Howe numbers Allen among the latter:

> Woody Allen was a reincarnated Menashe Skulnik, quintessential *schlemiel* of the Yiddish theatre, but now a college graduate acquainted with the thought of Freud and recent numbers of *Commentary*. . . . [He] exploited the parochial helplessness of Jewish sons, their feelings of sexual feebleness and worldly incapacity; but he did this with an undertone of wistfulness and affection that marked him off from most other Jewish comedians of his moment.[6]

No doubt there are those who would point out that Allen, tenderhearted though his personae might be, is hardly above dragging in bearded Hasidic Jews whenever he wants an easy laugh (indeed, earlocks and broad black hats have been paraded through Allen's films since the days of *Take the Money and Run*, and always for their value as a quick visual gag) and others who might argue that *Stardust Memories*—its parody on Fellini films notwithstanding—is, at bottom, a mean-spirited affair. Fortunately, the sour note one often finds creeping through the humorist's mask (e.g., Dorothy Parker, Ring Lardner, Don Marquis, James Thurber, and most especially Mark Twain) has not lingered long enough to produce a string of *Stardust Memories* sequels.

Nonetheless, given the Allen who continues to plug away at serious, Bergman-like efforts such as *Interiors* or *September*, one cannot entirely discount the possibility of yet another Allen film justifying his decision *not* to remake his earlier comedies ad infinitum. As those before Allen discovered, humorists live so long under the lesser shadows of writing light verse or of providing comic relief—in short, of not being considered *serious*—that they learn more about the ambivalent nature of contempt than is probably good for them. In *The World According to Garp* (1978), John Irving's narrator explains the situation this way:

> Why did people insist that if you were "comic" you couldn't also be "serious"? Garp felt most people confused being profound with being sober, being earnest

with being deep. Apparently, if you *sounded* serious, you were. Presumably, other animals could not laugh at themselves, and Garp believed that laughter was related to sympathy, which we were always needing more of. He had been, after all, a humorless child—and never religious—so perhaps he now took comedy more seriously than others.

However, I hasten to point out that Garp's arguments (most of which Woody Allen would second) do not convince the Mrs. Poole who had written an antifan letter accusing him, among other things, of laughing "at people who can't have orgasms, and people who aren't blessed with happy marriages, and people whose wives and husbands are unfaithful." The comic exchange ends, as it must, with Garp's final letter (in what turns out to be a pointless, frustrating exchange on both sides) and with this particular argument's bottom line: "Fuck you."

Stardust Memories has something of the same message for those, including God, who keep urging Sandy Bates (Woody Allen) to make funnier films, to tell funnier jokes, to replay it all again, Sandy. Small wonder that Bates turns testy and self-conscious. As he would have it, aggravation is everybody else. Others get in the way, complicate things, misunderstand, whatever—but you can't make films without them.

And *that*, of course, is the point about *Stardust Memories*. It is about the making of itself. Rather than a film that holds a mirror up to the cosmos, to a universe that riddles us with deaths that come too soon and loves that do not come at all, this time Woody Allen points his looking glass at the silver screen itself. In the concluding moments of the film the entire cast assembles in the rickety auditorium that has been the locale for the weekend's Sandy Bates retrospective, and they watch the film we have ourselves just watched. They file out full of wonderment and praise. Bates is a comic genius, they exclaim in unison, but we know better than to trust people on the payroll. After all, the film has bashed into senselessness those who might raise any objections. Besides, this film is *not* akin to the early Bates; rather, it points toward similarly reflexive moments in films such as *The Purple Rose of Cairo* or *Hannah and Her Sisters*.

In the final frame of *Stardust Memories*, Sandy Bates's quizzical face is fixed on the blank screen and the empty auditorium. Two unformed questions spread across his face: Was the film any good? Does it matter, one way or the other? Perhaps those are *always* the essential questions, but artists cannot overworry them and still remain artists. In Allen's case, working conditions unmatched in the American film industry have allowed him plenty of elbow room to play his hunches. *He* cannot say of Sandy Bates what Flaubert said of Madame Bovary—namely, "C'est moi!" Rather, Woody Allen is a case of Blakean persistence rewarded, of a person pursuing his neuroses until they become the very stuff of Art—an art, by the way, that included not only the Manhattan haunts that have become Allen's equivalent of Faulkner's "postage stamp of native soil" and the gallery of introspective, nervous schlemiels he has added to our stock of mental images, but also the generous doses of humanity that infuse his work with love as well as lovability. As to Sandy Bates's questions, it is fair to say that the jury is no longer out about Woody Allen, despite his being still very much in midcareer and showing no signs of either slowing down or standing still: his films *are* good and they *do* matter.

NOTES

1. Mark Shechner, "Woody Allen: The Failure of the Therapeutic," in *From Hester Street to Hollywood*, ed. Sarah Blacher Cohen, 232 (Bloomington: Indiana University Press, 1983). Subsequent references to Shechner are to this seminally important article.

2. Allan Bloom, *The Closing of the American Mind* (New York: Simon and Schuster, 1987), 146.

3. Bloom is quick to point out that Bruno Bettleheim's cameo appearance as one of Zelig's "witnesses" is further evidence of the Germanic strain in Allen's thought. What Bloom quite misses, however, is the marvelous self-parodies that intellectuals such as Irving Howe, Susan Sontag, and ironically enough, Saul Bellow (Bloom's colleague and friend at the University of Chicago) contribute to Allen's pseudodocumentary.

4. James Thurber, *The Thurber Carnival* (New York: Harper & Row, 1945), 175.

5. Phil Berger, *The Last Laugh* (New York: Limelight Editions, 1985), 114.

6. Irving Howe, *World of Our Fathers* (New York: Harcourt Brace Jovanovich, 1976), 571.

2

Woody Allen's New York

Leonard Quart

There was a time, not so long ago, when New York was less volatile and threatening, when its social desperation and agony seemed more manageable and avoidable. It was during that period—the 1930s through the 1950s—that Hollywood created a dream city out of both the iconography of New York's skyscrapers, penthouses, bridges, and neon lights and the intense street rhythms and theatrics on the ground. Crime, poverty, and fear continued to exist on those celluloid streets (e.g., *Dead End* in the 1930s, the weariness and cynicism of the documentary-style *The Naked City* in the 1940s), but the dominant tone inherent in Hollywood's depiction of the city was a buoyant one—cinematic New York, often even when it was corrupt, was a world of romantic possibility. And for decades that fiction about the city helped shape its citizens as well as a worldwide audience's vision of New York.

In 1930s screwball comedies like *Easy Living* (1937), musicals like *On the Town* (1949) and *The Band Wagon* (1953), and romances like *The Clock* (1945), the mixture of carefully selected locations and artfully designed sets evoked an exhilarating and humane world. The city in *On the Town* could elicit the most exultant and joyous of responses from its central characters, three sailors played by Gene Kelly, Jules Munshin, and Frank Sinatra, inspiring them together with their female partners to lift their voices in song and kick up their heels in dance. In fact, the "helluva town" of historic landmarks and ethnic nightclubs that the three sailors giddily race about on their shore leave, the imaginatively designed Forty-second Street arcade in *The Band Wagon* where Fred Astaire dances with a shoeshine man, and *The Clock*'s wartime portrait of caring, earthy New York milkmen and idyllic

13

nights in misty city parks along the Hudson, were almost the visual equivalent of Thomas Wolfe's overripe paeans to a city that had moved him to "grow drunk with ecstasy" and to feel that he "can never die."

Obviously, these cinematic evocations of the city never pretended to social realism or criticism. They were mainly interested in stylizing and mythologizing the social universe so an audience could escape into a more radiant, romantic, or exciting world for a couple of hours. The films were so constructed that all those small-town, middle Americans in the audience could identify with their counterparts in *On the Town* and *The Clock*, wandering around wide-eyed in the big city. Even in films that portrayed poverty in the New York slums and were genuinely concerned with social issues, class animosity, and injustice, like William Wyler's *Dead End* (1937), urban social problems unfolded on a meticulously and beautifully constructed stage set and were strikingly augmented by cinematographer Greg Toland's use of deep focus and light and shadow. In *Dead End* every fire escape, tenement stoop, roof, garbage can, and huddle of people conveyed more of a calibrated aesthetic effect than a statement about urban entrapment. From the vantage point of the 1990s, life in *Dead End*'s New York slum, despite its poverty and violence, looks pretty good—a vital neighborhood with a river view that was ripe for the kind of gentrification the film depicts as already in process.

The movie industry repeatedly used New York to project an image of a city that would excite the collective imagination and fantasies of its audience, offering them either upper-class glamour and success or working-class warmth and folksiness. The cinematic city was centered in neighborhoods like a moneyed, chic Upper East Side, a charming, bohemian Greenwich Village, a communal but impoverished Lower East Side, and a daffy, distinctively accented Brooklyn, whose mere mention would elicit laughs from movie audiences throughout the country. For the moviegoing public of the time, Brooklyn was the apotheosis of all the kindhearted, good-humored, raw, democratic virtues of America's urban, ethnic common man. And New York's fire escapes, pushcarts, town houses, elevated trains, office buildings, art galleries, night clubs, and quaint, checkerboard-tablecloth Italian restaurants dominated Hollywood's vision of the city in films ranging from screwball comedies like *The Awful Truth* (1937) to film-noir classics like Fritz Lang's *Scarlet Street* (1945). In the noir films the dark, shadowy, glistening wet streets of the studio back lots whetted the audience's appetite for fashionable corruption. For Hollywood, setting a film in a large city, more often than not, meant placing it in New York.

Since the mid-1960s, however, as the city began to unravel—its social problems more insoluble, its middle class leaving for the suburbs, the underclass growing in numbers and menace—Hollywood's image of New York began to change. From *Midnight Cowboy* (1969) to Scorsese's *Taxi Driver* (1976), Lumet's *Q&A* (1990), and countless violent exploitation films, New

York has been portrayed on the screen as a traumatized city overwhelmed by drug dealers, prostitutes, and street criminals; as permeated with garbage-laden streets and graffiti-scarred buildings; and with a jarring symphony of sirens and alarms constantly playing as an accompaniment in the background. Even so, this cinematic nightmare vision of New York can still make the city seem seductive. Scorsese's city in *Taxi Driver* is perversely beautiful and galvanizing—a rancid night world of steam hissing from manhole covers, hydrants spouting streams of water, and ominous figures shimmering in the oppressive summer heat. It's an inversion of the dream city—a luminous portrait of urban rot and foreboding—and it's almost as phantasmagoric a view of the city as *On the Town*'s sanitized version of an earlier, more serene New York. *Taxi Driver* remains the hallucinatory vision of one singular director in collaboration with his scriptwriter, Paul Schrader, with both men more interested in projecting their personal obsessions and demons onto the New York urbanscape than in documenting its social breakdown.

Despite the film being conceived and shot from the point of view of Travis Bickle (Robert De Niro), a character who is a paranoid and a psychopath, Scorsese's New York remains touched with a great deal of gritty reality. Living in New York there is no avoiding the precariousness and edginess that suffuses a great many urban encounters and neighborhoods, and the film echoes that sense of public danger and decay. Still, even in the turbulent New York of the 1990s—a city in constant financial and social crisis—a dark, sinister film like *Taxi Driver* offers up only one of many possible, very different New Yorks.

Clearly there are other visions of New York that can be conjured up on the screen. A film like Nancy Savoca's *True Love* (1989) provides an unsentimentally realistic portrait of Bronx working-class Italian Americans who live in a coherent world whose public life is neither violent nor fragmented. In fact, in *True Love*'s Bronx, the characters' confusion and pain is not brought on by social desperation or alienation but by the communal and familial pressure to conform to traditional codes of male and female behavior. In *Do the Right Thing* (1989), Spike Lee creates a Brooklyn block devoid of drugs or street violence and crime—a softened (artificially and radiantly lit), relatively benign version of an inner-city street. It's a block whose sense of community owes more to 1930s films about white working-class life, like Vidor's *Street Scene* (1931), than to inner-city life in the 1990s. Other Hollywood films use Soho, the Upper East Side, and Wall Street to capture arty, stylish, and high living slices of the city, which if neither spiritual sanctuaries nor totally cut off from the city's agony, are physically comfortable, livable, and to many, desirable worlds.

The most powerful antidote in films to the nightmare vision of New York is conveyed by Woody Allen. From *Bananas* (1971) to *Alice* (1990), most of Allen's films use New York locations and treat the city as one of the prime subjects of his work. Allen's city is foregrounded, it's one more character in his films. It's never merely used as a visually interesting or picturesque background for the narrative to evolve in or to complement the interaction of his characters. His Manhattan is an extension of Allen's protagonists' personalities—its streets are places to walk in, hold conversations, have random and absurd encounters, reflect on both one's private angst and the city's plight, and mute or escape one's anxieties. New York is also a public projection of Allen's protagonists' generally best selves and moments—a city of infinite promise, possibility, and grandeur. It's a city where, in Allen's most famous image in *Manhattan* (1979), with Isaac (Allen) and Mary (Diane Keaton) romantically silhouetted, sitting on a bench in the beckoning shadows of the Queensborough Bridge at dawn, Isaac can unambiguously assert, "This is really a great city, I'm knocked out."

Allen's New York is the sum of the striking and chic neighborhoods and icons his camera focuses on either in glorious long shot or in more intimate tracking shots—Fifth and Madison avenues, Central Park West, Bloomingdale's, Lincoln Center, the Hayden Planetarium, the Plaza, Zabar's, the Russian Tea Room, the Dakota, and so on. His city is basically limited to a large fragment of one borough, Manhattan—though both *Annie Hall* (1977) and *Radio Days* (1986) reconstruct scenes from his central characters' boyhoods in Brooklyn and Rockaway, the other boroughs are usually treated as if they have been severed from the city—an upscale section that runs from the Upper West Side through Central Park to the Village and Soho and from the east 80s to Gramercy Park. There are scenes set on the Columbia University campus with its grand McKim, Mead, and White buildings, but Harlem, Washington Heights, and even the Lower East Side barely make an appearance in his films.

Of course, Allen is no neorealist like early De Sica or a cinema verité documentarian like Frederick Wiseman, who in one work exhaustively compiled footage of much of the daily activity that takes place in Central Park. Allen's films aren't interested in exploring urban problems like racial tensions, AIDS, or crime, nor does he have an interest in providing a composite, wide-ranging portrait of urban life. His New York has a narrow social and racial base, it's limited to an upper-middle-class world of WASPs and Jews who are primarily artists, academics, or media people—people who share his world and values and are able to evoke some empathy from him. In this New York, the poor, African Americans, and Hispanics play almost no role. In fact, they don't even have bit parts in Allen's films.

As one can see, Allen's vision of the city is a carefully selective one—a world where social pain and threat never intrude on the private lives and agonies of his characters. It's a city of dreams whose streets range from a cool, symmetrical Park Avenue with its groomed green medians to the raw, powerful, cast-iron building blocks of Soho. Allen's directorial eye looks not

only at life on the streets but also at the aesthetics of the buildings themselves. As the architect David (Sam Waterston) says in *Hannah and Her Sisters* (1986), "People pass by vital structures in this city all the time, and they
never take the trouble to appreciate them." Allen forces us to look closely at
the peeling posters and classical pediments that adorn the Soho loft buildings, the terra-cotta reliefs on the richly decorated Alwyn Court building on
Fifty-eighth Street and Seventh Avenue, and the grace and elegance of the
tapering art deco towers and gargoyles on the Chrysler Building.

In *Manhattan*, Allen's protagonist is writing a novel about a hero who
"thrived on the hustle and bustle of the crowds and the traffic." But the films
keep the city's fever pitch, collective anxiety, and chaos under control. Allen's depiction of Central Park illustrates this perfectly. Allen is so urban
oriented and committed a director that he treats the natural world in his
films as a comic antagonist—as a landscape in which his protagonists are totally ill at ease. The only natural space that he can tolerate and embrace in
his films is Central Park, which he treats as both his backyard and version
of the pastoral ideal, albeit an urbanized one, surrounded by magnificent ed-
ifices like the Beresford apartment building on its west side and the Guggen-
heim on its east. And in his vision of the park, the litter, noise, homeless
people, and crowds at mass events that are an integral part of its reality have
been removed from view. What is left is a relatively quiet oasis—the ideal of
its original nineteenth-century designers, Olmstead and Vaux—where one
can watch the change of seasons, count lovers in hansom carriages and boats
on the lake, and play ball with one's son on the Great Lawn. One can even
seek the meaning of life in a discussion with a Hare Krishna follower, as in
a luminous scene in *Hannah*, where the screen is split into three bands—at
the top a dusky blue sky; in the middle a delicately shadowed, glowing gold-
green Sheep's Meadow where Hare Krishna followers are dancing; and at
the bottom of the frame, an anguish-ridden Mickey (Allen) in search of the
meaning of life. The park here is transformed into a slice of paradise, providing a moment of utter relief for a man in emotional difficulty.

An image in *Manhattan* of Central Park enveloped in snow, harking back
to nineteenth-century Currier & Ives prints, is also part of Allen's opening
montage in homage to the city. This breathtaking montage and the film itself
resurrects the New York of memory that Allen loves. It's a New York that
is a fitting object of a grand passion—the city of Dixieland, Willie Mays,
Cole Porter, and the Marx brothers. The montage itself is built on volup-
tuous images of an incandescent Park Avenue in winter, Broadway's neon
lights, and a dramatic aerial view of Yankee Stadium at night, mixed with
images catching the everyday vitality of the streets, culminating in a crescendo of fireworks lighting up the night sky over Central Park, all accompanied by Gershwin's pulsating *Rhapsody in Blue* on the soundtrack.

These are contemporary, familiar New York images, shot in a dazzling high contrast black and white rather than color, which Allen utilizes to project the city's continuity with, from his perspective, its more elegant and civilized past. These fabulistic images also act as a self-conscious reminder of the way many old Hollywood films once projected a portrait of a city that gleamed and soared. Of course, Allen's vision of New York is more deeply felt, personal, and knowing than Minnelli's in *The Band Wagon* or the coy portrait of supposedly liberated Greenwich Village life in *My Sister Eileen* (1955). It's the city as seen by a man who, without too many illusions and with full awareness of New York's social sores ("drugs, garbage, crime"), continues to love and burnish it ("New York was his town, and it always would be") and steadfastly refuses to allow New York's real tawdriness to encroach on his vision of the heavenly city.

Allen is not uncritical of the city in *Manhattan*, but the brunt of his critique is cultural rather than social and political. In the opening voice-over in *Manhattan*, Isaac intones that his novel will be about "New York as a metaphor for the decay of contemporary culture." But it's not the city's gnawing poverty, the breakdown of its social services, its gratuitous violence, or its crumbling infrastructure that Allen is concerned with. The decay he inveighs against is his friends' and social milieu's penchant for self-indulgently betraying their talents and relationships. It's that insecure, shallow, narcissistic, name-dropping world that angers the moralist in Allen. His character Isaac's prime insight is that "people in Manhattan are constantly creating these unnecessary neurotic problems for themselves because it keeps them from dealing with the terrible, unsolvable problems of the universe"—like death.

Taken as cultural analysis, Allen's attack on modern decadence is itself specious and shallow—a mixture of cafeteria existentialism and some genuine revulsion with a milieu of which he is a member in good standing. But nobody asks Allen to be a Tocqueville, Marx, or even a Christopher Lasch— it's sufficient that his satirical thrusts at sophisticated Manhattan behavior often hit their mark.

Despite his censure, it's this same Manhattan that Allen's characters, like Alvy Singer in *Annie Hall*, trek over the Brooklyn Bridge to passionately embrace and defend. In *Radio Days*, Allen's skillfully crafted, nostalgic evocation of growing up in Rockaway in the late 1930s and the World War II years while listening to old radio programs like *The Green Hornet* and pop songs like "Lay That Pistol Down," Manhattan is always there to provoke a boy's fantasies. In this sentimental film, built around a series of vignettes, lower-middle-class Rockaway is not an oppressive world. It is remembered as an utterly domesticated, innocent neighborhood of teenage girls sitting in soda shops and sighing in unison while listening to crooners on the radio, a neighborhood where violence in school was no more than a spitball fight, and sex was just boys hungrily looking through binoculars at a nude, Rubenesque woman dancing in her apartment to the strains of "Babalu."

These Rockaway memories are filled with charm and warm feeling. Allen even granting the clamorous, insensitive family life of his young alter ego—a nearsighted, quietly irreverent boy named Joe—a semi-Edenic glow. All the family's abrasion—his uncle telling his aunt "to take the gaspipe"—is treated as a comic conceit, and the neighborhood cozily encompasses white beaches and piers for promenading. Still, underlying these soft-focused reminiscences is the strong feeling that neighborhood life is constricted and that home life is nothing more than a place where Joe's family settles down to tedious evenings of endless bickering, playing cards, washing the dishes, and listening to the radio. It is Manhattan, with its radio quiz shows, restaurants with cheek-to-cheek dancing, and a Radio City Music Hall with carpeted corridors and grand spaces, that Joe truly longs for.

It's Manhattan in *Radio Days*, both the real and the imagined one, that provides Allen's young protagonist with a sense of transcendence. The pleasure and excitement of his infrequent trips to Manhattan is reinforced by radio programs like the breakfast show over which Roger and Irene preside. It is a show that conjures up images of sophisticated people living in glamorous Manhattan penthouses, spending their evenings at the Stork Club, formally dressed for dancing and engaging in civilized adultery and urbane chitchat with other radio celebrities. The film, however, does not romanticize the celebrities—they're unprepossessing, somewhat absurd figures. But for Allen, the high style and success that this Manhattan world provides is clearly preferable to the more prosaic virtues of Jewish, lower-middle-class Rockaway. It's not that Allen repudiates his own ethnicity or roots: his persona, especially in the early films, is modeled after the classic Jewish victim-schlemiel; Alvy Singer is obsessed with anti-Semitism and jokes about his Jewish identity and past in *Annie Hall*; and *Broadway Danny Rose* (1984) is, on one level, a homage to Jewish Catskill comics. It's not, however, Jewish upper-middle-class suburban life young Joe dreams about, but a cosmopolitan Manhattan, with all its spiritual imperfections (and, given Allen's romantic revelations and travails of a few years ago, an emotionally more Dostoyevskian and anguished Manhattan than any of his films have conveyed), that the adult Allen now inhabits.

In a concluding voice-over in *Radio Days*, Allen speaks of these memories as growing dimmer with each passing year. But it's clear from Allen's films that the stylized memories of a magical Manhattan New Year's Eve in *Radio Days*—moonlit skies, gossamer-like snow flakes, and a large neon Camel sign blowing smoke—still vividly color and shape his vision of the New York present.

Allen's New York is very different from the city of streets filled with wandering dispossessed souls, shards of broken glass, ruined buildings, and sporadic murderous gunfire that characterize the New York films of Scorsese and Lumet. He has consciously projected a city that may not be celestial but comes as close as possible to a luminous "city on the hill." Obviously, that city is far removed from the daily reality of dire social and economic statistics and screaming headlines, but in this city of continual flux, there are still neighborhoods, streets, and moments where the dreamscape is ascendant. Allen's indelible urban images offer consolation and hope for those who believe that the delicate balance between dream and nightmare in New York will be preserved into the next century.

3

The Narrator and the Narrative
The Evolution of Woody Allen's Film Comedies

Celestino Deleyto

Stardust Memories (1980) employs a pervasive stylistic strategy: a character looks straight at the camera, which occupies the position where Sandy Bates (Woody Allen), the film's protagonist, is presumed to be. The identification between camera and star-director apparently confirms his centrality in the Allen text. But then the other character's gaze gradually moves away and is eventually directed on-screen as Sandy comes into the frame. This pattern can be read, metaphorically, as a move away from the self-conscious, authoritarian author, who obliges the spectator to be constantly aware of the author's creative presence, toward the author's inclusion in a narrative of which he or she is only a part, in a film that includes the author and encompasses his or her intention within a wider frame, that of classical film narrative.[1] This tension between author and narrative is not always solved in the same specific way in Allen's films. Yet the strategy employed in *Stardust Memories* suggests a certain evolution with respect to the presentation of this conflict in earlier films, whose exaggerated metafictional nature seems a consequence of Allen's particular relationship with the texts as narratives. A gradual shift can be posited in the development of his filmic career from a privileged author-spectator relationship to an acknowledgment of the power of narrative and the limitations of the author as dominant creator and as viable artistic concept.

This hypothesis does not coincide with George McCann's reading, which sees a progression from genre parody to autobiographical works, with *Love and Death* (1975) as a bridge between the two periods (76). Parody in the Bakhtinian sense is also the starting point of Ruth Perlmutter's reading of *Zelig*, in which she relates this concept to issues of comedy and Jewishness in that film (206–7). Although my emphasis in this chapter is on narrative and comedy, I share with McCann and Perlmutter a general concern with metafictional aspects of Allen's films[2] and eventually concentrate on *Love and Death*, *Annie Hall* (1977), and *Manhattan* (1979) because they seem to constitute the arena in which the conflict between author and classical narrative is most crucially played, with *Stardust Memories* as a sort of epilogue or summary and the subsequent films of the 1980s and early 1990s bearing the consequences of the result of this "battle."

The starting point of Allen's early films, of course, can be found in his nightclub performances of the 1960s. The resistance to narrative of the early films can be directly related to this period. Steve Seidman has placed Woody Allen's films within the comedy film tradition he labels "comedian comedy," a tradition formed around performers who began their careers in other media, such as music hall, vaudeville, musical theater, or radio, and whose work previous to the cinema sets their films apart from other Hollywood films (2–3). As a result of his experiences doing stand-up comedy (reflected in his characterizations of Alvy Singer and Broadway Danny Rose), Allen developed the need for complete control over his work. McCann sees this goal as the reason behind each important move in Allen's career, "from writing gags to performing his own material to appearing in his own films to directing them" (63). But arguably, the structures of the 1970s films, and the centrality of the author or of the author figures in them, can also be related to the structure of the stand-up comic acts that preceded them. The issue of authorship, in spite of all the developments of modern criticism, is not even at stake in the case of Woody Allen.[3] Allen's desire to control his creation completely informs each of his most clearly metafictional works, *Annie Hall*, *The Purple Rose of Cairo* (1985), and the play *God* (McCann, 63).

The texts themselves, however, may tell a very different story, one that presents the progressive debilitation of the omniscient, all-powerful author in favor of the logic of the narrative, the power of convention and language, and the unavoidable textuality of experience. Babington and Evans, perhaps less radically, hold the same view, although in their account simultaneity and ambivalence replace evolution: "He is . . . a fragmented author, a de-*auteur*ising *auteur* . . . , someone who within his immediately recognisable persona at times even seems to acknowledge the post-structuralist principle of the author's de-centred contribution to a tissue of multiple voices and writings" (152–53).

The iconoclastic parody of classical cinema characteristic of the early films can be seen as part of a carefully devised project. The narratives themselves are not very compelling, coherent, or elaborate because they are not important: they are merely excuses for the comedian to tell his jokes and establish his special rapport with the audience. Allen wants to achieve the same sort of intimate relationship with film audiences that he is used to from his successful live performances, and he not only disregards but successfully deconstructs the narrative wrapping of his films. The comedian keeps popping up as comedian: sometimes in subtle ways, as in the ambiguous relationship established between his and Diane Keaton's characters through his jokes, in *Play It Again, Sam* (1972) and *Annie Hall*, and other times in somewhat cruder ways, such as the episode "Do aphrodisiacs work?" from *Everything You Always Wanted to Know about Sex* (1972). This segment is the first occasion, in fact, in which the character (a medieval comic) looks directly at the spectator, in what is taken as the logical way of reproducing the communicative situation of earlier live performances. The very weak story line of this episode is the excuse for the diegetic comedian to tell his jokes, mostly concerned with sex and language, and for the film to dramatize his relationship with the audience.

This textual strategy—the character looking at and talking directly to the spectator, therefore placing himself outside the story, in an updated version of the old theatrical aside—is combined, from *Play It Again, Sam* onward, with an omniscient and self-deprecating narratorial commentary carried out by the protagonist.[4] Narrational commentary had already appeared as a central feature of *Take the Money and Run* (1969), but as will happen later in *Zelig*, the voice-over was an ironically omniscient and frequently self-contradicting third-person narratorial voice, meant as a parody of similar devices in documentary films. The mixture of direct address to the camera and narratorial commentary used in *Play It Again, Sam* was repeated in *Love and Death* and *Annie Hall* and, in different modified and more complex forms, in *Stardust Memories, Hannah and Her Sisters* (1986), *Radio Days* (1987), *Another Woman* (1988; although, significantly, in this film the protagonist and first-person narrator is not a character played by Woody Allen), and the "Oedipus Wrecks" episode of the film *New York Stories* (1989). This strategy is crucial in the formation of the Woody Allen filmic persona in the 1970s and proves irresistible for the spectator: an ironic, self-indulgent even if self-criticizing narrator, who looks at himself as hero and does not often like what he sees, even though the charm is still there. The spectator identifies with the Allen persona not only because of what the characters are but also because of the way the narrators present them.[5]

In *Play It Again, Sam* the narrator is not content with asserting his control over the narrative, but beckons to the spectator so that she too occupies the same privileged position she had in the stand-up acts. It may seem, at times, that there are two independent centers of interest in the films: the narrative line and the imaginary axis that unites Allen and the spectator. This split can be most clearly seen in the opening scene of *Annie Hall*, with Allen talking directly to the camera in medium close-up, framed by an abstract, nonrepresentational background, and only gradually and reluctantly admitting that he is a character—Alvy Singer—forming part of a narrative. The audience that the Allen persona talks to is a very specific audience, probably even one whose heyday has now passed: "largely college-educated, mainly urban middle-class," and one that is trying to adapt to "the demands of a deconstructionist, postfeminist, post-Vietnam culture" (Babington and Evans, 155, 152).

Protagonist and audience are still the main concern in *Play It Again, Sam*, as they were in the live performances. Everything makes sense when Allan/Allen starts talking to us and introducing his character with the usual physical and psychological limitations, combined with his personal charm and wit. It even seems at times as if the character were constantly performing for a diegetic audience, especially when the Diane Keaton character (Linda) starts laughing at his jokes, apparently preferring them to the narrative of which the character she plays is an important part. Even though this is the only film among the first five in which voice-over narration occurs, all the early films feature the predominance of the cherished comic-audience relationship over the different narrative frames, which have been used only as filmic wrappings of the comic persona's addresses to the spectator. *Sleeper* (1973) certainly has a more complicated, but not necessarily more complex, plot than any of the earlier films, but that plot is still there largely to be parodied and to provide an attractive context for the jokes about the character's science-fictional arrival in the future, the development of the Allen persona, and the serious comments about love and death in the final dialogue, the first explicit acknowledgment of a tragic dimension to the Allen comic world.

Love and Death, which presents itself, even from the title, as one more parody, starts again with first-person voice-over narration: this time the object of the parody is nineteenth-century realist fiction. The plot, again very complicated, seems, in this respect, similar to that of *Sleeper*, one more excuse for the jokes and the more elaborate comic presentation of the tragedy of the modern man. *Love and Death* is the most sophisticated compendium yet of the Allen persona's views and thus a source of material that will reappear in subtler ways in the later films. But even if the narrative is still largely unimportant, we find in this film a self-conscious concern with narrative forms, a reflexive exploration of narrative rules, as if the film were striving for a more viable, more fruitful approach to narrative than the previous iconoclastic baring of conventions. An example can be seen in the strange dream of the waiters, whose connection with the rest of the narrative seems nonexistent. The lack of causality in the relationship between dream and context parodies classical narrative rules but also explores new ways of conveying experience that may better fit the Allen persona's attitude toward life. Immediately after the dream, young Boris discusses matters of universal causality and the role of God with father Nicolai. The exploration of narrative possibilities based on contingency rather than causality is, consequently, connected with the protagonist's response to life. However, this narrative, whatever form it takes, is not yet ready to acquire any semblance of realism.[6] Like *Sleeper*, which proved to be far less a science-fictional account of the world in 2173 than a contemporary vision of 1973 society, *Love and Death* is only superficially a faithful portrait of nineteenth-century Russia, with the characters often breaking into contemporary dialogues and exhibiting anachronistic patterns of behavior.

Causality is parodied, even though a linear, narrative view of life is implied in the protagonist's somber, tragic attitude toward existence. At one point he says, "Nothingness, nonexistence, black emptiness"; Sonja (Diane Keaton) asks, "What did you say?" and he replies, "Nothing, I was planning my future." Boris says these words on the eve of his duel, after he has been asking God for a sign of his existence (even a cough would do). Even though Sonja intervenes and breaks the spell, Boris again speaks directly to the audience, in close-up, outside the narrative, conveying his existential worries and asking us directly to share them. The character repeats this address to the spectator several times. When Sonja looks at the camera, however, it is a subjective shot: after finally marrying Boris and living happily with him for a few months, she says, "Oh Boris, I've never been so happy in my entire life," addressing Boris, who is clearly supposed to occupy the position of the camera. Both the realistic strategy—the subjective shot—and the metafictional one—direct address—serve the same purpose: to provide the spectator, particularly the male spectator, with a figure of identification. We can see, then, that the presence of the Allen persona is as pervasive as in the former films, the rest of the characters and the events being just functions, often not very clearly motivated ones, of the obsessive discussion of his own personality.

Love and Death, as much as the earlier works, is a film about Woody Allen, as self-centered as before, but one in which the exploration of self by the film-persona is presented in narrative terms, one that finds it more difficult to do away with the conventions it parodies, and one that is conscious of the critical tension at its core between comedian and narrative. This tension can best be perceived in the final section of the film. The weak and still largely uninteresting narrative line is disrupted once again for the two main characters to engage in a highly theoretical argument about the moral dimensions of murder. The scene, like the two similar dialogues earlier, draws its comic dimension from its inappropriateness to the context while simultaneously conveying Boris's riddling insecurity about life in general. Narrative has been openly parodied in the jail dialogue between Boris and his father and, more importantly, in the dialogue between Sonja and Natasha, after Boris's execution, in which Natasha tells Sonja an absurd, unbelievable story of octagonal love and Sonja answers with a piece of complicated philosophical speculation. When Boris's specter appears outside the window, the shots of the two women recall Bergman's *Persona* (1966) and look forward to one of Allen's least popular films, *Interiors* (1978). The reference to Bergman is apt here because the scene is suffused in the resigned, tranquil atmosphere of acknowledgment of death, followed by Boris's final address to the audience in which he summarizes the film's view of life. This final address ends with the following line: "The mind embraces all the nobler aspirations, like poetry, or philosophy, but the body has all the fun," which, as a final statement on life, seems remarkably unrelated to most of what has happened in the film but does encapsulate one of the most characteristic elements of the worldview presented by the Allen persona throughout Woody Allen's various works, one that will have a central position in the next film, *Annie Hall*. The final long take, filmed with static camera, is again a reference to Bergman, this time to the last shot of *The Seventh Seal* (1957). It shows Boris dancing along with the figure of Death to Prokofiev's music, disappearing at the end of the long line of trees and visually encapsulating the theme of the film in a much more powerful way than the former monologue. What is more important for the argument here, the shot is essentially narrative.

Love and Death is ostensibly presented as a parody of realist Russian novels of the nineteenth century, but more centrally as a parody of plot and causality. The voice-over narrator, a device that classical cinema took from the realist novel, becomes less and less interested in the verisimilitude of the plot and more interested in addressing the spectator and confronting her with the issues of death and the existence of God. Boris's final address is really the only thing that we are meant to take seriously, yet his goodbye formula, "That's about it from me, folks," and the last shot, together with the obvious allusion to Bergman's film, manage to undercut the authority of Allen's authorship, leaving the final word to narrative and showing the powerful creator as a fool in the hands of Death.

If the final shot of *Love and Death* seems to be pointing at the future, the opening shot of the next film, *Annie Hall*, returns to the first-person narrator convention in an even more exacerbated form than in *Play It Again, Sam* or *Love and Death*. This time we do not get a voice-over narrator but the on-screen character talking directly to the spectator. Significantly, Alvy Singer, the Allen protagonist, is a comedian by profession, although the most important aspect of the plot revolves around his relationship with women, particularly Annie. His opening monologue startles the spectator, who does not know exactly who she is dealing with: is this Woody Allen the director, introducing the film in a prologue scene, or is he talking to someone in the fictional world? Is he a character, and is this going to be a narrative film at all? The suspense lasts a relatively short time, but the metafictional beginning is there to announce the kind of film this is going to be. Almost inadvertently, the monologue breaks into narrative: "Annie and I broke up and I still can't get my mind around that." We find out, therefore, that this is not Woody Allen but a fictional character who, so far, looks very much like the actor-director. The film starts in a confessional mood: he is not talking to anybody in the fiction, he is telling us and expecting us to believe him. He looks so natural, so relaxed, and so intimate with the audience that we immediately take what he says at face value. When he says that he is not the morose, depressive type and that he was a reasonably happy kid, we believe him, but when he says he grew up in Brooklyn during World War II we start to doubt his happiness. Immediately after, the narrator says, so as to justify the discrepancy, "My analyst says I exaggerate my childhood memories." The voice-over both dominates the visual narrative and confirms the past as unreliable memory. In *Love and Death* we saw the stand-up comedian proving the narrative to be arbitrary and artificial, even though the ending was somehow more ambiguous. The beginning of *Annie Hall* confirms the same attitude, narrative taking now the form of unreliable memories. The spectator may choose to place more trust on the visual narrative, but the reliability of the initial flashback image of a small house directly under the Coney Island roller coaster is at least problematic, and it becomes more so as the scene develops. The narrator seems to keep a certain degree of control, even if he cannot control himself: "I have some trouble between fantasy and reality." The classroom scene, immediately following, confirms the unreliability of memory by having the adult narrator intrude in his own childhood memory as an adult and by having the children behave in a totally—and comically—unrealistic way. The role of memory with respect to the past is, therefore, presented as parallel to the creative role of the narrator with respect to the narrative in that both fictionalize reality by selecting and rearranging preexisting material.[7]

Alvy Singer is not, like Boris, parodic in the treatment of narrative material, but the film still diverts, in many ways, from classical narrative. The cinema queue scene, for example, presents a new subversion of narrative: characters talk directly to the camera, and even one of the famous (real) people who are being discussed—Marshall McLuhan—has the power to materialize. "If only real life was like that," says Alvy, once again talking directly to us. The arbitrariness of classical film narrative is exposed several times again in the course of the film. Take, for example, that flashback to Alvy's relationship with Allison, his first wife. The scene ends with another direct address to the spectator, but although the character talking is the one in the flashback and not the present-day narrator, his words are those of the divorced Alvy, talking about his past relationship with the woman who is still in the room. The Allen persona is still very much the center of film, and narrative conventions around him continue to dissolve and to prove arbitrary, unnatural. It may be said that the character is trying to control his own life in the same way as the narrator attempts to control the narrative.

In the previous scene, Annie accuses Alvy of being so egocentric that he thinks of her therapy in terms of how it affects him. The same critique can be applied to the whole narrative, which although it is called *Annie Hall*, is really much more about Alvy than Annie. But this figure, Alvy, has a very unstable ontological status that suggests the arbitrariness of classical narrative. Both characters look at the memory from the perspective of the present but still form part of the diegetic past, the flashback, apparently again having transgressed the boundary between the two narrative levels. In realistic terms, the scene reflects neither his re-creation nor her memory, but a sort of collective revisitation of her past.

The flashback that takes us back to the first time Alvy and Annie met is not motivated by a memory but directly introduced by the text. This time, the presentation is much more realistic, with the characters talking in the same relaxed, natural way that the narrator used to address us at the beginning, even if this classical style is interrupted by the famous subtitled balcony scene. Gradually, the narrative sets into a classical account of their romance, even though Alvy is throughout recognizable as the Allen persona (as when he tells Annie how "life is divided between the horrible and the miserable"). The whole of the middle section, which develops the relationship between Alvy and Annie, presents itself as real (with some slips into self-consciousness) but is obviously no more or no less real than what had gone before. It is as if, after undermining the classical method, the film itself attempts to use it and to persuade the spectator to suspend her reluctantly but definitively lost disbelief.[8]

The final scene, however, marks an open return to the self-conscious mode. The play, whose fictional status is ambiguous at first, is Alvy's attempt to put into practice the words we hear him say: "You are always trying to get things perfect in art because it's so difficult in life." It offers a "fictional" narrative of his relationship with Annie, but one with a happy ending. The distinction between life and art, which much of the film has tried to explore, is now clear, since it becomes gradually obvious that the action is part of a play. Yet the multiplicity of narrative levels and the foregrounding of conventions are fully at work now. What other narrative level are we supposed to separate this fiction from? Is Alvy Singer real within the film diegesis, after everything that has happened in it? Are we then to believe that Marshall McLuhan's materialization, at Alvy's fictional level, is realistic? Can Alvy and Annie's relationship not be interpreted, as it no doubt must have been at the time, as a stylized, wish-fulfillment version of Woody Allen and Diane Keaton's by-then finished relationship? Are Alvy's confessional moments with the audience still the only thing we can believe in? The problem remains that narrative structures have already intruded to such an extent in this film that they cannot simply be written off as a frame for the antics of the comedian. If the narrative disappears, then Alvy goes with it, and the Allen persona too, since they are fictions built by the narrative.

In the end, the cherished relationship between comic and audience proves as viable as the narrative mechanisms over which it has always been privileged. Too many questions about the real existence of the artist and his audience have been left unanswered, and simultaneously, narrative, plot, and fictional stories have become inseparable from the ways of expression of the comic. In *Manhattan*, after an opening scene in which a narrator struggles to find the right beginning for his story, the film will settle for classical narrative and the strategies inherited from the live performances will all but disappear. The diegetic dominance of the artist is replaced by a specific classical style, which has been associated with Allen's films since *Manhattan*.

In *Manhattan*'s prologue sequence, however, Allen is still talking about himself. We get his unmistakable voice-over, as a writer who is trying to begin a novel about New York. He tries several unsatisfactory openings, until he seems to hit on the right one: "Behind his black-rimmed glasses was the coiled sexual power of a jungle cat." What is interesting about this chosen alternative is how much more personal it is than the previous ones, how much more indirectly it describes New York, and how much closer it comes to the author and to one of the crucial component tensions of the Allen persona, as created in previous films: the intellectual who is trying to find an outlet for his (sexual) instincts. This mixture of intellectual and sexual urges will still characterize Isaac Davis, a writer who, unlike Allen in *Play It Again, Sam*, is very successful with women but still not without personal problems.

For anybody who has followed Allen's career, this first sequence must come as no surprise as an introduction to a similar kind of film as the enormously successful *Annie Hall*.[9] Expectations, however, are frustrated, and the film proves drastically different from the previous ones. The second scene breaks the established pattern and plunges into a classical style yet unknown in Allen, without self-consciousness or direct address to the audience. The lively dialogue is presented by means of classical establishing shots, analytical breakdown in shot-reverse shots and two or three shots, making the most of the wide-screen format and concentrating on the expressions of the characters, especially Isaac and Tracy. The dialogue concerns art, with Yale, a university lecturer, lecturing Tracy on some academic issue. But Isaac, who reminds us here of Alvy in the cinema queue, soon degrades art in favor of life. The main stylistic ways through which the film will present its story, and that will constitute its very personal style, are already obvious here: expressionistic mise-en-scène, particularly the lighting, framing, and double frames, with the tracking shot of the characters walking in the streets as the favored space in which to communicate real feelings. Although these tracking shots occur mostly in the first hour or so, their climax will be the montage following Isaac in the final scene as he runs to Tracy's apartment, a parodic reference to the last scene in Wilder's *The Apartment* (1960) or perhaps to Nichols's *The Graduate* (1967), but also a logical consequence of the stylistic choices made in the rest of the film. The tracking shot, usually framed in a recognizable New York cityscape, can, on the other hand, be related to the final shot of *Love and Death* (even though the characters' movements were presented there through a static camera) in that both stylistic choices emphasize narrative linearity and classical causality at the expense of the author.

The comedy in *Manhattan* departs from the anarchic, deconstructive, Bakhtinian spirit of the earlier texts and becomes a comedy of integration, however precarious, and triumph over human mortality, a weltanschauung closely linked to Freud's view of humor as liberating and as "something of grandeur and elevation" (428). It is as if, once again, classical comedy had tamed the comic spirit into narrative structure (Deleyto, 75–76). The film's alliance with the worldview of classical comedy can best be seen in its last scene. Isaac undergoes the classical moment of crisis out of which recovery (and discovery) will emerge, lying on his sofa, listing the things that make life worth living. He comes out with works of art: *Sentimental Education*, Cezanne's paintings, Mozart's 41st Symphony, etc. and ends up with what is felt to be the most important one, Tracy's face. At one level, his conclusion is one more version of the preference for life, reality, and experience as opposed to art and intellectual achievement. But throughout *Manhattan*, the camera has privileged the image of Tracy's face, insisting on close-ups of Mariel Hemingway as opposed to Diane Keaton, who is generally framed from a much greater distance. This concentration is particularly curious because Tracy's face is usually not very expressive. Like the beloved in Petrarchan and Elizabethan sonnets, it is like a blank page to be filled in by the imagination of the lyrical subject, in this case, by Isaac's gaze. In Shakespeare's sonnets, beauty is ephemeral and can be immortalized only through poetry. In *Manhattan*, it is Tracy's face that, the film argues, is worth immortalizing. But this object—Tracy's face—is not simply the face itself (Hemingway's face) but the image of it projected by the film, a very subjective image that includes as much of Isaac's fascination at her purity and honesty as of Tracy's character itself.

The close-ups of Tracy serve to contrast what is worth preserving with what inevitably dies, as represented by the skeleton in the anatomy classroom earlier in the film. Within the theoretical debate between life and art, or life and the mind, life comes out as triumphing, but only through the artificial perspective of the close-up, as if the film could not get away from its artistic solipsism. Tracy's face, from a metafictional standpoint, is not so much opposed to the artistic masterpieces that have preceded it as it is one more work of art, one that epitomizes all that is affirmative in this rather dark comedy.[10] It is also, through the development of Isaac's relationship to

Tracy, an argument in favor of classical narrative and closure.[11] Thus *Manhattan*'s comic solution to the problems of existence echoes the gradual evolution in Allen's oeuvre as well as the historical evolution of comedy from anarchic, carnivalesque parody to classical comic narrative.

After the trilogy *Love and Death—Annie Hall—Manhattan*, through which, gradually, narrative and plot have come to equal the importance of the stand-up comic and narrator, and even, in *Manhattan*, to take over, *Stardust Memories* represents a moment of crisis, at the same time as it parodically refers to Fellini's *8 1/2* (1963) and Sturges's *Sullivan's Travels* (1941). While Allen suggests an apparent return to the centrality of the creator (now not a comedian but already a film director), his persona now serves the demands of narrative structure. The subjective shots turned external I described at the beginning of this chapter illustrate how, for all its narcissism and self-consciousness, the text dramatizes the position of an author-director who has been turned into a part of the narrative process. Like Sullivan in *Sullivan's Travels*, Sandy Bates acknowledges, in the penultimate happy ending, and in the moment of happiness with Dorrie, the validity of comedy. *Stardust Memories* does not tell a linear narrative, but in a way, by mixing levels and continually turning reality, memories, and jokes into a film, it suggests that narrative in the end will win the day, in spite of its fictionality, in spite of its arbitrariness. In the same way, the author has also become part of a film and can only control the different snatches of films within that film. As if Allen's films had been trying to exorcise the ghost of the author-artist-comic-narrator, now they can move on. The author is acknowledged as one more fictional construct, formed of fragments of his films, audience, and critics' and intellectuals' responses, all part of the narrative process. At the same time, the obvious autobiographical nature of much of the film shows the ability of the Allen text (originally the ability of the comic) to turn personal experience into narrative, just as, later on in *Zelig* and *Radio Days*, history will also be turned into narrative.[12]

NOTES

The research toward this paper was carried out with the financial aid of the Direccion General de Investigacion Científica y Tecnica, Ministerio de Educacion y Ciencia, Spain, research project no. PS90-0117. I would also like to thank Constanza del Rio, Peter Evans, and the editor and anonymous readers of *Film Criticism* for their comments and suggestions on earlier drafts of the paper.

1. Robert C. Allen and Douglas Gomery provide a good definition of classical film narrative in the predominantly formal sense in which the term is understood here:

> This term designates a particular pattern of organization of filmic elements whose overall function is to tell a particular kind of story in a particular way. The story the Hollywood

film relates involves a continuous cause-effect chain, motivated by the desires or needs of individual characters and usually resolved by the fulfillment of those desires or needs. . . . All filmic elements in the classical Hollywood cinema serve the narrative and are subordinated to it. Editing, mise-en-scène, lighting, camera movement, and acting all work together to create a transparency of style so that the viewer attends to the story being told and not to the manner of its telling. (81)

2. On metafiction, see Waugh and Hutcheon.

3. Allen's opinion on the issue of colorization of old films could be taken as illustration: "What's at stake is a moral issue and how our culture chooses to define itself. No one should be able to alter an artist's work in any way whatsoever, for any reason, without the artist's consent. It's really as simple as that" (Allen, quoted in Brunette and Wills, 191–92).

4. Of course, this strategy defines, with some variations, other comic filmic personae, such as Groucho Marx, whose influence Allen has long acknowledged, and W. C. Fields, although their asides to the spectator are usually more openly critical and iconoclastic than Allen's. In any case, it is the specific characteristics of the Allen persona and its relation to the film narratives, and not its belonging to a comic tradition, that interest me here.

5. Seidman has explained the structure of direct address as a consequence of the style of performance and comic persona that Allen and other comedians bring to their films from their previous appearances in other media. He also argues that this and other devices of the "comedian comedy" conflict with the conventions of the classical Hollywood film, in which, for example, direct address to the camera is generally forbidden (15–19). See also Neale and Krutnik, 103–7.

6. I am assuming a connection between classical narrative and verisimilitude, and although realism and classical narrative do not necessarily go together, in the case of Woody Allen's films there seems to be a direct link between these two concepts, both negatively—the most artificial-looking films are also the least classical in construction—and affirmatively—films like *Manhattan*, *Broadway Danny Rose* (1984), *Hannah and Her Sisters*, or *Crimes and Misdemeanors* (1989)—give a greater impression of realism than the rest through their reliance on classical strategies of representation. However, the limitations of realism within classical narrative are brilliantly exposed in *Manhattan* through the use of close-ups of Tracy's face, as will be discussed later.

7. In his discussion of this scene, Sam B. Girgus relates Allen's "promiscuous use of time and space" to a tension between *histoire* and discourse in the film that produces a denial of artistic and creative closure. While his analysis of narrative desire allows Girgus to relate the film's narrative structure to certain ideological concerns such as gender relationships, there is no attempt to distinguish between classical Hollywood narrative conventions and the presence of the author persona in the film (25–42, esp. 26–27).

8. I am not trying to suggest that the spectator is constantly gulled and confused by the text's strategies. On the contrary, the film engages the viewer in a game that sharpens her awareness of narrative conventions and expands the range of comic response.

9. Yet as Girgus points out, the hesitant mode of the sequence can be read as undermining any transcendent authority (44).

10. The presence of a work of art at the moment of anagnorisis reappears in *Hannah and Her Sisters*, when Mickey (Woody Allen) overcomes his existential crisis as a result of the experience of watching the Marx Brothers *Duck Soup* (1933).

11. For a different reading of Tracy's face, see Girgus, 64–65.

12. In view of events in Woody Allen's personal life, the rupture with Farrow and subsequent court battle, one is tempted to suggest that narrative has now, to a certain extent, turned into personal experience, thus completing a cycle. I am indebted to Lloyd Michaels for this insight.

WORKS CITED

Allen, Robert C., and Douglas Gomery. *Film History: Theory and Practice*. New York: Alfred A. Knopf, 1985.

Babington, Bruce, and Peter William Evans. *Affairs to Remember: The Hollywood Comedy of the Sexes*. Manchester, UK: Manchester University Press, 1989.

Brunette, Peter, and David Wills. *Screen/Play: Derrida and Film Theory*. Princeton, UK: Princeton University Press, 1989.

Deleyto, Celestino. "Narrative Closure and the Comic Spirit: The Inconclusive Ending of *Bringing Up Baby*." In *Flashbacks: Re-Reading the Classical Hollywood Cinema*, ed. Deleyto, 161–84. Zaragoza, Spain: Servicio de Publicaciones de la Universidad de Zaragoza, 1992.

Freud, Sigmund. "Humour." *Art and Literature*. The Penguin Freud Library, vol. 14. Harmondsworth, Middlesex, UK: Penguin, 1991 (1928).

Girgus, Sam B. *The Films of Woody Allen*. Cambridge: Cambridge University Press, 1993.

Hutcheon, Linda. *Narcissistic Narrative: The Metafictional Paradox*. New York: Methuen, 1984.

McCann, George. *Woody Allen: New Yorker*. London: Polity, 1990.

Neale, Steve, and Frank Krutnik. *Popular Film and Television Comedy*. London: Routledge, 1990.

Perlmutter, Ruth. "Woody Allen's *Zelig*; An American Jewish Parody." *Comedy/Cinema/History*, ed. Andrew S. Horton, 206–21. Berkeley: University of California Press, 1991.

Seidman, Steve. *Comedian Comedy: A Tradition in Hollywood Film*. Ann Arbor, MI: UMI Research, 1981.

Waugh, Patricia. *Metafiction: Theory and Practice of Self-Conscious Fiction*. London: Methuen, 1981.

4

Woody Allen's Theological Imagination

Gary Commins

"To you, I'm an atheist. To God, I'm the loyal opposition . . ." Allen comes out of the Jewish tradition which, from its scriptural roots, has poked and prodded the powerful. In *Stardust Memories*, he turns this protest against a powerful God, saying "Thou hast a good job. Don't blow it."

Sandy Bates sits on a train. The only sound to break through the silence is that of a clock ticking. Bates looks around at the other passengers. Their faces are morose, morbid, haunted, suspicious. One man cries. People return his gaze without expression. The clock ticks on. He looks out the window to see another train just beginning to pull out of the station. A party is in full swing. People are laughing. A woman looks at him enticingly, flirtatiously. He calls the conductor over to examine his ticket. He must be on the wrong train. He gets up and tries to open the door to get out. A priest, among others, looks on distantly. The door is locked. The clock keeps ticking. The train pulls out. He yanks on the cord to stop the train. It falls into his hands. He bangs on door and window alike in frustration, unable to get out.[1]

If the actor on the screen were not Woody Allen, the audience would not be laughing. He brings humor to the absurdity and the tragedy of life. Throughout his works—movies, plays, books—Allen has consistently shown life to be a mystery rather than a problem that can be solved like a puzzle or a riddle. He takes up profound questions about the meaning of life, about evil and suffering, and about God with a profound sense of their inscrutability—and the dark humor of it all.

I

Allen delights in pairing ultimate concerns with silly ones. His mother-in-law in *Take the Money and Run* (1969) has conversations with God about "salvation and interior decorating." Elsewhere, he summarizes his parents' values as "God and carpeting."[2] He thinks about Jesus Christ: "If he was a carpenter, I wonder what he charged for bookshelves."[3] In a conversation with a nun, they agree that Jesus Christ was "extremely well-adjusted for an only child."[4] His philosophical statements become enlightening and wistful examinations of the inability of the human race to come to grips adequately with the universe: "Eternal nothingness is O.K. if you're dressed for it."[5] "Is knowledge knowable? If not, how do we know this?"[6] A philosopher "differentiated between existence and Existence, and knew one was preferable, but could never remember which."[7] He describes himself as a "teleological, existential atheist," which means "I believe that there's an intelligence to the universe with the exception of parts of New Jersey."[8] In *Stardust Memories* (1980), Sandy Bates carries on an imagined conversation with a superintelligent being:

Bates: Why is there so much suffering?
Being: This is unanswerable.
Bates: Is there a God?
Being: These are the wrong questions.

Right or wrong, these questions fill his works: questions about relationships, about the meaning of life, about God, about death, about morality, about alienation, about hope. His questions never find complete answers.

In New Orleans, a Haitian "conjure man," a leftover from a superstitious era, performs his spells on the street. Obviously, he provides passing entertainment for profit in a more scientific, sophisticated age. A policeman tells him to move on. They argue. "When it is over, the policeman is four inches tall."[9] In Woody Allen's world, nothing can be counted on and nothing can be counted out. Life is mystery. It cannot be solved. It is absurd. It does not make sense.

In the film *Love and Death* (1975), Boris is suddenly gripped by a terrible feeling from out of nowhere. His marriage had finally overcome the initial difficulty that his wife, Sonja, did not love him. Now triumphant, he is seized with an urge to commit suicide. He discusses the crisis with a friend:

Boris: I feel a void at the center of my being.
Friend: What kind of a void.
Boris: An empty void. I felt a full void a month ago but it was just something I ate.

He returns to such amusing distinctions between physical and existential nausea in many subtle ways. In the play "Death," a killer is on the loose. In the dark night, sweat beads up under everyone's clothing, sweat that always lies in wait for release by an omnipresent fear. Kleinman and a doctor hear a scream.

Doctor: Do you hear footsteps behind us?

Kleinman: I've been hearing footsteps behind me since I was eight years old.[10]

His characters are anxious, fearful, haunted. His leading men are almost always peculiarly Allenesque. They seem to attract an undue number of crises. They seem unable to pull their lives together. They seem very much like ourselves.

The only way to avoid the anxiety is through not really living. In *Annie Hall* (1977), the only "happy" couple Allen encounters has found happiness because neither one has any opinions, ideas, or thoughts. In *Love and Death*, the following exchange takes place:

Sonja: The only truly happy person I know is Berdykov the village idiot.

Boris: Well, it's easy to be happy, you know, when your one concern in life is figuring out how much saliva to dribble.

Is ignorance bliss? Perhaps. But Allen is certain that intelligence, knowledge, sensitivity to the misery of the human condition, an acute awareness of one's self and of others all breed anxiety, grief, and sometimes fear.

We only add to the problem if we try to avoid it, much as we might like to. In *Stardust Memories*, Sandy is told that "too much reality is not what the people want. . . . Human suffering doesn't sell tickets in Kansas City." In *Manhattan* (1979), Isaac reflects on a short story to take place in New York City in which people are "constantly creating these real unnecessary, neurotic problems for themselves because it keeps them from dealing with more unsolvable, terrifying problems about the universe." If people become preoccupied with these false, neurotic, manufactured problems, they will never come to face the truly important crises of life. They will live without integrity or courage. Honest ignorance is one thing, though scarcely admirable. Avoidance can never simulate the bliss of ignorance, although it seems that people will try.

If avoidance is one problem in coping with the world, another is humanity's desperate need for control. Allen consistently pokes fun at every attempt to come to a philosophically consistent approach to the human dilemma. Zelig, the human chameleon who changes his appearance to fit in with any group of people (an exaggerated form of altering one's personality to be accepted), finds himself analyzed by various groups. Marxists try to use him. Americans see him as a kind of Horatio Alger character. To the Jewish community, he reflects the experience of assimilation into American society. French intellectuals "see in him a symbol for everything." The drive to explain is the drive to control.

Two apocryphal stories of his experiences at New York University reveal his own view of philosophy. On his final in Existential Philosophy, he is faced with ten questions. He cannot answer even one. He leaves them all blank. For his efforts, he receives a "100."[11] On another occasion, "I cheated on my Metaphysics final. I looked within the soul of the boy sitting next to me."[12] For this, he is expelled from the university.

Allen consistently resists any "answers," and he subverts, through a comic reductio ad absurdum, all attempts to provide them. Zelig is told by a doctor that he has a tumor and may die in a few weeks. Ironically, the doctor dies instead. In *Sleeper* (1973), Miles finds that health foods are not really healthy, that science has failed him, and that politics and religion are dead ends. Allen tells a story of Socrates walking along in Athens when two youths from Sparta accost him for his money. "Socrates proved to them using simple logic that evil was merely ignorance of the truth. . . . And they broke his nose."[13] The secret of life according to Ho Sin: "Never to yodel."[14] Helmholtz, the great colleague of Freud, "proved that death is an acquired trait."[15] Allen chronicles attempts to understand someone by "psychoanalyzing him through his laundry lists."[16] Elsewhere, a restaurant critic sees in the tossing of a salad a "statement" about the meaning of life.[17]

Trying to control life with explanations puts people in awkward positions. In *A Midsummer Night's Sex Comedy* (1982), the rationalist Leopold, whose arrogant logical positivism grates on everyone's nerves ("I did not create the cosmos. I merely explain it."), says, "What a pity that people require more for their existence than the wonderful world about them." The physician, Maxwell, replies, "It's not always so wonderful down at the hospital." Leopold consistently refutes the existence of anything beyond the physical world as fantasy. At the end of the film, when he dies, he is transformed into pure essence, the ultimate punishment for his philosophy.

One of Allen's greatest stories about the failure to control one's own life and one's environment is "The Lunatic's Tale."[18] In this story, a formerly successful doctor, who once drove a Mercedes, wore expensive clothes, and was known for his wit and his backhand, is seen "roller skating unshaven down Broadway wearing a knapsack and a pinwheel hat." What caused his breakdown? He was in love with two women, one brilliant and reasonably attractive, the other the most beautiful woman he could imagine. A brain surgeon, he performed a transplant to put the brilliant brain into the perfect body. After successful surgery, he married the woman, then fell helplessly in love with a moderately attractive and not-too-intelligent airline stewardess. Hence his breakdown.

Not satisfied with undermining every philosophical, religious, and psychological attempt to explain the world, Allen subverts even the grounds on which their claims are made. Metterling attends "a production of *Oedipus*, from which Freud had to be carried out in a cold sweat." Even Freud can be convicted of projection.

II

For Woody Allen, as for Sartre, there is no exit from the conundrum. Like Sandy Bates on the train, Allen senses that there *must* be something else, some other possibility. But we cannot get there. We are caught.

Broadway Danny Rose tries to convince the cynical Tina of the importance of guilt. After all, his rabbi told him that we are "all guilty in the eyes of God."

Tina: You believe in God?

Danny: No, but I feel guilt about it.

There is no God, but there is guilt because of God. There is guilt with no possibility of forgiveness. A priest visits a man about to be executed. The man asks the priest if there is time to convert, and the priest replies, "This time of year, I think most of your major faiths are filled. . . . Probably the best I could do on such short notice is maybe make a call and get you into something Hindu." Even for that, he will need a passport photo.[19] Under hypnosis, Zelig recalls an event from his childhood. At the age of twelve, he asks a rabbi about the meaning of life. The rabbi tells him everything, but in Hebrew, and Zelig does not understand Hebrew. Then the rabbi wants Zelig to pay him six hundred dollars for Hebrew lessons. Every possibility has some kind of catch. And the catch locks the door.

Even death plays a major role in seeing to it that there are no exits from life. Throughout Allen's works, there are many references to what happens after death:

"What happens after we die? Is there a hell? Is there a God? Do we live again? All right, let me ask one key question: Are there girls?"

"I don't believe in an afterlife, although I am bringing a change of underwear."

On reincarnation: "Anything's possible, but it's hard to imagine if a man is president of a big corporation in his life, that he'll wind up a chipmunk."

Perhaps there will be an afterlife, "but no one will know where it's being held."[20]

Boris confronts Sonja in *Love and Death* with his anxiety about the meaning of life and the existence of God:

Boris: What if there is no God? . . . What if we're just a bunch of absurd people who are running around with no rhyme or reason?

Sonja: But if there is no God, then life has no meaning. Why go on living? Why not just commit suicide?

Boris: Well, let's not get hysterical! I could be wrong. I'd hate to blow my brains out and then read in the papers they found something.

Death is no exit. Certainty is no exit. Not even the anticertainty of atheism is an exit. Sonja tells a companion near the end of the film, "To love is to suffer. Not to love is to suffer. To suffer is to suffer. To be happy is to love. To be happy, then, is to suffer." And when one turns to desperation? Allen describes a time when he attempted suicide "by wetting my nose and inserting it into the light socket. Unfortunately, there was a short in the wiring, and I merely caromed off the icebox."[21] Even his act of desperation fails.

III

Given this view of the world, it is understandable that Allen pokes so much fun at religious people, practices, prejudices, and platitudes. Some of this is merely superficial; the comedian's goal is laughter, sometimes for its own sake. But even what seems superficial often leaves a serious aftertaste.

He tells the story of how he was approached to do an advertisement for a vodka company. In the course of the phone conversation, he explains with dignity that he does not do commercials, especially for a product he does not believe in. When he is told that they are offering fifty thousand dollars, he says, "Let me put Mr. Allen on the phone." He seeks out his rabbi for spiritual counsel, who supports his decision for personal integrity. Sometime later, as he is watching television, his rabbi appears in the commercial he was asked to make.[22]

Two priests in *Love and Death* fare little better. Father Andre, elderly and wise, advises sex with twelve-year-old blondes to solve Boris's depression. Father Nikolai ("always dressed in black with a black beard; for years I thought he was an Italian widow") when asked about Jews, produces sketches of the Russian Jew, with horns, and the German Jew, with stripes. A similar picture of ineffectiveness, narrow prejudice, and repression characterizes the priest in *Everything You Always Wanted to Know about Sex (But Were Afraid to Ask)* (1972). Here, in a scene set in a man's brain, the priest is discovered in the conscience department, where he has tampered with the conscience's normal functioning. The priest is repressed and repressive. The priest in a television commercial in *Bananas* (1971), on the other hand, is hardly that. Almost worse, this priest tries to sell New Testament cigarettes, saying, "I smoke them; (gesturing upward) He smokes them."

In *Sleeper*, Allen pokes fun at Billy Graham: "He knew God personally. He picked out his wardrobe. They used to go out on double dates together. They were romantically linked for a while." He also tells the story of two religious leaders of questionable repute: a fifteen-year-old maharishi sues Rev. Ding over which one is really God and therefore entitled to free passes to a theater. Both gurus are arrested before they can escape to Nirvana, Mexico.[23] Again, in *Sleeper*, Miles receives absolution from a computer. In *Take the Money and Run*, Virgil Starkwell's father proudly recalls that he "tried to beat God" into his son and feels like a failure because he had no success. In *Manhattan*, Isaac laments that, because he has quit his job, he will not be able to send as much money to his father. Because of this, his father will not get as good a seat in the synagogue and will have to be farther away from God.

Religious and philosophical platitudes are seen in an embarrassingly foolish light in Allen's work. Sonja assures Boris, in *Love and Death*, that people are made in God's image.

Boris: Do you think He wears glasses?

Sonja: Not with those frames.

This is merely a harmless diversion. But in "Notes from the Overfed," a misunderstanding of dogma has tragic and ridiculous consequences when filtered through a distorted mind.

> If God is everywhere, I had concluded, then He is in food. Therefore, the more I ate the godlier I would become. . . . In six months, I was the holiest of holies, with a heart entirely devoted to my prayers and a stomach that crossed the state line by itself. . . . To reduce would have been the greatest folly, even a sin![24]

Two of the darkest observations that Allen makes about religious platitudes come in quick succession in the film *Love and Death*. As he looks out at the battlefield at thousands of dead bodies, one of Boris's cohorts remarks, "God is testing us." Boris responds, "If He's going to test us, why doesn't He give us a written?" Allen justly attacks the appalling complacency involved in using such notions of a rational universe to explain away awesome tragedy. Temptations to offer explanations to every tragedy as a part of God's plan plague religious traditions. Shortly after this affront to human dignity, as Boris is digging graves, a priest remarks, "Mercifully, God was on our side." Again, Boris cannot let this ridiculous, horrible platitude linger: "Yeah. I'm sure things could have gone a lot worse if He wasn't. It might have rained." Clichés, empty words, especially when stamped with a religion's seal of approval, are enemies of the human race.

IV

Again and again, despite being put off by mindless religious and philosophical trivia, Allen pursues God, or at least the idea of God. He yearns to have his questions answered, even if the extraterrestrials fail him. Some of his crucial questions about God pertain to God's power and to human perceptions of that power. When Allen is called upon to play God as an actor in a couple of instances, he discovers that he does not have "a good voice for God."[25] Another time he resorts to method acting, which means that he goes around

New York in a blue suit, giving big tips to cab drivers and forgiving people "because He would have."[26]

In Allen's version of the story of Abraham and Isaac, Abraham is certain that he has heard God because "it was a deep, resonant voice, well-modulated, and nobody in the desert can get a rumble in it like that." Later, when Abraham is embarrassed that he did not get God's little joke, he asks if his willingness to sacrifice his son does not prove his faithfulness, only to be told by God, "It proves that some men will follow any order no matter how asinine as long as it comes from a resonant, well-modulated voice."[27]

One of the recurring themes in Love and Death is Boris's quest to receive some kind of sign from God: "If I could see a miracle, just one miracle. If I could see a burning bush, or the seas part, or my Uncle Sasha pick up a check." Or again, "If only God would give me some sign. If He would just speak to me once, anything, one sentence, two words. If He would just cough." Near the end of the film, when he finally sees an angel of God who tells him that he will be saved, he responds with the kind of trust one would expect of one who had been frustrated and insecure for so long: "I shall walk through the valley of the shadow of death. In fact, now that I think of it, I shall run through the valley of the shadow of death because you get out of the valley quicker that way." Relieved and hopeful because of God's promise and the angel's appearance, it still seems wise to take advantage of the situation quickly and not trust that such a good thing will last.

In addition to craving signs from God, Allen also craves justice. A proverb from "The Scrolls" says "My Lord, my Lord! What hast thou done lately?"[28] One is reminded of an occasion in the book of Judges when an angel comes to Gideon in the midst of the oppression under the Midianites. Gideon says to the angel, "If the Lord is with us, why then has all this befallen us?" (Judges 6:13) and then goes on to ask why God does not do all the good things God used to do. According to Allen, a rabbi tells a detective seeking God, "We're the chosen people. He takes best care of us of all His children, which I'd like to someday discuss with Him."[29] And a man whose relationships have failed wonders if he is "guilty of hubris. A man who has never thought of himself in an order higher than rodent, nailed for hubris?"[30]

The failure of either God's justice or God's power, or both, come together in two of Allen's works, Love and Death and "God (A Play)." After Boris has his vision of the angel, he is still executed and concludes that he has been "screwed." At the end of "God," the script states that, to save the messenger Diabetes, "Zeus, Father of the Gods, descends dramatically from on high and, brandishing his thunderbolts, brings salvation to a grateful but impotent group of mortals." Unfortunately, when the play is performed, Zeus fails to save Diabetes from execution because the machine that is supposed to lower the actor playing Zeus gets stuck and the lowering wire strangles him. "God is dead." So the actors, like the rest of us, are told to "ad-lib the ending."[31]

The questions of God's power and justice converge in the issue of theodicy. Allen's consuming questions about suffering are central to how, if ever, he will resolve his questions about God. Although, in a moment of romantic feelings, Isaac tells his adolescent lover, Tracy, that she is "God's answer to Job,"[32] he cannot let the question rest with that. Elsewhere, a man argues with his uncle that if there is a God, "why is there poverty and baldness?"[33]

Allen's fullest treatment of the question comes in his version of the story of Job. Among Job's hardships, God

> slew a tenth part of Job's kine and Job calleth out: "Why dost thou slay my kine? Kine are hard to come by. Now I am short kine and I'm not even sure what kine are." . . . And when Job's wife saw this she wept and the Lord sent an angel of mercy who anointed her head with a polo mallet, and of the ten plagues, the Lord sent one through six, inclusive.[34]

Later, there is this final confrontation when God speaks to Job in a way similar to that in the biblical story:

> "Must I who created heaven and earth explain my ways to thee? What hath thou created that thou doth dare question me?"
> "That's no answer," Job said. . . . Then Job fell to his knees and cried out to the Lord, "Thine is the kingdom and the power and the glory. Thou hast a good job. Don't blow it."[35]

As Allen's Job rightly asserts, God did not give an answer. There is no adequate answer in the Book of Job other than God's awesome presence. But, for Allen, that is not enough. There are no answers to human suffering. Where does that leave God in his theology?

In "Mr. Big," a detective is employed to search for God, aka Mr. Big. Near the end, he hears that there is no Mr. Big: "It's a syndicate. Mostly Sicilian. It's international. But there is no actual head. Except maybe the Pope." Later he finds that God has been murdered by an existentialist.[36] The play "God" offers a different answer. Diabetes is the messenger assigned the task of answering the king's "question of questions. Is there a god?" Since his life depends on giving a hopeful answer. Diabetes thinks it over for a moment and assumes that a yes will make the king happy. But as it turns out, this only upsets the king who believes that he will be judged for his sins and doomed for eternity.[37] The first answer: God is dead. The second: God is alive but that may not be such a good thing.

Finally, there is the answer in *Love and Death*, no more conclusive than these two, but more profound and probably closer to Allen's real position. Facing the audience, a man who was promised that he would be saved, only to be executed on time because God did not come through, says, "The important thing, I think, is not to be bitter. If it turns out that there is a God, I don't think that He's evil. The worst you can say about Him is that basically He's an underachiever."

V

What is one to do? Where can one turn? What paths might one take?

> Mankind faces a crossroads. One path leads to despair and utter hopelessness. The other to total extinction. Let us pray we have the wisdom to choose correctly.[38]
> I haven't seen my analyst in two hundred years. He was a strict Freudian. And if I'd been going all this time I'd probably almost be cured by now.[39]
> Do you think there's any difference whether we live under the Czar or Napoleon? They're both crooks. The Czar's a little taller.[40]

Often, it seems, the world of no exit and the underachieving God offers little hope of redemption. Analysis *might* cure a person after two hundred years. Political solutions elude the world in which leaders seek power to glorify themselves. The two paths laid before us make it hard to discern the right decision.

Political solutions are never really solutions in Allen's work. In the film *Bananas*, on the occasion of a successful revolution in the Latin American nation of San Marcos, the new leader declares all children under the age of sixteen officially sixteen years old. The national language will be Swedish, and each citizen's underwear is to be changed each half-hour and worn on the outside for easier inspection. In *Sleeper*, after the Leader's nose (all that is left of him after a moderately successful assassination attempt) is stolen as a result of the brilliant planning of the underground leader Erno, Miles Monroe declares that soon it will be time to steal Erno's nose. Elsewhere, a Latin American revolution ends with the new regime declaring a divine monarchy.[41] In *Love and Death*, Boris's desire to know what Russia will win by killing thousands of Frenchmen is never satisfied. Political solutions are impossible, because of human nature.

Even hopes for personal liberation meet with frustration. In *The Purple Rose of Cairo* (1985), Cecilia lives in the midst of oppression. She holds down a job as a waitress during the Great Depression of the 1930s. Married to a louse who drinks, womanizes, and never tries to get work, she is expected to wait hand and foot on him in return for all he does for her. Cecilia's one source of joy is going to the movies. They offer her a chance to escape. When she sits there, she hears Fred Astaire sing "Cheek to Cheek" (with the lyrics

"I'm in heaven"). Tom Baxter, a character from a movie she has seen several times, actually leaves the screen in his search for real life to join her. She falls in love with him, because he is perfect "but fictitious." Even after a fist fight with her husband, there is no blood on Baxter's face and not a single hair is out of place. The actor who plays Baxter, Gil Shepherd, also arrives on the scene, the dreammaker trying to round up the wandering dream. Baxter returns to the screen, spurned by Cecilia in favor of Shepherd. But Shepherd returns to Hollywood to project dreams onto the screen for others, leaving her hopeless. Cecilia is left to watch still another movie, once again in temporary relief from the pain of life. In the end, she hears Fred Astaire sing, "I'm in heaven," while she sits in hell. Personal liberation is sheer fantasy.

Fantasy of another kind makes false promises to Andrew and Ariel in *A Midsummer Night's Sex Comedy*. Years before, they had passed up the opportunity to make love together. Upon meeting again, they share the impression that if they had not missed that opportunity their lives would now be totally different—less filled with frustration and foreboding. But when they do have sex, they merely "bull their way through it." Their past dream anticipated no real liberation.

But there is a kind of fantasy that Allen seems to find at least somewhat promising. We see it in *Play It Again, Sam* (1972). Throughout the film, Allan Felix is in dialogue with his idol, Humphrey Bogart. At first, he can identify only with Bogart's toughness and independence, which he cannot hope to emulate successfully. But later, he sees through the tough exterior of Bogart's character to his vulnerable interior and realizes that he, like Bogart, is "short enough and ugly enough" to succeed on his own. Instead of an empty fantasy, *Play It Again, Sam* offers images for a new mode of self-understanding, images of strength through weakness, glory through humility, and self-love through self-sacrifice. The vision liberates precisely because it does *not* sweep us off our collective feet or take us out of the world. It frees us to be ourselves.

Allan is somehow able to see through Bogart's tough exterior and participates in his own liberation. Cecilia never gets past the glitter. She waits passively to be saved. For her, there is no movement from fantasy to reality. Her dreams leave her in the same place they find her. But Allan's dreams empower him to change his life. Is it possible that there is some exit after all?

Zelig's alienation, caused by his craving to be liked, seems incurable. Only the "love of one woman" changes his life, liberates him from his compulsive need to be hidden in the crowd, and frees him to become himself. Other moments of liberation also appear in Allen's films. Even though Tom Baxter fails to liberate Cecilia, his sincere innocence succeeds in reaching out to a group of prostitutes as he touches their humanity in a unique way. Even though Andrew's dream of freedom from frustration through a new relationship with Ariel fails, his wife finds her "curse" lifted when her infidelity is revealed openly. Even though Boris is executed in *Love and Death*, he dances down the road with Death as the film ends.

Allen has no illusions about the ease with which one might be set free from political, psychological, or spiritual misery. But he does reveal possibilities, even though they may be ambiguous. At the end of *Manhattan*, Isaac decides that he wants Tracy, his teenage lover, even though he had rejected her coldly for a woman nearer his age. The moment he arrives, Tracy tells him that she is leaving for London as he had encouraged her to do in the past. Isaac tries to change her mind but fails, finally heeding her plea to allow her to be free. The changing expressions on his face leave the viewer in some doubt as to whether he really accepts her liberation. But then a smile passes across his face for just a moment. He seems to.

Liberation is somehow possible in Allen's world, perhaps only because nothing can be counted on or counted out, not even the lack of an exit. So, in "Death Knocks," Nat tells Death, that most fearsome of figures, "I thought you'd be . . . uh . . . taller."[42] But if liberation is a possibility, an ethics of some sort is an absolute necessity.

Manhattan opens with a play on Camus' *The Fall*. Isaac singles out courage as the single most important human virtue: "If four of us are walking over a bridge and someone is drowning in icy water, would someone have the courage to save the person? . . . I can't swim so I never have to face it." He is concerned throughout the film with a "lack of individual integrity." When his friend accuses him of being self-righteous, saying, "You think you're God," Isaac retorts, "I gotta model myself after someone!" Yet, in his relationship with Tracy, he is clearly the oppressor who does not like it when she gets "too mature." In the end, when she tells him how much he hurt her, he can only say that it was not intentional. He still does not accept responsibility for his actions. His ambivalent acceptance of her move to London is the best he can do—and perhaps that is not too bad.

Broadway Danny Rose (1984) reveals Allen at his most optimistic. Danny's life is guided by simple, positive principles of behavior ("acceptance, forgiveness, and love") passed on by the wisdom of his Uncle Sidney, though, like Rose in *Interiors* (1978), he may not know why he believes in them. Rose is asked, "How do you know what's good?" She answers, "You just don't squeal." There are some things that you just know.

What Danny Rose knows is that all business relationships are also personal. As an agent, his compassion leads him to pick the worst acts in show business: a one-legged tap dancer, a one-armed juggler, a blind xylophone player, a parrot that sings "I Gotta Be Me." The only act he will not work with is a stuttering ventriloquist, though Danny later finds a way to help even him. His reward for such goodness? When his acts become famous, they leave him. As the story goes on, he is continually the victim of undeserved bad fortune. People are out to kill him even though he has done nothing. He risks his life for Lou Canova, the washed-up Italian singer, and Canova leaves him for another agent. Only in the end does Tina, the woman he met on an "adventure," return to him seeking his "acceptance, forgiveness, and love." And the local deli gives him the "greatest single honor" it can bestow by naming a sandwich after him.

In "God," after Zeus dies, the actors are told to ad-lib the ending. Woody Allen insists that our ad-libbing be done with compassion for others. An ethical life is possible, even necessary. Intellectual reflection often paralyzes many of his characters. Only an intuition, perhaps common sense, tells people how to live with integrity.

VI

"To you, I'm an atheist. To God, I'm the loyal opposition." This is where Allen, via Sandy Bates in *Stardust Memories*, locates himself. There are three aspects to living as the loyal opposition: he must protest, he must question, he must live a moral life. His protest is long and loud against the sufferings of humanity—and against any religion that offers cheap answers to humanity's deepest questions, any religion that can look at tragedy complacently and say, "God is on our side" or "God is testing us." Such religion denigrates human life and yearning. The loyal opposition has the responsibility to reveal such corruption.

Allen comes out of the Jewish tradition that, from its scriptural roots, has poked and prodded the powerful. He turns this protest against a powerful God, saying, "Thou hast a good job. Don't blow it." *If* you are a powerful God, act like it and straighten things up! Again and again, human suffering and the omnipresence of death haunt him. He wants a God who will agonize and act with love in response to the human condition.

He raises questions about conventional religious and philosophical wisdom. Like the writings in Job, Ecclesiastes, Lamentations, and many psalms, he refuses easy answers and cheap comfort. Wisdom in the Hebrew Bible comes from being faithful to one's experience and one's reflection on that experience. Allen insists that faith (if it is a possibility at all) arises from human experience, especially the experiences of suffering, absurdity, and mortality.

Rabbis argue with God. Allen carries on this tradition but from one step removed. He argues with the idea of God. In many ways, this distinction might be likened to that in the American black community between gospel music and the blues. Gospel music deals with life, its sufferings and aspirations, in relation to God. The blues also deal with life, but leave God almost invisible in the background.

In the midst of his protest and his unanswered questions. Allen relies on wisdom again. Uncle Sidney's philosophy of life in *Broadway Danny Rose*, like Proverbs, forges a way to live in a world that cannot be comprehended. Danny even finds that, in the end, rewards come to him. The more traditional, conventional wisdom literature of the Hebrew Bible proclaims that the righteous will be blessed. Job and Qoheleth (Ecclesiastes) dispute that claim. In this one instance, Woody Allen sides with the more hopeful tradition. He concludes that people can live morally, with integrity, with humanity.

VII

What is the value of Woody Allen's theological imagination for those of religious conviction? On some occasions, he speaks through his characters to demean the importance of his own quest. He is "self-indulgent and pretentious";[13] he is told that his adolescent concern about God's silence only "dignifies your own psychological and sexual hangups by attaching them to grandiose philosophical issues";[44] an ex-wife's book says, "he had complaints about life but never any solutions. . . . In his most private moments, he spoke of his fear of death, which he elevated to tragic heights when in fact it was mere narcissism."[45] In spite of these doubts, he makes some important contributions. He reminds us of the limits of human understanding. He reminds us that revelation often partakes simultaneously of hiddenness.

Thomas Merton would have appreciated Allen's deep sense of the absurdity of life, and his sense of humor about it. According to Merton,

> it is only when the apparent absurdity of life is faced in all truth that faith really becomes possible. Otherwise, faith tends to be a kind of diversion, a spiritual amusement, in which one gathers up accepted, conventional formulas and arranges them in [the] approved mental patterns, without bothering to investigate their meaning, or asking if they have any practical consequences in one's life.[46]

Woody Allen and Thomas Merton share an abhorrence of religion or philosophy that makes sense only on paper.

It would be foolish to say Allen's works function to bring the world to faith in God. But by setting before our eyes something of the absurdity of life, he does make faith in God, where it exists, more faithful to human experience—truly an appropriate act of the "loyal opposition."

Allen does not stand alone in considering God an underachiever. In fact, this has been one of the great insights of both Jewish and Christian tradition as one ponders Israel's defeats and exiles; Judaism's suffering of oppression, pogroms, and holocaust; and the Jerusalem career of Christianity's Messiah. It bears noting that the figure who redeems Allan Felix is a Humphrey Bogart who is short and ugly. Perhaps the power of redemption, the power to liberate, comes not from Zeus descending onto the stage to intervene but through the power of love that enters into the world in vulnerability. This is a different kind of power, and a very different kind of God.

NOTES

1. *Stardust Memories*. All works by Woody Allen, unless otherwise noted.

2. *The Nightclub Years, 1964–68*.

3. *Love and Death*.

4. *Nightclub Years*.

5. "My Philosophy," in *Getting Even* (New York: Warner Books, 1971), 31.

6. "Spring Bulletin," ibid., 49.

7. "Remembering Needleman," in *Side Effects* (New York: Random House, 1980), 3.

8. *Sleeper*.

9. "Reminiscences: Places and People," in *Side Effects*, 81.

10. "Death (A Play)," in *Without Feathers* (New York: Random House, 1975), 67.

11. *Zelig*.

12. *Nightclub Years*.

13. "God (A Play)," in *Without Feathers*, 164.

14. "Fabulous Tales and Mythical Beasts," in *Without Feathers*, 181.

15. "Conversations with Helmholtz," in *Getting Even*, 85.

16. "The Metterling Lists," in *Getting Even*.

17. "Fabrizio's: Criticism and Response," in *Side Effects*.

18. *Side Effects*, 71–78.

19. "The Condemned," in *Side Effects*, 15.

20. *Love and Death*; "Conversations with Helmholtz," in *Getting Even*, 90; "Death (A Play)," in *Without Feathers*, 78; and "Early Essays," in *Without Feathers*, 102.

21. "Selections from the Allen Notebooks," in *Without Feathers*, 4.

22. *Nightclub Years*.

23. "Nefarious Times We Live In," in *Side Effects*, 88.

24. "Notes from the Overfed," in *Getting Even*, 69.

25. *Stardust Memories*.

26. *Nightclub Years*.

27. "The Scrolls," in *Without Feathers*, 23–24.

28. Ibid., 25.

29. "Mr. Big," in *Getting Even*, 104.

30. "Retribution," in *Side Effects*, 145.

31. "God (A Play)," in *Without Feathers*, 141, 173–75.

32. *Manhattan*.

33. "Notes from the Overfed," in *Getting Even*, 67.

34. "The Scrolls," in *Without Feathers*, 22.

35. Ibid.

36. "Mr. Big," in *Getting Even*, 105–9.

37. "God (A Play)," in *Without Feathers*, 170–72.

38. "My Speech to the Graduates," in *Side Effects*, 57.

39. *Sleeper*.

40. *Love and Death*.

41. "Viva Vargas," in *Getting Even*. 98.

42. "Death Knocks," in *Getting Even*, 40.

43. *Stardust Memories*.

44. *Manhattan*.

45 Ibid.

46. Thomas Merton, *Disputed Questions* (New York: Farrar, Straus, & Giroux, 1960), 166.

5

Woody Allen's Comic Irony

Christopher Morris

Woody Allen's films can be effectively analyzed in terms of certain literary paradigms and structures of comedy. This synchronic approach is useful because of Allen's own expressed interest in questions of genre and because his work consistently exhibits sophisticated awareness of theories of comedy—Bergson's and Freud's most notably.[1] Such an approach is also innovative, for a generic analysis of Allen's films will indicate Allen's distinctive ironies, which at their most artful seem deployed with an almost psychoanalytic interest to prompt his viewers to the acceptance of some reality principle toward which his film comedy points. The disadvantages of such a generic approach are also clear, however: consideration of the problematic film *Interiors* (1978) must be omitted, and the important subject of Allen's artistic development can only be hinted at.

In keeping with his essentially black comic vision, the structure of Woody Allen's films inverts that traditional, circular pattern of romantic comedy first outlined by Northrop Frye and C. L. Barber,[2] in which the action moves from an urban center hostile to lovers through a retreat to a green world associated with nature, to arrive at a return of reconciliation in the city. Allen inverts this paradigm first and most obviously by showing that the green world offers nothing, not even heightened consciousness, that might serve as an acceptable antidote to his alienating cityscapes. The ostensibly more "natural" woodland life of the rebels in *Sleeper* (1973) is just as vapid as the sterile, fascist regime that oppresses them. The blue Pacific vistas in *Play It Again, Sam* (1972) merely exacerbate Allan Felix's romantic frustrations: instead of experiencing some enabling transformation there, he's beaten up by hoodlums at a roadhouse. In *Manhattan* (1979), Isaac's brief tryst in the country with Mary Wilkie does nothing to enhance their affair; indeed, they still perceive their lovemaking as "acting." And perhaps the most bitter of Allen's permutations of the green world is the New Jersey swampland of *Broadway Danny Rose* (1984): fleeing the Mafia, Danny and Tina wander through the high weeds only to be startled by an actor bedecked in a Flash Gordon cape and costume, fresh from shooting a television commercial nearby. This parody of the notion of being rescued in and by a green world suggests Allen's recurrent theme—that it is impossible by a change of scenery to escape the neuroses and dislocations of contemporary life; Allen's green worlds offer no succor.

But it is the ironic nature of the comic "reconciliation"—Frye's "comic balance" (165) or Barber's "clarification" (10)—that more tellingly measures Allen's subversion of these comic paradigms. The ambiguous, minor key endings of *Play It Again, Sam* and *Annie Hall* (1977) are well-known; but even in the films that end with lovers apparently united—like *Zelig* (1983) and *Broadway Danny Rose*—the romantic resolutions are, on closer inspection, self-indicting. For example, Zelig's married life to Dr. Fletcher is reduced to an anonymously written paragraph; in effect, his putative happy ending is of a piece with the film's evocation of a human identity submerged in and defined by interpretive communities outside itself. And the fact that Zelig dies still curious as to the outcome of *Moby Dick* may be a final symptom of the persistence of his pathetic desire, never fully erased, to fit in. Also, while Danny Rose seems to find happiness with a repentant Tina, his quixotic nobility is finally just one more story told by the gossiping comedians whose narration frames the film. In fact, the endings of Allen's films parody the concept of reconciliation itself.

Similarly, Allen has also experimented with the converse of the formula; positing endings in which the viewer is asked to consider apparently outrageous behavior as constituting the final comic resolution, thereby undermining received expectations of the comic integration like heterosexual love. Besides parodying television genres, two skits in *Everything You Always Wanted to Know about Sex* (1972) end with the image of traditionally aberrant behavior—transvestism and fetishism—as harmless, even more genuine expressions of humanity than the unctuous, Philistine yet supposedly normal society that serves as its context. Thus the transvestite Sam and his forgiving wife are morally superior to the wealthy, supercilious suburbanites they visit. And the rabbi's fetishism is certainly more honest than the sneering voyeurism of the game show that indicts itself through the use of look-alike actors who impersonate television personalities.

Such ironic reversals of the comic pattern outlined by Frye and Barber constitute the broad structure of Allen's mature films, one that rejects American myths of normalcy, assimilation, and integration just as intransigently as did Allen's nightclub monologues, especially his famous story about being captured by the Klu Klux Klan. At the core of Allen's theme is the insistence on some irreducible individuality that resists assimilation and for which such social integration remains a lie. The development of this theme can be traced in various images of the parade.

In his early films, Allen's personae struggle behind, outside, or on the periphery of the parade. Virgil Starkwell drags his cello and chair in an effort to keep up with his high school band; later as part of a chain gang, he must limp along while his fellow prisoners ride bikes, in *Love and Death* (1975), Russian troops ahead of Boris march too fast and new troops march into him from behind. These early slapstick images satirize the notion of social integration in a conventional Chaplinesque manner.

In the later films, Allen's parades become ominous, bitter icons. Zelig's immersion in the ticker tape parades that begin and end the film suggest the ultimate interchangeability of conformity and individualism. There is an uncomfortable similarity between both American and Nazi crowd scenes. In *Broadway Danny Rose* the parade acquires Felliniesque values: the comedians and entertainers, cheered by the crowd, seem only smaller versions of the vacuous Superman looming apocalyptically over the parade's end. The moral consequences of Danny Rose's assimilation into this society are implied by one of Allen's rare dissolves, which momentarily melds a huge frozen funny-faced float into Danny Rose's baffled, weary features as he makes yet another effort to act with integrity in a world ready to betray him at every turn. In the fates of Zelig and Danny Rose, Allen depicts assimilation or social integration as the occlusion or devouring of the individual by and in an omnivorous community of Heideggerian idle talk: the press, the media, the modern interpreters of Zelig (like Saul Bellow, Susan Sontag, and the other contemporary analysts who predictably find his life of interest only insofar as it offers evidence to confirm their biases); or the bantering, sometimes incoherent comedians for whom Danny Rose is only an object of humor, the source of another good story, or the name of a sandwich. Such is the black comedic version of traditional assimilation or reconciliation.

True reconciliation of characters with each other or with society as a whole is impossible in Allen's film world because his most memorable settings are envisaged as unremitting wastelands. Society is "bananas," which, as John Irving reminds us, is a euphemism for bullshit (146). In it we bring our daily tithe or worldly goods or excrement—the Freudian equivalence is deliberate—to literally raise the status of moronic dictators. Like Virgil Starkwell, we flay pointlessly at boilerplate slag heaps in the sun. In *Love and Death* the predominant setting is warfare on a boundaryless grassy space framed by empty heavens. One of the lessons of *Annie Hall* is the spuriousness of Alvy's disingenuous distinction between the authenticity of New York and superficiality of California. And the montage that begins *Manhattan* (1979) reveals the city of Heisenberg's uncertainty principle: it chaotically changes before our eyes faster than any generalization about it can be uttered. These settings—like the New Jersey swampland in *Broadway Danny Rose* that Allen daringly likens to North Vietnam—suggest that the hope of an eventual comic return to some normative community is doomed at the outset.

In these distinctionless landscapes, Allen's lovers vainly struggle to act out the one familiar comic imperative that might create authentic love, the exchange of identities or reversals of positions that—by positing some genuine human reciprocity—may enable lovers to discover a personal freedom denied to them by society. Barber writes, "Just as a saturnalian reversal of social roles need not threaten the social structure, but can serve instead to consolidate it, so a temporary, playful reversal of sexual roles can renew the meaning of the normal relation" (245). Allen's early comedies sought to develop this formula: through their mutual rescues and coordinated disguises as doctors, Miles and Luna overcome their initial suspicions and find love. In one of Allen's closest approximations to the classical myth of the green world, the restoration of Miles's identity is assisted by the role playing by which Luna becomes Marlon Brando and Miles, Blanche DuBois. But the extent to which such an exchange of positions, roles, or identities can promote real love—tenuous at best in *Sleeper*, *Bananas* (1971), or *Take the Money and Run* (1969)—is completely rejected in the later films. The love of Alvy Singer and Annie Hall grows when he is able to give up the role of entertainer and listen as a member of the audience to Annie's song—literally to consider *her* as "singer." Yet it is just such a moment of hypothetical reciprocity that exposes their love to assimilation by an aggrandizing social order epitomized in the sleek California emptiness of Tony Lacey.

In *Zelig* this pattern is repeated: we're led to hope that love can apparently grow when Dr. Eudora Fletcher and Zelig exchange the roles of psychiatrist and patient. And in *Broadway Danny Rose* a momentary escape is facilitated when a man and woman left bound together in the traditional missionary position—Danny Rose is on top—stand up and loosen their bonds with simultaneous wriggling. By the traditional logic of comedy, these acts of reciprocity should awaken true love. But as we've seen, Allen raises these classical expectations ironically, only to undermine them with nihilistic conclusions that challenge the possibility of romantic or social harmony.

Appropriately, it's in *A Midsummer Night's Sex Comedy* (1982) that Allen destroys the Shakespearean pattern most convincingly. There, the exchange of traditional positions is satirized when, in a role reversal, Adrian aggressively pursues her reluctant husband Andrew in the kitchen. To the accompaniment of "The Lord's Prayer," sung by Leopold in the next room, she nearly rapes Andrew while atop him, only to learn that his backside is "on the burner." But the whole notion of the "green world" is undermined by the characterization of nature as "a restaurant." Shakespeare's innocent exchange of partners, supervised by the benevolent magic of Oberon and Puck, gives way to an almost obsessive promiscuity that leaves each character trapped in selfhood. Like the modern analysts of *Zelig*, each character in *A Midsummer Night's Sex Comedy* interprets reality only as a confirmation of preexisting biases: the various in-character readings of the swamp gas or will-o'-the-wisp indicate their inability to achieve authentic reciprocity, despite their manic bed-hopping. Instead, the spirit world or poetic imagination that Shakespeare celebrated becomes for Allen only that hedonistic "highest moment of ecstasy" that produces simultaneous orgasm and death for Leopold.

The inability of traditionally conceived role reversals to release Allen's neurotics from their solipsistic prisons finds a correlative in a parallel irony: though often the ideal self-transformation induced by comedy is figured forth by what Frye calls "the point of ritual death" (179) and rebirth, in Allen's hands such regeneration is always spurious. Maxwell's botched suicide in *A Midsummer Night's Sex Comedy* does nothing to change his egomania. And perhaps the most elaborate example of false rebirth occurs in *Stardust Memories* (1980). There, Sandy Bates stumbles into an oneiric green world after his car breaks down on a country road. In a kind of Walpurgisnacht vision, the world in the phantasmagorical form of his friends and lovers passes before him, confessing its inadequacies through its clichés. Nevertheless, still hoping to resolve both an artistic and a sexual impasse, the director interrogates his imaginative phantoms, pressing for answers but finding in their place only empty ascension balloons. This ironic green world ends with Bates's assassination at the hands of a once-loyal fan, betrayed by the director's evident loss of purpose. Now, in the paradigm outlined by Frye and Barber, such a symbolic death should presage some eventual reintegration of character. But Bates's ambiguous rebirth at the end of *Stardust Memories* does nothing to resolve the dilemmas he had faced earlier. On the contrary, when he returns to the film festival being held in his honor, his identity is even more elusive: it is impossible to place him finally in either art or life. Far from re-creating him anew, Bates's false regeneration only distances him farther from the world. His dark glasses—like his defenses—are easily reassumed at the end of the film.

In their futile search for regenerative harmony, Allen's artists and lovers (and audiences) are often bitterly mocked by the soundtracks, which use music ironically both to undercut such expectations and to provide artistic instances of the integrity and concord unavailable in life. A simple example is the sentimental Marvin Hamlisch song praising "loving, giving and sunshine" following the crude comparison between lovemaking and boxing that concludes *Bananas.* But nowhere is the ironic function of the soundtrack more important than in *Manhattan*, in which wordless orchestral versions of Gershwin tunes provide a disparaging commentary—for viewers who do know the lyrics—on the principal characters' delusions. For example, the pseudosophisticated Mary Wilkie is ridiculed as "a little babe who's lost in the woods." Later, the love of Isaac and Tracy, ostensibly celebrated in a romantic hansom cab ride through Central Park, is mocked, since we know Isaac's flirtation with Mary has begun, by unsung lyrics that would characterize them as "a twosome that just can't go wrong." The cynicism of Isaac's self-conscious pursuit of Mary is evident when the tune for the lines "I never had the least notion / that I could fall with such emotion" is heard as the accompaniment to his two-timing. There are six other examples of such musical irony in the film; these are discussed in the notes.[3] But in addition to defining the self-deceptions of Allen's characters, the New York Philharmonic's lush renditions of the Gershwins' simultaneously witty and romantic tributes to human love establish in the film a normative ideal—an example of harmony once achieved, at least—that further serves to measure the contemporary decadence depicted. The characters are writers or would-be writers, but their creative achievements pale in comparison to those of the Gershwins. Yacowar (198) points out that Jill's book is spiteful gossip; Yale postpones a book on O'Neill to buy a Porsche; Mary writes a novelization of a film as eagerly as she edits Tolstoy's letters; Isaac's book about Manhattan is unwritten, contradictory. In contrast to this self-indulgent artistic posturing, then, the Gershwins' music stands as an enviable testimony to harmonics so clearly missing from contemporary life. Finally, in a film representing urban lives as isolated, atomistic, and devoid of natural ties, it is significant that Allen chooses as his homage to harmony, as if to *il maglior fabbros*, the collaborative work of brothers.

One valid objection to the foregoing account of Allen's ironic, black comedy is that it is too black, that stressing Allen's inversion of comic paradigms omits the provisional reconciliations, the laughter, and the undeniable moments of love that surely distinguish Allen's world from, say, that of Beckett. There can be no doubt that such moments as Isaac's outburst to Tracy ("You're God's answer to Job: 'I may do a lot of bad things, but I can also make one of these'") reflect a kind of genuine hope for human love that seems everywhere else denied by Allen's corrosive irony. One means of resolving this paradox is to recall that irony often serves as a defense against libido and thus Allen's multilayered defenses may enable him to shape a statement about love acceptable to contemporaries, much as the Gershwins' innovative jazz rhythms and witty rhymes mitigated against their inherently sentimental statements.

But this explanation leaves the definition of love still unresolved in the films. A better explanation may be found in *Annie Hall.* There, genuine, lasting love is consigned to the realm of art, not life. It is the provenance of the play Alvy directs and the songs he recalls. The importance of the irony of the film's closing with "Seems like Old Times" lies not with its evocation of nostalgia: the film so exquisitely modulates Alvy's growing acknowledgment of real loss that we must view any retreat to the past as illusory. Instead, the irony resembles that of the transference in psychoanalysis: the song ends with "you," meaning not just Alvy but the film audience, to which the temporary revelation of genuine love has been disclosed, only to be repudiated, through art. Thus the song returns Alvy and the audience to the reality principle, to the theater, to the incoherence of life, which Allen's ironic temperament has so persistently worked on us to accept, without tears.

NOTES

1. Two examples of Allen's many permutations of the Bergsonian notion that laughter is precipitated by the momentary conversion of the organic into the mechanical are Allan Felix's fight with a hairdryer and the dissolve that likens Danny Rose's face to a parade float. Allen refers explicitly to Freud's *Jokes and Their Relation to the Unconscious* at the beginning of *Annie Hall.* An ultimately oversimplified but workable description of part of Freud's theory is voiced by Jack, the instructor of screen writing, in *Stardust Memories.*

2. Frye coined the term *green world* to indicate the place of retreat or metamorphosis to which lovers repair in Shakespeare's comedies (182). Barber bases his paradigm on a "saturnalian pattern," which involves a movement through a festive "release" to an ultimate "clarification" about the nature of love (3–15). Barber indicates the complementarity of his pattern and Frye's at p. 11. This paradigm has not gone without challenge, of course. Kiniry, for example, argues that "not all comedies . . . end with a return to normality" (76). Testimony to the continuing utility of both Frye's and Barber's paradigms is evident in Charney's essay (157, 164). Gurewitch agrees with Barber that comedy is based on a saturnalian paradigm but argues that true saturnalianism is a mode of farce, which is "comic art in its most irrational form" (47, 129). Gurewitch also challenges the notion that a restoration of social order is necessary to comedy. Allen's ironic use of classical comic paradigms shares the subversive spirit of farce, ridiculing the arbitrariness of the social order, but always envisages that order as inescapable.

3. Exercising his visiting rights, Isaac takes his son from Jill for lunch and shopping, to the theme of "Love Is Sweeping the Country." The lines "All the sexes from Maine to Texas / Have never known such love before" provide an ironic commentary on the film's depiction of a society in which divorce, lesbianism, and single-parent families are more common than ever; in addition, the lines may disparage the father-son "love" exhibited by Isaac: in the guise of sophisticated (but defensive) banter, Isaac jokes with his son about picking up women at the Russian Tea Room. And like many divorced parents, Isaac buys his son's affection, yielding to his request for a large model boat in a toy-shop window.

"'S Wonderful" is heard as the accompaniment to Isaac's tryst in the country with Mary. This sequence begins ironically, with the deliberate ambiguity of whether the car on the highway contains Isaac and Mary or Isaac and Tracy. But the song's reference to "paradise" is obviously undercut by the continuing posturing of Isaac and Mary.

In Isaac's apartment, he and Mary dance to "Embraceable You," and it is jarring to recall the phrase "irreplaceable you" in the context of the film's kaleidoscopic partner swaps. During the discussion of the publication of Jill's book, which recounts Isaac's marital embarrassments, the song "Lady Be Good" seems grimly appropriate. But as in "Someone to Watch Over Me," the allusions to a "lonesome babe in the wood" all "alone in a big city" work to undermine Isaac's protestations of innocence.

The songs played during the concluding sequences—"Strike up the Band" and "But Not for Me"—deride the whole notion of romantic expectation and consummation. Isaac's middle-age, out-of-breath race through the streets of Manhattan parodies the ending of *The Graduate* while the Gershwin march ridicules romantic quests as delusions. Given the overwhelming likelihood that Tracy's anachronistic innocence will not survive the London stage, it is difficult to see "But Not for Me" as soliciting sentiment or nostalgia; like *Annie Hall*, *Manhattan* ends with a statement of love's impossibility in life.

WORKS CITED

Barber, C. L. *Shakespeare's Festive Comedy: A Study of Dramatic Form and Its Relation to Social Custom.* Princeton, NJ: Princeton University Press, 1959.

Bergson, Henri. *Laughter.* In *Comedy*, ed. Wylie Sypher. Garden City, NY: Doubleday, Anchor, 1956.

Charney, Maurice. "Comic Premises of *Twelfth Night*." In *Comedy: New Perspectives*, ed. Maurice Charney, 151–66. New York: New York Literary Forum, 1978.

Freud, Sigmund. *Jokes and Their Relation to the Unconscious.* Trans. James Strachey. New York: Norton, 1960.

Frye, Northrop. *The Anatomy of Criticism.* Princeton, NJ: Princeton University Press, 1973.

Gurewitch, Morton. *Comedy: The Irrational Vision.* Ithaca, NY: Cornell University Press, 1975.

Irving, John. *The Hotel New Hampshire.* New York: E. P. Dutton, 1981.

Kiniry, Malcolm. "Jacobean Comedy and the Acquisitive Grasp." In *Comedy: New Perspectives*, ed. Maurice Charney, 73–86. New York: New York Literary Forum, 1978.

Yacowar, Maurice. *Loser Take All: The Comic Art of Woody Allen.* New York: Ungar, 1979.

6

Self-Deprecation and the Jewish Humor of Woody Allen

Mark E. Bleiweiss

Just when the evidence of his public life seemed to imply that Woody Allen is a self-hating Jew, his new film *Crimes and Misdemeanors* (1989) opens to shed a fresh light on the comedian's enigmatic spiritual identity. Not only are all of the central characters Jewish—unheard of in Allen's other major works—but the rabbi, Ben, represents the major ethical figure. With Judaism portrayed positively, Allen appears to have matured significantly from the days when he would introduce Jewish themes only to deride them. Yet *Crimes* still leaves us with many questions about the role of Judaism in Allen's life. To gain a cogent understanding of these questions, we need to survey the history of Allen's career and of Jewish humor.

Sigmund Freud set the precedent for studies of Jewish humor when he suggested that Jewish humorists are the butt of their own jokes. In *Jokes and Their Relation to the Unconscious* (111–12), Freud said that Jewish jokes "are stories created by Jews and directed against Jewish characteristics. . . . I do not know whether there are many other instances of a people making fun to such a degree of its own character."

Freud observed that the Jews denigrate their own character flaws and not Judaism itself and that they direct their criticism against the stereotype of the Jew rather than against the actual Judaic system of life. This self-deprecation, while existent in the humor of other ethnic groups, represents the most prevalent feature in Jewish humor.

Many scholars question whether humor was a widely accepted characteristic of the Jews before Freud published *Jokes* in 1905. Since Freud's analysis, not only do scholars recognize Jewish humor as an integral part of modern Western culture, but most endorse the basic distinction of Jewish humor as self-deprecatory. Freud defines humor in general as a socially accepted outlet for repressed ideas and notes that "by the help of a joke, internal resistance is overcome . . . and the inhibition lifted." By studying humor, we find truths about people's identity that their inhibitions otherwise might conceal. If humor can be used to analyze cultural or ethnic identity, what does the self-deprecatory nature of Jewish humor reveal about the Jews? By denigrating their characters, do Jewish humorists like Allen actually disclose feelings of self-hatred? We first will explore various interpretations of how Jewish humor reflects Jewish identity and then will focus on Allen himself to determine what his humor reveals about his identity as a Jew.

In his book *Jewish Humor* (49), Avner Ziv distinguishes the main perspectives from which scholars approach Jewish humor as emotional, sociological, and intellectual. While all three approaches overlap—intellectual and social factors directly influence emotions, for instance—Ziv outlines their basic differences. He explains that, in reaction to their tragic history, Jews use humor as an emotional defense mechanism. Rather than cry at the abuse others inflict on them, Jews laugh to ease their pain. Their own foibles provide the best target for their laughter, not only because they are most familiar with the subject, but because by laughing at themselves first, they may prevent others from following suit. Unlike the individual experience of crying, the Jews share their laughter with one another, and through common emotional release, they can look to one another for comfort.

Martin Grotjahn, another early student of Jewish humor, focuses on this emotional component. He develops the idea that Jews indicate their own flaws first to prevent others from using these shortcomings as justification for anti-Semitic persecution (114).

Maurice Samuel has a more sympathetic approach in his focus on the emotional aspect of humor. He sees Jewish self-deprecation as an escape from the tragic realities of Jewish life rather than as a justification for retaining flaws (210–11).

Freud's disciple Theodor Reik also describes self-deprecation in Jewish humor as an emotional defense mechanism, yet he differs from Grotjahn and Samuel in his analysis. Whereas Grotjahn attributes the pleasure Jews derive from their humor to their natural ability to belittle themselves, Reik affirms Samuel's thesis that self-deprecating humor enables Jews to rise above their tragic history. Yet Reik takes the argument one step farther than Samuel by suggesting that this self-deprecation is actually masochistic in its severity. He concludes that masochism, even outside a humorous context, has been essential to Jewish survival in the Diaspora over the last two millennia (222).

Yet all of the emotionalists remain conspicuously silent about whether self-deprecation implies self-hatred. Perhaps this silence itself indicates that

Jewish humorists actually reveal their openness toward their Jewish identity. Given the difficulty of identifying as a Jew in a largely anti-Semitic world, the fact that these humorists even discuss Judaism, albeit negatively, shows that they are to some degree self-affirming Jews.

While both the emotional and the sociological approaches to Jewish humor draw from Jewish history, scholars who take the latter approach are more concerned with how Jews express frustration with their precarious social status through humor than with how they use humor as a defense mechanism. Because the majority of Western Jewish humorists trace their roots back to Eastern Europe, scholars focus on the ghetto as the origin of Jewish social identification. The ghetto was traditionally a small, crowded section in the poor part of town in which, because of its claustrophobic nature, conflicts between Jews abounded. When, in their humor, Jews criticize the secluded Jewish life that ghettos represent, they perhaps unwittingly give voice to their disdain for this part of their cultural and ethnic heritage.

In his own study of the social component of Jewish humor, Ziv focuses on the folk characters of the *luftgescheften*, the *schadchen*, and the *schnorrer*, all of whom played a dispensable, yet integral role in the everyday life of the traditional ghetto. Because they were inclined to complain, gossip, beg, and commit other *chutzpadik* acts, they became prime targets for humor. Each character represented a negative Jewish stereotype perpetuated inside as well as outside the ghetto walls and the rest of the Jews were quick to distance themselves from such objects of abuse. Ziv observes that the Jews from the ghetto did not mean to offend any specific person through their ridicule of these characters—which would have been difficult anyway since few, if any, Jews openly identified as *luftgescheftens*, *schadchens*, or *schnorrers*—but that all Jews shared at least some of their faults. The humor that appeared to be directed outwardly was, in fact, a subtle form of self-criticism. Yet because Jews laughed at their own personal flaws without being abusive, they revealed an admirable form of humility rather than any deep-seated self-hatred.

Although Dan Ben-Amos also denies that Jewish humor reveals self-hatred, he is one of the few students of Jewish humor to reject Freud's thesis on self-deprecation (113). He agrees with Ziv that many Jews mock negative Jewish stereotypes but claims that they laugh exclusively at other Jews who embody these stereotypes rather than at themselves. To substantiate his argument, he draws from a study of Jewish dialect jokes by Richard Dorson in which the majority of the American Jewish comedians use a Yiddish accent in relaying their jokes (152). By using a foreign accent and thus establishing a fictional persona, the comedian distances himself from the subject of his joke. The issue of self-hatred in humor thus becomes irrelevant to Ben-Amos because the jokes are not ultimately about the narrator himself but about his invented persona. That the comedian does not identify with his persona is neither a positive nor a negative indication of his own Jewish identity.

While Ben-Amos bases his criticism of Freud on more contemporary data, most modern scholars do not support his conclusions. Stanley Brandes argues that no comedian could distance himself so thoroughly that his persona's beliefs and prejudices do not in any way reflect his own (239). To be able to mimic the Yiddish accent accurately, as the comedians do in Dorson's study, requires a thorough understanding of Jewish culture, irrefutably linking the supposedly objective comedian with his created persona.

Even if the narrator could somehow distinguish himself from his persona, the jokes the persona tells must reveal something about the narrator's own identity. After all, by Freud's definition, humor reveals truths that its creators might otherwise conceal. Kurt Schlesinger elaborates Freud's thesis by suggesting that, despite the seemingly ambivalent attitude of comedians toward their humor, "hostility is not absent from such wit, but it is . . . expressed . . . with the invocation of indirection, nuance, and intellectuality" (319).

In short, the comedian must express true thoughts with subtlety, allowing the listener to figure out the meaning of the humor. If narrators blatantly mock themselves rather than subtly deprecating a fictional persona, they probably lose their sense of humor in the process. Schlesinger argues that the comedians who mock groups with which they deny cultural affiliation more often than not actually identify as members of such groups.

When Jews indulge in self-deprecation, they attempt to quell their anxiety by keeping their values in perspective. Humor provided the Jew from the ghetto with an opportunity to rise above everyday struggles and realize the absurdity of problems from an objective viewpoint. Even the liberated Jew who is self-mocking, according to Schlesinger, reveals more the desire to retain sanity than any self-hatred through humor.

Though similar to Schlesinger in her analysis, Heda Jason argues that Jews did not mock themselves until after they left the sheltered ghetto community. In the ghetto, Jews mainly interacted with other Jews, so they had "no need to 'self-efface,' or as we would rather say, to 'justify' [himself or her]self before anyone" (53). They certainly knew of anti-Semitism but, because non-Jews were not a part of everyday life, did not feel any awkwardness with their Jewish identity. Once they became a distinct minority outside the ghetto, prominent cultural traits like observance of kosher dietary laws made them an unpopular, and even threatening novelty in Central Europe, Western Europe, and America. With external pressure to forget customs and assimilate into Western society, Jews began renouncing the values of religious tradition. Though embarrassed by misunderstood customs, Jews did not necessarily hate the Jewish heritage. Instead, Jews remain confused by incompatible cultural ties with both Western society, in which there is at least a legal status of equality, and Jewish background and traditions.

Although most of the sociological scholars of Jewish humor address the subject of self-hatred, none attribute the Jews' self-deprecation to hatred for their Jewish culture. Schlesinger sees the Jew's self-mockery as an attempt to retain sanity, Jason observes that self-mockery reveals the Jew's feeling of cultural ambiguity, and Ziv actually suggests that Jewish self-mockery is a healthy form of humility. Even Ben-Amos, in his rejection of Freud's basic definition of Jewish humor, does not link self-deprecation with self-hatred. Yet none of the scholars go into enough depth to disprove the possibility that Jewish humorists are self-hating. Like scholars of the emotional aspect of Jewish humor, sociologists leave the problem essentially unresolved, perhaps relying on scholars of the intellectual component of Jewish humor to form decisive conclusions on whether Jews' self-deprecation reveals their self-hatred.

The intellectual approach to Jewish humor, as to other areas of Jewish folklore, is rooted in the Torah—the core of Jewish life—which contains the Jews' monotheistic moral code and principles of justice. While the Torah does not assume that the Jews will live up to all of its rigorous ethical requirements, it does maintain that each Jew must struggle to do the best of his or her ability. Like Christian theologian Paul of Tarsus, many Jews who lived in European ghettos before the Enlightenment did not understand that the Torah allowed for the occasional moral blunder, and they criticized the Jewish way of life with its impossibly high moral demands as untenable. When, with increasing tolerance sparked by the Enlightenment, European authorities liberated Jews from the ghettos, many Jews were faced with the seductive opportunity to completely reject the Torah by assimilating into non-Jewish society. These Jews developed humor to rationalize their assimilation and to condemn the supposed zealots who maintained tradition. In a sense, humor was a natural outgrowth of the guilt that assimilated Jews felt by accepting the easier route of secularism. At the same time, having rejected Judaism without yet being absorbed into the non-Jewish society left many of these Jews alienated from both cultures. Because their Jewish background was responsible for their feelings of alienation, many assimilated Jews inevitably began to resent their Jewish identity. The intellectual outlet of self-deprecating humor therefore both reconciled their guilt feelings and revealed their "need to search for self-identity," yet most scholars question whether it actually vocalized feelings of self-hatred.

In discussing modern Jewish identity, Sander Gilman defines self-hatred as the outsider's inability to gain acceptance from the majority group. Usually incapable of concealing his distinctive Jewish characteristics and convinced at the supremacy of secular Western culture, the assimilated Jew often concludes that the "contradiction must be within [himself or herself], since that which [he or she wishes] to become cannot be flawed. . . . The fragmentation of identity that results is the articulation of self-hatred" (2–3).

Professor Alan Dundes of the University of California at Berkeley further points out that the individual, no matter how distinct he or she may want to appear from an ethnic group, ultimately must define an identity in relation with that group (239). Yet in identifying as a member of his or her ethnic group, the self-hating Jew begins to believe that stereotypes attributed to traditional Jewish characters, like those Ziv describes, actually bear resemblance to his or her own idiosyncrasies.

Psychoanalyst Edmund Bergler draws from the sociologists' study of humor when he attributes the Jews' self-deprecatory humor to the sheltered intellectual life of the traditional ghetto (111). The ghetto's oppressiveness and provincialism so distorted the modern Jew's understanding of Judaism that it was no wonder so many Jews were quick to assimilate after the Enlightenment.

Although most of the sociological scholars of Jewish humor address the subject of self-hatred, none attribute the Jews' self-deprecation to hatred for their Jewish culture.

The intellectual potential of the Jew was limited to the parameters of his ghetto's physical and psychological walls. Even the sacred Torah, Bergler continues, was of little comfort to the oppressed and impoverished Jew when it relentlessly demanded that he strive harder to improve himself and his community. Jewish humor reveals the Jew's dissatisfaction with life in general, but it does not reveal self-hatred simply because anti-Semites, the ghetto, and the Torah—and not the Jew—ultimately cause his misery.

Naomi and Eli Katz concede that the Jew's self-deprecating humor reflects the struggle with cultural identity, yet they differ with Bergler's reasoning that blames the Torah's high moral demands as much as provincialism and anti-Semitism for Jewish self-deprecation. For the Katzes, Jewish humor does not mock Judaic values as much as Jewish American stereotypes. "Rather than being anti-Semitic," the Katzes explain that Jewish humor "is anti-greenhorn, anti-immigrant, and possibly anti-poor" (219). The Jewish American humorist mocks those negative qualities usually attributed to first-generation immigrants who, fresh from the Eastern European ghetto, were less successful in assimilating into American culture. Such self-deprecation does not imply hatred of Jewish ethnicity or of Judaism as much as hatred of the first-generation Jew himself, since the stereotypes being criticized refer to a specific folk caricature rather than to the Jewish system of ethics. In fact, the Katzes note that the Jewish American caricature has become such a familiar figure that most second- and third-generation Jews "no longer regard [the caricature] as ignorant or embarrassing, but rather as quaint and 'warm'" (220).

Focusing on the issue of intellectual transition, Salcia Landmann claims that the shift from the mentality of the ghetto to that of the New World has been the only source of self-deprecation in Jewish humor. With the disappearance of the first-generation caricature and the relatively successful assimilation of Jews into America's mainstream culture, Landmann predicts the impending decline of the phenomenon of Jewish humor defined by Freud because Jewish humorists will soon have nothing new to mock (203). Bernard Rosenberg and Gilbert Shapiro refute Landmann's prediction by indicating a new dilemma for second- and third-generation American Jews. "Where we previously hated ourselves for being Jews, we now frequently hate ourselves for not being Jews" (72). In other words, whereas previous self-deprecating humor revealed the narrator's rejection of his Jewish identity, modern self-deprecating humor indicates the guilt assimilated Jews feel for not preserving Jewish traditions.

Some scholars take the extremely positive view that self-deprecating humor, rather than revealing any self-hatred, serves to help Jews improve intellectually. Joseph Dorinson concludes that self-deprecation, without being threatening or humiliating, permits Jews to deal honestly and openly with problems (451). Ziv concurs: "Self-disparaging humor makes possible self-criticism, and enables a man to take a more courageous look at his negative aspects. . . . Self-disparaging humor is a sign of maturity and of self insight" (56).

Both Dorinson and Ziv readily admit that Jews have as many problems as non-Jews—if not more because of their confused cultural identity—but in the attempt to identify these character flaws, Jews take one step closer to improving them.

Elliott Oring best summarizes the views on the intellectual component in Jewish humor as a paradox in the modern Jew's cultural identity. "When a man passionately proclaims his Jewishness and refuses to accept the inferiority that is deemed his, yet secretly or unconsciously reviles his heritage and is utterly convinced of his inferior status, then that man is in a real sense *meshugge*" (118).

Oring identifies the qualities of the modern Jewish mind that are as distinctive as self-deprecation is to Jewish humor—contradiction and confusion. Of the disparate views scholars present on the intellectual component of Jewish humor, all would probably confirm Oring's observation. While most of these scholars note the correlation between self-hatred, as Gilman defines it, and the self-deprecation of the Jew's humor, all heavily qualify what this self-hatred reveals about the humorist's Jewish identity. Where Bergler generalizes by suggesting that the self-deprecating humorist resents his entire Jewish heritage, the Torah included, the Katzes point out that most self-deprecating Jews actually do not hate their own Jewishness as much as the Jewish American caricature to which their cultural identity links them (221). Some of this self-deprecation, Rosenberg and Shapiro add, cannot be labeled as self-hatred at all, but as intense guilt that the humorist transforms into apparent self-hatred (75). Finally, when used correctly, Dorinson (39) and Ziv (56) note the positive value self-criticism can have for Jews who want to improve their character flaws.

Perhaps the emotionalists and the sociologists seem to avoid the intellectual issue of self-hatred because such a catchphrase is too broad to reflect the actual nature of Jewish identity with any accuracy. True, there are elements of Gilman's self-hatred in Jewish humor as there are in other forms of Jewish folklore, but the Jew's cultural identity is more three-dimensional than the two words imply. In the case of Woody Allen, often condemned as a self-hating Jew, his humor reveals that he identifies as a self-affirming Jew in many ways. Nevertheless—whether self-hating, self-affirming, or both—no Jew can be characterized by many of the generalizations made by many of the scholars in this study. Identifying with an ethnic group, Dundes observes, "tends to reduce the individual to a number" (257). Woody Allen's Jewish identity is not only the result of the Jewish-American emotional, sociological, and intellectual experience but of Allen's complex personal experience as well.

In examining both his persona's attitude toward his Jewish identity and the limited information about the comedian's Jewish background itself, many critics see self-hatred as one of Woody Allen's most distinctive characteristics. While I argue against such a simplistic, and often inaccurate, labeling of the complex subject of cultural and religious identity, Allen's private and public self-deprecation admittedly gives the impression of self-hatred. His persona's nebbish appearance and awkward presence send clear signals that he is not comfortable with himself. He seems unsympathetic and occasionally hostile to Jewish causes and institutions. The first time he revealed any interest in Israel was when he publicly criticized the government for the Intifada (Allen, "Am I Reading the Papers Correctly?," 34). He often denigrates his Jewish identity without regard in both interviews and professional work. Many in his audience might even find "self-hatred" too generous a description of a man who seems to deprecate his ethnic culture so maliciously. But, the various scholars of Jewish humor would point out, Allen's self-deprecation does not necessarily imply self-hatred. Ironically, in many ways his humor reveals his self-affirmation as a Jew.

Just as Brandes refutes Ben-Amos's claim that the humorist separates himself completely from his created persona, Maurice Yacowar—in his thorough and insightful analysis of Allen's career, Loser Take All (13)—equates much of Allen's identity with that of his persona. Yacowar notes that the two entities are so inseparable that Allen has never ceased playing his persona in any of his movies, written works, or monologues. Of his strong identification with his persona, Allen says that "what I'm really interested in is creating an image of a warm person that people will accept as funny, apart from the joke or the gag" (13).

The real Allen clearly does not share his persona's extreme neurosis and low self-esteem, both of which he exaggerates for the sake of humor. Yet to make his persona appear human enough for audiences to identify with him, Allen instills his own personal warmth into all of his roles.

Allen's persona seems to disclose the real Allen's self-hatred by appearing deliberately gawky. Yet if this reflected his true nature, he would probably try to conceal his awkwardness rather than play on it. Allen does not depreciate his appearance out of self-hatred as much as out of the desire to humble himself before audiences who might otherwise idolize him. Consequently, as Richard Schickel remarks, he forces his audience to identify with him "just by appearing, bent like a question mark, his delivery hesitant, his eye contact with the audience non-existent, looking as if he might bolt and run at any minute" (33).

Allen's intent is neither to mock his Jewish identity nor even the American Jewish caricature from which he tries to distinguish himself, even though that caricature shares his shifty, hesitant, and clumsy characteristics. Rather, he increases his persona's warmth by stressing his imperfections. His emphasis on the imperfect, far from mocking Jewish values, actually reflects the Jewish notion that we must all learn to accept unchangeable shortcomings so that we can function in our everyday lives.

At an early age, Allen concluded that his sheltered, distorted, and inadequate Jewish upbringing characterizes all of Judaism. He explains that his parents "represent the heart of the Old World: their values in life are God and carpeting." As a result, "only philosophy, magic, and the clarinet became [Allen's] constant avocations," said Eric Lax (31), because each of these individualistic disciplines were devoid of the hypocrisy of his Jewish community. Through these introverted pastimes he learned to have faith only in himself instead of any higher moral being.

In his short biography, Lee Guthrie observes that, although Allen went to Hebrew school for eight years and observed various Jewish customs, Allen "figured out there was no God when he 'first learned to think' at age four or five" (13–14). Based on his wisdom at age five, Allen essentially rejected Judaism and any other form of monotheism for the rest of his life. As his character Mickey confesses in *Hannah and Her Sisters*, he simply "got off on the wrong foot" with Judaism and God.

While most of his work touches on elements of Allen's life history, his film *Radio Days* is the closest he has come to producing an autobiography. Through a series of anecdotes, Allen recalls various comic incidents that revolved around the most popular American household device of the 1930s and early 1940s, the radio. In the process, the audience has a glimpse of Allen's childhood in the Flatbush community, in which meaningful Jewish observance was virtually nonexistent. One particularly telling scene depicts a hypocritical neighbor committing the double sin of sneaking an unkosher pork chop during the Yom Kippur fast. While pointing to the neighbor's blind observance of rituals like kashrut and fasting, which he neither believes in nor understands, Allen also reveals his own ignorance of the meaning of these Jewish traditions. The ritual of kashrut refines the observer's moral discipline by limiting the kinds of foods that can be eaten and requiring those animals allowed for consumption to be killed in the least painful way possible. Fasting during Yom Kippur similarly serves to discipline the observer who, for at least that one day in the year, tries to restrain bodily desires to concentrate on sincerely repenting for misdeeds. To people like the neighbor and Allen himself who do not understand the ethical value of such rituals, both fasting and keeping kosher appear foolish and unnecessary.

Allen reveals not only his contempt for Jewish traditions, but of organized religion in general as an obstacle to rational, decent behavior. In one of his monologues, he recalls a great love affair that did not lead to marriage because of the principals' religious differences—he was an agnostic and she was an atheist, "so we didn't know what religion not to bring the children up in" (Allen, *Getting Even*, 24). The one-liner pokes fun at the dilemma of intermarriage between Christians and Jews in America, considered particularly serious in the Jewish community because of the fear of complete assimilation and rejection of Judaism by children of intermarried couples. With enough natural assimilation and intermarriage to dilute the Jewish population, the Jewish system, which tries to encourage the pursuit of morality from generation to generation, may not survive. The concern Jews have for preserving this ethical system of life is not shared by atheists and agnostics who, because they do not affirm any ethical system, usually expect their children to choose their own system of beliefs. Allen's joke responds to what seems an absurd invasion of privacy rather than a concern for preserving morality in the world. As in *Radio Days*, Allen mocks what he does not understand.

Allen best proves his ignorance of Judaism in his response to criticism from a Jewish organization, B'nai B'rith, about a sacrilegious sketch in *Everything You Always Wanted To Know about Sex* (1972) in which a rabbi is guest on a game show called *What's My Perversion?* As contestants look on, the host asks the rabbi to act out his favorite fantasy, which consists of his being whipped by a beautiful girl while his wife sits at his feet eating pork. This time Allen mocks both kashrut and rabbis themselves who, Allen maintains, perpetuate an illusion of holiness while they actually experience the same unholy desires as laymen. When B'nai B'rith expressed its disapproval of the scene, Allen responded, "B'nai B'rith complained about whipping the Rabbi. . . . I've never considered Rabbis sacred as I've never considered organized religions sacred. I find them all silly. Costumed and bearded just like popes, to me it's all absolutely absurd" (Probst, 261).

When Allen criticizes rabbinical self-righteousness, he misunderstands that the rabbi is not an exalted figure, but an Everyman who admits experiencing human passions. *Rabbi* simply means "teacher," implying that the rabbi (it is hoped) is a role model for how to live a decent life.

Allen believes that rabbis are forbidden from indulging in bodily pleasures because such indulgence is simply sacrilegious. If he had any significant knowledge of Jewish life, he could not be so critical. In serving as role models, rabbis usually try harder not to become slaves to their bodies not only because they fear appearing sacrilegious, but because by giving in to their body's demands, they risk compromising their moral ideals. If rabbis such as the guest on *What's My Perversion?* occasionally fail to achieve ideal ethical discipline, they merely reveal human shortcomings, and because they make no pretense to exceptional righteousness, they are not hypocrites. The rabbi's modest clothing symbolizes ethical discipline that he strives to maintain. His traditional beard complements that discipline and serves as a sign of knowledge and observance that befits a traditional Jewish role model. Allen's denigration reveals his superficial knowledge of the role of the rabbi.

While Gilman attributes self-hatred to ignorance—such as Allen's ignorance of the ethical value of kashrut, the Yom Kippur fast, the Jewish concern about intermarriage, and the role of the rabbi—Allen nonetheless may have reasons other than self-hatred for criticizing these Jewish institutions. As a popular artist, he needs to remain accessible to all contemporary audiences rather than just Jewish audiences. Allen's harsh response to B'nai B'rith was probably directed against the critics and their comments more than any Judaic ideal or symbol. In criticizing Allen, the leaders of B'nai B'rith indirectly forced him to take responsibility for his Jewish identity in his work, which the nonobservant Allen perceived as an unfair demand. In his personal life, Allen feels he has the right to decide freely how he will identify, but his art deserves to remain culturally indistinct. His self-defense is well justified in many ways. Jews did not become God's chosen people to conceal Jewish moral values from others but rather to spread these ideals to the rest of the world. When Allen tries to make the ideals universally accessible, he unknowingly affirms the Judaic ideal of *tikun olam* (repairing the world).

As long as his Jewish identity does not threaten the accessibility of his art. Allen maintains a disinterested attitude toward his background. When film critic Natalie Gittelson noted the predominance of jokes in his work that in some way involve Jewish themes, Allen responded by downplaying the importance of his identity. "When asked, Allen adds the fact of being Jewish never consciously enters his work. . . . 'Of course any character I play would be Jewish because I'm Jewish,'" she wrote, quoting Allen (106). Allen sees his Jewish identity as playing as small a part in his art as his freckled complexion and his scrawny build. He may feel frustrated by all these traits at times, particularly when they limit his sexual prowess, but he believes that the most important elements of character are talent and hard work. Allen appears to take accusations of Jewish self-hatred lightly simply because, like his complexion and build, he cannot change his Jewish identity.

While Allen downplays the importance of his Jewish identity in his work, not only are many of his characters Jewish, but much of his subject matter deals either with explicit Jewish themes or with general Judaic ideals, from the Japanese characters who speak Yiddish in *What's Up, Tiger Lily?* to the satire on the Jewish American's attempt at social acceptance in *Zelig*, to the scathing portrayal of a Jewish mother in his short "Oedipus Wrecks." Allen may not consciously admit to the large role his Jewish identity plays in his work—at least compared with the supporting role his freckles and his scrawny build play—but, as Freud would argue, Woody Allen's humor reveals what his conscious mind otherwise conceals.

Far from completely renouncing his Jewish heritage, much of Allen's humor that appears to condemn the Jews and their religion actually condemns self-hating Jews themselves. In one monologue, he describes an intellectual who "suffered untold injustices and persecution from his religion mostly from his parents . . . they could never accept the fact that their son was Jewish" (Yacowar, 79). The joke relies on several ironic twists. First, his parents resent him for being Jewish, something he got from them in the first place, when he should logically resent them. Second, of all the anti-Semitic people in the world, he suffers the most abuse from those who should love and accept him the most. Finally, the stereotype of Jewish parents holds that they cannot accept their children's decision to reject their heritage rather than affirm it, which as the joke implies, Allen does. This third irony suggests that Allen identifies positively as a Jew and, through his subtle criticism, he actually distances himself from self-hating Jews. Allen's joke ultimately makes the issue of self-hatred ridiculous because people cannot change their identity and thus they will only become frustrated by resenting what they cannot change.

The underlying message in Allen's self-deprecating humor is that, mostly because of his Jewishness, he feels like an outsider. He rarely, if ever, actually refers to himself as an outsider, probably because he assumes that alienation is a natural part of his identity as a member of a minority. Since he blames his Jewish identity for feelings of alienation, Allen logically appears self-hating, yet he is wise enough not to blame his identity alone for feelings of social alienation. The main source of his alienation, like that of most outsiders, lies in our contemporary social framework and not just in his identity as an ethnic minority. Because his humor attracts such large and diverse audiences, most of his fans must also identify as or be empathic to outsiders for them to appreciate his work so much.

Allen's identification as an outsider enables him to look at his life objectively and keep his personal problems in perspective. Guilt and suffering recall what the sociological scholars of Jewish humor attributed to the ghetto experience. With high moral demands placed on them by their religion, and paranoia caused by anti-Semitic persecution, Allen believes it natural for Jews to identify as outsiders. Feelings of guilt and suffering are not limited to Jews, but belong to all people who aspire to Western culture's impossible ideals of power, status, and financial success. When people inevitably fail to achieve these ideals, they feel guilty and even suffer for not succeeding where so many others seem to have succeeded. They ultimately feel like outsiders. Those exceptions who do not aspire to these ideals also become outsiders simply because of their unusual values. In Allen's world, where everyone feels alienated, the only outsider ironically would be those who do not consciously identify as outsiders.

Even the all-American title character in one of Allen's most popular films, *Annie Hall*, suffers as an intellectual outsider, especially when she spends time with the seemingly sophisticated Alvy Singer, played by Allen. Allen the director focuses not just on the problems involved with alienation but on how the individual deals with these feelings in everyday life. Both of the film's main characters manage to overcome their sense of inadequacy, which leads to their alienation. Annie takes literature classes and advances her singing career, and Alvy looks at his life with characteristically Jewish self-mockery.

Like Freud, Allen sees Jewish humor as a paradox. Jews understand their shortcomings—in this case, the inability to accept those who accept them—but often feel destined to retain them. Jews who strive for acceptance into non-Jewish society can never feel satisfied because, as soon as non-Jews accept them, they assume that those non-Jews themselves cannot be social insiders or they would not accept Jews.

The figure of the outsider may suffer from feelings of alienation, but he also enjoys a sense of quirkish individuality that an insider often sacrifices for the sake of social acceptance. In an age of technology and uniformity when people try to control characteristics that might distinguish them from what is socially accepted, Allen's uniqueness is a refreshing change of pace. The Jewish robot tailors in the futuristic film *Sleeper* (1973) exemplify the importance of the Jewish talent for retaining individuality. The tailors are unique. They even resist conforming to a robot's image of impersonality by retaining their warmth and humor through constant bickering in thick Yiddish accents. When Allen appears to mock the Jewish stereotype of bickering tailors, he actually praises their Jewish individuality for distinguishing them from other robots. The theme of Jewish individuality appears in a later scene in which two of the film's non-Jewish characters try to re-create a Flatbush dinner scene to deprogram the brainwashed Miles, played by Allen.

Allen elaborates on the theme of Jewish individuality in *Zelig*, in which a Jewish American wants to be accepted by non-Jewish society so badly that he completely loses his own personality. Through his study of *Zelig*, Allen mocks those Jews who try to discard their Jewishness. The result of his personality loss is his chameleon-like nature, which enables him to both physically and mentally assume the characteristics of people nearest to him. When he goes into the kitchen of a Chinese restaurant, Zelig becomes indistinguishable from the Chinese chefs. In an all-black jazz band, Zelig appears as a black clarinet player. In the company of rabbis, Zelig grows a beard and *peot* (curled sideburns). Allen's comic portrayal subtly jabs those assimilated Jews who imitate non-Jews to gain acceptance and lose their own identity in the process. Allen's criticism is partially self-directed since he himself desires acceptance from non-Jewish society: Zelig's playing of the clarinet, Allen's own trademark instrument, may represent Allen's intention of including himself in his criticism. But at least Allen does not forfeit his individuality, as his quirky persona demonstrates, in his attempt to fit into American society. Although he criticizes the rabbi's beard in his earlier response to B'nai B'rith, Allen eventually shows his appreciation of such uniqueness in his study of Zelig.

Allen's identification as an outsider also helps him retain his moral integrity. In one of his monologues, he recalls going to a costume party in the Deep South dressed as a ghost when a car of Ku Klux Klansmen mistake him as one of their own. He tries to fit in with the gang by saying "you-all" and "grits," but the Klansmen eventually discover his Jewish identity and prepare to lynch him. As he awaits his death, he sees his life pass before his eyes "as a kid in Kansas, swimmin' in the swimmin' hole, fishin' and fryin' up a mess o' catfish." Suddenly he realizes that this is not his life. He is to be hanged in two minutes and the wrong life is passing before his eyes. Trapped by the alien Klan, Allen cannot even find refuge in his own memory. But his image of a hopeless outsider is not depicted with the animosity of a self-hating Jew. Allen readily accepts his position as an outsider because it places him on a moral pedestal above the vigilante Klansmen. If his being Jewish means he is not guilty of murderous acts of bigotry, Allen gladly accepts his minority status. True, he may have to fear for his safety as an outsider, but Allen's ingratiating wit usually protects him from any harm. In the finale of the story, the Jewish identity that made him an endangered outsider at one time now becomes his ticket to social acceptance as he leaves his newfound friends, the Klansmen, having sold them two thousand dollars' worth of Israeli bonds.

Not only does Allen affirm his identity as an outsider, but he has no desire to try to function in any way as a social insider. Mark Schechner points to his unconscious hesitancy to adapt to non-Jewish society, even when he makes a concerted effort. Schechner mentions one scene in *Annie Hall* when "the gourmet in Alvy Singer suddenly yields to the nervous boy from Brooklyn who isn't quite ready to handle the aggressive, snapping traif [unkosher food] that his dreams have conjured up" (235).

Allen may occasionally resent the inferior status his outsider identity forces him to accept, but he cannot be considered self-hating because he recognizes that no matter what his ethnic identity he would still suffer from feelings of alienation in modern American society. While the Jewish culture has its limitations, Allen must finally admit—either consciously or unconsciously—that his humor owes part of its genius to his profound understanding of his outsider identity.

Allen consciously distances himself from the Jewish religion and culture, but his films nonetheless embrace Jewish ideals. Self-deprecation prompts humility and often even self-improvement rather than self-hatred. Allen summarizes his atheistic moral philosophy in which self-improvement serves as a central objective: "We've got to find the transition to a life-style and a culture in which we make tough, honest, moral and ethical choices simply because—on the most basic grounds—they are seen to be the highest good" (Gittelson, 32).

He does not reconcile the contradiction within his philosophy that, if there is no moral source higher than humans, morality is relative to the individual and conflict becomes inevitable. Yet at least Allen tries to pursue the "highest good" in his moral choices by struggling to find the most ethical way of treating other people. Similarly, most of the stories in the Torah can be interpreted as giving the affirmative answer to Cain's question, "Am I my brother's keeper?" in their emphasis on the individual's responsibility to work for peaceful human relationships. Allen unknowingly affirms the Jewish value of *tikun olam* by struggling to make ethical choices.

Although Allen may appear to have most faith in his artistic or intellectual abilities, especially since he has no faith in God, he realizes that these pursuits are ultimately empty when they are devoid of ethical meaning. In one monologue, he describes how a ballet performance of "The Dying Swan" sold out because of rumors that bookies fixed the performance so that the swan would live (Yacowar, 18). In addition to the absurdity of the idea that criminals would take interest in ballet, Allen subtly suggests that art has the same potential for corruption as any underworld activity. With the same intent, Allen tells the story of two policemen who lose their tear gas and are forced to perform the death scene of *Camille* to coax kidnappers from a house (18). Allen reduces the sophistication of great literature to the banter of crime stories. Yet Allen values artistic and intellectual pursuits insofar as they provide outlets for his morality plays. In this sense, Allen is even a kind of a rabbi himself who teaches his audience the importance of striving for integrity in the otherwise morally decadent modern world.

While Allen's persona always struggles to make moral choices, his pursuit is most apparent in his role of Isaac Davis in *Manhattan* (1979). Isaac is frustrated by the absence of moral decency in his previously cherished urban society. As the film begins, Isaac starts to realize that art and intellectualism have replaced morality in Manhattan society by becoming ends in themselves rather than means of expressing moral issues. Most of Isaac's peers deny his moral imperatives in their indulgent pursuit of pleasure. In one scene, Isaac criticizes his irresponsible, selfish friend Yale for undermining their friendship and cheating on his wife:

Yale: Well, I'm not a saint, okay?

Isaac: But you—you're too easy on yourself. . . . You—you rationalize everything. You're not honest with yourself . . .

Yale: You are so self-righteous, you know. I mean, we're just people, we're just human beings, you know. You think you're God!

Isaac: I—I gotta model myself after someone!

Unlike Yale, who uses his human status as an excuse to maintain immoral conduct, Isaac prefers to follow a remote ideal rather than conform to the corrupt values that surround him. In an earlier scene, Isaac objects to Yale's indulgence in buying a new Porsche, which he claims just "screws up the environment." Yale defends himself by calling the car "a work of art," thereby supporting Allen's argument on the emptiness of art as an ethical ideal. Instead of artists or intellectuals, Isaac chooses God as a role model not necessarily because he believes in the Judeo-Christian deity but simply to follow the ideal of moral excellence attributed to that God. The main difference between Isaac and Yale is that both accept their human limitations, but only Isaac makes the effort to rise above them and pursue higher ideals.

His struggle, like any good person's struggle, will last throughout his life, yet he will conceivably improve with age because he will have learned from his past mistakes.

Perhaps the strongest evidence of the affinity Allen feels for the Judaic ideal of ethical struggle appears in his short story "Remembering Needleman." The story describes the moronic title character, a self-proclaimed Nazi, and his outlook on life. Like Allen, Needleman does not believe in God, yet he does not share Allen's moral concerns. Allen draws Needleman as an absurd, yet frighteningly believable character whose amoral philosophy leads him to the following conclusions: "After much reflection, Needleman's intellectual integrity convinced him that he didn't exist, his friends didn't exist, and the only thing that was real was the I.O.U. to the bank for six million marks" (Allen, 5).

Allen again criticizes the danger of intellectuality when it has no moral basis, and even points out the evil that can result from such amorality. The six million marks represents the Nazi toll of Jewish lives, which is also the only real element in Needleman's life. Needleman never takes responsibility for his actions, so he tries to rationalize his evil behavior instead. When he fell out of his box at an opera he was too proud to admit his mistake, so he "attended the opera every night for the next month and repeated it each time." He feels guilty for the Nazis' crime of genocide only as a person feels guilty for not repaying a monetary debt. The story serves as Allen's most pointed condemnation of immoral people like Needleman whose distorted values make them lose their sense of moral justice.

Allen goes as far as praising the Jews' often vulgar, yet ethically minded, attitude toward life in comparison with Protestant genteelness in his film *Interiors* (1978). The film focuses on how three daughters cope with changes in their family life, told from the point of view of one of the daughters, Joey. Joey's father, Arthur, leaves her mother, Eve, because he can no longer endure her cold and exacting nature. He marries Pearl, who attracts him with her vibrant and loving nature. Eve clearly embodies Protestant values while Pearl embodies Jewish values, although neither actually identifies her ethnic origins. Eve is obsessed with cleanliness and appearances, as her ice-gray interior design suggests. Like her elegant vases, she has little moral integrity nor even emotions beneath her aesthetically pristine exterior. Similar to Yale in *Manhattan*, she represents the meaninglessness of sophistication as an end in itself. Pearl, on the other hand, has all the vitality, independence of spirit, and vulgarity of Allen's Jewish persona. At her wedding with Arthur, she insists on dancing with all the members of her new family, while they—perhaps under Eve's influence—respond coldly to her affection. Pearl's sensitivity to Joey's awkwardness reveals that she takes nothing for granted, so intense is her appreciation of life. What is vulgar in Pearl's nature can also be seen as life affirming, especially in contrast with Eve's morbid nature. Allen depicts Pearl's character more sympathetically than any other character in the film, probably because he idealizes her love of life. In an earlier monologue, he explains that "somebody truly close to life will always be regarded as vulgar by cultivated, brainy people." With his praise of Pearl's appreciation of life. Allen elaborates his theme of the importance of morality in our sophisticated, yet decadent modern society.

In the same way that he points to the potential immorality in art and intellectualism, Allen pokes fun at philosophical wisdom that does not apply directly to everyday morality. In *Love and Death* (1975), Boris (Allen) attempts a syllogism to rationalize his plan of assassinating Napoleon: A: Socrates is a man. B: All men are mortal. C: All men are Socrates. That means all men are homosexual.

Allen reduces the ancient piece of mathematical wisdom to meaningless philosophical banter by his irrelevant conclusion. In Allen's world, philosophy has the same amount of importance to our everyday actions as a junky detective comic book. Yacowar attributes part of Allen's comic genius to his use of bathos, the reduction of the grandiose to the trivial, while Schechner parallels Allen's use of bathos with Yiddish comedy (191). In addition to revealing his genius through such reductions, Allen reveals his moral skepticism in which he understands that, like art and intellectualism, philosophy itself can lead to evil if it has no moral basis.

Morality for Allen is not just a matter of philosophical speculation, but a way of life grounded in the everyday reality of eating, sleeping, sex, and other forms of human behavior. If Allen was better informed Judaically, he would realize that—far from focusing on any abstract, metaphysical matters—the Torah and the rabbinical texts that are the core of Judaism concentrate on the ethical regulation of human activities.

Throughout his films and other work, Allen reveals a positive affirmation of the Jewish ideals that his Jewish upbringing must have instilled in him. As a Jew who constantly distances himself from Judaism, Allen would probably deny the influence of Judaism in his life and argue that his morality is the result of his natural goodness. Yet the prevalence of his pursuit of moral integrity, particularly in films such as *Manhattan* and *Interiors*, suggests his Jewishness must have had some influence on him for him to idealize self-improvement as the first step to repairing the world. Despite the commendable objectives of his system of beliefs, he does not affirm any organized system of morality. That has several negative implications. First, because he does not believe in a higher moral source than humanity, he has no defense against moral relativism in which matters of right and wrong are reduced to each individual's opinion. Second, with no moral system, Allen has no way of transmitting ideals to future generations that may not have access to his artistic works. Finally, Allen's belief in the pursuit of moral integrity in no way obligates him to fulfill all of his moral objectives because he does not have to answer to a higher authority. He may not hate his Jewish identity, but by not meeting the requirements of his religion, Allen unwittingly reveals his moral laziness.

In January 1988, Woody Allen wrote an article in the *New York Times* expressing his concern over Israel's controversial policy for treating Palestinian demonstrators. He explains in the article that, as a supporter of Israel, he questions the ethical soundness of the Israeli government's violent and even "wrongheaded approach." While his article initially seems to reflect his moral conscientiousness, Allen may have had an ulterior motive in writing for the *Times*. Because of his anti-Israel stance, many Jewish and even non-Jewish critics denounce Allen as a "self-hating" Jew. Some mistakenly recall Allen's self-deprecation as a Jew throughout his career as further evidence of his self-hatred, without understanding the true, often self-affirming, nature of his Jewish identity that his article reveals. Of all the responses to the article, Charles Krauthammer's observation in the *New Republic* is probably the most accurate in its appraisal. "It is important for Israelis to know that diaspora Jewry will not support a policy of deliberate brutality. . . . But it is quite another thing when the protests are designed for the American press and aimed at an American audience. . . . Woody Allen was not writing to move Shamir or Rabin. He was trying to reassure his tablemates at Elaine's: not me," said Krauthammer (29).

Allen's personal statement about his Jewish identity, if not clear in his artistic work, is apparent in his *Times* article. He affirms the struggle for moral integrity in principle yet is unwilling to follow his ideals in his actual personal activities. He distances himself publicly from Jews and plays the role of voyeur, rather than active participant. As in *Crime and Misdemeanors* in which he broadly posits that the universe has an arbitrary judicial system, he remains painfully silent in dealing with how decent people like the rabbi should confront moral crisis. In his outburst about the Arab-Israeli conflict, Allen ultimately reveals what he has tried so hard to conceal about his personal life—that his persona's admirable struggle to become a better human being does not reflect in Allen's personal integrity. In this sense, Freud's idea that humor reveals what the conscious mind otherwise conceals works backward. Allen's humor, far from revealing any admirable moral strength, actually supplements Allen's otherwise morally lazy actions. Woody Allen is the incarnation of Grotjahn's warning that self-criticism often leads to self-justification and concurrent ethical complacency.

WORKS CITED

Allen, Woody. *Getting Even* (New York: Random House, 1971).

———. "Remembering Needleman: At the Cremation," *The New Republic* (July 24, 1976), p. 5.

———. "Am I Reading the Papers Correctly?" *The New York Times* (January 28, 1988).

Ben-Amos, Dan. "The 'Myth' of Jewish Humor," *Western Folklore*, 32 (1973).

Bergler, Edmund. *Laughter and the Sense of Humor* (New York: Grune & Stratton, 1956).

Brandes, Stanley. "Jewish American Dialect Jokes and Jewish American Identity," *Jewish Social Studies*, 45 (1983).

Dorinson, Joseph. "Jewish Humor: Mechanism for Defense, Weapon for Cultural Affirmation," *Journal of Psychohistory*, 8 (1981).

Dorson, Richard M. "Jewish-American Dialect Stories on Tape," *Studies in Biblical and Jewish Folklore* (1960).

Dundes, Alan. "Defining Identity through Folklore," *Identity: Personal and Socio-Cultural* (1983).

Freud, Sigmund. *Jokes and Their Relation to the Unconscious* (New York: W. W. Norton & Co, 1960).

Gilman, Sander. *Jewish Self-Hatred: Anti-Semitism and the Hidden Language of the Jews* (Baltimore: John Hopkins University Press, 1986).

Gittelson, Natalie. "The Maturing of Woody Allen," New York Times Magazine (April 22, 1979).

Grotjahn, Martin. *Beyond Laughter: Humor and the Subconscious* (New York: Mc-Graw-Hill, 1966).

Guthrie, Lee. *Woody Allen: A Biography* (New York: Drake Publishers, Inc, 1978).

Jason, Heda. "The Jewish Joke: The Problem of Definition," *Southern Folklore Quarterly*, 31 (1967).

Katz, Naomi, and Eli Katz. "Tradition and Adaptation in American Jewish Humor," *Journal of American Folklore*, 84 (1971).

Krauthammer, Charles. "No Exit," *The New Republic* (March 14, 1988).

Landmann, Salcia. "On Jewish Humor," *Jewish Journal of Sociology*, 4 (1962).

Lax, Eric. *On Being Funny: Woody Allen and Comedy* (New York: Charterhouse, 1975).

Oring, Elliot. *The Jokes of Sigmund Freud: A Study in Humor and Jewish Identity* (Philadelphia: University of Pennsylvania Press, 1984).

Probst, Leonard. *On Camera* (New York: Stein & Day. 1975).

Reik, Theodor. *Jewish Wit* (New York: Gamut Press, 1962).

Rosenberg, Bernard, and Gilbert Shapiro. "Marginality and Jewish Humor," *Mainstream*, 4 (1958).

Samuel, Maurice. *In Praise of Yiddish* (New York: Stein & Day, 1971).

Schechner, Mark. "Woody Allen: The Failure of the Therapeutic," *From Hester Street to Hollywood* (Bloomington, Ind: Indiana University Press, 1983).

Schickel, Richard. "The Basic Woody Allen Joke . . ." *New York Times Magazine* (January 7, 1973).

Schlesinger, Kurt. "Jewish Humor as Jewish Identity," *International Journal of Psychoanalysis*, 6 (1979).

Yacowar, Maurice. *Loser Take All: The Comic Art of Woody Allen* (New York: Frederick Ungar Publishing Co, 1979).

Ziv, Avner, ed. *Jewish Humor* (Tel Aviv: Papyrus Publishing House, 1986).

7

Beyond Parody
Woody Allen in the 1980s

Maurice Yacowar

In the beginning was the parody. From *What's Up, Tiger Lily?* (1966) through *Sleeper* (1973), Woody Allen developed his film artistry through forms of genre parody. In addition to providing the beginner with convenient sets of conventions to play against, the parodic stance was appropriate for his persona as frustrated outsider. Allen's nebbish persona provided a continuity across the wide range of film types that he parodied for his first ten years (and with his prose, theater, and television work as well). As a result his series of formal frolics seemed like a running autobiography, the candid, self-exposing confessions of a loser whose garb of heroic and romantic aspirations just did not fit. Each new chapter widened and deepened his audience's identification with his image.

Allen achieved a new level of sophistication when he ventured into philosophic parody in *Love and Death* (1975). But his mature period began with *Annie Hall* (1977). From Alvy Singer's opening address to his audience, this film presented an art that grew more personal as it abandoned his familiar persona. Allen's expression was no longer mediated by conventions of film (or literary) types. As well, Alvy Singer was more like Woody Allen—someone occasionally liable to success whether in comedy or in love—than like his earlier nebbishes. Allen consolidated this growth in *Interiors* (1978), from which not just his persona but even his image was excluded altogether. Still, the values for which he had come to stand were personified by the character of Pearl (Maureen Stapleton). When Allen reappeared on-screen in *Manhattan* (1979) his character was explicitly defined as a moral corrective

78

to self-absorbed and compromised urbanity. Thus the TV comedy writer quits his job to write a novel about the decay of culture.

In the 1980s Allen's cinema has extended this growth toward a more personal and profound vision. His next five films are rooted in the artist's experience rather than in the genre conventions that provided his earlier style and subjects. The parodist now speaks directly. The ostensible loser's autobiography has given way to the mature artist's concerns. The form of his first films has become a metaphor for his major themes: the social and cosmic limitations both upon art and upon life. As the persona has become subordinated to the material, Allen's image-referential work has matured into the harder-headed cinema that is self-referential. As the artist grew more confident both in his skills and in the capacity of his audience, his cinema ripened.

Stardust Memories (1980) has justly been called Allen's *8 1/2*, a fragmentary vision of the teeming limbo between an artist's experience and its transformation into art. Often what seems to be a life event is revealed to be a scene in a film-within-a-film. Indeed, when Jessica Harper and Marie-Christine Barrault leave the cinema chatting about Sandy Bates's (or Woody's?) open-mouth screen kisses, even the main plotline is exposed as a film. What we had assumed to be a film-within-the-film was actually a film-within-the-film-within-the-film. This array of mutually reflecting mirrors establishes one of the film's major themes: the insubstantiality of art in the context of a disintegrating cosmos. The film dramatizes the range of social and economic pressures that assail the artist in proportion to his success. But it also acknowledges the ephemerality of the art itself.

There are many moments of parody in *Stardust Memories*, because that is the level of art—popular, familiar, formulaic, trivial—that Sandy Bates tries to transcend, to the dismay of his fans and counselors. The specimens of Bates's films recall Allen's earlier genre parodies: a stiff-smiled musical ("Three Little Words"), a monster thriller ("Sidney Finkelstein's hostility has escaped"). But more than parody Allen emphasizes tonal homages and allusions to show a filmmaker deriving his personal voice from a great tradition, specifically Bergman and Fellini. For example, the UFO convention in the field and the inner-film characters' walk along the beach of carrion are pure Fellini.

Indeed the opening train scene seems to put Bates on a Bergmanian track, yearning to switch his ticket for the vigor of Fellini's world. Hence the pivotal contrast between two moving close-ups of Bates's neurotic ex-lover, Dorrie (Charlotte Rampling). The first is what is called Sandy's last meeting with her. A montage of brief, jagged, repetitious phrases suggests the tensions and fragility of a psyche that is shivered if not indeed shattered. The discontinuous footage expresses both the character's halting speech and self-control and Sandy's (and our) unsteady hold on the moment. This stark baring of a troubled soul is the Bergman locus. The Fellini comes later, when

Sandy searches "for something to hang onto . . . something to give my life meaning." He finds it in recalling a treasured moment: we hear Louis Armstrong sing "Stardust" and see Dorrie in assured, peaceful repose. Since this shot is continuous and Rampling is farther away from the camera, this scene has none of the unsettling effects of the earlier. But Allen's art equally preserves the painful and the treasured. In another shot a Fellini line of dancing nuns can be seen in the background, while in the Bergmanian fore Bates tries to talk Dorrie out of her pre-filming anxieties. When Bates and Daisy discuss *The Bicycle Thief*, Bates affirms the double development of modern cinema beyond the social concerns of neorealism: in effect, Fellini's thrust into the realism of the imagination and Bergman's into that of the soul.

The language of allusion and homage is personalized when Allen weaves in echoes of his earlier films. Sandy's cosmic despair recalls little Alvy Singer, peering into his quivering tomato soup, wondering why he should do homework when the universe is doomed. The lobster scenes in *Annie Hall* lurk behind the rabbit and bird scenes here. Both films are (in Alvy's words) "sifting the pieces" of memory, loss, and thwarted aspiration. Sandy's memory of the fight in the Jewish school play recalls the many comic Jewish images in Allen's work, as do his gags on masturbation, the artist's pretense to being a god, and his attempt to assert an order in art that life does not allow. These patterns of cross-reference, parody, and allusion establish the public language at the filmmaker's disposal. As Sandy Bates strives to outgrow parody, Allen's film declares its independence from his fans' demands for a simple comedy. As even the space visitor tells Sandy, "I especially like your early films, your funny ones."

Stardust Memories is extremely troubling. This is partly due to its unpredictable shifts between different levels of reality. It is doubly unsettling because it preempts the charges that might wrongly be laid against Allen's work: "pretentious," "self-indulgence—I think the man has lost his mind," "They try to document their private suffering and fob it off as art," "I like a melodrama *mit* a plot but *nicht kein philosophia*," "Too much reality is not what the people want." Notwithstanding Allen's implicit claims for a brave, realistic cinema, this film's most problematic element is its unmitigated caricature of Bates's fans. Without exception they are viewed as self-promoting exploiters and grotesques ("Can I have your autograph? I was a Caesarean," "Would you sign it 'To Phyllis Weinstein, you unfaithful, lying bitch'?"). Bates turns a rape victim into a joke ("I know you didn't resist, knowing you"). The furnishing of Sandy's sister's home is a savage satire on middle-class domestica. Even a valid observation is undermined by its speaker (e.g., the self-promoting psychiatrist's diagnosis of Bates's Ozymandias melancholia: "He saw reality too clearly; he had a faulty defense mechanism"). Further, because Allen plays Bates, Bates's grotesque audience comes to stand for Allen's; they are us. Allen's self-satire in Bates does not balance his satire against all others. As a result, it is tempting to take Bates's arrogance and misanthropy as Allen's; however, the conventions of fiction should preclude this judgment. This film's virulent satire makes it a work of far greater valor than discretion. His later films rework the themes of *Stardust Memories* but without its discomfiting prophetic vision.

As if to make amends for the lack of distance in *Stardust Memories*, Allen then produced a work of sweetness and light, in which the moral anatomy was not centered upon his role. In *A Midsummer Night's Sex Comedy* (1982) the plot uncrosses mismatched lovers, but its larger concern is the tension between man's physical and ethereal natures. Speculations about the occasional coincidence of love and sex establish this theme. The film's major movement is the conversion of the arrogantly materialist philosopher, Leopold (Jose Ferrer), into a romantic spiritualist; the man of culture rediscovers his savage impulses. Leopold is suitably liberated from the limits of the flesh and narrow intellect by the candid and open Dulcy Ford (Julie Hagerty), who despite her inferior education can both beat him in chess and literally fuck him to death, which frees him into a greater life. With her animal vibrations, Dulcy both validates and transcends Leopold's materialist vision of man.

The film derives from the end dance of *Love and Death* more than from the Shakespeare namesake. Allen plays a pathetic kind of Prospero, the inventor Andrew. The spirit-character Ariel is here an earthy, liberated woman (Mia Farrow). Conversely, the libido figure of Caliban is elevated into the articulate but lecherous doctor, Maxwell (Tony Roberts). Even his jokes are keyed to his devotion to the appetites. When Ariel remarks that Raphael fainted at his first sight of the Sistine Chapel, Maxwell quips, "Had he eaten?"

One framing strategy proves that there are more things in heaven and earth than are dreamed in Leopold's philosophy. Allen often keeps his camera stationary so that action and speech flow beyond the frame. That is to say, life continues beyond what a particular sense may convey. Thus we see Andrew fly but we only hear him crash off camera. In Andrew's key conversations (with Maxwell, with wife Adrian, with Ariel) the characters move in and out of the frame. The unseen world remains realized by what we hear. This wholly realistic technique prepares for the miracles later: first, the magical projections by Andrew's "spirit box" and, ultimately, the revelation of immortal romantic spirits glowing in the forest night.

The film's magic also has a personal dimension as Allen's affirmation of art. Andrew's metal globe anticipates filmmaking, since it projects images of romantic potential for its characters to realize. These images the materialist Leopold dismisses: "What pathetic delusions we frightened mortals cling to." Where Leopold claims, "I didn't create the cosmos; I merely explain it," Andrew's inventions change his world by allowing the lovers to increase their understanding. Allen creates the cosmos of this film but refuses to "explain" it. He prefers the mysteries of magic and love. An incidental emblem for Allen's art can be found in Andrew's wedding gift for Ariel and Leopold: a machine that can either take the bones out of a fish or put them back in. His creation is gloriously independent of its audience's desires (Leopold loathes fish). It is also like a Woody Allen comedy in that it can pander to a taste for mushy matter (the deboned fish) or it can provide a work with backbone and difficulty (the reboned fish). In a simpler vein, Andrew functions as antimaterialist even in his profession of stockbroker; "I help people with their investments until there's nothing left." As the stockbroker makes nothing of something, the artist makes another kind of nothing—the ethereal visions of his art—out of the "things" of experience, or something of nothing. This film makes much ado about various kinds of nothing.

In *Zelig* (1983) Allen makes a considerable something out of nothing in terms of his hero's personality. His central character has the miraculous capacity to assume the physical and personal character of whomever he's with. This ability endangers his integrity because of his eagerness to blend in with others. Zelig personifies conformity: "It's safe to be like the others . . . I want to be liked." The Zelig craze satirizes the faddishness in American popular culture and the arts but also the American tendency toward social uniformity. In a public interview someone flatly states, "I wish I could be Leonard Zelig," that is, literally a non-Zelig who is like everyone else. He embodies Allen's common quip that his one regret is that he is not someone else. But Zelig is also an artist figure. In addition to the Jungian explanation of the artist—"I've never flown before in my life and it shows what you can do if you're a complete psychotic"—Zelig is the ultimate actor and the victim of both his own success and his celebrity. His career may reflect Allen's fickle fortunes, especially the reviewers' rejection of *Interiors* and *Stardust Memories*. Thus Zelig is loved and imitated, then loathed and abused ("America is a moral country, a God-fearing country. In keeping with our puritan society, I say lynch the little Hebe.") Paradoxically, this unique film is based on the principle of imitation. As Zelig is unique because he can become anyone else, the film is a distinctive work that is essentially a parody. Indeed it is so radically a parody that it seems to belong to a different order than Allen's earlier forays into the form.

Zelig is set forth as a parody of the Metrotone newsreels of the 1930s that Orson Welles took as a starting point for *Citizen Kane*. True to his antiheroic disposition, though, where Welles pursued the impenetrable enigma of a powerful man, Allen pursues the mystery of a peripheral nebbish who is only distinctive for his ability to become indistinguishable. But if *Citizen Kane* and the quoted blips from a putative Hollywood biography of Zelig provide a public context of parody, there is also a personal context. Allen mischievously parodies Warren Beatty's *Reds*. The search through Europe by Dr. Fletcher (Mia Farrow) for Zelig (Allen) parodies the search by Louise Bryant (Diane Keaton) for John Reed (Beatty) in *Reds*. Of course, Ms. Keaton was Allen's love and star before she moved on to Beatty in both capacities. Allen parodies Beatty's "witnesses" with the testimony of such real public figures as Susan Sontag, Saul Bellow, Bruno Bettelheim, and Irving Howe, even as their remarks advance the most explicit themes of the film: the social and personal dimensions of assimilation, alienation, and integrity.

Conversely, the reality of these witnesses is itself undermined by the conviction with which Allen slips his character into what seems to be newsreel footage of historical figures (Babe Ruth, Tom Mix, the pope, Hitler—the usual suspects). Here as in *Stardust Memories* Allen details the exploitation of the artist. "Among fanatics he was a handy symbol of iniquity"; the French intellectuals "see in him a symbol of everything." Everyone projects his own needs or weaknesses upon Zelig. Thus the doctor who says Zelig has a brain tumor dies of one himself. Hordes of exploiters, including Zelig's "half sister," cash in on the chameleon craze. Zelig is Allen's most outrageous assertion as an artist: he rewrites history by blending his own image into documents of the past. Here the artist is going one better than inventing a cosmos: he is re-creating the one we think is the real one, as recorded on documentary film. For all its continuation of the themes of *Stardust Memories*, however, Allen's and Gordon Willis's stunning craftsmanship and Allen's distance from his character make for a more comfortable, however more radical, experience.

In *Broadway Danny Rose* (1984) Allen returns to his more familiar format of moral comedy. Allen plays a sad sack theatrical agent who attracts a stable of losers. His acts are emblems of an incomplete humanity struggling for self-respect and fullness: a one-legged tap dancer, a blind xylophonist, a one-armed juggler, and a skating penguin dressed as a rabbi. One is a comic version of the larger theme of integrity and finding one's own voice: a parrot who sings "I Gotta Be Me." The film details Danny's betrayal by his one hit client, a one-hit Italian crooner, Lou Canova (Nick Apollo Forte), whose career is revived by the nostalgia craze. As in *Zelig*, the artist is subject to the whims of a faddist and forgetful public.

The plot centers upon Danny Rose's misadventures with Canova's girlfriend Tina (Mia Farrow, perhaps mining her experience in the Frank Sinatra society). Proving Canova's lack of integrity both in his professional and his domestic life, Tina leads him out of his marriage and away from his agent. But Danny Rose teaches Tina about integrity, commitment, and the need for conscience and guilt. In other words, Danny Rose has the same effect of moral awakening on Tina that the Allen characters had on Diane Keaton's WASP princesses from *Sleeper* through *Manhattan*. As Danny puts it, "You gotta suffer a bit or what's the point of life?" In Tina's view, "Who's got time to feel guilt? . . . You gotta do what you gotta do. Life is short." But

Allen does not leave his hero a saint. At film end, when Tina returns to apologize, Danny at first rejects her overture of friendship, then recants and chases after her to forgive. Their reunion is commemorated in the Danny Rose Special at the Carnegie Deli: cream cheese on a bagel with marinara sauce. The absence of meat suits the agent's poverty; the mix combines his Jewish palate with the Italian flavor of his new relationship with Tina.

Although Danny's virtue goes largely unrewarded in his career, the sandwich signifies his esteem in the minor heaven of show business. The respect for integrity (if only as a risible oddity in a callous world) is established by the plot's framing. A group of actual club comics sit around schmoozing in the famous deli. Sandy Baron tells Danny Rose's adventure as the ultimate story of this loser. The kind of respect in the afterlife for which Isaac strove in *Manhattan* is dramatized here in the comedian's chronicle of Danny Rose's exploitation and defeat. The comedians' cynical respect is a kind of showbiz canonization. Also, the framing device distances Allen's role. He is reduced to a character in the story Baron is telling, like the characters in the inner films of *Stardust Memories* and *Zelig*.

Supported by the Italian American music and setting, the film evokes Fellini's fascination with the tawdry eccentrics of show business. But instead of Allen's usual Jewish contrast to the American mainstream, here he parallels the subcultures of Jewish showbiz and Italian semicriminality. The Italians at a party tear up money; Danny later rues the expense of a hotel hideout. Tina blandly asserts herself in any situation, while "the landlocked Hebrew" is at sea as soon as he crosses the bridge into New Jersey. On the other hand, both ethnic societies establish the moral imperative of self-acknowledgment. "Keep Italian in your heart," sings Canova; the Jewish comedians leaven their chat with Yiddish and proverbs. The characters have more difficulty acknowledging their professional beginnings than their ethnic roots. Danny persists in faithful, self-sacrificing service to his acts despite his bitter lesson from experience that "people like to forget their beginnings." His successful acts always leave him. Both subcultures share exuberance, familial warmth, camaraderie, and an appetite for food and fun. But in their key contrast, the Italians are motivated by a hard code of social honor and image, in contrast to Danny's personal conscience. Without the core of integrity, Canova's familial warmth is a hollow image compared to the extended family with whom Danny celebrates a frozen-turkey Thanksgiving dinner.

Danny Rose's characterization is among Allen's most inventive. His hands keep moving, as if in choreographed routines, punctuating his nonstop chatter, platitudes, oaths, and anecdotes—Catskills gush. Danny's restless hands and words seem to be his only way to ward off chaos. From the moment he enters Tina's apartment and finds her in full tantrum against Lou, Danny manfully tries to use slogans, stories, and euphemisms to calm the storm.

Similarly, he uses a three-word formula to stave off his performers' anxiety: "Strong—Smile—Star."

As Danny's mannerisms and morality are feeble attempts to keep his chaotic world in order, Allen achieves another kind of order in casting real comedy heroes as themselves in the film. The deli storytellers include the real Will Jordan, Corbett Monica, Jackie Gayle, Howard Storm, Morty Gunty, and Allen's longtime producer Jack Rollins. Milton Berle, Howard Cosell, Sammy Davis Jr., and Big Bird also appear as themselves. As in *Zelig*, Allen plays on the tension between these real people and his fictional characters to establish the ethic of being oneself. As the fictional folk move among the real, Allen's central couple scamper among the less real giant heads stored for the Macy's parade. These heads may represent the enlarged egos of modern man and the great icons of showbiz (the two are not always the same). The image also seems emblematic of Allen's comedy, where moral rigor gives weight to the comedy of caricature. Without such moral weight a person can turn into a cartoon. Thus when a hood's gunshot releases helium from a float, the escaping gas gives all the characters' voices the queer speed of cartoon speech.

Related to the theme of inflated personality is the image of Mia Farrow, here stretched between stiletto heels and a plastic hairdo. She strips down to her more familiar Vulnerable Waif image when Tina studies herself in a mirror and resolves not to move to Hollywood with Canova but to seek out the betrayed Danny. This relates to the recurring metaphor of the false front. Danny is a "beard" when he agrees to take Canova's girlfriend to his performance for him. Barney Dunn becomes Danny's "beard" inadvertently when he suffers the assault intended for Danny. Danny's star ventriloquist has a stutter, but his "front," his dummy, has none. Even the recurring shots of the front of the Carnegie Deli establish the idea of a front, behind which teems a complex of moral confusions and choices. *Broadway Danny Rose* reminds us of the moral imperatives behind fame and fortune.

The moral distinctions between real and false people also occupy Allen in *The Purple Rose of Cairo* (1985). Not only does he not appear, it's his first feature without an Allen surrogate. Mia Farrow stars as Cecilia, a Depression-era New Jersey housewife married to the brutish Monk (Danny Aiello). She escapes her dreary life with frequent visits to the Jewel cinema. While she is watching a Hollywood romance, *The Purple Rose of Cairo*, for the fifth time, one of the characters, explorer Tom Baxter (Jeff Daniels), steps off the screen into the "real" world and begins to court her.

While Cecilia begins to live out her film fantasy, Tom starts to learn about the real world; when he takes her into the screen world she upsets the plot. Eventually she abandons the screen character to accept the romance of Gil Shepherd (also Jeff Daniels), the Hollywooden actor who played Tom Baxter. Gil seems also to have fallen in love with the plain Cecilia, who is more "real" than the Hollywood bimbos he has known, as she is more real than the fictional characters in the inner film's world. "To hear that from a real person!" the actor exults at Cecilia's compliment. Ultimately he chooses the Hollywood world over the "real" woman and abandons her. Having chosen the real, imperfect Gil over the ideal but fictional Tom, Cecilia resigns herself to sustaining her romance with the vicarious pleasures of the escapist film. Fred Astaire seems to taunt her with his "Heaven, I'm in heaven," as he dances "Cheek to Cheek" Gingerly.

This film again expresses Allen's sense of the artist restricted by his audience's demands for a cinema that is familiar, simplistic, reassuring. Several audience members complain that the interrupted film is not meeting their expectations. As one indignant client puts it, "I want what happened in the movie last week to happen this week. Otherwise what's life all about anyway?" Again the film-within-a-film sets up a series of reflecting mirrors. The basic "conceit" in this witty, metaphysical fiction is the confusion about which of its several worlds is really "real." In addition to the obvious antithesis of explorer Tom's screen life and Cecilia's world, when Cecilia first leaves Monk he yells after her that she'll be back after she learns "what it's like in the real world." There is some sad validity to his implication that even her sordid marriage is a refuge from the even harsher world outside.

The two romantic men in Cecilia's life find their own confusions. Fictional Tom Baxter stumbles into the brothel world, but his naïveté and romantic purity turn the "real" whores (Dianne Wiest et al.) into the cliché of the sentimental heart-of-gold mother manqué. Actor Gil Shepherd's courtship of Cecilia takes them into a quaint little pawnshop where they enjoy the kind of musical interlude that usually happens only in unrealistic films. Allen intercuts actor Gil's date with the "real" Cecilia with character Tom's experience with the seamier romance of the brothel. In both cases idealism triumphs, albeit only momentarily. On the other hand, Tom Baxter anticipates with relish a romance where the kiss is not followed by a fade-out (one of the film's many parallels to Keaton's *Sherlock, Jr.*). But even this is an illusion; few of us could fairly lay claim to his assumption that we "make love without fading out." We may be free from the cinematic device but not from the failings of the flesh. Life in the inner film is equally false, however: Cecilia finds that the "champagne" served in the film's Copacabana is ginger ale. And despite the eternal romance in the inner film there is an unaccommodated resignation in the chanteuse's repeated song "Let's Take It One Day at a Time."

Boredom afflicts life on both sides of the screen. Indeed, in the inner film the first line spoken is the playwright character's "Jason, I'm bored." The New York socialites of the film can take refuge from their boredom by flying off to Egypt. The explorer they meet there flies back with them for a madcap Manhattan weekend. Their respite from routine palliates the dreariness in their audience's lives. As the screen characters provide an image of impossible freedom for their audiences, the real world promises freedom for the fictional characters. "I'm free, after 2,000 performances," exults Tom Baxter when he escapes into the life of the woman who has been escaping into his. Tom's role gives him both powers and compulsions: "I'm sorry. It's written into my character to do it so I do it." The free, affluent character prefers the life of the unscripted: "I want to live. I want to be free to make my own choices." Of course, this freedom is itself an illusion; we see how restricted Cecilia's and Gil Shepherd's choices in life really are, subject as they are to social, economic, and psychological pressures. Indeed, Cecilia's escapist fascination with her films keeps her from confronting the real problems in her life. The Van Johnson and Zoe Caldwell characters in the inner movie seem to take a more realistic view of life on our side of the screen:

Van: I wonder what it's like out there.

Zoe: They don't seem to be having much fun.

Van: I want to go too. I want to be free. I want out.

Zoe: Quiet. That's Communist talk.

When Tom violates the distance between the inner film and the "real" world, the inner plot breaks down. When "it's every man for himself," the Copacabana maitre d' breaks into a tap solo, what he's "always wanted to do." Thus "the real people want their lives fictional and the fictional want their lives real." As in *Zelig*, in other words, everyone wants to be someone else.

On the other hand, the fictional world offers a consistency and at least the illusion of human perfection that reality cannot. As Tom puts it, "Where I come from people don't disappoint. They're consistent, reliable." Significantly, the character who proves most unreliable, a betrayer, is Gil Shepherd, the actor who played the perfect, reliable Tom Baxter. Probably we must reject the moral defeatism of Gil's line to Tom: "You can't learn to be real. It's like learning to be a midget. . . . Some of us are real, some of us aren't." From Allen's perspective, the ideality of the fictional character has more weight and substance, that is, more of a kind of "reality," than the exploitative vanity of the "real" but insincere Hollywood star. It's the latter who fails to learn to be "real" either from Cecilia or from the idealized character he portrays. Allen keeps making movies because he must feel that we can learn to be real.

Again Allen deals with the insubstantiality of the fictional characters; indeed after the lack of self in *Zelig* and the role-within-the-story that Allen played in *Broadway Danny Rose*, it is appropriate that from this film he is absent altogether. Paradoxically, this time it is his absence that establishes him in the familiar Allen role as God in the cosmos of the film. Curiously, the inner film has a credit for the producer, Raoul Hirsch, but none for a director. So there is a confusion over the source of being. Claiming full responsibility for his role, Gil will share credit only with his dialogue coach ("a genius"); but the actor refuses to accept responsibility for what his character goes on to do when he asserts his independence. Character Tom rather places the writers in the function of God. In his beginning was the word. In this light Allen's film can be read as a theological parable of the confusions and despair that afflict a world with no belief in God. This reading is supported by Milo O'Shea's presence in the inner film as the stereotype stage priest. As Cecilia puts it, a life without God would be "a world without point and no happy ending," which is what she ultimately gets. And with no God to direct his creatures' fates the only good shepherd is the culpable Gil Shepherd.

Allen's film ends with a sentimental close-up as resonant as the last shots in *City Lights* and *Manhattan*—with the same pathos, resignation, and ambivalence. As Cecilia watches the Hollywood musical, her teary melancholy slowly gives way to the joy of her vicarious experience. When she chose Gil, she told the fictional Tom, "I'm a real person . . . I have to choose the real world." She chose the real world but the false man. At film end she has in one sense returned to the real world but to the only romance and joy she can find in it: Hollywood fantasy. This is a solace dearly bought. Where inventor Andrew's romantic art solved the characters' problems, here the art leaves the victim with only the illusion of satisfaction, her voids unfilled.

The Purple Rose of Cairo is a culmination of Allen's discussion of the ambivalence of the filmmaker's art. Its technical freshness and wit provide a palliative that was lacking in *Stardust Memories*. But Allen has not settled into the compromise that Cecilia made, her retreat from an uncompromising reality to the false security of the fantasy cinema. Allen's vision and concern remain constant despite the flex and frolic of his comic forms.

Through parodies Woody Allen learned how to make films. In his features in the 1980s, Allen no longer makes film parodies but films about the implications of parody. His more recent works, realistic anatomies of fantasy, affirm the artist's need to break free from conventional forms and rhetoric. The need to find and to free one's own voice is, of course, not restricted to the artist. Zelig as Everyman must learn not to try to be like others, not to go through others' forms, others' faces. While the parodist takes an important first step toward self-realization in subverting the conventions or language that he is expected to use, integrity requires that one break free even from the conventions subverted. As *The Purple Rose of Cairo* demonstrates, however, the social condition betrays the human one by not allowing freedom from roles, conventions, the repressions of our manifold realities, on either side of the silvered screen. In Allen's continuing spiritual autobiography, the artist continues to flee his prescribed roles.

8

Woody Allen and Fantasy
Play It Again, Sam

Wes D. Gehring

Fantasy has always been associated with the comedy world of Woody Allen.[1] The pervasiveness of his comic antihero stance, what Maurice Yacowar focuses on as the comic outsider (78, 112)—in his films, short stories, and stand-up comedy albums—has come to represent a pivotal view of the frustrations of modern society. And fantasy has been crucial in these presentations, be it the short sketches from *Everything You Always Wanted to Know about Sex (But Were Afraid to Ask)* (1972; where antihero consistency is maintained even when he appears as a sperm) or that moment of supreme self-satisfaction in *Annie Hall* (1977) when Allen suddenly pulls Marshall McLuhan out of nowhere to put down a pompous intellectual. Director Allen even underlines the fantasy magic of this moment by then giving his comedy character the direct address line, "Boy, if life were only like this."

For the student of comedy, it is quite natural to link the frustrations and fantasies of Allen's world with an earlier author who helped bring the comic antihero to center stage in American humor—James Thurber. In fact, if one's sense of a comedy chronology were a bit shaky, it would seem logical to note the Woody Allen–like nature of James Thurber's classic fantasy "The Secret Life of Walter Mitty":

> Captain Mitty stood up and strapped on his huge Webley-Vickers automatic. "It's forty kilometers through hell, sir," said the sergeant. Mitty finished one last brandy. "After all," he said softly, "What isn't?" The pounding of the cannon increased. There was the rat-tat-tatting of machine guns. . . .

Something struck his shoulder. "I've been looking all over this hotel for you," said Mrs. Mitty. "Why do you have to hide in this old chair?" (51)

It is important to keep in mind, however, that the Allen fantasy does not always represent the escape from frustration associated with Walter Mitty's secret life. For example, in *Bananas* (1971) Allen dreams that the monks carrying him on a cross are beaten out of a parking place by a second cross-toting group of monks; one fantasy in *Play It Again, Sam* (1972) even has *the* Bogey getting shot by Allen's ex-wife.

Frustration in comedy fantasy is, of course, nothing new. Charlie Chaplin was shot in the heaven scene from *The Kid* (1921, after he has succumbed to sin); and in the more modern variation on this in *The Seven Year Itch* (1955), Tom Ewell gets conflicting fantasy messages from heaven and hell about what to do when upstairs neighbor Marilyn Monroe comes visiting . . . but goodness wins, if you can call that a victory.

What is unique about Allen's depiction of frustration in the fantasy world is that it occurs so often. In fact, in a film like *Sleeper* (1973), where Allen is defrosted in a Big Brother–like world two hundred years in the future, the whole movie might be termed a science fiction fantasy of frustration—a comic nightmare. As John Brosnan has noted, Allen actually had done science fiction trial runs for *Sleeper* the previous year (1972) with some of the episodes from *Everything You Wanted to Know about Sex*, particularly one involving a giant, mobile, killer breast (218).

But except for underlining the deep-seated nature of his comedy persona's frustration (which can cause real-world problems to show up in his fantasies), this aspect of Allen's imaginary world does not offer the viewer much new insight. However, when examined in tandem with more truly escapist fantasy elements in his work (also the more dominant), some rather interesting insights are revealed.

This is best exemplified in *Play It Again, Sam*, which Allen himself described as "fun to write because it dwelt on fantasies and I could write all these romantic things you could not live out in real life (Lax, 68)." By casting Bogart (played by Jerry Lacy) in a number of the fantasy scenes, Allen raised viewer identification to the last degree. And without discarding occasional fantasy frustration, he was able to construct a story around such traditional Woody Allen requirements as his relationship with women, movie history, and personal identity. The film has no fewer than eighteen often lengthy fantasy scenes (his longest and most consistently integrated use of film fantasy at the time) and is his most effective balancing of the fantastic and the real for both comic effect and maximum viewer identification.

The film opens with Allen in a theater watching the close of *Casablanca* (1942). As the film cuts back and forth between Bogart on screen and its antihero audience member, it is clear that Allen has momentarily become

Bogart. He underlines this after the close of *Casablanca* (and his first fantasy) by saying, "Who'm I kidding? I'm not like that. I never was, I never will be. Strictly movies."

For the next several minutes the film avoids fantasy, allowing the viewer to become acquainted with the real-world situation of Allen's character. It is familiar ground: Allen is a film journalist who is feeling especially frustrated sexually because his wife has recently divorced him. Most of this information is provided through two flashback scenes with his ex-wife (Susan Anspach), which help prepare the viewer for the next bit of fantasizing.

When Allen asks himself, "What's the secret to being cool?" Bogart appears and essentially tells Allen to toughen up. The naturalness of Bogart's appearance is helped by the fact that Allen's apartment is like a Bogart museum, with posters from *Casablanca* and *Across the Pacific* (1942; another Bogart film) dominating everything, while smaller bits of Bogart memorabilia, like stills and books, lie scattered about. Allen tries Bogart's prescription of bourbon and soda and passes out. The result: his depression continues.

Next enter his supportive friends (Diane Keaton and Tony Roberts), who make it a point to play matchmaker. But Allen is so depressed now that his third fantasy occurs. It is a short vision of his ex-wife on a wild date with a Hell's Angel type, while she knocks Allen, "He fell off a scooter once. And broke his collarbone."

His friends manage to get him a date, and as Allen dresses, Bogart again appears. His message is, be more earthy: tone down the mouthwash, deodorant, aftershave, and baby powder, or "you're gonna smell like a French cat house." Encouraged by Bogart, mimicking Bogart's mannerisms and inflections, and with a reflection of a Bogart poster in the mirror before him, he fantasizes the seduction of his blind date—curing her of frigidity.

As might be expected, however, the blind date is a horrible failure, as are his next several interactions with different women, from a suicidal girl who is interested in Jackson Pollock to a drug user who nearly gets Allen's face redesigned by taking him into a biker's night spot (more Hell's Angel types). This series of failures is reminiscent of the comment by Shelley Duvall's character in *Annie Hall* (1977), "Sex with you is really a Kafkaesque experience," and is the longest passage of the film without a fantasy break. Fantasies will, however, occur regularly for the rest of the film, appropriately starting with an appearance by his ex-wife, who tells him, "You're not the romantic type."

After she goes, Allen does not exactly negate her message when he ponders, "I wonder if she actually had an orgasm in the two years we were married—or did she fake it that night." In fact, there is more of the same in the very next scene, when Allen calls the home of a girl he took out in high school eleven years ago and finds that she has *still* left explicit directions with her parents not to give Allen her number.

By this point in the film the viewer has started to realize, though it has not yet become apparent to Allen's character, that this frustrated outsider just happens to have a lovely rapport with Diane Keaton. Since she is married to his best friend, she is the only girl he has not been trying to impress—a classic example of the success of being yourself.[2] And since her nonstop businessman husband is also a "phone man" (a continuing gag finds him constantly calling his answering service to leave new numbers where he can be reached), Keaton and Allen have lots of time together.

To top off the logical nature of their budding relationship is the fact that, despite her beauty, Keaton is as insecure as Allen; this is compounded by her husband's marital neglect. That all of this should culminate naturally in an innocent affair has been foreshadowed in the comically touching scene in which he gives her a plastic skunk for her birthday, the skunk being her favorite animal.

It is not long, therefore, before his neat fantasy (number seven), finds him briefly imagining the seduction of Keaton. Appropriately enough, this fantasy is immediately followed by feelings of guilt, which just as logically bring Jerry Lacy's Bogart to the rescue, trying to downplay the guilt. This soon becomes the most important fantasy since the *Casablanca* opening, because Allen's ex-wife then appears and proceeds to argue with Bogart about what Allen should do. It is a pivotal fantasy because it brings together for the first time the two poles of Allen's fantasy world—the castrating ex-wife and the macho legend, who will eventually do battle for control of Allen's real world. The scene is given an added comic touch by taking place in a supermarket (something Allen accents at the fantasy's close by saying, "Fellas, we're in a supermarket!"). From this point on, his imagination will become much more active.

On the way home from the market Allen fantasizes how much easier it would be if his friends were getting divorced, and if Roberts had asked him to take care of Keaton. The fantasy, though very brief, maintains an otherwise beautiful consistency with the rest of the movie by having Roberts leave by plane (echoing the *Casablanca* opening airport scene and anticipating its return at the close) and also by continuing and topping the telephone-number gag—he is meeting an Eskimo lover at "Frozen Tundra six, nine two nine oh."

At home now, preparing for a dinner date with Keaton (Roberts is out of town on business), Allen imagines all his advances being misunderstood, with the cry of rape quickly dispatching this nightmare fantasy. Understandably sobered, he plays it very detached upon Keaton's real arrival.

Bogart soon appears as sort of an on-the-job date counselor. It will represent his longest scene thus far in the film, as well as his funniest. Allen, like

Buster Keaton in *Sherlock, Jr.* (1924), effectively uses this example of a "real" screen lover to guide his own love life. And once again the mise-en-scène of Allen's apartment enhances the effectiveness and believability of Bogart stepping out of the shadows to coach Allen. That is, the Bogart posters seem to turn up in every shot, and bits of room decor ape the Moroccan set design of the original *Casablanca*, from the beaded curtain in the kitchen to the living room's rattan chair and shutters. But just as Allen is about to become Bogart's A student, the ex-wife appears and guns the teacher down. Needless to say, this is a bit disconcerting to the pupil Allen, especially since the fantasy assassination takes place right over the living room couch on which he is courting Keaton. However, Bogart's pointers are not wasted, because everything comes to pass; thus, a long take of one very passionate Allen-Keaton kiss is intercut (once again courtesy of Allen's imagination) with a similar Bogart-Bergman kiss from *Casablanca.*

The next scene finds Allen and Keaton in bed the morning after, and though we seem to have returned to total reality (that is, if you can accept Allen in bed with anyone), the cue still seems to be taken from Bogart—a huge film poster of *Across the Pacific* appears over the bed, completely dominating the couple. In fact, this morning-after scene actually opens on a close-up of the poster, in which Bogart is scoring a one-two punch, as if suggesting a sexual pun on what has occurred the night before.

Allen and Keaton decide they have found something good and that Roberts must be told. Since Keaton insists she will tell him, Allen ends up with time alone to imagine how his best friend will respond. Thus Allen's next three fantasies represent different possible reactions from the cuckolded husband. The first (number thirteen overall) is a monocle and pipe parody of two English gentlemen discussing things ever so rationally. Allen defuses any further possible hostility by giving Roberts a terminal disease anyway and closes the scene with proper British civility—a toast and "Cheers."

Cuckolded-husband fantasies two and three are both movie parodies and do not run quite so pleasantly for interloper Allen. The first plays upon Allen's guilt and finds Roberts walking into the sea à la the first two versions of *A Star Is Born* (interestingly enough, director Allen will use the scene again, this time seriously, in his later *Interiors* [1978]). In *Play It Again, Sam*, however, even any lingering chance of melancholy is undercut by Roberts's parting soliloquy on the beach: "Why didn't I see it coming? Me, who had the foresight to buy Polaroid at eight and a half."

In the final fantasy of this trilogy it is Allen, however, who bites the dust. Passing a theater playing the Italian film *Le Coppie* (with a large display poster acting as a backdrop for the fantasy opening), Allen imagines Roberts as a humiliated, hot-tempered Italian out for revenge. The knife-wielding husband corners Allen, who is a most unlikely baker (defending himself with some of the limpest dough ever to put in a movie appearance), in his establishment. The little baker never has a chance.

Allen is, however, suddenly and comically jarred back to reality when, outside his apartment, he runs into Roberts. Though Allen fears the worst, Roberts only senses trouble and does not suspect his friend. He pours out his love for Keaton to Allen and then leaves our comic antihero Romeo with even more guilt. Not surprisingly, Allen decides he cannot break up the marriage. Thus his number-one anxiety becomes how to let Keaton down easily; this will not be simple, since "I was incredible last night in bed. I never once had to sit up and consult the manual."

The next two fantasies occur as Allen rushes to the airport to tell Keaton he has reconsidered, while Keaton is rushing to the airport to tell Roberts she has reconsidered (Roberts is, of course, just rushing . . . off on more business). In the first fantasy Keaton takes Allen's decision poorly, and it quickly turns into a melodrama parody, with Keaton asking for a mysterious letter (*Casablanca*'s letters of transit?) and then pulling a gun. The fantasy closes just in time as Allen screams, "Don't pull the trigger, I'm a bleeder."

This near miss then cuts directly to Allen's second fantasy on the ride to the airport—Bogart is his cab driver, ready to give him more pointers, as well as settle him down. Bogart actually stops the car and shows Allen how to break it off with a dame (appropriately, again played by a gun-toting Keaton). This, along with Bogart's praise of Allen's sacrifice "for a pal," prepares Allen for the big romantic finish with Keaton.

This final fantasy brings us full circle to the film's opening, only this time instead of cutting back and forth between fantasizing audience member Allen and the projected image of *Casablanca*, both the situation (romantic triangle preparing for airport farewell) and the mise-en-scène (incoming fog and the separate starting of the plane's propellers) of *Play It Again, Sam* actually re-create *Casablanca*. Then, when the plane is safely away, Bogart assumes the original Claude Rains role by joining Allen in his walk into the enveloping mist.

Unlike earlier fantasies, however, in which Allen blindly tried to ape the complete Bogart persona, the closing scene uses the Bogart legend as a point of reference to aid Allen in the final liberation and acceptance of his own identity. That is, Allen essentially plays the part on his own; Bogart is not even giving him cues from the wings, as he did earlier in the apartment. And though Allen does restate part of Bogart's farewell speech from *Casablanca*, it is the act of a mature person merely using past experience, rather than the alienated incompetent in search of a style that opened the movie.

Allen's own character capsulizes it quite nicely when he says, "I guess the secret's not being you [Bogart]; it's being me." Moreover, as if to keynote this, even Bogart and Allen break up their stroll at the close; after the former's, "Here's looking at *you*, kid," Allen walks off into the darkness of the night (and into his future?) alone, but not quite so lonely.

These then have been the eighteen fantasies in *Play It Again, Sam*. As for fellow antihero Walter Mitty, the fantasies have, at times, provided Allen with unique adventure (hobnobbing with Bogart) in what is normally a rather banal life. At the same time, as already noted, there have been balancing fantasy frustrations. Yet possibly the key difference here between Allen's fantasy life and Mitty's lies not so much in the latter point (important as it may be) but rather in the fact that Allen's comedy persona (unlike Thurber's) is allowed to take his fantasy beyond mere distraction, using it to learn both to be himself and to accept himself. (At the close of *Manhattan* [1979], his girlfriend will echo that same message when she tells him, "You have to have a little faith in people.")

In achieving this level of maturity, the Allen film persona no doubt needed both poles of fantasy, from the confidence Bogart could provide to the occasional fantasy frustration that kept his values in perspective—which eventually steered him away from being just a Bogart clone. And this final maturation has become the norm for much of his later work, be it the eventual touching acceptance of Annie (Keaton) as friend instead of lover in *Annie Hall*, the realization late in *Stardust Memories* (1980) that the real joys of life can be locked in the most simple moments, the message of *A Midsummer Night's Sex Comedy* (1982) to seize the opportunities of life, finding the capacity to forgive at the close of *Broadway Danny Rose* (1984), and the touchingly upbeat conclusion of *Hannah and Her Sisters* (1986), which celebrates the fundamentals of comedy and life itself—marriage and an approaching birth. None of these situations, of course, leave him with any real answers to a man's eternal questions (the same might be said of the Chaplin-like exit of Woody in *Play It Again, Sam*). But they do leave his character in a much healthier state of mind for coping with the darker side of existence.

In terms of comedy theory, the dominant element in *Play It Again, Sam* is the fantasy identification with Bogart and a situation in which the viewer could relate to having him as a special tutor. The actions of this film fall under what genre theorist Northrop Frye calls the "drama of the green world," with the green world representing the ideal romance of another place, such as our imagination (182). More specifically this type of comedy "begins in a world represented as a normal world, moves into the green world, goes into a metamorphosis there in which the comic resolution is achieved, and returns to the normal world" (182).

In *Play It Again, Sam*, Allen's character has moved from a frustrated normal existence to a fantasy "green world" apprenticeship with Bogart (certainly a key romantic ideal to anyone immersed in film culture). A metamorphosis takes place (Allen learns to accept himself), and he then returns to the normal world (necessitating the solo walk off at the film's close) after Bogart has tendered Allen something of a "graduation" toast by way of his, "Here's looking at you, kid." Through this interaction with one of the legends of cinema history, director Allen has tapped a seemingly universal romantic fantasy among the viewing public.

Allen, moreover, accents the universality of the Bogart figure by the realistic manner in which this macho symbol appears and interacts with today's most prominent example of the comic antihero. There is nothing like the white ball of light that heralds the arrival of the good witch Glinda in *The Wizard of Oz* (1939), nor even the special glossy environment one associates with the goddess of death in *All That Jazz* (1979). No, Bogey just drops in at Allen's apartment, appears at your typical A & P, and turns up behind the wheel of a cab.

This realistic tone in the fantasy scenes is consistent with the majority of other such excursions in Woody Allen's films. It also might help explain the tendency for Allen's more exotic fantasies never to reach the final print stage, from his playing a spider caught in Louise Lasser's "black widow" web (shot for *Everything You Always Wanted to Know about Sex* [Yacowar, 145]) to the giant chess game using real people (shot for *Sleeper* [Rosenblum and Karen, 261]), with Allen appropriately playing a white pawn about to be sacrificed but not without a comically lovely bargaining argument: "Hey fellas, it's only a game. We'll all be together later in the box" (Rosenblum and Karen, 261).

The generally natural tone of these fantasies, particularly the Bogart scenes in question, might best be classed under what Siegfried Kracauer labels "fantasy established in terms of physical reality" (90). That is, the plot of *Play It Again, Sam* takes

> the existence of the supernatural [in this case Bogart] more or less for granted, its presence does not simply follow from these visuals . . . the spectator must from the outset conceive of them as tokens of the supernatural. (Kracauer, 91)

Thus, even to relate to the fact that a fantasy is in progress whenever Bogart appears, one must already be a practicing member of the modern world's biggest fantasy club—the filmgoing public. And by getting the joke (a mixture of Allen's inadequacies and Bogart giving home lessons in self-assertiveness), we go a long way toward becoming part of it—for who has not felt similar inadequacies, at least in comparison to our favorite cinema superhero, be it Bogart or 007?

Allen represents his own best example of such a fantasy world (daydreams peopled with cinema heroes) even as a child:

> I remember seeing *Tom, Dick, and Harry* advertised and saying, "I can't wait to see that." It was one of those things that became a part of my conscious, because I lived in the movies and identified with that. (Lax, 69)

His comedy persona in *Play It Again, Sam* actually restructures part of his life to use the experience of his film fantasy existence, slipping in and out of this other world as someone else might do with an old pair of shoes. An example is the farewell break with Diane Keaton that uses the *Casablanca* model for its inspiration. Interestingly enough, all this activity tends to flirt with the tongue-in-cheek message of Oscar Wilde's delightful "critical" essay "The Decay of Lying"—"Paradox though it may seem . . . life imitates art far more than art imitates life" (680). That is, by so immersing himself in Bogart (with posters, movies, books, other assorted memorabilia, and an almost total Bogart mind-set), Allen's screen persona both consciously and subconsciously tries to imitate film art—namely, the world of Bogey. Allen stops trying to be Bogart only when he inadvertently achieves romantic success (through the relationship with Keaton) by simply being himself. His closing walk off symbolizes a literal as well as physical break with Bogart. And thus his posture changes from trying to ape art to constructively applying it to a less-than-perfect lifestyle.

This "be yourself" lesson parallels the closing message of America's favorite fantasy, *The Wizard of Oz*; there too the viewer is reminded (by way of Dorothy's refrain—"There's no place like home") that individual happiness can only be found within oneself. For this same reason, Allen's *Purple Rose of Cairo* (1985) has the saddest of conclusions. Overworked Depression-era waitress and film fan Mia Farrow does not live happily ever after with movie idol Jeff Daniels—who had literally stepped off the screen at her local theater. The heartbreaking close comes about because Farrow cannot move beyond the mere fantasy escape level of the movies, just as Daniels's AWOL screen shadow does not know how to act in real life. Fittingly, the film's last image of Farrow is alone again—at the movies.

Fantasy for the Allen comedy persona has a continuing duality that he struggles with in each film (will he use fantasy as mere escape or as a step toward maturity?), and much of this chapter has examined the struggle in the light of an opening reference to Thurber's most celebrated short story—the escapist "Secret Life of Walter Mitty." To come full circle, however, an apt closing observation on this duality might best be drawn from Allen's own most celebrated short story, "The Kugelmass Episode," which won the O. Henry Award as best short story of 1977 (the same year *Annie Hall* won an Academy Award as best picture).

"The Kugelmass Episode," rather reminiscent of the Mitty story, examines the life of an unhappily married professor (Kugelmass) out to put some excitement back in his life, preferably on a sexual level. His adventure, or escape, will come in the form of a fantasy-like invention that can transport a subject into the world of the written word. For Kugelmass, this means an opportunity to date "any of the women created by the world's best writers" (Allen, 44). Walter Mitty could not have gone for it any faster. Thus Kugelmass ends up having an affair with Emma Bovary. But there are complications when the invention breaks down, causing the frustrated professor no end of grief, mental and financial. Therefore, when the crisis is over, he maturely swears off these fantasyland time trips, happy in the fact that at least his wife has not found out and grateful that "I learned my lesson" (Allen, 54).

But Kugelmass's maturity is short-lived, and he tries another "trip" (this time into sexy *Portnoy's Complaint*), but the fantasy quickly becomes an eternal comic nightmare. The machine shorts out and is destroyed, the operator-inventor dies of a heart attack on the spot, and poor Kugelmass, instead of finding himself projected into *Portnoy's Complaint*, turns up in

an old textbook, *Remedial Spanish*, . . . running for his life over a barren, rocky terrain as the word *tener* ("to have")—a large and fairly irregular verb—raced after him on its spindly legs. (Allen, 55)

Quite clearly, Allen is warning us that total fantasy escape can be dangerous (as it is later in *Purple Rose*) if it is not directed toward the character growth of a *Play It Again, Sam*. Otherwise, we might end up like poor Kugelmass —forever running away.

NOTES

1. The original version of this article was selected for presentation at The Second International Conference on the Fantastic in the Arts (Florida Atlantic University, Boca Baton, Florida), March 18–21, 1981.

2. Matchmaking friends, being a fool on blind dates, and acting natural around wives of friends were all drawn from events following his breakup with his second wife, Louise Lasser (Lax, 215). Diane Jacobs draws upon the same Lax interview in . . . *but we need the eggs: The Magic of Woody Allen* (41).

WORKS CITED

Allen, Woody. *Side Effects.* New York: Random House, 1980.

Brosnan, John. *Future Tense: The Cinema of Science Fiction.* New York: St. Martin's Press, 1978.

Frye, Northrop. *Anatomy of Criticism.* 1957. Princeton: Princeton University Press, 1973.

Jacobs, Diane. . . . *but we need the eggs: The Magic of Woody Allen.* New York: St. Martin's Press, 1982.

Kracauer, Siegfried. *Theory of Film: The Redemption of Physical Reality.* New York: Oxford University Press, 1960.

Lax, Eric. *On Being Funny: Woody Allen and Comedy*. New York: Manor Books, 1975.

Rosenblum, Ralph, and Robert Karen. *When the Shooting Stops . . . the Cutting Begins: A Film Editor's Story*. New York: Penguin, 1979.

Thurber, James. "The Secret Life of Walter Mitty." *The Thurber Carnival*. New York: Harper & Brothers, 1945.

Wilde, Oscar. "The Decay of Lying." In *Critical Theory Since Plato*, ed. Hazard Adams. Chicago: Harcourt Brace Jovanovich, 1971.

Yacowar, Maurice. *Loser Take All: The Comic Art of Woody Allen*. New York: Ungar, 1979.

9

Love and Death and Food
Woody Allen's Comic Use of Gastronomy

Ronald D. LeBlanc

On the basis of its title alone, *Love and Death* (1975) seems designed largely as a tribute to some of the lasting achievements of nineteenth- and twentieth-century Russian culture. Indeed, Woody Allen in this film spoofs (warmly and gently) many of the giants of classical Russian literature, music, and cinema to whom he was indebted for inspiration, ideas, and techniques as a writer and filmmaker. The movie, as a result, contains numerous allusions to Russian artists, ranging from Dostoyevsky and Tolstoy to Eisenstein and Prokofiev. The score for *Love and Death*, for example, includes selections from Prokofiev's composition for Eisenstein's *Alexander Nevsky* (1938) as well as from Prokofiev's *Lieutenant Kizhe Suite* (1934) and *Love for Three Oranges* (1921);[1] cinematic allusions, meanwhile, are made to Eisenstein's *Potemkin* (1925) and to Bondarchuk's *War and Peace* (1968). The central target of Allen's parody, however, is the nineteenth-century Russian novel and specifically the "loose and baggy monsters" of Tolstoy and Dostoyevsky. Set in tsarist Russia during the time of the Napoleonic wars and centered upon a bespectacled hero who plans to murder the French emperor, *Love and Death* prompts immediate associations, of course, with Tolstoy's classic *War and Peace* (1869).[2] There are distinctively Dostoyevskian echoes, on the other hand, in the film's theme of a man sentenced to death and then reprieved at the last moment (*The Idiot* [1868]), in the trio of brothers who make up the Grushenko family (*The Brothers Karamazov* [1880]), and in the moral dilemma that confronts the hero when, à la Raskolnikov, he contemplates the act of murder (*Crime and Punishment* [1866]).[3] This Dostoyevsky connection is humorously laid bare in Allen's film during the jail-cell conversation between Grushenko and his father on the eve of Boris's execution, when names from the titles and heroes of Dostoyevsky's works are called forth in a comic litany of literary reference.[4]

If the film's artistic and philosophic ambitions are to pay homage to the two towering figures of nineteenth-century Russian literature, Dostoyevsky and Tolstoy, then the bathos at work in *Love and Death*—a bathos that repeatedly deflates and reduces the film's serious, elevated ideas—calls to mind yet another great nineteenth-century Russian writer: Nikolai Gogol. It is entirely possible that during his younger years, when he took to reading various Russian, Scandinavian, and German authors, Allen became acquainted with the works of Russia's greatest comic writer.[5] The question of direct influence aside, an affinity with Gogol suggests itself in the way that Allen captures the absurdity of human life and the anxieties of modern humans, casting them both in a grotesquely comic light. Like Gogol, Allen possesses the gift for humorously deflating the pretensions of his fictional characters—be those pretensions social, political, sexual, or philosophical. One device, common to both Gogol and Allen, for bringing about this comic deflation is the use of food imagery. In Gogol's works, as many critics have noted, the demands of the stomach are invariably made prominent and predominate over those of the heart or head. A central concern of nearly all his fictional characters, especially in the early Ukrainian tales, is how well—and how often—they will be able to satisfy their appetite for food and drink. Indeed, an entire book, Alexander Obolensky's *Food-Notes on Gogol* (1972), has been written on this very subject.[6] Woody Allen, for his part, has written a gastronomic version of *Notes from the Underground* in his short sketch "Notes from the Overfed," a work that derived, in the author's words, from "reading Dostoyevsky and the new *Weight Watchers* magazine on the same plane trip."[7] Allen has been quoted as saying that he finds all food "funny" and at one point actually considered calling his Russian film either *Love, Food and Death* or *Love, Death and Food*.[8] Gastronomy, therefore, was obviously meant to figure quite prominently in the comic design of this film.

Woody Allen's comic use of gastronomy is, of course, hardly unprecedented. In Western literature, food and drink have traditionally served as symbols of life and sensuality, and robust, earthy humorists—from Rabelais and Cervantes to Fielding and Sterne—fully exploited the comic possibilities that presented themselves whenever their heroes sat down at table to satisfy their hunger, that most basic and primitive of human instincts. In his study of Rabelais and the medieval popular-festive tradition, Mikhail Bakhtin has outlined how in carnivalized literature—with its atmosphere of license, gaiety, and liberating laughter—eating served to reflect the sense of freedom, collectivity, and abundance that was experienced in the "inverted" world of popular folk culture. The banquet imagery in *Gargantua et Pentagruel*

(1532) thus conveys the democratic spirit that is unleashed during carnival festivities, when the laws, prohibitions, and restrictions that dominate everyday life within official culture are temporarily suspended and all are suddenly made equal.[9] With the rise of the modern realist novel, however, food imagery in literature came more and more to acquire a decidedly mimetic function, providing a metonymic device for satirizing contemporary bourgeois life. Literary realists in nineteenth-century France, for instance, regularly exploited fictional meals as psychological and sociological synecdoches through which to criticize the personalities of their characters as well as to condemn the values of the society in which they lived.[10] Gustave Flaubert (whom Victor Brombert accuses of suffering from an "alimentary obsession") used extensive gastronomic and gustatory imagery in *Madame Bovary* (1857) as a way to expose the shallowness and bankruptcy of the heroine's bourgeois way of life. "Bovarysme," as reflected in the daily eating rhythm at Emma's household, suggested the very monotony, triviality, and vapidness of middle-class existence.[11]

With comic writers, such as Molière and Gogol, however, the enjoyment of food is used not only to condemn the banality of bourgeois philistines (à la Flaubert), but also to continue to celebrate in Rabelaisian fashion the pure physical joy of life and its primitive sensual pleasures. A similar aim seems to inspire Woody Allen, for one of the primary roles that food imagery plays in his films is to remind us—amid all the lofty philosophical speculation engendered by abstractions such as "love" and "death," "war" and "peace," "crime" and "punishment"—of immediate physical sensations and instinctual urges. The act of eating, by returning us to our bodies, helps to affirm the élan vital of human life. This reminder is especially relevant for the anxiety-ridden modern human, of course, since these two aspects of a person's being—the psychological and the physiological, the cerebral and the instinctual—have become divorced from each other. Indeed, one of the most important lessons that Boris Grushenko comes to learn by the end of *Love and Death* is that humans are hopelessly split between mind and body. "The mind embraces all the nobler aspirations—like poetry and philosophy," the hero explains. "But—the body has all the fun!" That corporeal "fun," as Allen makes abundantly clear throughout his film, is to be had in satisfying appetites both sexual and gastronomic.

When Sonja, assuming the pose of a Dostoyevskian infernal woman (like Nastasia Filippovna in *The Idiot*), intones in an early scene of the movie that she could well be considered "half-saint and half-whore," Boris, who champions the life of the instincts throughout *Love and Death*, comments sagely, "Here's hoping I get the half that eats."[12] The implication here is clear, of course, that Grushenko is also hoping he will get the half that enjoys engaging in sex. Divided between the aspirations of the intellect and the urges of the body, Boris Grushenko—as another paradigm of the basic Woody Allen cinematic persona—is a seemingly sex-starved individual whose libidinal desires, he would have us believe, are never adequately satisfied.[13] Although Boris is attracted to cousin Sonja largely because she is able to engage in deep philosophic discourse with him, what he is really yearning for throughout the movie is sexual gratification. *Love and Death*, as a result, comes to constitute what Foster Hirsch calls a "schlemiel comedy"—"a mingling of sex and philosophy, as a search for sex shares the stage with the quest for the meaning of life."[14] And in this film the search for sex predominates because Allen, as Maurice Yacowar notes, consistently "subordinates philosophy to the appetites and senses."[15] Like sex, eating is for Allen an activity that debunks the sterile and futile philosophizing of intellectuals and reaffirms instead life's essential vitality by satisfying one of man's most basic appetites. Not surprisingly, food and sex are often linked together in his films, a connection perhaps most graphically illustrated in *Bananas* (1971), where the director pays tribute to the famous scene of erotic dining in Tony Richardson's film version of *Tom Jones* (1963).[16]

In *Love and Death*, this connection between food and sex is made clear in the scene where Sonja, convinced that Boris will die on the following day as a result of his duel with Count Anton Inbedkov, agrees at last to have sex with the hero. When she suggests that they go upstairs to make love, Boris says, "Nice idea! I'll bring the soy sauce." Similarly, an invitation to tea by the beautiful, inviting, and promiscuous Countess Aleksandrovna is interpreted by Boris as an opportunity to "run a quick check" of her erogenous zones. Later, after Boris and the countess have succeeded in consummating their lovers' tryst, the shot of their postcoital satisfaction is accompanied by the same balalaika music that had been played earlier in the film at the Grushenko party scene, where people were shown merrily eating, drinking, and dancing. The Freudian connection between bed and board is also established in the Boris-Sonja relationship, especially during the early stages of their married life together, when the hero is desperately seeking to win his bride's heart. The conjugal tension the couple feels is made palpable in scenes that alternate in locus between the bedroom ("Don't—not here!" Sonja objects when Boris starts to caress her in bed) and the kitchen (Sonja shatters the wine glass in her hand and sweeps the dishes off the table onto the floor). Indeed, when Boris finally does succeed in winning Sonja over and gaining her love and affection, that change in their marital relations is presented not in bed but at table, where we see the couple not only enjoying Sonja's first soufflé (so heavy that it breaks the table in two) and her dishes made out of snow ("Oh, sleet—my favorite!") but also holding hands and talking of having children together.

This linking of the sexual with the gastronomic sharply distinguishes Allen's use of food imagery from that of Gogol, whose characters, in a so-called retreat from love, reflect their creator's own aversion to sex and generally regress from genital to oral modes of libidinal satisfaction.[17] "Food, and not love," Obolensky writes with regard to Gogol, "is the usual motivation in his stories."[18] With Woody Allen, on the other hand, food and sex go together naturally as objects of desire; his characters seek the "half that both eats and fornicates." Thus Allen's fascination with eating, as Douglas Brode points out, results in a tendency to use food as a symbol for sex rather than as its substitute.[19]

In any event, food—whether it be the geometrically correct blintzes of Grushenko's mother, the cookies fed to the village idiot Berdykov, the herring and wine sauce secreted upstairs by the fish merchant Voskovec, or the bowls of snow food prepared by Sonja (the "frigid" bride)—serves as a source of pleasure in *Love and Death*, gratifying the senses and providing a strong affirmation of life in the face of all the destruction caused by war, violence, and death. This life-affirming role of food is humorously noted in the deathbed scene where Voskovec has no sooner passed away than his widow is encouraged to forego bereavement and continue with the process of living. "The dead pass on and life is for the living," the bedside doctor tells Sonja. "I guess you're right," she responds. "Where do you want to eat?" This exchange reveals that for the characters in *Love and Death*, eating and living are nearly synonymous activities. And the food that most strongly symbolizes life in this movie is wheat. Thus when Boris visits Sonja on the eve of his duel and contemplates his near-certain death at the hands of the noted duelist, he rhapsodizes comically about the "staff of life":

> To die . . . before the harvest. The crops, the grains, fields of rippling wheat. All there is in life is wheat. . . . Oh, wheat. Lots of wheat. Fields of wheat. A tremendous amount of wheat. . . . Yellow wheat. Red wheat. Wheat with feathers. Cream of wheat.

Later, after Boris's death, as the twice-widowed Sonja tries to convince herself that life must go on, she and Natasha strike a Bergmanesque pose (compare with *Persona* [1966]) and utter repeatedly, "Wheat." "Wheat," Boris interrupts. "I'm dead; they're talking about wheat." Hours earlier, as Boris sat in a prison cell awaiting execution for his attempted murder of Napoleon, his dread of impending death had been somewhat allayed by the sight of a cart filled with delicious French pastries ("Of course, it was a French jail, so the food was not bad").

This motif—eating as synecdoche of living—is comically inverted, however, when the Russian army reaches the front and witnesses a scene of widespread devastation in which the bodies of numerous dead soldiers are strewn across a smoke-filled battlefield. "Boy, this . . . this army cooking will get you every time," Boris remarks to his comrades. Allen plays here on the comic dichotomy between what food ought to be (an object not only of pleasure but also of sustenance, a source of life) and what, in the army, it really is: namely, something so poorly prepared that it makes ill and even kills those who eat it.[20] Similarly, when Boris returns to Sonja in a posthumous visit following his execution and tries to describe for her what death is like, he tells her that it resembles the food at a familiar restaurant ("You know the chicken at Tresky's restaurant? It's worse!").

War, like death, is likewise often juxtaposed to eating in *Love and Death*, as Allen uses food, the symbol of life affirmation, as a device for comically deflating military pretensions. Napoleon's invasion of Austria is attributed to a shortage of cognac ("Is he out of Corvoisier?"), while the Battle of Austerlitz is reduced to a game of American football, complete with cheerleaders exhorting their team on and vendors peddling red-hots (blinis) and beer to the Russian troops. Later, during the Napoleonic invasion of 1812, the destructive war that has been raging for the last seven years in Europe is reduced to a ridiculous culinary contest between the leaders of the two most powerful armies in the world. The battle is over which dish will be developed first: the pastry named after Napoleon or bocuf Wellington? Conversely, when Boris, an avowed pacifist (and "militant coward"), objects to joining in the fight to stop Napoleon, those of his countrymen who advocate war try to change his mind by arguing that the French army poses a threat to the two things the hero holds most dear: women and food. "What are you going to do when the French soldiers rape your sister?" Boris is asked when he refuses to enlist. Later, during basic training, when Boris again questions the wisdom of going to war to stop Napoleon, the aftermath of French rule in Russia is described in gastronomic terms: "Imagine your loved ones conquered by Napoleon and forced to live under French rule. Do you want them to eat that rich food and those heavy sauces? Do you want them to have soufflé every meal and croissant?"

The joke here, of course, is not only that the quality of life under foreign occupation should be measured in terms of diet (rather than, say, political liberties and individual rights) but also that the soldiers would prefer bland Russian food to tasty French cuisine. A similar absurdity is sounded when Boris, who urges that Russian crops be destroyed in advance of the French troops, notes that "it's tough to light borshcht."

Whereas Allen uses food (like sex) as an affirmation of life and a source of enjoyment in the face of the destruction threatened by war, the dread caused by fear of death, and the abstraction from life inherent in philosophical speculation, he at the same time recognizes that eating is a paradigm not only of pleasure but also of power. Although in *Love and Death* to eat signifies primarily to taste (*goûter*), there are nevertheless instances in the film when to eat means to destroy and devour (*manger*).[21] Food, in other words, can serve as a means of domination as well as a source of enjoyment. We have already seen intimations of this in Allen's juxtaposition of food and eating to war and death: army food kills, death is worse than the chicken at Tresky's restaurant, under French rule Russians will be forced to live on a diet of Gallic cuisine. The most memorable instance of eating as power and domination, however, occurs early in the film when Boris and his cousin Sonja present competing perceptions of nature. To Sonja's teleological view of nature (and particularly her Leibnizean idea that this is "the best of all possible worlds"), Boris provides a sufficiently cynical, Voltairian response, positing instead a Darwinian universe of natural selection: "To me nature is the . . . you know . . . I don't know . . . spiders and bugs and . . . and . . . and big fish eating little fish and . . . and . . . and . . . plants eating, uh, plants, and animals eating animals. It's like an enormous restaurant. That's the way I see it."

The restaurant, a civilized place normally associated with elegant dining, where eating is a pleasurable activity (*goûter*), is here comically transformed into a primitive jungle of cannibalistic beasts where, in accord with the law of survival of the fittest, to eat is to dominate, to destroy, and to devour (*manger*).[22]

The metaphor of nature as an enormous restaurant, although used comically here, manages nonetheless to make a serious statement about the dog-eat-dog world in which we live.[23] Humans must exist with the fear of being devoured by forces larger than themselves and, ultimately, by death itself, which is portrayed in Allen's film, appropriately enough, as a "grim reaper" who is ready to harvest human lives. If young Boris Grushenko's strange and vivid dream of waiters stepping out of coffins to dance a Viennese waltz served as sufficient warning to him that he "would not grow up to be an ordinary man," it also prepares the viewer to see a connection between food and death—between dancing waiters in the enormous restaurant of life and Boris traipsing with the grim reaper in a dance of death in the film's finale.

It seems ironic that food and drink, which are used throughout *Love and Death* mainly as a way to affirm life in the face of war, death, and the sterility of intellectual speculation, should also be used in this and other Allen films as effective metaphors for posing ultimate questions about humans, life, and the universe. In *Annie Hall* (1977), for instance, Alvy Singer's opening comedy monologue includes a food joke that encapsulates a stark view of the human condition:

> There's an old joke. Uh, two elderly women are at a Catskills mountain resort, and one of them says: "Boy, the food at this place is really terrible." The other one says, "Yeah, I know, and such . . . small portions." Well, that's how I feel about life. Full of loneliness and misery and suffering and unhappiness, and it's all over much too quickly.[24]

In *Love and Death*, as Boris and Sonja debate the moral ramifications involved in assassinating Napoleon, Kant's categorical imperative is alluded to in a food joke that once again resorts to the restaurant metaphor:

Boris: Sonja, Sonja, I've been thinking about this. It's murder. What if everybody acted like this? It'd be a world full of murderers. You know what that would do to property values?

Sonja: I know. And if everybody went to the same restaurant on the same evening and ordered blintzes, there'd be chaos. But they don't.

"I'm talking about murder," Boris deadpans, "she's talking about blintzes."

Although Sonja's analogy here attempts to deflate her husband's moral qualms, the actual effect is to lend Kant's imperative greater concreteness and thus to communicate it more effectively. In both instances, therefore, Allen uses food jokes not just for laughs, but also for serious commentary about life.

This seriocomic element in Allen's films once again brings to mind the example of Gogol, whose major contribution to Russian literature, critics have contended over the years, consisted of his ability to mix serious social critique with amusing representations of characters, settings, and events. His satiric comedies—with their grotesque exaggerations, absurd illogicalities, and comic distortions—prompted in their audiences "laughter through tears." Like Gogol, Woody Allen seeks in his film to convey a serious message about the human condition, while poking fun not only at the message itself but also at some of the artistic vehicles traditionally used to convey it. As a parody of the Russian philosophic novel and the Hollywood film epic, *Love and Death* thus combines serious metaphysical concern with rich comic form. The artistic result is, as Benayoun puts it, "a farce based on ideas," where the ideas themselves are not necessarily debunked and discredited.[25] In keeping with the seriocomic designs of Allen's Russian film, gastronomy plays a double role as both a deflator of philosophic pretensions and a conveyor of ultimate questions. Eating in *Love and Death* may be said to serve as a remedy for—as well as a reminder of—the modern malady of alienation, the propensity toward chronic depression that Allen elsewhere labels "Ozymandias melancholia" (compare with *Stardust Memories* [1980]). As paradigm of pleasure (*goûter*) as well as power (*manger*), food here affirms the physical joy of human existence at the same time as it reminds us of life's inherent cruelty, injustice, contingency, and meaninglessness.

Gastronomy, however, provides Allen—as it did Gogol—with an appropriate metaphor not only for human life but also for artistic creation itself. Gogol, whose passion for Ukrainian cuisine and Italian pasta is well documented, often spoke of the writer as a "chef" and of the literary work as a "dish" served up to the reader. Thus when overly eager Russian readers clamored for the appearance of part 2 of his masterpiece, Gogol responded that "*Dead Souls* are not like bliny, which can be prepared in an instant."[26] And in his essay, "A Few Words about Pushkin" ("Neskol'ko slov o Pushkine" [1835]), Gogol observed that, to understand and appreciate the great Russian poet, one must be to a certain extent a sybarite, who has long since had his fill of coarse and heavy foods and who now eats no more than a thimble full of game fowl and savors such a dish, one whose taste seems utterly indefinable, strange and totally unpleasant to a person accustomed to swallowing the concoctions of a peasant cook.[27]

Woody Allen likewise resorts to gastronomic metaphors to explain his art, especially when expressing his desire to be recognized as a serious filmmaker rather than merely another cinematic funny man. "Drama is like a plate of meat and potatoes," he notes in an interview in *Newsweek.* "Comedy is rather the dessert, a bit like meringue."[28] Funny films, he observes elsewhere, are "like eating ice cream all the time," and many of his own comic pieces in the *New Yorker* he has dismissed as "sheer dessert."[29] Love and Death, in this context, offers its audience a complete meal: both the main course and the dessert, both the "meat and potatoes" and the "meringue." By blending serious philosophic concerns and artistic intentions together with broad physical comedy, witty verbal humor, and clever literary and cinematic parody. Woody Allen has concocted here a veritable smorgasbord—a funny film that seeks to satisfy the viewer's hunger for humor as well as his appetite for substantial intellectual and aesthetic nourishment. Like so many of Allen's films. *Love and Death* provides us with what one critic calls "chicken soup for the soul."[30]

NOTES

1. The score for the film was originally intended to be made up entirely of music by Igor Stravinsky, claims Ralph Rosenblum, who served as film editor for *Love and Death.* "I listened to a lot of Stravinsky," writes Rosenblum, "and found his [music] too overpowering for the film. He was like a tidal wave, drowning every part of the picture he came in contact with. As an alternative, I introduced Woody to three compositions by Sergei Prokofieff." See Ralph Rosenblum and Robert Karen, *When the Shooting Stops,* 270 (New York: Viking Press, 1979).

2. Most reviewers of *Love and Death* regarded Allen's film primarily as a parody of Tolstoy's novel. Geoff Brown, for instance, called it a "demented version of *War and Peace.*" See *Monthly Film Bulletin* 42, no. 502 (1975): 241. Michael Deskey, meanwhile, referred to *Love and Death* as a "cockeyed, minor *War and Peace.*" See *Films in Review* 26 (August–September 1975): 435. Finally, Judith Crist, in a review titled "War and Punishment, Crime and Peace—Or Something Along Those Lines," called Allen's film "a perfect pastiche of *War and Peace.*" See *New York* 8 (1975): 66.

3. Robert Benayoun, in his book *The Films of Woody Allen,* trans. Alexander Walker (New York: Harmony Books, 1985), regards the hero Boris as a Raskolnikov in the army (42). See also Benayoun's review of *Love and Death,* titled, appropriately enough, "Raskolnikov au régiment (*Amour et guerre*)," in *Positif* 175 (1975): 56–58.

4. Father: Remember that nice boy next door, Raskolnikov?

Boris: Ya.

Father: He killed two ladies.

Boris: No! What a Nasty Story!

Father: Bobok told it to me. He heard it from one of the Karamazov Brothers.

Boris: He must have been Possessed.

Father: Well, he was a Raw Youth.

Boris: A Raw Youth? He was an Idiot!

Father: And he acted Insulted and Injured!

Boris: I hear he was a Gambler.

Father: You know—he could be your Double.

Boris: Really? How novel!

5. According to biographers. Allen in the late 1950s (after unsuccessful undergraduate stints at New York University and City College) hired a tutor to guide him through some of the world's great literature. Allen mentions Gogol's masterpiece, "The Overcoat" ("Shinel" [1842]), in his short story "A Little Louder, Please." See *Getting Even* (New York: Random House, 1971), 105–6. The severed nose of the leader in *Sleeper* (1973), it seems to me, might well allude to Gogol's comic grotesque tale "The Nose" (1836).

6. Alexander Obolensky, *Food-Notes on Gogol* (Winnipeg, Canada: Trident Press, 1972). See also Natalia M. Kolb-Selelski, "Gastronomy, Gogol, and His Fiction," *Slavic Review* 29, no. 1 (1970): 35–57; Jan Kott, "The Eating of *The Government Inspector*," *Theatre Quarterly* 5, no. 17 (1975): 21–29; and Ronald D. LeBlanc, "Satisfying Khiestakov's Appetite: The Semiotics of Eating in *The Inspector General*," *Slavic Review* 47, no. 3 (1988): 168–99.

7. *Getting Even* (81). Another Allen story from this collection that involves a food motif is "Yes, but Can the Steam Engine Do This?" which chronicles the invention of the sandwich by the Earl of Sandwich (35–40). In another anthology, *Side Effects* (New York: Random House, 1980), Allen includes such gastronomic pieces as "The Diet" (63–69), which reduces Kafka's *The Trial* to a tale of dieting; "A Giant Step for Mankind" (91–98), which traces the development of the Heimlich maneuver as a result of scientific research; and "Fabrizio's: Criticism and Response" (123–29), which travesties the restaurant review, using it as a platform for literary, cinematic, and political criticism.

8. "Food is funny in itself. It makes me laugh," Allen confessed in an interview with Robert Benayoun. "I even thought of calling my Russian film *Love, Food and Death* or *Love, Death and Food*! I had a scene cut, which I shot in Paris, where Diane Keaton and I are on the way to assassinate Napoleon and stop at the home of a Jewish couple, at Yom Kippur, and eat a full dinner, only our plates have no food on them. It was very funny, but not usable." See *The Films of Woody Allen*, 162.

9. Bakhtin delineates his theory of carnivalization in both *The Problems of Dostoevski's Poetics*, trans. Caryl Emerson (Minneapolis: University of Minnesota Press, 1984), 101–80; and *Rabelais and His World*, trans. Hélène Iswolsky (Cambridge, MA: MIT Press, 1968). Richard Berrong presents a critique of Bakhtin's theory of carnivalization in his book *Rabelais and Bakhtin: Popular Culture in "Gargantua and Pentagruel"* (Lincoln: University of Nebraska Press, 1986). For a study of Rabelais'

use of gastronomy, see Michel Jeanneret, " 'Mon patrie est une citrouille': thèmes ali-
mentaires dans Rabelais et Folengo," in *Littérature et gastronomic* (Papers on French
Seventeenth-Century Literature, Biblio 17), ed. Ronald W. Tobin (Paris: Papers on
French Seventeenth-Century Literature, 1985), 113–48. See also Jeanneret's book,
Des mets et des mots: banquets et propos de table à la renaissance (Paris: Corti, 1987).

10. See, for example, James Brown, *Fictional Meals and Their Function in the
French Novel, 1789–1848* (Toronto: University of Toronto Press, 1984).

11. Victor Brombert, *The Novels of Flaubert. A Study of Themes and Techniques*
(Princeton, NJ: Princeton University Press, 1966), 49–51. For studies that examine
the use of gastronomy in Flaubert's novel, see Lilian R. Furst, "The Role of Food in
Madame Bovary," *Orbis Litterarum* 34 (1979): 53–65; and James Brown, "A Note
on Kitchens in *Madame Bovary*," *USF Language Quarterly* 17, nos. 1–2 (1978): 55–
56. Allen himself uses Flaubert's novel (or at least its heroine) in his story, "The Kugelmass Episode." See *Side Effects*, 41–45. Jonathan Culler discusses this story in
"The Uses of Bovary," *Diacritics* 11, no. 3 (1981): 74–81.

12. As Kevin Smith (a former student of mine) once pointed out to me, Sonja's
line may well refer not only to the heroines of Dostoyevsky but also to the lyric
persona of Anna Akhmatova, the twentieth-century Russian poet whose verse was
harshly condemned in 1946 by Andrei Zhdanov (Stalin's watchdog over the arts) as
"the poetry of a half-crazy gentlelady who tosses between the bedroom and the
chapel." "Half-nun and half-harlot, or rather both nun and harlot," Zhdanov wrote
of Akhmatova, "her harlotry is mingled with prayer." Quoted in Edward J. Brown,
Russian Literature Since the Revolution (New York: Collier, 1963), 227.

13. See, for example, Ross Wetzsteon, "Woody Allen: Schlemiel as Sex Maniac,"
Ms. 6, no. 5 (November 1977): 14–15.

14. Foster Hirsch, *Love, Sex, Death, and the Meaning of Life: Woody Allen's Comedy* (New York: McGraw-Hill, 1981), 134.

15. Maurice Yacowar, *Loser Take All: The Comic Art of Woody Allen* (New York:
Ungar, 1979), 168. "In *Sleeper* most of Woody's jokes are about bodies; in *Love and
Death* he kids the mind," notes Hirsch. "This is a comedy about intellectual affecta-
tion: big words and abstract concepts keep getting in the way of Boris and his sometime girl friend Sonia, who reluctantly becomes his wife. The two of them fall into
pseudo-intellectual discourse when what they would really rather do is fall into bed."
See *Love, Sex, Death, and the Meaning of Life*, 76.

16. Hartmut Kiltz has devoted an entire book to the theme of erotic dining in
nineteenth-century European literature. See his *Das erotische Mahl: Szenen aus dem
"chambre separee" des neunzehnten Jahrhundert* (Frankfurt: Syndikat, 1983). James
Brown explores the connection between food and fornication in the nineteenth-
century French novel in his book *Fictional Meals and Their Function in the French
Novel*. See especially 12–14, 42–43, and 50–51.

17. Hugh McLean, "Gogol's Retreat from Love: Toward an Interpretation of
Mirgorod," in *American Contributions to the Fourth International Congress of Slavi-
cists* (The Hague: Mouton, 1958), 225–44. For treatment of Gogol's aversion to sex,
see Simon Karlinsky, *The Sexual Labyrinth of Nikolai Gogol* (Cambridge, MA: Harvard University Press, 1976); Daniel Rancourt-Laferriere, *Out From Under Gogol's
Overcoat: A Psychoanalytical Study* (Ann Arbor, MI: Ardis, 1982); and Tommaso

Landolfi's short story, "Gogol's Wife," in his *Gogol's Wife and Other Stories*, trans. Raymond Rosenthal et al. (New York: New Directions, 1961), 1–16.

18. Obolensky, *Food-Notes on Gogol*, 6.

19. Douglas Brode, *Woody Allen: His Films and Career* (Secaucus, NJ: Citadel Press, 1987), 45.

20. Army cooking had been satirized earlier in the film when Boris, who is told to clean the latrine as well as the mess hall, asks how he will be able to tell the difference between the two.

21. For the distinction between *goûter* (or eating as pleasure) and *manger* (or eating as power and violence), I am indebted to Ronald W. Tobin. See his article "Les mets et les mots: gastronomie et sémiotique dans *L'École des femmes*," *Semiotica* 51 (1984): 133–45.

22. Another comic inversion of the restaurant—at a more graphic level and in reverse order (that is, from the primitive jungle to the civilized world)—occurs in *Bananas* (1971), during the hilarious scene where Fielding Mellish orders sandwiches and coleslaw for his band of South American revolutionaries at a local jungle "deli."

23. Douglas Brode (wrongly, I think) subsumes nearly all the food imagery in Allen's films under this enormous-restaurant metaphor, arguing that hunger—emotional and psychological as well as physical—is largely what motivates the behavior of Allen's characters, from the early *Don't Drink the Water* (1969) to *The Purple Rose of Cairo* (1985). See *Woody Allen: His Films and Career*, 81, 89–92, 110–11, 123, 138–40, 155–56, 178, 235–39, and 247–49.

24. See the screenplay for *Annie Hall* in *Four Films of Woody Allen* (London: Faber & Faber, 1983), 4. Another food joke with broad existential implications occurs at the end of *Annie Hall*, when Alvy Singer says: "I—I thought of that old joke, you know, this—this—this guy goes to a psychiatrist and says, 'Doc, uh, my brother's crazy. He thinks he's a chicken.' And, uh, the doctor says, 'Well, why don't you turn him in?' And the guy says, 'I would, but I need the eggs.' Well, I guess that's pretty much how I feel about relationships. You know, they're totally irrational and crazy and absurd and . . . but, uh, I guess we keep goin' through it because, uh, most of us need the eggs." See *Four Films of Woody Allen*, 105.

25. Benayoun, *The Films of Woody Allen*, 42. This combination of the farcical and the intellectual leads, in Benayoun's opinion, to "a satirical meditation on the thought processes themselves," to "a comedy of procrastination," which suggests a parallel, he maintains, not with Gogol but with Chekhov.

26. See the letter to S. T. Aksakov of March 6, 1847, in the fourteen-volume complete collection of Gogol's works, *Polnoe sobranie sochinenii* (Moscow-Leningrad: Akademiia nauk, 1940–1952), 12:187. The translation here is mine.

27. Gogol, *Polnoe sobranie sochinenii*, 12:54.

28. Quoted in Benayoun, *The Films of Woody Allen*, 41. In an interview with *Esquire*, Woody Allen used a similar gastronomic metaphor to characterize his work. "A comedy, for me, has the quality of being a little dessert, a diversion," he said. "The real meat and potatoes are serious films." Quoted in Douglas Brode, *Woody Allen: His Films and Career*, 34.

29. See Benayoun, *The Films of Woody Allen*, 161; and Eric Lax, *On Being Funny: Woody Allen and Comedy* (New York: Charterhouse, 1975), 224.

30. Frank Pierson, as quoted in Douglas Brode, *Woody Allen: His Films and Career*, 18.

10

Powerful Man Gets Pretty Woman
Style Switching in *Annie Hall*

Devin Brown

In this chapter I extend the argument made by Scotton (1983, 1985, 1988) that style switching, one type of code switching, is a feature of powerful language and can be used as a self-enhancing strategy. While the data from Scotton 1985 were taken from the speech of television interviewers, the data for this study come from the Woody Allen movie *Annie Hall*. In the absence of other accesses to status such as looks, power, or wealth, the character that Woody Allen plays uses style switching to establish his status, particularly in wooing the character played by Diane Keaton. While Scotton's studies have associated style switching with the negotiation of power between speakers, a second factor that can be associated with it is attention to audience.

By way of introduction, before examining this effect of audience, consider two quite different types of style switching. First imagine, if you will, the case of the freshman composition student who, upon getting back his or her paper, finds a red "27d" in the margin, which indicates a particular error to look up in the *Harbrace College Handbook* (Hodges et al., 1990, 282). Error 27d reads, "Avoid needless shifts in tone or style." *Harbrace* offers two examples of this type of error and a suggestion for improvement:

> Journalists who contend that the inefficiency of our courts will lend to the total elimination of the jury system are **nuts**. [Replace *nuts* (slang) with a word like *wrong* or *uninformed*.]
> The darkness of the auditorium, the monotony of the ballet, and the strains of music drifting sleepily from the orchestra aroused in me a desire to **sack out**.

Next consider this utterance, included in the data from Scotton 1985, that was made by Tom Snyder, a nationally syndicated talk show host, during a televised interview: "Why didn't you just want to continue being a magician? I mean, what the heck, sir, you're all dressed up in a magic suit."

Scotton takes her title ("What the heck, sir?") from this phrase and her claim is roughly this: rather than being some type of linguistic error stemming from a deficiency on the part of the speaker, style shifts (by which she means style switches) and lexical coloring (a speaker move similar to and, as Scotton notes, not always distinguishable from style switching), when used by a person with command of the requisite styles in his or her linguistic repertoire, become powerful language features that allow the speaker to "negotiate his/her personal rights and obligations in effect during the exchange, relative to those of the addressee" (Scotton 1985, 107). Snyder's casual-style phrase "what the heck," a down switch from the middle consultative style used for most of the interview, is followed by an up switch to the formal-style "sir." Scotton offers other examples of style switching taken from interviews conducted by Tom Brokaw, Dick Cavett, Phil Donahue, Jane Pauley, Tom Snyder, and Mike Wallace, and she shows how these style switches, deviations from the unmarked or expected choice, can be powerful language strategies intended to change the rights and obligations balance within the conversational exchange.

Thus what is an error, or at least a power-diminishing move, on the part of the freshman writer with an imperfect control over the formal academic style that is required in a written essay, becomes a power-increasing move when made by speakers with full command over the various styles they switch to and from. Just as Ervin-Tripp found that the same style directive, a bald imperative, when used by different speakers had different implications, similarly here, a style switch can convey either linguistic inability or linguistic versatility, depending on the skill of the person who makes it.

Another aspect of the style switching exhibited by the six interviewers, one that Scotton does not address directly, is the role that audience plays. Bell has done a lengthy study on language style as audience design, and he notes that in radio programs for mass communication, such as interviews, which have more than one participant, the mass auditors (his term for *audience*) are likely to be more important to a communicator than the immediate addressees, that is, the person or persons being interviewed. The question arises: would the television interviewers Scotton studied (1985, 1988) have used the style switches and other powerful language features to the same extent if there had been no audience present? For example, is it conceivable that Tom Snyder would have made a style switch like "what the heck, sir?" while he was talking to Tom Petty alone backstage before the show?

This chapter examines the general relationship between style switching and audience, in particular the style switching in *Annie Hall*, and suggests that this style switching is motivated both by a desire to negotiate the rights and obligations of the speakers as fits Scotton's theory of markedness and also by an appeal to an audience that (1) will enjoy witnessing this display of linguistic versatility and (2) will enjoy being defined as in-group members, that is, as people who get the encoded intent that this style switching carries. I have two goals here: (1) to show how Scotton's approach as described above can be applied to a another corpus of data, namely the language found in *Annie Hall*, and (2) to push Scotton's work a step farther by showing how audience can be added as a variable in interpreting the meaning of style switches. Finally, while my data come from a particular Woody Allen film, I argue that the linguistic issues addressed here are not limited to this somewhat special data set but are characteristic of discourse in general.

THE POWERFUL SPEAKER AND HIS AUDIENCE

From urban ghetto rapping to traditional rural storytelling, audience-based oral discourse has always been a part of our culture, and those who possess the ability to speak in these special forms have been held in esteem. Audience-based discourse is part carefully planned and part spontaneous, and often highly conventional; and while it may share some of the characteristics of regular (non-audience-directed) speech, the frequency or purpose of these characteristics may be somewhat different. For example, audience-based oral discourse may include speech exchanges that contain powerful language features, but here the primary purpose of these features may not be to negotiate power with the addressee, as Scotton's 1985 study suggests and as it is in a normal conversation, but to appeal to the audience.

Linguistic versatility, in particular the ability to deftly switch from style to style and with each switch to encode additional information concerning the speaker's relationship to addressee, addressee's group, the topic, or any combination of the three, is in some ways like athletic versatility, musical versatility, or versatility in any other area of human endeavor: other people, the audience, can derive pleasure simply from witnessing a display of this special skill. The ability to jump nimbly from code to code or from style to style, a skill that other people do not have and so will pay to observe, becomes a status marker for whoever has it and can make him or her a celebrity. Some of the raters who assessed the data and identified style shifts in Scotton (1985, 110) felt that Snyder was "playing around" or showing off with his language. Scotton (1988, 204) mentions this dimension of style switching, which "asserts interactional power for the speaker by displaying his/her multiple identities" and is a type of symbolic boasting:

> It has been suggested that women, who traditionally have often been denied access to occupation and education, turn to one status marker which is available

to them, language. So too people of either gender without access to the status markers of physical appearance, power, and wealth often claim access to power through their abilities in athletics, music, or language.

How many comedians, masters of powerful language, can we list who could not have appealed to an audience on the basis of their looks? We might mention comedians such as Woody Allen, short, scrawny, and myopic, or the late John Belushi, plain and pudgy. It might be argued that Cyrano de Bergerac's linguistic abilities were a direct result of the length of his nose. Certainly the lexicon that Dick Cavett displays in front of an audience is as large as he is small. Conversely, someone either as ruggedly handsome as Paul Newman and Clint Eastwood or as physically powerful as Arnold Schwarzenegger and Sylvester Stallone may feel little need to give attention to developing powerful language abilities, or even to saying very much at all. If some people find an audience by being the strong silent type, others must find it by being the wimpy style-switching type.

Besides the story of the competition for Roxanne's affection between the powerfully speaking Cyrano de Bergerac and the powerfully attractive Christian, literature also holds Longfellow's narrative poem of Miles Standish, who calls upon his more eloquent-speaking friend John Alden to help him win the hand of Priscilla. In *Annie Hall*, Woody Allen plays a character who employs his powerful language abilities in the attempt to woo Annie, who is played by Diane Keaton. Allen's character, Alvy Singer, is very much like the character that Allen displays in public. In fact, in this film Allen often seems to be speaking directly to the camera as his public self. So for the sake of simplicity, in this paper I will not distinguish between Woody Allen and the character he plays in *Annie Hall*, although obviously the two are not identical.

STYLE SWITCHING IN *ANNIE HALL*

Using language from a film rather than naturally occurring speech as the source of data for this chapter might seem to put the arguments here on a somewhat shaky foundation, particularly if we hope to extend the observations found here to language in general. I chose the *Annie Hall* corpus because its style switching is both richer and more refined than that found in "real" speech and hence easier to use as illustration. However, it is our assessment of this style switching that is the issue here: assessments that are equally "real" whether they are being applied to the language from a film or from a transcript of naturally occurring language. Just as Scotton's findings were not limited to comments about the way that Tom Snyder and others exploit language, my claims made in this chapter about the relationship between style switching and audience are not intended to be restricted merely to the style switching found in *Annie Hall*, nor to the films of Woody Allen or even to films in general, but apply to style switching and our assessment of it wherever it may occur.

Annie Hall opens with Woody Allen alone on camera, speaking directly to his audience. After two brief jokes, one of which he attributes to Freud, Allen tells us, "Annie and I broke up and I still can't get my mind around that. I keep shifting the pieces of the relationship through my mind and examining my life and trying to figure out where did the screwup come, you know?"

Throughout the film. Allen makes both down switches in style, such as the one that occurs in "where did the screwup come, you know?" and up switches. The film's other characters either (1) remain in the same style or (2) are capable of making one style shift, that is, they move to a single different style and then stay there for an entire exchange. This distribution of style choice in the film sets off Allen's switches of style as marked and fit the markedness model proposed by Scotton in her 1983 study. First we will look at some of Allen's style switches and then turn to the lack of style switching by the other characters.

While Joos (1961) found it useful to distinguish five general styles, following Scotton (1985, 113), I note in this chapter only three: an unmarked middle style, a marked casual style, and a marked formal (sometimes legal or technical) style. In the previous example, we see a down switch from the opening neutral or middle style to casual style. While there may be general agreement that "style" represents subdialectal variation, considerable disagreement may arise over exactly how many styles exist and what appropriate cover terms for them should be. I do not give a precise definition of each style, but I claim that in this film Allen switches between three basic styles—casual, middle, and referential—and four specific styles that Allen identifies himself by mimicking them—academic style, *Rolling Stone* style, California style, and film-critic style—and that his switching depends on what he hopes to gain by manipulating these styles.

Another style switch by Allen comes early in the film, where we see a scene from the past in which the Allen character and his first wife, a university professor, are at a party of academicians. She remarks on the impressive credentials of those in attendance. "There's Henry Druckard. He has a chair in history at Princeton. The short man is Hershell Cominsky. He has a chair in philosophy at Cornell."

The Allen character expresses his scorn for one-dimensional men whose identities are defined by their degrees or their style. He expresses his criticism by switching to the role of an outsider, by pretending to misinterpret:

Allen: Oh yeah? Two more chairs they got a dining room set.

Later, Allen further displays his claim to multiple identity by demonstrating his ability to switch to academic style while ridiculing it in this exchange with his wife:

Allen: I'm so sick of spending evenings making fake insights with people who work in dysentery.

Former wife: Commentary.

Allen: Oh really? I heard that commentary and dissent had merged and formed dysentery.

As the party nears its close, Allen's former wife catches him hiding in a back bedroom watching a New York Knicks basketball game, and Allen wants to attack her on the bed.

Allen: While all those Ph.D.s are in there, you know, discussing modes of alienation, you and I will be in here quietly humping.

In this last utterance Allen makes a triple switch from middle to academic to casual. Unlike the first example of "where did the screwup come," where the effect was to display to the audience his identity as a normal person with genuine sincerity about the pain of breaking up, here the Allen character exhibits his ability to switch to academicese in "modes of alienation" and then expresses his contempt for such one-dimensional eggheads by his switch to the casual "humping." The brief switch to the middle style "quietly" adds to his demonstration of verbal prowess.

Who is this demonstration for? In one sense Allen's style switches have a dual purpose: (1) to demonstrate his superiority to his local audience, in this case his wife but later other women, and (2) when he speaks in soliloquy or during those times when his local audience does not get that he is style switching, to demonstrate his superiority to his film audience.

If Allen's style switches may be seen as assertions of superiority or power, as seen in the last example, they may also be viewed as demonstrations of verbal virtuosity, performed simply because someone is watching. Bell (1984, 176) notes that the "use of a language which is unintelligible to any interlocutor defines that person out of the audience." I suggest that an inability to recognize the humor in Allen's style switches defines an out-group and that perhaps one of the appeals of his humor is that it also thus defines an in-group, those who are sophisticated enough to get it.

We have seen two of Allen's down switches. If his switching is in part done to demonstrate his verbal prowess to his audience, we might expect this prowess would also contain the ability for up switches. And in fact it does. In one segment, the Allen character is playing before an audience at the University of Wisconsin. "College audiences are wonderful," he tells Annie, acknowledging his awareness of audience, particularly one that will understand his referential style switches. In one story with a referential style shift he tells the crowd of students, "I was thrown out of NYU my freshman year for cheating on my metaphysics final. I looked within the soul of the boy sitting next to me." Later he adds, "I was suicidal, as a matter of fact, and would have killed myself but I was in analysis with a strict Freudian, and if you kill yourself they make you pay for the sessions you miss."

"You were wonderful," Annie tells him after his performance, "I think I'm starting to get more of the references."

In another scene, Allen has been called over to Annie Hall's apartment to kill some spiders that were in her bathtub. While he is in the bathroom he sees a bar of black soap, and we have this exchange:

Allen: What is this, you got black soap?

Hall: It's for my complexion.

Allen: What are you joining, a minstrel show?

After the killing of the spiders, Annie Hall is crying and the Allen character asks, "What did you want me to do, capture and rehabilitate them?"

Here then are four examples of up switches to the referential style, a style defined by its reference to a certain kind of knowledge—here, of metaphysics, of Freudian analysis, of minstrel shows, and of penal theory—which the average person might not be expected to have.

An exchange that clearly illustrates Allen's view that his style-switching ability is his status marker, his way to show that he is special, his way to get girls, occurs when he and Annie are talking together for the first time. In discussing Annie's photography, out of nervousness Allen finds himself shifting permanently to one style—that of an innocuous, smooth talker. At this point we get to see the character's thoughts about his language written on screen while he is talking:

Allen: (says) Still, you need a set of aesthetic guidelines to put it into social perspective, I think.

Allen: (thinks) Christ, I sound like FM radio. Relax.

Woody Allen is distinguished from the other characters by his ability to switch styles. Annie Hall does not style shift. In fact, several times Allen asserts his status by indicating her linguistic deficiencies, in particular her limitation to casual style lexical choices. As they are getting to know each other after their first tennis date, Allen makes sure that he gets in several style switches that establish him as a possessor of powerful language features:

Allen: I love what you're wearing.

Hall: This tie was a present from Grammy Hall.

Allen: Who? Grammy? Grammy Hall? What'd you do, grow up in a Norman Rockwell painting? Your grammy? My grammy never gave gifts. She was too busy being raped by Cossacks.

Allen makes light of a book of Sylvia Plath poems he finds in Annie's bookcase:

Annie: Some of her poems seem neat.

(Annie defends.)

Allen: Neat? I hate to tell you, this is 1975. "Neat" went out, I would say, at the turn of the century.

This assertion of linguistic superiority continues. The Allen character makes clear his verbal power over both Annie and her former boyfriends. After the couple have been dating for a while, they get into a discussion of Annie's past loves. In a flashback we see one of them, an actor, who tells Annie, "Acting is like an exploration of the soul. It's very religious, like a kind of liberating consciousness. It's like a visual poem."

Because of the somewhat surreal nature of this film, the Allen character has been able to watch this flashback. He replies, "Is he kidding with that crap?"

Allen tells Annie Hall that considering her former loves, she is fortunate to be going out with him:

Allen: I think you're pretty lucky I came along.

Hall: Oh really? Well, la di da.

Allen: La di da. If anyone ever told me that I would be taking out a girl who used expressions like "la di da."

Hall: Oh yeah, that's right. You really like those New York girls.

Toward the middle of the movie, the Allen character accuses Annie of having an affair with her college professor. This exchange occurs:

Hall: We're not having an affair. He's married. He just happens to think I'm neat.

Allen: Neat? There's that word. What are you, 12 years old? That's one of your Chippewa Falls expressions.

Hall: Who cares? Who cares?

Allen: Next thing you know he'll find you "keen" and "peachy," you know. Next thing you know he's got his hand on your ass.

Annie, who knows that an attack on language by Allen constitutes his attempt to exert his status or power over another person, responds with, "You've always had hostility towards David."

In the preceding data, we have seen an inability by Annie Hall to speak in anything other than the casual, everyday style, which is characterized by expressions such as "la di da" and "neat." Allen notes his greater stylistic range both in comparison to Annie and to his potential rivals.

After Annie Hall leaves Allen and goes to California, Allen goes on a date to see a maharishi with a reporter for *Rolling Stone*. This character's speech is characterized by a shift to *Rolling Stone* style, a style that Allen trivializes by switching to it in the following exchange:

Reporter: The only word for this is transplendent. It's transplendent. It's unbelievably transplendent! I was at the Stones concert in Altamont where they killed that guy, remember?

Allen: Oh yeah, were ya? I was at an Alice Cooper thing where six people were rushed to the hospital with a case of bad vibes.

Here it should be pointed out that the reporter is completely unaware that Allen is trivializing her speech style; this style switch is done for the benefit of the audience, which realizes that in this style switch Allen is demonstrating his higher status. While the reporter can shift from casual to *Rolling Stone* style, this style is only one of many Allen is capable of. In the film, certain speakers, like the reporter and Allen's former wife, are capable of a single style shift. This style shift creates an identity for them and a boundary marking both an in-group and an out-group, with speakers of the jargon on the inside. Allen's multiple styles, which often only the audience is privy to, also create a boundary, marking him as special, something more than the single shifters. The reporter's use of *Rolling Stone* style is her attempt to mark herself as an in-group member. Her inability to realize that Allen's style switch is not genuine marks her as a out-group member. The audience's awareness that through his style switch Allen is ridiculing her speech-marked identity designates them as in-group members.

Another time when Allen switches to another speaker's style occurs when he and Annie go to a party in California. Again Allen demonstrates both (1) his ability to use the style of the partygoers and (2) his contempt for the people who use that style. This contempt is made clear by the fact that only the audience realizes Allen's style switch is deprecatory. We witness the following exchanges in California style:

Californian 1: Will you take a meeting with her?

Californian 2: I'll take a meeting with you if you take a meeting with Freddy.

Californian 1: I took a meeting with Freddy. Freddy took a meeting with Charlie.

Californian 2: You take a meeting with her.

Californian 1: All the good meetings are taken.

        *   *   *

Californian 3: Right now it's only a notion, but if I get some money I think I can turn it into a concept and later turn it into an idea.

        *   *   *

Californian 4: I forgot my mantra.

Allen's response and assertion of multistyle superiority are shown in the following sarcastic switches to California style:

Allen: I came out here to get some shock therapy, but there was an energy crisis.

        *   *   *

Allen: (to his friend and a woman they have met) You guys are wearing white. It must be in the stars. Uri Geller must be on the premises.

        *   *   *

Allen: (ordering food) I'm going to have the alfalfa sprouts and a plate of mashed yeast.

In another scene, the Allen character and Annie Hall go to the show and are in line in front of an obnoxious film professor who is speaking over-loudly to his date in film-critic style. Here Allen makes a style switch to a fourth type of style, film professor style, and then switches back to casual to indicate his power to his audience:

Film professor: Granted, *La Strada* was a great film. Great in its use of negative imagery more than anything else. But that simple cohesive core, meaningful patterns leading from one to another. . . . I found it incredibly indulgent. He really is. He's one of the most indulgent film makers. Weltan-schauung is what it is . . .

Allen: (to Annie) They probably met by answering an ad in the *New York Review of Books*: "Thirtyish academic wishes to meet woman who is inter-ested in Mozart, James Joyce, and sodomy."

To conclude, in *Annie Hall*, the Allen character's claim to status rests on his language skills, in particular on his ability to style switch between casual, middle, and referential as well as to switch back and forth between the styles of those around him—academics, reporters, Californians, and film profes-sors. This style switching is motivated (1) by a desire to renegotiate the rela-tionship between himself and the other characters and (2) by the desire to demonstrate his verbal prowess to his audience, both the audience on film in *Annie Hall*, whom he is trying to impress, and the audience watching the film to whom Allen the writer-director-actor is trying to appeal.

An interesting parallel exists between this work and Shaw's *Pygmalion*. The male leads in both are masters of other people's linguistic repertoires, and in each of their minds this ability, this possession of multiple identities, marks them as superior. In both works, the female lead becomes the pupil of the male. In the end, Annie Hall develops her own status markers, includ-ing the ability to style switch, and leaves Allen, much as Eliza Doolittle, now a powerful language speaker herself, leaves Professor Henry Higgins at the end of *Pygmalion*. But unlike Eliza, who returns to Henry when he ac-knowledges her as his linguistic equal, Annie Hall goes to live with Tony Lacey (played by Paul Simon), a character with more status than the Allen character because, besides being a Harvard graduate and well-spoken, Lacey is also a famous rock star with lots of money and a huge California mansion. In this exchange near the end of the film, we witness Annie's display of her newly acquired ability to switch to referential style:

Allen: So you're not going to come back to New York?

Hall: What's so great about New York? It's a dying city. You read *Death in Venice*.

Allen: You didn't read *Death in Venice* until I bought it for you.

Allen gets his one last assertion of status before Annie goes to stay with

Lacey. Allen and Annie are at a party at Tony's, and Tony is showing off one of his status markers, his home, to Allen and Hall. Allen knows that Lacey has an interest in Annie, so he must display his own status and language and denigrate Lacey's. Lacey is name-dropping and Allen cannot resist joining in the name-dropping, status-asserting game:

Tony: This is a great house. Really, everything. Saunas, Jacuzzis, three tennis courts. Know who the original owners were? Nelson Eddy and Legs Diamond. Then you know who lived here?

Allen: Trigger?

WORKS CITED

Allen, Woody, and Marshall Brickman. *Annie Hall*. Directed by Woody Allen. United Artists, 1977.

Bell, Allen. "Language Style as Audience Design." *Language in Society* 13 (1984): 145–204.

Ervin-Tripp, S. "Is Sybil there? The Structure of Some American English Directives. *Language in Society* 5 (1976): 25–66.

Hodges, John C., Mary E. Whitten, Winifred Horner, and Suzanne Webb. *Harbrace College Handbook*. 11th ed. New York: Harcourt Brace Jovanovich, 1990.

Joos, Martin. *The Five Clocks*. Bloomington: Indiana University Research Center in Anthropology, Folklore, and Linguistics, 1962.

Scotton, C. M. "The Negotiation of Identities in Conversation: A Theory of Markedness and Code Choice." *International Journal of the Sociology of Language* 44 (1983): 115–36

———. "What the Heck, Sir?" Style Shifting and Lexical Colouring as Features of Powerful Language." In *Sequence and Pattern in Communicative Behavior*, ed. R. L. Street and J. N. Cappella, 103–19. London: Edward Arnold, 1985.

———. "Self-Enhancing Codeswitching as Interactional Power." *Language and Communication* 8 (1988): 199–211.

11

Annie Hall and the Issue of Modernism

Thomas Schatz

There is an essential paradox in the historical development of the commercial cinema: as the medium's technological evolution has enhanced its capacity for representation, its narrative and thematic evolution has been toward codification, convention, and artifice. While, on the one hand, the modern spectator recognizes the close affinity between his or her perception of images on the screen and of their represented objects in reality, the cumulative effect of the cinema's narrative conventions causes a strong perceptual countercurrent. Spectators generally have learned to negotiate the film story and its ideology only indirectly in terms of their own experience; essentially, they negotiate the story in terms of previous experience of the form itself. Thus the modernist (or postrealist) would contend that the inherent photographic realism of the indexical imagery ultimately is negated—or at least severely qualified—by the symbolic, iconographic codification of those images within the conventions of narrative cinema.

Structuralist analysts (identified, significantly, as either theorists or critics) propose, in the tradition of de Saussure, to glean the myriad "systems of signification" in which any act of narrative discourse participates. The term *modernist* generally is assigned to any narrative that manifests a certain degree of self-awareness—or in more fashionable parlance, self-reflexivity—regarding the narrative, thematic, or formal conventions at work in the circuit of discourse in which it is communicated. Modernism is opposed to one of several terms—traditional, classical, realist, conventional—that designates a narrative system whose function is to conceal its codes (its formal and narrative conventions) and sustain a hermetically closed, logically consistent, formally transparent fictional world. The modernist text, in its self-reflexive

123

stance, is said to subvert the codes of both classical narrative discourse and the production-consumption modes that sustain it. But I should affirm that this opposition is not absolute—the two represent conceptual, functional parameters. The difference between the classical and modernist text is essentially one of *degree* and not of *kind*, in that the qualities of modernism are latent in all narratives.

Roland Barthes, perhaps the most articulate proponent of narrative structural analysis, has confronted this issue by suggesting that narrative fiction is dominated in both its creation and apprehension by two antithetical but related qualities: the *lisable* and the *scriptable*. It is significant that these French terms have been translated into English somewhat differently. Jonathan Culler, in his *Structuralist Poetics*, translates the terms as "readable" and "unreadable," whereas Richard Miller, in his 1974 translation of Barthes's *S/Z* (New York: Hill and Wang), opts for the terms "readerly" and "writerly." As this discrepancy suggests, the classical-modernist opposition might be construed of the individual analyst. Miller's position assumes that the readerly-writerly distinction has to do with the "attitude" and emphasis of the author and reader; Culler, on the other hand, stresses that *readable* and *unreadable* "are functional concepts rather than classes of texts."[1] Ultimately, both viewpoints seem not only accurate but complementary, and consideration for each will enable the analyst to avoid the kind of interpretive trap that snares Judith Mayne in her essay "*S/Z* and Film Criticism" when she states that "we can find many writerly texts—most 20th Century literature courses depend upon them."[2]

Barthes would disagree—or rather, he would indicate that the authors of these texts (Proust, Joyce, Faulkner, etc.) encourage a writerly attitude on the part of the reader. Barthes's conception of the unreadable or writerly is that of an absolute conceptual parameter that is itself unattainable in practice. The fact that a novel or film—or any kind of narrative—can be *named* as such indicates that it is, at least to some degree, "readable." Without participating in the conventions of the form, the writer-creator is without a means of expression; "to write" becomes virtually inconceivable. Barthes further posits that the author's participation in the conventions of his or her form, far from being a creative restriction, actually determines the communicable as well as the aesthetic basis for the work's apprehension and evaluation. As he states in *The Pleasure of the Text*, "There are those who want a text (an art, a painting) without a shadow, without a 'dominant ideology'; but this is to want a text without fecundity, without productivity, a sterile text. . . . The text needs its shadow: the shadow is *a bit* of ideology, *a bit* of representation, *a bit* of subject."[3] The writerly text, then, is not only unreadable from the audience's viewpoint but also unwritable from the author's.

The fact that Barthes himself uses the *lisable-scriptable* opposition only in establishing the conceptual framework for his analysis, and then in effect abandons it in the actual analysis, further underscores its theoretical value and its practical limitations. What Barthes clearly needs is a concept to mediate the opposition and reinforce the fact that all texts are both *lisable* and *scriptable* in varying degrees. Thus the notion of the "plural" text. "To interpret a text," contends Barthes, "is not to give it a (more or less justified, more or less free) meaning, but on the contrary to appreciate what *plural* constitutes it."[4] Barthes applies this notion to various aspects of narrativity, indicating that the more overtly plural (i.e., modern) text will subvert conventional codes along these broad guidelines: to portray characters, objects, and events as a "galaxy of signifiers" without stipulating their "meaning"; to develop a narrative structure that allows the reader various points of access (which generally is accomplished through some manipulation of the traditional chronology of exposition, complication, resolution); to elaborate the ironic interfacing of author, narrator, and character and thereby subvert the traditional conception of the central character as a primary organizing sensibility within the text.[5]

Keeping in mind both Culler's and Barthes's observations that the *lisable-scriptable* opposition is conceptual rather than historical, we cannot overlook the fact that modernist authors, by definition, exhibit a writerly attitude toward the narrative textual system in their tendency to subvert its conventions, and that this tendency necessarily must be related to the historical development of narrative tradition. Scholes and Kellogg, in their relatively conservative *Nature of Narrative*, survey the evolution of the narrative from oral tradition through the modern novel and film. In their discussion of the modern narrative, Kellogg and Scholes posit formal qualities roughly similar to those suggested by Barthes. It is characterized by thematic ambiguity, by an ironic interrelationship among author, narrator, and character (and, by extension, the reader or viewer) and by a convoluted narrative temporal structure.[6] Further, if we consider those narrative analysts and art historians who have studied the evolution of art forms, the notion of self-reflexivity or subversion of convention does indeed seem to be a necessary development indigenous to the historical process. Henri Focillon, in *The Life of Forms in Art*, suggests that "forms obey their own rules . . . and there is no reason why we should not undertake an investigation of how these great ensembles . . . behave throughout the phases which we call their life. The successive states through which they pass are more or less lengthy, more or less intense, according to the style itself: the experimental stage, the classical stage, the age of refinement, the baroque stage."[7] Leonard B. Meyer, in *Music, the Arts, and Ideas*, presents a similar progression: from "preclassical" through "classical" and eventually into a "mannerist" stage."[8] Christian Metz assumes a more overtly structuralist tone in *Language and Cinema* when he describes the Western genre as progressing from a "classical" stage, into "parody" and "contestation," and finally into a stage of self-critical "deconstruction."[9]

Implicit in each of these viewpoints is the conception of an art form evolving toward a stage of self-reflexivity, a stage at which its conventions are subverted in a fashion that is pleasurable for both artist and audience. That Western literature has long since entered its mannerist stage seems obvious enough, and it would appear that the commercial cinema is following its lead (liberated perhaps, at least in this country, by network television's having assumed the classical supportive function of the mass media: that is, to deliver to the passive viewer in conventional terms a reaffirmation of the aesthetic and sociopolitical status quo). As a form enters its mannerist stage, the artist in effect is challenging the audience to reject the necessary passivity of classicism (wherein the conventions are mutually understood and deemed inviolate) and to become actively involved in the text. Scholes and Kellogg, discussing the unreliable narrator in fiction, suggest that "its frequent use in modern fiction is also an aspect of the modern author's desire to make the reader participate in the act of creation."[10] Barthes, in the typically materialist jargon of structuralism, states that "the goal of literary work (of literature as work) is to make the reader no longer a consumer, but a producer of the text."[11]

What these analysts are advocating—and, indeed, this may well be the vocation of any modernist movement—is an essential reconstitution of both the creative and the perceptive activity of narrative production. Because of the modern text's preoccupation with the *process* of producing and conveying messages, any search for meaning—particularly meaning construed as the author's intent—is subordinated to a concern for the understanding and interpretation of formal and thematic conventions. That is, a concern for the *how* over the *what*; or rather, a realization that in certain texts the how actually *is* the what, that the mediation is the meaning. Implicit in this perspective is a conception of the reader or spectator as analyst, especially regarding highly plural texts. As Geoffrey Nowell-Smith has observed, "The process of deconstruction/reconstruction that is continually taking place within the codes is inseparable from an activity of deconstruction/reconstruction present in the relation of the spectator to the text. . . . In the last analysis it remains the spectator who determines the role and production of the sign."[12]

With a genuinely modernist text, the inseparability of the author's and spectator's familiarity through self-reflexivity provides the basis for the work's effect. As I will suggest in the forthcoming discussion of *Annie Hall*, the spectator is cued from the opening sequence to the self-reflexive nature of the text and is encouraged to read the narrative as something other than a sequential development toward some transcendent truth. As opposed to a 1950s genre film like, say, Sirk's *All that Heaven Allows*, which can be read as either classical or modernist depending on the analyst's perspective and approach, Allen's film immediately establishes its self-referential stance in a number of ways: the ironic, generally ambiguous interrelationship of author, narrator, and character; by extension, the ambiguous, problematic status of the text in relation to "reality"; the convoluted, metaphoric-associative plot structure (at least at the outset); the establishment of a context for repeated authorial intervention; and the ultimate subordination of the messages communicated to the process of narrative communication. *Annie Hall,* then, is a film that virtually demands that the viewer adopt a modernist perspective, that the viewer conduct what Barthes would term a "writerly reading" of the text.

I do not mean to imply, however, that *Annie Hall* is by any means an "unreadable" text. On the contrary, the film's eminent readability is indicated by the breadth of its critical and popular success, although the range of the film's appeal belies its accessibility at different levels of viewer engagement. *Annie Hall* is a narrative that is alternately modernist and classical, that at different points in its development foregrounds the tale, the teller, and the act of telling. While at one level the viewer is engaged by the rather conventional—and conventionally mediated—courtship of Alvy Singer and Annie Hall, that viewer's reading of the courtship is radically affected by both the structure and the generally ambivalent tone of the narrative. The tale of Alvy and Annie's courtship is literally and figuratively the core of the narrative, but the presence of the Allen *persona* as narrator and the rhetorical dynamics of his narration prevent the viewer from negotiating the film as primarily a courtship narrative. In fact, the "teller telling" aspect of the narrative so utterly determines the nature of the told that the telling itself assumes, finally, the status of tale.

With the opening monologue sequence of *Annie Hall,* we are cued both to the ironic status of the film's central character (its narrative focus, its organizing sensibility) and also to its general narrative strategy. By revealing at the outset not only the outcome of the courtship story but also the reasons for that outcome, Allen/Alvy functions to foreground the process of narrativity and redirect our conception of the film's ultimate meaning. In the opening sequence, we see Woody Allen (whom we know, having just seen the credits, to be the director and coauthor of the film) in medium close-up before a flat pastel backdrop delivering a stand-up comedy routine. After telling what he calls the "key joke" in his adult life concerning his unwillingness to belong to any club with low enough standards to allow him membership, the stand-up comic and narrator poses the film's motivating and typically self-conscious question: "Annie and I broke up—where did the screwup come? A year ago we were in love."

Through the framing device of the stand-up comedy routine, which is sustained throughout the film by means of various cinematic devices, Allen establishes a pretext for authorial intervention and character aside that repeatedly underscore the ironic author-narrator-character relationship. The comic narrator, in his ambivalent status as both author and character, both

Allen and Alvy, functions throughout to subvert the film-reality distinction and to disrupt the autonomy of the hermetic fictional world. Further, the comedy routine presents itself as the primary narrative level, with the court-ship story as essentially another comic bit within the routine—albeit one that is developed at considerably greater depth and length than the other bits. In fact, until the courtship story begins some time later in the film, the stand-up comedy format dominates the narrative construction. That is, the events depicted follow an associative, metaphoric pattern of construction rather than the sequential, chronological pattern of most classical Hollywood nar-rative films.

Annie Hall is composed of roughly seventy distinct narrative sequences (with the term *sequence* indicating an event that is differentiated spatiotem-porally from the events preceding and following it), and the sequences them-selves are organized into what I would term three distinct movements. The narrative logic of the opening movement, which is comprised of twenty se-quences, derives from the stand-up-comedy-routine format: the organizing principle is the comic narrator's life, with the sequences following an asso-ciative rather than a chronological pattern. Those sequences may be de-scribed briefly as follows:

1. Opening monologue (key joke, motivating question)
2. Alvy as child with psychiatrist (discussing the expanding universe)
3. Exterior of Alvy's home under the roller-coaster in a New York City amusement park
4. Alvy as both a child and grown-up comic narrator in Alvy's grade-school classroom (discussing future occupations)
5. Alvy as comedian on Dick Cavett's television program
6. Alvy's mother deriding Alvy while peeling carrot
7. Alvy walking with Rob/Max (discussing anti-Semitism)
8. Alvy and Annie at theater (late for *Face to Face*)
9. Alvy and Annie in line at another theater (discussing sex, McLuhan— "boy, if life were only like this")
10. Alvy and Annie in bedroom (discussing sexual and communication problems)
11. Alvy meets Allison (first wife) at Adlai Stevenson rally
12. Alvy and Allison in bed seven years later (discussing second assassin theory re Kennedy's death); coitus interruptus
13. Alvy and Annie attempt to boil lobsters
14. Alvy and Annie on pier (discussing earlier lovers)
15. Annie as high schooler with greaser date
16. Annie one year earlier with actor-lover (during which sequence Alvy and Annie enter frame, comment on Annie's relationship with lover)
17. Annie and Alvy on pier (she mentions second wife)

18. Alvy and second wife at hip New Yorker party
19. Alvy and second wife in bed—interrupted by siren (Alvy heads for another cold shower)
20. Alvy and Rob/Max emerge from the men's shower and prepare to play tennis with Annie and another woman (Alvy is about to meet Annie for the first time)

From this point in the narrative, commencing with Alvy and Annie's meeting and courtship, the narrative assumes a classical, "realist" tone and structure. The following twenty sequences, which trace their courtship and eventual cohabitation through their first separation, are presented in chronological order and without direct authorial intervention or camera-directed asides. As opposed to the associative, metaphoric sequencing in the opening movement, the sequencing in the courtship story honors the Aristotelian-mimetic unities of space and time, as well as character, following a linear, metonymic structure. Once the Alvy-Annie relationship begins to deconstruct, however, so does the dependence on conventional sequential narrative structure. The end of the second courtship movement is signaled by distinct ruptures in the preceding narrative flow. The sequence in which Alvy and Annie argue in the street over the relationship with her poetry professor and eventually separate is accented by two significant departures from the metonymic narrative structure: the first is a flashback to an earlier, chronological, unspecified confrontation between Annie and Alvy over the value of her psychoanalysis; the second is Alvy's stopping people on the street after Annie has left him and questioning them concerning the nature of human relationships, an event that signals the return of the self-conscious narrator into the diegetic world of the film as well as a tendency for the characters within the film to step out of their assigned roles. With this narrative disruption of the courtship story, the film recovers its ironic, self-reflexive tone, which had been suspended since the opening movement. The third movement, which traces the gradual dissolution of Alvy and Annie's relationship, does sustain an essential chronological sequential structure although it is disrupted by frequent ellipses (recalling the two-sequence relationship with Allison that spanned a Stevenson rally and Kennedy's assassination seven years later), as well as flashbacks, voice-over intervention by the comic narrator, and camera-directed character asides. With the initial breakup of the romantic couple, Alvy's character once again becomes, like Vonnegut's Billy Pilgrim, "unstuck in time"—and unstuck in character as well.

There is a sense, finally, in which we might consider the courtship movement (sequences twenty through forty) as a classical text imbedded within a primarily modernist one. During the courtship narrative, Alvy is in a state of mental and emotional security, his disposition is determined by his relationship with Annie, and he—like the narrative itself, which is an extension of his own psyche—enjoys the only period of sustained unselfconsciousness in the film. During the courtship, Alvy essentially remains in character (i.e., Alvy Singer as opposed to Allen/Alvy or Allen). During this movement, we do not sense the ironic interfacing of author, narrator, and character, and consequently we are during the second movement at the highest level of emotional and empathetic engagement with Alvy Singer and Annie Hall as fictional characters, and we are relatively unaware of the narrative and cinematic conventions whose manipulation is foregrounded in the opening and closing movements of the film.

But despite the relative autonomy of the classical courtship story, that movement does not completely elude the spectator's self-reflexive deconstruction due to its position within the larger narrative context. In fact, there are a number of formal and thematic elements in the opening movement that tend to subvert our reading of the courtship story as a traditional romantic narrative. In the opening monologue sequence, the comic narrator informs us that he and Annie have broken up and asks, "Where did the screwup come?" This question would seem to generate certain expectations, but in fact the narrator has already answered the question. The comic narrator prefaces the Groucho Marx gag about clubs with low enough standards to allow him membership with the statement that it is the "key joke in my adult life regarding my relationships with women." So whereas the narrative development would seem on one level to be based in the dual-plot, detective story convention—where, in this case, the narrator attempts throughout the narrated flashbacks to "solve" the question of the screwup—actually the screwup itself is explained within the context of the Marx gag within the opening monologue, and is further reinforced as a *model* of Alvy/Allen's sexual relationships during the opening movement.

Thus Allen's self-conscious persona, like the narrative extension of his character, is the victim of a tendency toward overdetermination of meaning—or in modernist terms "the tyranny of the signified"—and his involvement with Annie can be viewed as an attempt to establish a spontaneous, intellectually unencumbered relationship, an attempt that is doomed to failure. *Annie Hall* is, in this sense, an examination of the process of human interaction and interpersonal communication, and the questions raised at the outset are never resolved. Human relationships are both an elemental necessity (as Allen/Alvy says in the closing scene, "we need the eggs") and also a practical impossibility due to the general self-conscious alienation suffered by members of contemporary American culture—or at least by characters in Woody Allen films. Allen/Alvy's obsession with interpersonal (and, by implication, cinematic) communication virtually overwhelms the entire narrative enterprise at the conclusion of the film. After Annie has left for a Southern California recording career, Alvy meets her in a health food restaurant, reaffirms his love for her, and proposes marriage, only to be rejected by Annie, who wants to remain friends and avoid the hostility of marital proximity. Following a slapstick car crash sequence underscoring Alvy's dejection, the restaurant scene is reenacted on an empty stage by two characters closely resembling Alvy and Annie, only this time Annie accepts the proposal. Alvy turns to the camera and asks, "What can I say?—it was my first play."

Alvy Singer's first play, perhaps—but also Woody Allen's ninth film. Once again, and with abrupt finality, the ironic interfacing of author, narrator, and character ruptures the diegetic world of the narrative, this time to the point of casting the entire conceptual basis for the film into utter ambiguity. Are we to assume that the author-narrator—that is, Woody Allen the filmmaker—is any less manipulative for the sake of dramatic effect than is Alvy the playwright? Apparently not, which renders the status of the entire comic narrative unreliable and problematic.

Although its treatment in the narrative assigns the Alvy-Annie relationship a certain privileged status—at least within the comic narrator's autobiographical routine—it finally is relegated to the level of being yet another manifestation of the Groucho Marx gag model. The comedy routine itself, however, sustains its narrative integrity throughout, and thus there is a sense in which the film's narrative is a closed, hermetic one. Although the comic narrator intrudes directly on the Alvy-Annie story, especially during its dissolution, Woody Allen the *author* never *directly* intrudes on the comedy routine or the narrated autobiography. Thus Allen is able to play the film both ways, as it were, as a closed courtship story within a self-reflexive narrative context that is itself ultimately closed. We read *Annie Hall* both paradigmatically and syntagmatically—both metaphorically and metonymically—because of this narrative interfacing. The stream of associated events that follow the opening monologue sequence, including the courtship story, are finally paradigmatic variations on the model of the Marx gag, on the narrator's limited self-esteem and his inability to sustain interpersonal relationships. The integrity of the comedy routine itself, however, indicates Allen's final acceptance of at least the minimal conventions of narrative and character—it is the bit of representation, the bit of subject that Barthes spoke of earlier. In conclusion, then, we feel about narrative communication much the same way that Allen/Alvy feels about interpersonal communication: it may be crazy, but we need the eggs.

NOTES

1. Jonathan Culler, *Structuralist Poetics* (Ithaca: Cornell University Press, 1975), 190.

2. Judith Mayne, "*S/Z* and Film Criticism," *JumpCut*, nos. 12–13 (1977): 42.

3. Roland Barthes, *The Pleasure of the Text*, trans. Richard Miller (New York: Hill & Wang, 1975), 32.

4. Roland Barthes, *S/Z*, trans. Richard Miller (New York: Hill & Wang, 1984), 5.

5. Ibid., 5–6.

6. Robert Scholes and Robert Kellogg, *The Nature of Narrative* (New York: Oxford University Press, 1966), 240–65.

7. Henri Focillon, *The Life of Forms in Art* (New York: George Wittenborn, 1942), 10.

8. Leonard B. Meyer, *Music, the Arts, and Ideas* (Chicago: University of Chicago Press, 1967), 109.

9. Christian Metz, *Language and Cinema* (The Hague: Mouton, 1974), 151–62.

10. *Nature of Narrative*, 265.

11. *Pleasure of the Text*, 4.

12. Geoffrey Nowell-Smith, "Moving on from Metz," *JumpCut*, nos. 12–13 (1977): 10.

12

Autumn *Interiors*, or the Ladies Eve
Woody Allen's Ingmar Bergman Complex

Bert Cardullo

If without knowing anything whatsoever about the work of either director, one had seen Ingmar Bergman's *Autumn Sonata* right after Woody Allen's *Interiors*, one might easily have concluded that the Swedish filmmaker had attempted to imitate the American. For these works share the same cinematographic and editing style, the same concentration on a handful of overwrought characters, and the very same subject—namely, maternal domination. Of course, the reverse sequence is the correct one: since 1971, if not further back, Woody Allen had yearned to make what he thought of as a European film, preferably in the monastic style of Ingmar Bergman. Finally, in 1978 with *Interiors*, he made it, and fortuitously if not felicitously it resembles (at least in outline) the particular Bergman number that happened to be released in America at almost the same time. Since our view of the film Allen made depends to a great extent on the model he employed (the quintessential Bergman movie), we would do well to ask ourselves of what that model consists before judging the carbon copy.

Among the many obsessions of Ingmar Bergman that American critics have failed to note, or failed to question closely, is his pervasive resentment in his art of the achieved man and occasionally the career woman—doctor, lawyer, professor, business executive. From the evidence of his numerous films, Bergman hates every professional except the artist. Predictably, since he is a puritan, his defense of the artist as somehow sacrosanct has engendered a feedback of guilt: periodically, having enshrined the creative personality in one context or another, he seems driven to follow up with a thumping self-accusation of the artist as charlatan or as detached and inhuman being. You may be sure that Bergman in his heart does not believe this, but he needs to hear an answering echo that absolves him of his own accusation.

Thus *Autumn Sonata* is characterized by the same kind of ambivalence that undermined the artistic veracity of *Wild Strawberries* in 1957. In the earlier film, Bergman's portrait of an old professor, whose egoistic frigidity lost him an idyllic sweetheart and produced an impotent son, was at odds with the visibly sympathetic performance of Victor Sjöström. Just as Bergman was reluctant in *Wild Strawberries* to follow the implications of his own scenario by destroying the professor figure entirely, so in *Autumn Sonata* he sets up Ingrid Bergman as a concert pianist–cum–mother who is supposed to have crippled her two daughters (one child being insufficient for the force of his accusation); then the auteur becomes so enamored of the personality he has given his character that he is hard put to convince us she could possibly be either as indifferent or as ruthless as her articulate daughter maintains.

To synopsize this picture accurately for anyone who has not seen it is almost impossible since what takes place in *Autumn Sonata* beyond the severely limited action is completely a matter of individual interpretation. Every statement made by the characters is open to question, and the whole moral issue on which the film hinges is never depicted. The damaging relationship of which this mother-daughter confrontation is supposed to be the climax is not visualized in flashbacks so that viewers can judge for themselves; it is, rather, wholly summarized in verbal terms through the daughter Eva's accusatory retrospect.

At the beginning, reading her diary while she awaits the visit of her celebrated mother, Liv Ullmann as Eva seems pretty clearly, in her spinsterish appearance and manner, to be a manic-depressive type, melancholy and retentive but prone to fitfulness as well. We glimpse her husband hovering in the background, from which he scarcely emerges during the subsequent encounter; and we learn that since her son drowned some years ago at age fourteen Eva has kept his room as it was when he died and moons over photographs of him. This morbid devotion to the irretrievable contradicts the leading statement she reads from her diary: "One must learn how to live. I work at it every day." We further discover that, before her marriage, Eva had lived with a doctor, and that she had once had tuberculosis. Not until later in the film do we become aware that she is looking after her bedridden sister, who suffers from a degenerative disease that has affected her speech and movement and whom her mother believes to be in a nursing home.

When the mother arrives at this outpost of Ibsenism (Bergman's setting, for a change, is among the Norwegian fjords), it is not too surprising that, after the first affectionate exchanges are over, as Eva listens obediently to her parent's necessarily self-absorbed chatter (she has come, after all, from the world of professional music as practiced in European capitals), the daughter all the while regards the mother with mingled amusement and suspicion. In no time at all, suspicion has become hostility, and step by step Eva rebukes her mother's self-secured authority in a crescendo of bitter reproaches that mounts steadily into the realm of hysteria. The younger woman makes the distressed elder responsible for all the ills of her life and blames her, besides, for the condition of the drooling sister upstairs, whose presence in the house is an unwelcome shock to the fastidious visitor.

Following a long sequence of passionate denunciation by her daughter, which she stems only at momentary intervals, the mother, inwardly shaken but outwardly collected, leaves to fulfill another musical engagement. Then after a few solicitous suggestions from her husband—who, again, has passively remained on the sidelines of this internecine struggle being waged under his roof—Eva writes a letter to the departed woman in which she retracts the burden of the accusation she had hurled and makes a pathetic bid for love. This letter is in part read over the image of the mother, traveling south for her next concert.

Critics have generally received this film as if it were indeed a straightforward indictment by the neglected daughter of a selfish parent, which means that they accept at face value the allegations of the daughter and pay no attention either to the personality or the remonstrance of the mother. In fact we have only the daughter's word that her mother's inattention drove her into a messy relationship with the briefly mentioned doctor. What part any of this played in her contracting tuberculosis is never clarified. How satisfactory or unsatisfactory her present marriage is, one is left to infer. Whether her mother had an affair with someone named Marten without telling her husband, Josef, depends on which of the two women you believe, and what bearing this has on anything else is never made clear. One is also left to decide whether the mother's absence at a crucial hour was the impelling cause of the sister's disabling condition.

It is possible to take the other view, that Bergman intended the Liv Ullmann character to reveal herself unmistakably as a self-pitying neurotic, whose charges are patently canceled by the clearly delineated superiority of the mother. (One of the most telling moments in the film would then be Ingrid Bergman's correction, at the piano, of her daughter's playing of a Chopin sonata: if the girl is to give the piece an authentic interpretation, declares the mother, she must avoid sentimentality and understand that the music should express "pain, not reverie.") However, even this view of Bergman's strategy may be ingenuous; it is much more in his line to establish an impeccably distinguished persona, poised against an unattractive spinster who is nonetheless married, to make the latter's accusations appear at first unlikely, then the more convincing, precisely because the accused has the more sovereign air. (This mechanism was invented by Strindberg in his play *The Stronger*, from 1889.)

In truth, near the end of *Autumn Sonata*, Bergman loses confidence in his own gambit. He cuts, in the most excruciatingly obvious way, from the sick daughter writhing helplessly on the floor, to the entrained mother coolly informing her agent that her visit home had been "most unpleasant": in other words, she shrugs it off. Unless we are to suppose she is acting, this is outrageously unbelievable; it totally contradicts the character of the woman we have witnessed, in merciless close-up, for the preceding hour. Evasive or hesitant she may have been when justifying a given response or action recounted by the vindictive Eva, but never for a moment did one feel that she was radically false. Equally unacceptable, as the film ends, is the abrupt change of heart that dictates Eva's remorse for the vehemence with which she has been arraigning her mother—thereby canceling, at the last minute, the substance of the movie's unrelenting inquisition.

Critics in America consistently underrate this Swedish inability of Bergman's to commit himself to the terms of a moral choice he has ostensibly initiated—unless, that is, he knows for certain he has a target to which absolutely no one will object. There is small point in trying to weigh truth in the antithesis he has contrived for *Autumn Sonata*. At any latter-day Bergman movie, including the slightly earlier *Serpent's Egg* and the subsequent, aptly titled *From the Life of the Marionettes*, one cannot be sure whether this director-screenwriter is unaware of the dramatic incongruities that he creates through poor motivation or whether he doesn't really care. He seems indifferent to plot because a plot is an action consistent with the revealed nature of its characters, and Bergman seems unable to perceive consistency; his characters say what he wants them to say, to an end he alone has chosen, as opposed to what they would say if allowed to speak for themselves.

He used to be a master of comedy, as in his gloss on Renoir's *Rules of the Game* (1939), *Smiles of a Summer Night*—itself more or less remade by a spent Woody Allen as *A Midsummer Night's Sex Comedy* in 1982. For in secular, and even more so divine, comedy you can give free rein to the improbable, just as you can in a religious allegory like Bergman's *Seventh Seal* (if not in existential meditations of the kind exemplified by his "faith" trilogy of *Through a Glass Darkly*, *Winter Light*, and *The Silence*, which secured the reputation of Ingmar Bergman in America in the early- to mid-1960s). Lately, in 1992's *The Best Intentions* and *Sunday's Children*, both of which he wrote if not directed—actually even before them in *Fanny and Alexander*—Bergman has become a purveyor of the probable or the consistent only through the form of self-absorbing autobiography.

With all this in mind, we should not expect the mundane inventions of *Autumn Sonata* to have objective credibility; the characters' motives are flimsily explored, the actualities of their lives not dramatized but reported after the fact. If Eva knew so much about her mother's devices of evasion, for example, as well as about her own victimization at her parent's hands, she would long since have ceased to be a victim—or at the very least she would have remedied those absurd outer signs of her condition thrust on her by Bergman via his wardrobe department: I mean the old-maid's provincial hair bun and the disfiguring eyeglasses. Women's faces, preferably under stress, are what Ingmar Bergman likes to photograph; objective coherence he no longer cares to cultivate. Like many other films in his canon, *Autumn Sonata* is a private tribunal. Bergman himself is the confessor, prosecutor, and plaintiff and as neutral or uncommitted a judge as he can risk being.

Which brings us to Woody Allen and his perplexing, abject desire to make a film in emulation of the remote Swede, even to the point of using the arche typal Bergman actor Max von Sydow to confer legitimacy on his work. Impressed by the austerity of Bergman's style and by what he reads as the master's tragic view of life, Allen was faced at the outset with the dangerous problem of imposing a stark Swedish ethos on urban American material. Ever since *The Virgin Spring* in 1960, Bergman has as often as possible shut out not only the world of nature but also the world of people and things, of society at large, so that his agonists can battle nakedly with each other (or with a surrogate God), undistracted by the alternative points of view, the cultural frivolities, or even the earthly vistas that tempt the commonality of mankind. Allen's *Interiors* is far more populous than *Autumn Sonata* or any other late film of Bergman, so our comprehension of it is not delayed or derailed by a ground level of universal, symbolic reference; it can be summarized as a story line that holds together. Motivation or inducement, however, is another matter.

If *Autumn Sonata* is ambivalent because Bergman is playing a game with appearances, *Interiors* is eventually ambiguous because the calamities represented are in excess of the cause alleged. *Interiors* should have been the tragedy (or even the comedy) of a man's attempt, alternately assisted or opposed by his three daughters, to win his own soul by ridding himself of their mother, his wife. I say "should have been" because Allen's conception of that man is so feeble (in the Bergmanian tradition of the ineffectual male), and the performance of E. G. Marshall is so uninflected, that he emerges as a far less sympathetic character than the compulsively meticulous wife played with twitchy naturalism by Geraldine Page.

Arthur, as he's called, persists in his bid for freedom—he wants to go to the Mediterranean, presumably to be reborn—against the warnings of his plaintive wife, who threatens suicide before actually attempting it, and against the querulous protests of his daughter Joey, more closely identified with her mother than her sisters are, probably because her own identity is insecure (as yours might be, too, if you were burdened with a name normally reserved for the opposite sex). The father-husband returns from Greece uttering the same banalities as before—nothing about him has changed, not even his ties—together with a personable if clownish woman whom Joey indignantly and correctly describes as vulgar. When Arthur marries the creature, mother, sure enough, walks into the sea. Loyal Joey is all but drowned in a vain attempt to save her, and she in turn is resuscitated by the unrefined stepmother: which proves that this name-flashing tourist may be an ox in the drawing room, but when it comes to fundamentals she is the pragmatist who saves the day.

Implicitly, Eve the mother deserves her fate, for in the explanation given her (too late) by Joey, she felt herself too good for this world and so created another, of interiors—of decor and decorum—that had demanded, from those around her, responses too strict for any of them to meet. Yet it is difficult to imagine that everyone around Eve is as derailed as they all seem to be by an excess of good taste; to repeat, the calamities represented are in excess of the cause alleged. (No one suggests, incidentally, that an exquisitely dictatorial mother might have been the answer to a visibly bland father.) The articulated miseries of the daughters and their men are strenuously reached for and hence appear contrived. They are phony excavations of the interior—of interior life—whereas Allen's specialty has always been the humorously objective observation of exteriors, the coolly comic send-up of surfaces. Diane Keaton plays intelligently an unintelligent poet whose self-contempt is fairly inexplicable, since her ignorance should be her bliss. Similarly, her husband, a churlish literary genius who's fearful that he is not as good as the critics say, decides to assert his misgivings by trying to rape his sister-in-law, a television actress given to drug addiction.

As I suggested earlier, the whole embroilment is distorted by Allen's insistence on telling his story in a style alien to the milieu he provides, a style that transposes the tenor of an American metropolitan setting into the hushed and claustrophobic atmosphere of Bergman's Baltic. He opens *Interiors* with unornamented credits, no simultaneous visuals behind them, no music. The exposition features single-shot close-ups of two sisters, each looking out a different window, followed by a medium shot of a male who, gazing at an urban panorama, commences a narration to himself and to the audience—a familiar Bergman beginning. Allen's man has his back to the camera, perhaps to alleviate the shock of our eventual recognition that he is none other than the tepid Marshall, informing us, in an unlikely outburst of rhetoric, that suddenly in the course of his contented marriage he "found an enormous abyss opening at [his] feet." Too much of the dialogue thereafter is like this, the sort of talk that, in earlier Woody Allen vehicles, would have speedily led to a verbal pratfall, but here only makes for tragicomedy of the unintentional kind.

Allen tries hard—perhaps too hard—to keep his settings from becoming as cluttered or static as his language, staging crucial scenes at the dining table and in the bedroom, then in an empty church and at a beach house in an attempt to exile the everyday domestic world. Self-consciously he employs a camera at rest, passively framing close-ups of faces or middle-distance shots of a stationary group, except for moments when he is recalling other Bergmanian strategies. The most conspicuous of these is the tracking shot of two sisters conversing as they walk along the beach, which sententiously evokes the world of *Persona*. With every sequence Allen thus appears to have asked himself not, "How can I best shoot this?" but, "How would Bergman shoot it?"

Moreover, he ends his film with a strict reversion to the Bergmanian format that, at the same time, summons a whole repertory of understated curtain tableaux from post-Ibsenian drama. After church and the business with the white roses and the coffin, the three sisters are aligned in profile (a reminder of the opening shots, as well as of Chekhov's greatest play), staring at the sea. One says, "The water is calm," and another solemnly replies, "Yes, it's very peaceful." That Allen should have been trapped by so obvious an error as to believe that you can depict tragedy by imitating the surface of it from someone else's (already superficial) version—this, I must say, is truly amazing.

He was less gullible when less assured as a director. According to the biography of him by Lee Guthrie (which, significantly, was withdrawn from distribution shortly after the opening of *Interiors*), the comedian once admitted that, although he admired the films of Bergman, they could only be a *bad* influence on his work "because they're so antithetical to comedy."[1] He went on to explain that Bergman interested him more than any other filmmaker, owing to "the consummate marriage of technique, theatricality and themes that are both personally important to me and that have gigantic size—death, the meaning of life, the question of religious faith" (75).

In a later declaration, Allen was prepared to throw previous caution to the wind and reach for just those "gigantic" themes, which he was now translating as "more personal" than those of his contemporaries. From the same source, we get the following statement: "I'm not sure any American film maker makes the kind of movie I want to make. I don't want to do films like *Bonnie and Clyde* or *Mean Streets* or *Badlands*. . . . To me, serious American movies always have one foot in entertainment—and I like more personal drama, though there may not be a market for it. The drama I like is what you see in the plays of O'Neill and Strindberg and Ibsen—and in foreign films" (173).

God forbid that a "serious" movie should have one foot in the swamp of entertainment! And as if *Annie Hall* and *Crimes and Misdemeanors*, to name only two of Allen's seriocomic films, don't try to entertain at the same time as they confront—however lamely or indecisively—significant themes. But there you have it: the puritanical hunger for the High Serious, the discontent with authentic veins of American subject matter. Such material may not be shot through with the subtle values of living to be found in European movies—you know, all that wisdom, refinement, and tendresse—but it is nonetheless vital in its consideration of the harsh characteristics of so much of American life: baseness, greed, and brutality.

Incidentally, this coupling of O'Neill and Strindberg on the part of Allen is meaningful. Strindberg was the artistic stepfather of Eugene O'Neill, who successfully transplanted the Swede's suffocating ethos into American settings and who, for his part, like the Bergman of *Smiles of a Summer Night*, managed to write only one comedy (*Ah, Wilderness!* in 1932) among his many works for the theater. The Swedes flattered O'Neill and his solemn sensibility back by staging all his plays at Stockholm's Dramaten in addition to awarding him the Nobel Prize in 1932 (before he had written his great naturalistic dramas, I might add). Strindberg is also, of course, the single most influential figure behind all Bergman's work, although the filmmaker seems to substitute excessive love for women for the dramatist's extreme antipathy toward them.

Indeed, the "rehearsal" in *After the Rehearsal* is of one of Strindberg's plays, a number of which Bergman himself has directed for the theater, and *Autumn Sonata* may derive its inspiration from that mad master's chamber drama titled *The Ghost Sonata* (1907). For all its avant-garde theatrical devices, this early twentieth-century work is not unrelated in theme either to its Bergmanian namesake or to Allen's *Interiors*, for Strindberg attempts in his autumnal *Ghost Sonata* to penetrate the naturally deceptive or mediating facade of verbal language, as well as of bourgeois exteriors—not only through the visual eloquence of scenic design, but also through the abstract purity of musical form.

The sympathetic link between these Swedes and the Americans is the fundamental puritanism they culturally share. (Bergman's Nordic damnations are taken far less seriously, for example, by the English, the Italians, or the French.) It has been said that the smothering family atmosphere in certain Bergman films, even as in Strindberg's naturalistic *The Father* (1887) and O'Neill's *Long Day's Journey into Night* (1941), appealed to Allen by reason of his special Jewish vulnerability to comparably oppressive parents in his own environment. I would not wish to pronounce on this probability, if probability it is, but I suspect that the driving force behind Allen's wistful Bergman worship is rather an aspiring intellectual's love of conceptual perfection and a confusion of it with the less-is-more aesthetic of Scandinavian reductionism, together with an obsessive love for women that Allen confuses with a desperate need to validate his narcissistic love for himself.

Be that as it may, the truth is that it takes more independent imagination, greater cinematic scope, and a richer sense of life's poetry to make *Bonnie and Clyde* (1967), *Mean Streets* (1973), or *Badlands* (1973); *Midnight Cow-*

boy (1969), *The Wild Bunch* (1969), or *Chinatown* (1974); *Raging Bull* (1980), *House of Games* (1987), or *Tender Mercies* (1983) than it does to make *Interiors*. Unlike a host of American movies in which the citizenry's blindest self-satisfactions with the status quo are upheld or in which the most immoral and fantastic projections of callow romanticism, spurious religiosity, or miserable sentimentality are indulged, these films insist on writing down contemporary American society as they see it: a society alarmingly animated by powerful minority factions that are debased and selfish when they are not downright criminal and that is grotesquely peopled by a fringe of parasites surrendered to listless perversions or violent exploitations or, alternatively, populated by a growing number of decent yet subsocial creatures who lead unexamined if not unworthy lives; that is forever encumbered by a floating majority, pitifully bewildered, vulgarized, and juvenile; and that is sadomasochistic at its core, hence wanting in all resolution, guidance, and dignity except perhaps in time of war. If this is not the whole truth about the American experience, it is that part of the truth most commonly suppressed for public consumption.

What, by contrast, is Woody Allen's *Interiors* centrally about? Certainly not "the meaning of life"—a silly predication for any work of art, just as it would be silly to argue that *Autumn Sonata* is really about the nonexistence of objective truth. And though the rejected wife and mother kills herself, *Interiors* is in no awesome way about death. The people involved are not tragic, although some of them would like to be; they tend instead to be hysterical, obtuse, or pathetically abusive. Their behavior more closely resembles that of the pseudointellectual New Yorkers of Paul Mazursky's films, who simultaneously know too much about one another and bitch all the time at their own limitations. Is this quality what makes the movie, for Allen, "more personal"? Is this the quality that he admires in *Scenes from a Mall* (1980), Mazursky's absurd take, starring Allen himself, on Bergman's *Scenes from a Marriage*?

As his first screen "drama," then, *Interiors* is an embarrassing episode in Woody Allen's career, to be followed by such others as *September*, *Another Woman*, and *Alice*. It represents a feeble struggle to escape from his more authentic self, an incredible concession to the snobbish misgiving that comedy is an inferior art—something that doubtless would be news to figures as diverse as Aristophanes and Molière, Charlie Chaplin and Billy Wilder. *Interiors* additionally reveals a filmmaker's mistaken assumption that one can create great art by consciously setting out to do so, according to this or that recipe, instead of intuitively using artistic means to capture for all eternity an image or idea of humanity.

Allen used to be a funny guy, heretofore having exercised a welcome talent for parody and a shrewd recognition of the clichés by which many American urbanites live, if he has not allowed his comedic talent to develop much beyond the gag-and-skit stage of *Take the Money and Run*, *Bananas*, *Everything You Always Wanted to Know about Sex*, *Sleeper*, and *Love and Death* (1975; which is the stage where he began as a writer for television in the 1950s). As a showman, he has developed a professional eye when choosing a cinematographer, a lively ear for the musical score, and a refined taste in actresses. (Although not in actors: witness his casting of himself in the leading roles of his comic and semicomic films, which a better actor [such as Dustin Hoffman] would make even wittier, yet his exclusion of himself from his utterly serious movies, where he could perhaps do some humorous good!)

What on earth compelled, indeed continues to compel, Allen to settle for less and sell his art short by aping a mode of cinema in which he has had to inhibit himself, instead of releasing his better inspiration or instinct, is a problem for him to resolve; the movies may be the last place in which he can do so. He certainly didn't help his cause with such a narcissistic meditation on the filmmaking experience as *Stardust Memories*, itself a rip-off of Fellini's *8 1/2* (1963), even as the comic fantasy of the vastly overrated *Purple Rose of Cairo* is lifted in reverse form from Buster Keaton's *Sherlock, Jr.* (1924).

And to say that he has resolved his artistic dilemma by striking a balance between the solemn and the funny in movies like *Annie Hall*, *Manhattan*, *Hannah and Her Sisters*, even *Crimes and Misdemeanors* and *Husbands and Wives*, is to miss the extent to which such pictures fail as genuine—dare I say Chekhovian?—tragicomedy. Rather than combining the serious and the comic into a unique new form, they just irresolutely lay the two elements side by side, or overemphasize one at the expense of the other, against the backdrop of culturally rich, culturally hip, psychically neurotic New York, which these films expect to do the real work of "meaning" for them. In movies like these. Allen is continually sending love letters to himself and to that province of provinces, Manhattan, and I for one don't enjoy reading other people's mail. A woman once told me that I should see *Hannah and Her Sisters* with someone I love. I don't know what she could have meant by this exhortation, given the film's solipsism, and I'm glad I didn't see it with her!

But, some people will say, those artsy Europeans, especially the French, love Woody Allen. Yes, well, they loved Samuel Fuller and Don Siegel not so long ago, and look where that got us. Europeans think that Americans (read: New Yorkers) are fabulously nutty at the same time that they believe America (read: New York) is wonderfully glamorous. *That's* why they love Woody Allen, Manhattan diarist. New Yorkers and all who aspire to be New Yorkers like *Annie Hall*, *Manhattan*, and *Hannah and Her Sisters* (among other Woody vehicles) because these films congratulate them on their choice of city in which to live and because these people think that Allen is the cinema's answer to drama's Chekhov: serious, comic, and deliciously melancholic, all wrapped up in the same tidy little package. One, just one, difference between Allen and Chekhov (it's difficult to join their names in the same sentence) is that the latter had some distance on himself and life, to put it mildly. Irony played a large part in his art, as did his knowledge of the theatrical tradition that had immediately preceded him. Allen loves himself and New York so much, he's nostalgic about both before the fact, to the point of making it and his own person the real subject of his movies.

Penultimately, it may be worth remarking that while Bergman's *Autumn Sonata* and Allen's *Interiors* alike are postulating the destructive consequences of perfectionism in life as in art, each film's director has, in his own way, been aesthetically pursuing the absolute or the ideal like mad: Bergman, the recreant preacher, with immaculate cinematic compositions that achieve their immaculateness at the expense of worldly or natural conception: Allen, the derelict stand-up comic, by aspiring to place himself among the most mirthless geniuses of our era. And both men, in the case of *Autumn Sonata* and *Interiors*, by not-so-coincidentally choosing central characters with the primal name of Eve.

Allen has said that such films of his as *Manhattan Murder Mystery* and *Mighty Aphrodite*—itself a parody of the original murder mystery *Oedipus the King* (430 BC)—mark a return to his "earlier, funnier" brand of filmmaking, to which I can only respond, "too little, too late." So desperate is he to return to previous form or prior success that his 1996 movie *Everyone Says I Love You* nearly abandons reality altogether for the childish world of musical comedy, a world toward which Allen's Gershwin-and-Porter-driven soundtracks have been moving for some time. (Allen himself plays the clarinet, sometimes professionally, which tells me he may have missed his true vocation.) Except that "real" New York, in the form of carefully selected views of Manhattan's loveliness, is still on hand in this movie to be adored and to provide the action with a backdrop—ironically, the best word to describe the direction Woody Allen's career has taken since he went deep years ago and made the fateful *Interiors*. As for the oft-made, desperate-seeming remark about what a competent *director* Allen has become, all that I can say is, with his bankroll and artistic support system, I too could become a competent director after so many pictures. To echo André Bazin on auteurs, competent director, yes, but *of what*?

LIST OF WOODY ALLEN FILMS MENTIONED (AS DIRECTOR)

Take the Money and Run (1969)
Bananas (1971)
Everything You Always Wanted to Know about Sex (1972)
Sleeper (1973)

Love and Death (1975)
Annie Hall (1977)
Interiors (1978)
Manhattan (1979)
Stardust Memories (1980)
A Midsummer Night's Sex Comedy (1982)
The Purple Rose of Cairo (1985)
Hannah and Her Sisters (1986)
September (1987)
Another Woman (1988)
Crimes and Misdemeanors (1989)
Alice (1990)
Husbands and Wives (1992)
Manhattan Murder Mystery (1993)
Mighty Aphrodite (1995)
Everyone Says I Love You (1996)

LIST OF INGMAR BERGMAN FILMS
MENTIONED (AS DIRECTOR)

Smiles of a Summer Night (1955)
Wild Strawberries (1957)
The Seventh Seal (1957)
The Virgin Spring (1960)
Through a Glass Darkly (1961)
Winter Light (1962)
The Silence (1963)
Persona (1966)
Scenes from a Marriage (1973)
The Serpent's Egg (1977)
Autumn Sonata (1978)
From the Life of the Marionettes (1980)
Fanny and Alexander (1982)
After the Rehearsal (1984)

NOTE

1. Lee Guthrie, *Woody Allen: A Biography* (New York: Drake, 1978), 75. Hereafter cited by page number.

13

Woody Allen's *Manhattan* and the Ethicity of Narrative

Christopher J. Knight

Like Shakespeare's so-called problem plays, Woody Allen's *Manhattan* raises all kinds of difficulties with respect to genre classification and basic interpretation. Is it a comedy or a serious drama? Is it a critique of a decadent milieu, or does it itself exemplify what is apparently critiqued? Is the narrative actually Isaac's representation, or is he himself one represented character among others? Is Tracy the object of some perverse Humbertian desire, inscribed within a patriarchal system of representation, or is she a fitting Other for Isaac, twice divorced and twenty-five years her senior?

Of course, the temptation when dealing with an Allen film is to mix and match characters or actors with their assumed counterparts (e.g., Isaac and Mary with Woody Allen and Diane Keaton or with Alvy and Annie in *Annie Hall*). Such is the consequence of fame and of repertory casting. Yet if one only compares *Manhattan* (1979) to *Annie Hall* (1977), the film with which it is most coupled in people's minds, one will be forced to note the extraordinary unlikeness. True, both films take as their main theme the difficulty of perpetuating friendships and, more pressingly, love relationships in the contemporary city. But the two films have very different points of view. In the earlier film, *Annie Hall*, the point of view is clearly that of Alvy Singer. The story is his story, even as the subject is, more or less, about another (Annie). And while Alvy is not a completely unsympathetic character, the way he frames his story forcefully reminds us, as Laura Mulvey writes, of just how often woman comes to stand in patriarchal culture as signifier for the male other, bound by a symbolic order in which man can live out his fantasies and obsessions through linguistic command, by imposing them on the silent image of woman still tied to her place as bearer of meaning, not maker of meaning. (7)

The same thing cannot, I think, be said of *Manhattan*. True, the film opens with Isaac Davis reading drafts of his manuscript; yet he addresses himself not, like Alvy, to the audience but to himself. His is an overheard conversation with himself. He does not frame the narrative but is part of that narrative, and the difficulties he experiences in fixing upon the best opening for his book (which is to say the best reading of New York City, his subject) thematize the difficulties of interpretation itself. The desire "to get things right," it seems, always must reside with the fact that we continually get things wrong, that error is an inevitable component of the epistemological ambition.

When compared to *Annie Hall*, then, the sense of framing or of space in *Manhattan* seems much more Shakespearean. By this I mean that there seems to be room for a multiplicity of voices and life styles. A lesbian ethic (practiced by Jill and Connie) shares the same space (albeit not always harmoniously) with that of a guarded, Jewish, liberal male chauvinist (Isaac), which shares the same space with that of a Waspish, heterosexual feminist (Mary), which shares the same space with that of a Waspish womanizer (Yale), and so forth. Certainly, a certain privileging takes place, as the camera and the narrative itself are proportionately more attentive to Isaac. (He is in most of the film's scenes.) Yet the privileging is not of a particularly coercive color. It does not, that is, require a silencing of all the other voices, but rather assumes this otherness as being a necessary part of what any one voice is about. The film's title is not *Manhattan* without reason.

Yet if *Manhattan* is as much about a milieu as about a singular character, this does not mean that it forfeits the right to articulate an ethic as such. Certainly, to look back again to *Annie Hall*, Alvy Singer, as both narrator and framer, was in a special position to make ethical judgments. This did not mean, or force the viewer to accept, however, that these judgments were synonymous with the film's ethic. Rather, this overriding ethic was not anything that could actually be reduced to words per se. Instead, it functioned in a more allegorical fashion, suggesting rather than stating, exemplifying rather than positing. As Hillis Miller has written about the significance of allegory,

> Allegory, like parable, is a way of hiding and revealing at the same time. It hides for those who seeing see not and make the fatal mistake of reading literally. It reveals to those who can see what is hidden behind the veil of the thematic narrative. Allegory makes the esoteric exoteric. It says something otherwise in the agora or public square, where all who run may read. (25)

And if it might be said that the ethic of Annie Hall is not synonymous with that offered by Alvy Singer, it can be even more readily said with respect to *Manhattan* that its ethic does not reduce itself to any one voice. It is not, for instance, reducible to Isaac's remarks "about decaying values" nor is it reducible to even Tracy's more generous judgments. But if this is so, what then is the ethic of Manhattan? And what is its relation to the "law as such." The answer, according to some of the more recent and influential thinkers on the matter of ethics, would appear to have something to do with narrative itself.[1] Miller himself writes, "Ethics itself has a peculiar relation to that form of language we call narrative,"[2] so much so that one could say that "without storytelling [there can be] no theory of ethics" (14).

What seems particularly noteworthy about narrative here, be it film narrative or any other kind, is that it begins to set up a series of expectations that, while not immediately cognizable, are nevertheless recognized as being part of a promise, a promise whose fulfillment always resides in the future. As Derrida writes, narrative "gives or promises," particularly in the experience of its aporicity, "the thinking of the path, provokes the thinking of the very possibility of what still remains unthinkable or unthought, indeed, impossible" (132). It suggests the law as such.

But if narrative shows rather than tells what the law as such is, it will require a more particular kind of response from us. Specifically, it will require that we not try to reduce it or pin it down. It will require a certain act of renunciation on our part. And because it does so, renunciation itself becomes part of the ethical equation—an equation that is not necessarily bound by history. (Derrida speaks "of a sort of narrative [rather than historical] fable—or rather, that of a story which certain people know how to tell about something which, finally, is not historical" [36].)

Allegory and renunciation, then, become ways of broaching the matter of the law as such. The ambition becomes not to discover (this not being possible) but to discern this other, this thing that is never seen face to face but always as if through a glass darkly. The consequence is that one is required to put even the "key question" forward in terms of an example, as Isaac (half drunk and sitting at a table at Elaine's restaurant) does in the film's opening scene:

> Listen to this example I'm gonna give. If four of us (*Smacking his lips together*) are walking home over the bridge (*Inhaling*) and then there was a person drowning in the water, would we have the nerve, would one of us have the nerve to dive into the icy water and save the person from drowning?[3]

The film itself, which of course constitutes what might be thought of as simply a larger pattern of exemplification, offers no dogmatic declarations, no definitive answers, yet at the same time it does push in the direction of what, in its own right, might be called the law of renunciation; it does promote the belief that less is more. This being the case, many of the film's characters can be judged in terms of the degree that they acknowledge this unstated law. Not surprisingly, Mary and Yale, the two characters least respectful of the law, are also the two characters who at film's end, when fortunes are usually if prematurely tallied, appear to be less well situated, it being understood that their romance has an extraordinary quality of the temporary about it. Mary, for one, often seems to set herself in adverse relation to the law of renunciation. Most pointedly, she refuses to give up her hold upon Yale, even as he is a married man and even as holding him requires that she seriously injure both Emily and Isaac. Mary, as she says, does not wish to be a "home wrecker," yet at the same time she cannot seem to find the happy balance between fulfilling one's own needs and giving way to the bona fide needs of others. What she deserves is construed by Mary less in terms of what she gives up than in terms of what she is. As she, in a moment of frustration, most revealingly says, "It's just—I'm beautiful and I'm bright and I deserve better" (228).

Yale also has a hard time acknowledging the law of renunciation. Like Mary, he chooses to hold on to what (his extramarital affair with Mary) when held can only once again lead to his hurting two of the most important people in his own life, Emily and Isaac. Yale thinks that, as he himself says, "I'm not the type for affairs" (237), yet he is far from strict with himself on this point. Not only has he had affairs before, but he is also unprepared to acknowledge the ethical relevancy of his behavior. Falling back upon the weak, even pathetic, defense that, in his own words, "I'm not a saint" (265), Yale, when confronted by Isaac about what he has been and is doing, refuses the obvious ethical dimension: "Don't turn this into one of your big moral issues" (264). Yet if it isn't a moral issue, what is it? Yale does not rightly know; he just knows that while he encouraged Isaac in his affection for Mary, he nevertheless holds first claims on Mary's affections for the reason that he "liked her first!" (264)

Again, the point is that Yale, like Mary, prefers, for selfish reasons, not to do anything more than faintly acknowledge the moral categorical imperative. This leads to a situation in which Isaac must lecture Yale on the point of his omission:

But you—you're too easy on yourself, you don't see that?! You know, you . . . you—that's your problem, that's your whole problem. You—you rationalize everything. You're not honest with yourself. You talk about . . . you wanna—you wanna write a book, but—but, in the end, you'd rather buy the Porsche, you know, or you cheat a little bit on Emily, and you play around the truth a little with me, and—and the next thing you know, you're in front of a Senate committee and you're naming names! You're informing on your friends! (265)

As Miller, Derrida, and before them, Kenneth Burke emphasize, the categorical imperative has a distinctly linguistic aspect about it. While we are not obliged "to say that the grounding is 'nothing but' language" we are obliged to acknowledge "that it is at least language (as distinct from 'the sense')" (440). That is, language, by its nature, "drives toward the 'ultimate' of itself. And the ultimate is 'Justice,' a kind of completion whereby laws are so universalized that they also apply to the lawgiver" (440). The simplest way of stating this (Kant's principle of the categorical imperative) in linguistic terms, says Kenneth Burke, whom I have been quoting, is to "suppose that I begin with a purely selfish, utilitarian command, '*Thou* shalt not kill *me*.' Next, I universalize the pronouns, so that everyone is a *thou* and everyone is a *me*. When this cycle is formally completed, I end by 'freely' commanding *myself* not to kill *others*" (440).

It is in this sense (that of the judge who is then judged by his or her own completed linguistic act) that Isaac must be understood. But before giving our attention to Isaac, the most problematic character here, we should perhaps turn our attention to Tracy, for she of course represents, in her respect for the law of renunciation, the antithesis of both Mary and Yale. At age seventeen, Tracy is, ironically, the film's most mature character. She is not an ideal character, as some might suspect her of being, but a woman who chooses to live her life in a particular way, a way that in itself involves difficult decisions. Of course, the most difficult decision that Tracy makes is to date a man twenty-five years older than herself. While the film does not problematize this decision as it is understood from Tracy's point of view, it is nevertheless a decision that is enacted out within the film's borders and therefore subject to being the object of our own selective attention. And here, as I say, Tracy freely chooses to bestow her affection upon Isaac even as it means giving up, in Isaac's less-than-kind roll call, "Billy and Biff and Scooter and, mm, mm, you know, little Tommy or Terry" (246).

The point is that, while Isaac chooses to dismiss his potential rivals as no more than adolescent boys, it is not likely that these same boys would treat Tracy in as patronizing a fashion as he himself does. That is, few would likely be so unkind as to turn back Tracy's avowals of affection with such rejoinders as, "You should think of me . . . sort of as a detour on the highway of life" (189). That Tracy puts up with such insensitivity is not indicative of the fact that she has no options; rather, it is a demonstration that she sees this behavior in its larger context. Which is to say that while Isaac can be boorish and unconsciously hurtful, he is also a man of wit, charm, and conscience, qualities that are not lost on Tracy.

Tracy herself does not idealize love, at least not necessarily, and when pressed to define it by Isaac, she does a better-than-passing job of concretizing the emotion, telling him, "We have laughs together. I care about you. Your concerns are my concerns. We have great sex" (245). At the same time, this emotion is expressed within the context of giving up, of renunciation. That is, loving Isaac the way she does, Tracy chooses not to extend this same quality and kind of affection to any other. It is both singular and special, and its singularity enhances its specialness both for the giver and the receiver. Thus it is at film's end that Tracy can say to Isaac, as she prepares to leave for a six-month acting program in London, "What's six months [away from one another] if we still love each other?" Her meaning, of course, is that what is given up in terms of time spent alone, apart from one another, will be more than made up for in the aftermath when they are once more together. Less is more, if they truly love one another.

All of this—Tracy's ability to give up something real and concrete in the present for something that unpalpably presents itself as a promise to be fulfilled in the future—follows from a basic trust in the relations about her. Trusting in these, in the unreadable laws that even in their unreadableness still hold out, in Derrida's words, "an other thinking, an other text, the future of another promise" (133), Tracy is able, by extension, to place her trust in people themselves, in the belief that "not everybody gets corrupted" (271). For, as she tells Isaac, "Look, you have to have a little faith in people" (271).

Those who care about Woody Allen's films know this last scene—and here I am speaking not only in more narrowly circumscribed narrative terms but also in cinematic terms, terms that include in addition to the spoken text, camera angles, montage, actors' gestures (such as Tracy's brushing of her hair, her chuckle, Isaac's final half smile)—to be the closest thing to perfection in his work. It expresses all that his films, cumulatively taken, would say, though saying just what this is, remains of course not so easy. Still, this expressed ethic has something to do with respect, respect for a law that is known allegorically only. This law, in turn, has a decidedly ethical dimension, though again what exactly this dimension is remains, and will remain, problematic. In any case, Tracy here is one who, through her own will, decides to live in as much harmony with this law—that is, with her sense of it—as possible. To give way to sentiment, she is, in Isaac's words, "God's answer to Job" (277).

Yet if Tracy is in fact "God's answer to Job," why then does Isaac treat her as badly as he does? The point is that of the four characters (Mary, Yale, Tracy, and Isaac) who most take hold of our attention here, Isaac is the one who presents the greatest difficulties in terms of our response. He is, as I said before, the most problematic character. And he is problematic for the reason that while, unlike both Mary and Yale, he would judge others in the light of an intuited ethical and transcendental law, he (when the "*thou* shalt not . . ." directed toward others completes its full linguistic circle and comes back to "*I* shalt not . . .") himself does not always shine at his best when measured this way. Which is to say that, while Isaac is a man of conscience, he does not always find it possible to live by it.

As I said earlier, Isaac appears most unlikable and most unethical in his treatment of Tracy, particularly in the way that he drops her. For if throughout his relationship with her, he has treated her in an offhand manner because, in Isaac's thinking, she was too young, the way that he drops Tracy appears more than just insensitive, but also deceitful. Isaac, of course, chooses to break up with Tracy for the reason that he has already entered into another relationship with Mary, though this is not, at first, the reason that he gives to Tracy for wishing to separate. Rather, he explains things in terms Tracy herself recognizes as being advantageous not to him but to her. He does not, he says, want her to get "too hung up on" him. When she protests that she is not "hung up on" him but "in love with" him, he resorts to that most self-serving of arguments in this situation: that neither she nor he knows what love is—"You can't be in love with me. We've been over this. You're a kid. You don't know what love means. I don't know what it means. Nobody out there knows what the hell's going on" (245).

In any event, Isaac, despite twinges of conscience ("Why should I feel guilty about this?" [246]), gets what he immediately wants: a breakup with Tracy so that he might more fully pursue his affair with Mary. He acts then not in a completely unforgivable way but nevertheless in a way that puts a distance between himself and the audience and that lends support to the otherwise too emphatic tone of his ex-wife's charge, put forward in her scandalous publishing success, *Marriage, Divorce and Selfhood*, that

> he was given to fits of rage, Jewish, liberal paranoia, male chauvinism, self-righteous misanthropy, and nihilistic moods of despair. He had complaints about life but never any solutions. He longed to be an artist but balked at the necessary sacrifices. In his most private moments, he spoke of his fear of death, which he elevated to tragic heights when, in fact, it was mere narcissism. (259)

At the same time, here, it needs to be said that neither Isaac's weak showing during his breakup with Tracy nor his ex-wife Jill's overly harsh estimation of his character represents the final word respecting his person. It might once again be seen as a sign of his hubris that Isaac, jokingly, admits to modeling himself after God: "I gotta model myself after someone!" (265). Yet this would be to see things too narrowly, to see only the hubris but not the real concern with moral and ethical values, values that (as the joking reference to modeling himself after God suggests) are not unconnected with religious longings and beliefs. Certainly, it seems that the numerous references (even when made in the form of expletives) to God and even to Jesus present themselves as a sort of veiled appeal to authority. And what goes along with these appeals is an interest in the Socratic question of how one should live one's life, an interest in the ethical question itself. A good illustration of this is, of course, that scene in which Isaac pulls Yale out of his classroom and across the hall into another classroom, empty except for two skeletons near the door:

> Jesus—well, what are future generations gonna say about us? My God! (*He points to the skeleton, acknowledging it at last*) You know, someday we're gonna be like him! I mean, y-y-y-y-you know—well, this is what happens to us! You know, uh, it's very important to have—to have some kind of personal integrity. Y-you know, I'll—I'll be hanging in a classroom one day. And—and I wanna make sure when I—thin out that I'm w-w-well thought of! (265)

The point is that despite his lapses Isaac does possess a remarkable "personal integrity." This integrity is not rooted in talk only (though his conversation is, as we have seen, unusually peppered with discussions of ethical import) but also in action. Examples, both small and large, are numerous enough, but we might do well to concentrate on just two: the first, Isaac's ethical stance vis-à-vis Mary; the second, his ethical stance vis-à-vis Tracy. Respecting the former, Isaac finds himself, soon after meeting Mary, not only her confidant but also her potential lover. That is, Mary, frustrated by Yale's unavailability both in terms symbolic (he is married) and real (he spends weekends with his wife), starts, in a small way, to make overtures to Isaac, asking him out for a walk in the park, then a bite to eat. There is nothing wrong with this, yet with Isaac, one senses that he is being drawn into a situation that is as yet not clearly defined, that has every potential for developing into a triangular affair. To his credit, Isaac, who has developed a real interest in being the recipient of Mary's affection, nevertheless hedges when Mary presses him about further dates, politely pushing such get-togethers into some distant, indefinite future: "I don't think it's such a good idea for me. I'm, you know, I'm working on this book" (224). In fact, Isaac does not actually assume the role of Mary's lover until he has been urged to do so by Yale, who now—at least for the moment—is of the opinion that he needs to put his own house in order, that he is not one for affairs. So while Isaac once found it necessary, in his earlier trip to the Hayden Planetarium with Mary, to restrain himself from "a mad impulse to throw [her] down on the lunar surface and commit interstellar perversion with [her]" (241), he now finds his path to Mary's heart unblocked. In a sense, by his respecting the law of renunciation ("I would never in a million years, you know, interfere in anything like that" [240], referring to the prior affair of Mary and Yale), Isaac is rewarded according to the formula that less is more. But here, of course, things are a little more complicated.

They are more complicated because the context is more complicated. While Isaac waits for Mary to be free of Yale, he dates Tracy, leading her on not so much by what he says—for he is always quite adamant about theirs being a short-term affair ("You know, I want you to enjoy me, my—my wry sense of humor and—astonishing sexual technique, but never forget that, you know, you've—you've got your whole life ahead of you" [189])—as by what he does: that is, he continues to date her. Isaac can, if he chooses, close the gap in one of two ways: he can actually break up with Tracy, or he can acknowledge to her and to himself that his affection is more profound than temporary. In time, of course, he does both.

Clearly, Isaac is the most problematic character here, for the reason that he is so torn between two poles: between acting in accordance with his conscience or in accordance with his more immediate self-interest. Like Yale, Isaac is not a saint, yet he would choose to be one if the getting there were not so difficult. As things stand, Isaac is conscious of having compromised his own values, though the testimony to this consciousness does not come so readily. Still, it does come in moments such as the one in Elaine's cafe when Isaac, having had too much to drink, starts, in response to Yale's complimenting Tracy, to blather about how he could beat up Tracy's father:

(*Drinking his glass of wine and nodding his head*) Mm, but she's seventeen. (*Smacking his lips together*) I'm forty-two and she's seventeen. (*Coughing*) I—I'm dating a girl wherein I can beat up her father. It's the first time that the phenomenon ever occurred in my life. (183–84)

Here, I do not mean to suggest that Isaac makes an ethical mistake by dating a seventeen-year-old woman, twenty-five years his junior. My only point is that the fact bothers Isaac, bothers his conscience. He identifies the matter as a serious ethical question, one about which he is uncertain. This uncertainty, in turn, colors all his interactions with Tracy. That it does so is, as I have said, most unfair to Tracy. Later, given the nature of Isaac and Tracy's affection for one another, the matter will be recognized as really being a moot ethical issue. But the way things stand at first, the age difference does pain Isaac and not without reason, for the depth of his affection for Tracy, and hers for him, has neither been tested nor securely established.

Tracy herself is the first to use the word *love* in connection to their (Isaac and Tracy's) relationship. Yet even when she does so ("I think I'm in love with you" [189]), there is a note of qualification in her voice, a note that, while it soon disappears, is significant as it indicates just how short-lived the relationship is and how unformulated as yet are the terms of the commitment. Isaac too will come, eventually, to understand that his feeling for Tracy is more than infatuation, that it is love, but he is at first too obsessed with the matter of age difference to recognize this. Ideally, he should have worked out his feelings on this matter before engaging Tracy in a relationship. That he did not is less a sign that he acted wrongly with respect to

Tracy than that he acted crudely and insensitively. Nevertheless, Tracy finds herself unfairly abused, abused for the fact that she is seventeen.

Isaac, then, does treat Tracy badly, but he also redeems himself by eventually being honest with himself, by acknowledging the depth of his affection for Tracy and by relegating the issue of age to the closet where, in this instance, it belongs. As he says to Emily in a kind of postmortem discussion of their individual love lives (that is, before he convinces himself of the rightness of seeking Tracy out): "I think of all the women that I've known over the last years, when I actually am honest with myself . . . tsch, I think I had the most relaxed and the most, you know, the nicest times with her" (266).

Having made the confession, Isaac is at first reluctant to act upon the belatedly recognized fact that he loves Tracy. He is reluctant for ethical reasons. He has already hurt Tracy too much and does not yet trust himself not to hurt her again. Asked by Emily why he does not phone Tracy, Isaac says: "No, I would never do that. I think I blew that one" (267). Love requires trust—in oneself as well as in another—something that Isaac is just beginning to fully understand. Still, his regard this way for himself (not to speak of Tracy) is not so deficient that, in the end, he would allow it to hold him back from pursuing her affection. When he does so, running down to Gramercy Park where she lives, the outcome presents itself as a culminating lesson in the law of renunciation: Tracy's affection is his if he can but wait six months for her return from London. The suspicion is that he can.

Woody Allen's *Manhattan* is a moral tale, but the moral (presented as it is by way of exemplification rather than statement) is not singularly or absolutely ever read. The parable-like nature of the narrative allows one to get where one could not get any other way, but the disheartening fact is that having been taken there, one can only passingly state where it is one has been. In *Manhattan*, one is, I would argue, afforded, allegorically, a glimpse of an ethical law that when stated might be spoken as a law of renunciation. That other laws might be glimpsed and passingly read is understood; that other critics will do so in the future is accepted almost as an absolute.

NOTES

1. I particularly have in mind Hillis Miller in *The Ethics of Reading* (New York: Columbia University Press, 1987) and Jacques Derrida in *Memoires for Paul de Man*.

2. From Miller's paper, "Is There an Ethics of Reading?" presented at the School for Criticism and Theory, Dartmouth, summer 1986. My argument here is inspired by Miller's own.

3. While I do not wish to confuse the film with its published script, I will, for the sake of convenience, mark quotations from the film with pagination information in the latter (*Four Films of Woody Allen*), 182.

WORKS CITED

Allen, Woody. *Four Films of Woody Allen*. New York: Random House, 1982.

Burke, Kenneth. "A Dramatic View of the Origins of Language and Postscripts on the Negative." In *Language as Symbolic Action*. Berkeley and Los Angeles: University of California Press, 1966.

Derrida, Jacques. *Memoires for Paul de Man*. New York: Columbia University Press, 1986.

Miller, J. Hillis. "Is There an Ethics of Reading?" Paper presented at the School for Criticism and Theory, Dartmouth, summer 1986.

Mulvey, Laura. "Visual Pleasure and Narrative Cinema." *Screen* 16, no. 3 (Autumn 1975).

14

Ciao, Woody
Stardust Memories

Louis Giannetti

Woody Allen's *Stardust Memories* (1980) did not do well at the box office, and though the film received a few favorable notices, the critical consensus was generally negative. The principal complaints: (1) the movie is narcissistic and self-indulgent, and the protagonist (a thinly veiled self-portrait) kvetches nonstop because the world does not devote itself to making Woody Allen happy; (2) the film is derivative, its debt to Fellini's *8 1/2* (1963) verging on plagiarism; (3) the picture is arty and pretentious; and (4) most damaging of all, it's not funny. Most of these complaints are superficial and ungenerous. Woody deserved better.

The charge of narcissism is implicitly based on the assumption that Woody Allen and Sandy Bates, the film's protagonist, are essentially the same person. Certainly there are similarities: both are well-known filmmakers, both are New York Jewish intellectuals, both are wryly ironic, and both have problems dealing with women and their own feelings about women.

But there are also important differences. Woody is often political in his comedy; Sandy is uncomfortable with politics. Woody has total independence as an artist; Sandy is at odds with his producers, who meddle with his work to make it more commercial. Woody's biggest box office hits, *Annie Hall* (1977) and *Manhattan* (1979), are works from the same period and were strongly admired critically; Sandy's latest films were critical and commercial bombs. Woody has a strong need for privacy and rarely grants interviews or promotes his films publicly; Sandy is surrounded by fans, interviewers, critics, business associates, groupies, and moochers. Woody is clear-sighted about his artistic goals and knows what he wants and how to get it; Sandy is confused, ambivalent, artistically paralyzed. In short, Woody is real. Sandy is fiction. It's surprising how many confuse the two.

Bad poets borrow, good poets steal—or so said T. S. Eliot, who was not above a little literary larceny himself. Woody does much the same with Fellini's *8 1/2*. That is, he steals, he doesn't borrow. The maestro has been pillaged before: by Paul Mazursky in *Alex in Wonderland* (in which Fellini makes an appearance) and Bob Fosse for *All That Jazz*. In fact, *8 1/2* has almost become a genre unto itself—a ready-made form with its own aesthetic conventions. Artists in every medium are attracted to genres because they provide a structural framework, a set of expectations to play off, or subvert.

Allen doesn't imitate *8 1/2*, he transforms it, creating ironic and comic contrasts between the world according to Federico and the somewhat less grand world according to Woody. For example, the fantasy sequence at the opening of *Stardust Memories* is both a parody of, and a homage to, the opening of *8 1/2*. Sandy Bates, looking forlorn and depressed, is sitting in a stationary train car, waiting. When he glances at the other passengers, he sees nothing but Fellini-like grotesques, looking more forlorn and depressed than himself. The scene, eerily silent, is photographed in the same surrealistic style as *8 1/2*. Sandy looks out his window, and in a train car parallel to his own, he sees a swinging party in progress, filled with beautiful people. A gorgeous chick tantalizes him with a come-hither smile, then kisses her window pane seductively. Excited, Sandy leaves his seat to switch train cars, but as he does so, the train pulls out, reducing our hero to impotent hysteria as he flails at the car door.

Actually, *8 1/2* is itself a variation of the *Grand Hotel* formula. (So named after the 1932 MGM movie that featured an assortment of characters from different walks of life, unified by their presence at the same hotel.) Fellini's startling innovation was to intercut scenes from the protagonist's past, fantasies, and dreams with the realistic episodes that take place at a bizarre health spa, where the film director hero hopes to shore up his sagging spirits as well as his body. Mired in a midlife crisis—both personal and artistic—he's immobilized by indecision.

Similarly, in *Stardust Memories*, Sandy Bates is the main attraction at a weekend film culture seminar, which takes place at the movie's principal locale, the Stardust Hotel, an old-fashioned hostelry snuggled in a woodsy setting. While there, he meets an assortment of weird characters. Some of them are real, some imagined, some from his past, others from his fantasies, dreams, and nightmares. Like Fellini, Allen intercuts these episodes in such a manner as to deliberately disorient the viewer. We're never sure if what we're watching is real, a flashback to Sandy's past, or a projection of his anxieties and fears. Sometimes all three are fused simultaneously. Like Fellini,

Allen is suggesting that the differences can be merely academic. To Sandy, they're all "real"—broken images from the mosaic of his fractured psyche.

The film's structural complexity allows a maximum of flexibility and expressiveness, freeing Allen to explore a variety of themes. A conventionally plotted movie, on the other hand, would have restricted him to a much narrower range. (Unity, consistency, and singleness of purpose have never been Allen's strong points, anyway.) Most of the ideas he explores revolve around his three thematic staples—art, love, and death. They include the search for the perfect woman, the transience of love, self-contradiction, the enervating toll of celebrity and fame, the lack of faith in relationships, artistic illusion versus crass reality, the inexorability of decay and death, and the search for meaning in the moral void of contemporary life.

These are serious themes, but the movie is often funny as well. Unfortunately, unlike *Annie Hall* and *Manhattan*, Allen is not always successful in integrating the comedy with the seriousness. Rather, the two tend to alternate, serving as foils to each other. The *range* of his humor, however, is broader in this work than in any other Allen film. Much of the comedy in this picture is found in the slapstick sequences from Sandy's earlier movies— like the *Frankenstein* parody/homage in which Sandy tries to fuse the beautiful body of one woman with the brilliant intellect of another in an attempt to create a perfect woman.

Not all of the slapstick is meant to represent Sandy's earlier, funnier films. One of the most endearing episodes deals with Sandy's problems with his housekeeper-cook. Flaky, jittery, and bewildered, she can barely see through her Coke-bottle eyeglasses, much less perform such subtle tasks as lighting the oven without creating a conflagration in the kitchen. One of the silliest scenes is the UFO convention, during which Sandy defensively attempts to justify himself to a group of disappointed extraterrestrials: like everyone else, they prefer his earlier, funnier films to his recent work.

The scene in which Sandy visits his neurotic sister and her wacko husband is a comic gem. As the door opens on our hero, the surprised sister lets out a squeal of delight. She ushers him into her living room, which is crowded with party guests and is furnished in a cacophony of bad taste. A fat and grossly unattractive female, her face battered and bruised, is introduced. Without a hint of embarrassment, the sister announces that the poor creature was gang-raped. Obviously a proponent of letting it all hang out, the woman calmly explains to everyone within earshot that she didn't fight her attackers, but suffered her indignities stoically. Boisterously vulgar and a little bit cruel, the sequence—like most of Allen's best comedy—is absurd, human, and rather touching.

The visual style of *Stardust Memories* is richly textured. In his beginning years as a filmmaker, Allen was relatively unconcerned with such aesthetic niceties as cinematography, editing, and mise-en-scène. His emphasis was almost exclusively on performance and script. Hence, his early films, like *Take the Money and Run* (1969), have a cheap, home-movie crudeness to them. *Bananas* (1971), though punctuated with outbursts of comic brilliance, is often sloppy in its visuals. Allen eventually developed more facility as a stylist. The images of *Everything You Wanted to Know about Sex (But Were Afraid to Ask)* (1972), an anthology film, are frequently inventive. Even more compelling is the pop surrealism of *Sleeper* (1973). None of these movies, however, could be described as technically distinguished. *Love and Death* (1975) is the weakest film of this period. Its script is slapdash, its acting amateurish, and its visuals a throwback to the crudities of his novice years.

With *Annie Hall* (1977), Allen began to pay more attention to his visual style. The movie was photographed by Gordon Willis, one of the most gifted of contemporary cinematographers. Willis is at his best in atmospheric low-key films. Most of his major assignments have been dark films: *The Godfather*; *The Godfather II*; *Klute*; *All the President's Men*. He also photographed the exquisitely mounted—and underrated—*Interiors*. It was in this movie that Allen proved himself as a directorial technician, for the ideas and emotions are communicated as much by the mise-en-scène as by the acting and script. In *Manhattan* Allen was able to fuse the spontaneity of his early works with a polished visual style, without sacrificing his wit as a writer or his charm as a star. The film's black-and-white photography is rhapsodic in its romanticism: evocative, tender, poetic. Willis believes that a good movie leads the audience along, allowing them to get caught up in the film without being aware of what the people behind the movie are doing. He prefers "magic" to tricks.

Stardust Memories is steeped in magic, thanks in part to Willis's cinematography—once again in low-key black and white. It's no small measure of his artistry that he is able to pay homage to the cinematography of Gianni Di Venanzo in *8 1/2* without sacrificing his own ideas. Willis's most poetic images have a stark simplicity to them, as he often prefers what isn't there to what actually is. The characters are frequently photographed as fragile silhouettes at dusk or as white specks against a black background. Sandy Bates's all-white apartment provides some striking white-on-white compositions. The film also features several arresting process shots that correspond to the various levels of reality in the movie. In one sequence, for example, we see a flashback of "The Amazing Sandy"—a magic act that Sandy performed as a boy. Suddenly Sandy's present-tense mother and psychiatrist appear in front of this past-tense sequence, commenting on its significance as a determining factor of his spiritual malaise.

The stylistic sophistication of *Stardust Memories* is by no means confined to the cinematography. Allen has studied the masters well. In addition to *8 1/2*, there are visual allusions to Fellini's *La Dolce Vita* and *Amarcord*. The influence of Allen's other cinematic idol, Ingmar Bergman, can be seen in a variety of scenes. For example, the sequence in which Sandy visits a mental hospital where his former lover, Dorrie (Charlotte Rampling) is a patient is strongly indebted to Bergman's *Persona*. The episode is shot in a series of medium close-ups of Dorrie talking to the camera, which simulates Sandy's point of view.

Allen's staging is occasionally reminiscent of the works of Antonioni as well. The characters are often separated by architectural obstructions or confined to space cubicles in the mise-en-scène. A good example of the Antonioni influence can be seen in a single-take sequence in which Sandy places a transatlantic telephone call to another lover, Isobel (Marie-Christine Barrault). The screen is split roughly in half. Though we can hear Sandy's voice clearly, he is hidden from view behind a wall on the right half of the image. We are allowed to see only his hand, which is dangling a pair of sunglasses, on the left side of the frame. (Throughout the film, Sandy uses his sunglasses to keep people at a distance and to soften the harsh glare of reality.) Sandy's evasiveness is conveyed through the juxtaposition of his tender words with the cool endistancing of the mise-en-scène—paradoxically revealing while it's concealing.

Not that *Stardust Memories* is without faults. Allen sometimes lapses into the Neil Simon disease—the inclusion of snappy one-liners that are often funny but out of character or inappropriate to the dramatic context. In his harshly critical review of the film, Andrew Sarris points out that Allen's tone is sometimes confused, and confusing. The scene he cites takes place in Sandy's apartment, which is decorated with a huge photographic blow-up of the famous TV image of a handcuffed Vietcong guerrilla being shot point-blank by a South Vietnamese officer. During this sequence, Sandy complains that he can no longer make funny movies in a world filled with human suffering. Are we meant to take this seriously, Sarris asks, or is Allen satirizing Sandy's more-sensitive-than-thou pretentiousness? The sequence is also clumsily staged, perhaps because its tone *is* confused.

The most damaging flaw of the movie concerns its three main female characters. Two of them are sketches rather than fully developed personalities. Isobel, an earth-mother figure, has two children by a former marriage—which Sandy helped to destroy. He is attracted to her in the abstract, terrified by the reality—especially the reality of her yelping youngsters. Isobel is given little to do in the movie except to symbolize the concept of domesticity. Similarly, Daisy (Jessica Harper) is a mysterious girl Sandy meets—and is attracted to—on his film-culture weekend. She is apparently bisexual, a sometime violinist, and lives with a pompous young film professor. Her function is primarily to sympathize with Sandy and accompany him on various expeditions.

The major female character is Dorrie, the great love of Sandy's life. She is unpredictable, bright, vulnerable. She also drives him up the wall with her paranoid insecurities. Charlotte Rampling, who plays the character, is a fine-looking woman and an accomplished actress, but she lacks warmth and personal charm. (Where was Diane Keaton when Woody needed her most?) It's difficult to see why Sandy puts up with Dorrie, why she haunts him even after their affair has long since soured. We have to take her irresistibility on trust: it's not much dramatized.

Stardust Memories is probably too ambitious and diffuse for audiences in search of easy entertainment. Though the film is flawed and uneven, it towers above the dismal fare of American cinema from the same period. In time, it'll probably be critically upgraded. It may even become a classic. For the record, when Fellini's *8 1/2* was released in 1963, virtually every commentator in Europe and America dismissed it as formless, narcissistic, and self-indulgent. Even Pauline Kael, perhaps our finest critic, pronounced the movie incoherent. In a 1972 poll of international critics, conducted by *Sight and Sound*, the prestigious British journal, *8 1/2* placed fourth in their list of the ten greatest films of all time.

15

Painful Laughter
The Collapse of Humor in Woody Allen's *Stardust Memories*

Paul Lewis

At the edges of humor lurk despair and fear and helpless pain. Have you heard the one about the farmer's daughter and the traveling rapist? What did one tumor say to another? How many corpses does it take to change a light bulb? If these questions were presented not as part of an essay on painful humor but as actual joke lines, how would you react to them? Would you be disgusted, sickened, or amused? Or would you feel torn between the impulse to laugh and a feeling that these are subjects too painful to laugh about?

The proximity of humor to pain has long been recognized. Aristotle, the father of superiority theories, described comedy as a depiction of minor deformities, imperfections, and miseries. Not overestimating the human capacity for compassion, Thomas Hobbes defined humor as the "sudden glory" that arises when people apprehend "some deformed thing in another, by comparison whereof they suddenly applaud themselves."[1] This element of sadistic delight led Baudelaire to his extreme conclusion that humor is an expression of satanic perversity. And Freud argued that wit is a disguised venting of normally repressed sexual and aggressive impulses, a *game* of attack and ravish or attack and destroy.

Empirical psychologists have demonstrated that this celebration of pain has a point of diminishing returns, that, for instance, great pain is not the stuff of humor. Laughing at the pain of others requires a lack of identification with and a distance from those who are suffering.[2] The more widely pain is distributed, the more intense it is, the more difficult it becomes to laugh at it. It is one thing to giggle at an old man's flatulence; it is another thing to learn that it is the result of inoperable and terminal disease.

In recent years students of humor, both psychologists and literary critics, have fixed on the view that humor requires our awareness of an incongruity as a necessary, if not a sufficient, condition. We laugh when we realize that our sense of the expected has been temporarily subverted, disrupted, or jarred. In *The Art of Laughter*, Neil Schaeffer summarizes a good deal of current thinking when he argues that humorous "laughter results from an incongruity presented in a ludicrous context," that is, "a context based on the absence of rationality, morality, and work."[3] Refuting Freud's view that wit is a safety valve for immoral impulses, Schaeffer argues that humor is amoral, that it arises in an atmosphere in "which moral concerns temporarily, at least, are constrained from interfering" (28). Schaeffer's point is that during the experience of humor the moral sense enters a state of "suspended readiness" (30). Our willingness to enter into the spirit of any particular joke is based on our sense that it would not be wrong to laugh at whatever the joke exploits.

In the early and largely unconscious stages of our reaction to a joke, a conflict may arise between our impulse to be offended by inappropriate humor—to say, "There is nothing funny about that"—and a counterimpulse to laugh. Although different issues or subjects bring this conflict to life for each of us, the conflict itself is universal, a device or at least an indicator of self-definition. Humor supports and clarifies our sense of values by delineating that about which we are in dead earnest, which reminds me of a Tom Swifty many people would find offensive but for different reasons. One group laughs at women's libbers, another at born-again Christians, another at Moonies, and another at gays. Our laughter creates inverted images of our nonlaughing selves, leering fun-house reflections, but there are parts of ourselves—ideas, subjects, situations—that we refuse not to take seriously.[4]

The instant in which we consider the acceptability of a given joke seems to me to be an unwelcome but valid metaphor of humor in our age. It is unwelcome because we would rather not see obstacles in the path of humorous pleasures, rather not regard ourselves as unamused and unamusing. But it is a valid metaphor because the pressing incongruities of a world minutes from global death but teeming with life, torn between need and abundance, between stupidity and beauty, can seem anything but funny.[5] In a world of woe no pain is minor or remote.

The problem is larger than trying to decide whether particular examples of painful humor—Mel Brooks's "Springtime for Hitler," references to spastics or cripples, ethnic jokes—are in poor taste. The problem has to do with the nature of humor in our inescapably genocidal century. Humor in our day seems suspect, like reading a newspaper filled with tales of cruelty and mutilation—of a babysitter who smothers children, of an old woman raped by teenagers, of poisons moving up the food chain and into our bodies, of the random slaughter of civilians—and then coming to the funny pages. In this context, that is, in the context of our lives, humor can seem inappropriate or superficial or immature: a cocktail party on board the Titanic.

Defensive irritation can arise on both sides of this conflict. If one seriously questions the value of humor, some people will quickly protest that humor, so productive of delight, needs no defense. I can hear Sir Toby Belch roaring mindlessly down the centuries at the compulsively serious Malvolio, "Dost thou think, because thou art virtuous, there shall be no more cakes and ale?" But, as Sir Toby needed to learn, there is no easier way to offend than by treating with humor what the other regards as sacred or malevolent or dangerous. "But seriously, folks," is the ironic refrain of the stand-up comic, but successful comics know there are limits to what serious subjects can be joked about safely.

The dispute between Sir Toby and Malvolio is another fitting image of the plight of humor in our time, perhaps because it is increasingly difficult to maintain a sense of balance, to avoid feeling that either everything or nothing is funny. The minor deformities, the lesser miseries, that were the source of most traditional comedy and joking still make us laugh, but they can seem beside the point. Cuckolds and misers, seducers and nerds, all seem remote from our fears, improper representatives of what we need most to change. The result is that humor has become a mixed blessing: either a mindless evasion or a painful reminder of our condition. Unable to keep pain at a distance, we are caught between the punch line and its punch, held in the moment before laughter.

The conflict in our culture between the longing for and a suspicion of mere laughter was demonstrated by the reception of Woody Allen's *Stardust Memories* (*SM*; 1980), a comic exploration of misery.[6] Perhaps because of its apparent obsession with neurotic urbanites, Allen's work in general, as he often points out, has not achieved the box office success of less thoughtful comedies. But the critical hostility and popular neglect *SM* received was unusually severe. Unwilling to confront Allen's questions about humor, many filmgoers were offended. Others found the film unpleasant, which indeed it is if we define pleasure as the successful denial of painful truth.

In the film, Allen plays the part of Sandy Bates, a writer-director idolized as a comic genius but trapped by his sense that the world is too depressing to support or justify or allow humor. Over and over during a film weekend at the Stardust Hotel, Bates is assaulted by a chorus of fans and reviewers demanding that he stick to comedy, that he continue to make funny films. But Bates does not want to talk about his early comedies, which in some moods he now regards as "stupid little films" (1:14). His despair is cosmic; at the outset he asks, only half in jest, "Hey, did—did anybody read on the front page of the *Times* that matter is decaying? Am I the only one that saw that? The universe is gradually breaking down. There's not gonna be anything left" (1:13–14). The action of the film is Bates's anguished search for a point of view that will allow him to deal honestly with his sense that pain is inescapable and still satisfy his admirers.

Critics have been too quick to see Bates's problem as a thinly disguised re-creation of Allen's own dilemma as an artist, an exercise in perverse, self-punishing narcissicism.[7] Robert Hatch argues that, because this is "the most intensely personal of his pictures," *SM* comes as close as Allen can to being tiresome," and Pauline Kael, seeing Sandy Bates as "the merest pretext . . . of a character," argues that the film suffers from Allen's inability to "step back from himself." An interesting version of this criticism is Stanley Kauffmann's complaint that Allen is "trying to equate the world with his own view of himself, smearing dat ole debbil Jewish self-hate over everyone." And for Judith Crist, *SM* is a long "kvetch." But we need not accept at face value Allen's assertion that the film is in no simple way autobiographical to see that Bates's tsuris is a metaphor for a universal dilemma.[8]

Another common criticism of *SM* is that, by failing to be either humorous or serious, it achieves only a desperate unpleasantness. Extending the biographical fallacy, Robert Asahina insists that as much as Allen "wants to be considered a serious film maker and philosopher, the comic in him is hungry for laughs, and the conflict produces a movie neither funny nor profound. . . . Sandy makes gratuitous references to Vietnam and to the Holocaust . . . in a desperate stab at *unearned* gravity."[9] About Sandy's enlarged photograph of the Saigon murder of a helpless Vietcong captive, Pauline Kael wonders, "Is this evidence of Bates's morbidity, or is it how he proves that he's politically or socially with it? Is there any way it can't be a joke? What is going on in this movie?" What is going on in *SM* is an examination of the limits of joking. The conflict between humor and sorrow is not the inadvertent mood of the film but its central thematic concern.

"To be or not to be," says Jack Benny over and over again in the Ernst Lubitsch classic comedy about the Nazi occupation of Poland, interrupting Hamlet's suicidal soliloquy to ogle his wife's lover and to allow the audience to recover from a siege of laughter. To laugh or not to laugh, wonders Sandy Bates as he looks around at a world ruled, to put it as cheerfully as possible, by ugliness, stupidity, and pain. The issue is captured perfectly in a metaphor that both begins and ends the film, revealing Bates's evolution. At the start of *SM* we are shown the ending of the film Bates is working on. In the film, Bates is in a train car surrounded, like a preppie in Dachau, by freakishly unpleasant passengers: weepers, starers, and nose pickers. Amid the crush of grief, Bates feels trapped. Across the track he sees another train, this one filled with female college students and fraternity revellers, dressed in furs and drinking champagne. These two trains—one characterized by untempered sadness, the other by foolish mirth—are an allegory of Bates's problem: how to acknowledge human pain and maintain a sense of humor, how to ride both trains or neither. The sequence that ends Bates's film but starts Allen's concludes with a twist: both trains are headed to the same garbage dump; in the end, as Bates later explains, "no one is saved."

We quickly gather that Bates is plagued by personal difficulties: he is being audited by the IRS; his doctor has had him using carcinogenic shampoo for eight months; his producers want to take over the final editing of his film; he is unable to make a commitment to another person; and he is depressed by the death of a young friend. "The guy was thirty years old, never sick a day in his life, and then suddenly, out of left field, amyotrophic lateral sclerosis. It was horrible! He was laying there in the hospital, his body degenerated like Lou Gehrig" (1:13). Everywhere Bates turns he is forced into contact with either a fan demanding humor or a reminder of human suffering. Among the flow of admirers seeking to have him autograph their left breasts or to inscribe an autograph to "Phyllis Weinstein, you unfaithful, lying bitch" (4:3) move a horde of philanthropists seeking the great filmmaker's help in raising money for leukemia victims or political prisoners. Gasping for breath in the face of this onslaught, it is no wonder that Sandy is coming to feel that there is finally nothing funny about life.

The rhythm of *SM* throbs back and forth between laughter and pain, poking at the ragged edges between the two. Bates's description of his friend's death is preceded (but not prepared for) by satirical portraits of his press agent, manager, and accountant:

Sandy: What . . . do you want me to say? I don't want to make funny movies anymore. They can't force me to. I . . . I look around the world, and all I see is human suffering.

Manager: Human suffering doesn't sell tickets in Kansas City.

Sandy: Oh!

Press Agent: They want laughs in Kansas City. They've been working in the wheat fields all day.

Sandy: Hey, fellas, I'm getting a headache. Can I please get some privacy?

Accountant: Your problem is ya never got over Nat Bernstein's death.

Sandy: Of course I never got over . . . The guy was thirty years old . . .
(1:12–13)

Just as we begin to relax and enjoy the exposure of the greasy commercialism of these manipulators, Allen snaps us out of a humorous frame of mind, shifting contexts abruptly. How can we relax, he forces us to ask, when the pain that people do not want to see after a day in the wheat fields is everywhere? This rhythm is the only constant in a film that shifts from past to present, from memory to desire, from interior to exterior images. Never are we allowed the comfort of an uninterrupted laugh; always pain waits. Another early conversation, this one in a flashback to Bates's relationship with a disturbed woman named Dorrie, illustrates this emotional dynamic:

Dorrie: That aftershave. It just made my whole childhood come back with a sudden Proustian rush.

Sandy: Yeah? That's 'cause I'm wearing Proustian Rush by Chanel. It's, it's reduced. I got a vat of it.

Dorrie: (chuckles) Mm. Why don't I just run down and get some food and we'll stay in tonight and I'll cook.

Sandy: Well, the last time you cooked the kitchen looked like Hiroshima. (1:15)

It is easy to be outraged by particular events or remarks in *SM*. Pointing to the capricious nature of fate, Bates observes that "if I'd been born in Poland, or in Berlin, I'd be a lampshade today" (3:40). We are not intended to sit back and laugh about concentration camps; we are intended to pause at the brink of humor and wonder what this concentration camp of a world has left us to laugh about.

The scene in which Bates escapes from the hotel to visit his sister is typical in the way that it vacillates between dark humor and tragic mirth. The tone for this scene is set as Bates arrives in the middle of a yoga party and is reintroduced to his sister's friend, Irene, a short, unattractive woman who has the signs of a recent beating on her face. Immediately we learn that Irene has been brutally robbed, beaten, and raped. Bates's sister makes a point of providing full details: that Irene was tied to her bed and raped repeatedly. We have just enough time to notice that Irene's T-shirt has the word *sexy* written on it. Before this bit of antihumor has a chance to sink in, we follow Bates through the living room and into his sister's bedroom where his brother-in-law Sam is incongruously "meditating and exercising" (3:12). Death, it seems, sits on Sam's bobbing shoulders as he pedals an exerciser, smokes a cigarette, and gets nowhere at all:

Sam: I had two heart attacks . . . before I got the bicycle.

Sandy: And since?

Sam: I also had two. (3:13)

And the scene ends with a private chat between Bates and his sister about their parents. She says "Dad's gonna be eighty. . . . In good shape. Mom's blind in one eye . . . deaf in one ear." And groping for a gag, Sandy breaks in, "Oh, I hope the same side of the head, right? Because that's important so she's even" (3:17).

Death, rape, old age: the stuff of life, but also the very raw materials of humor. The issue in *SM* is clear: humor, though much in demand, seems somehow to be in poor taste. Those who most desire laughter—the voracious fans, the money-hungry studio moguls, the trainload of revellers—all lack judgment and depth. In a world of pain, of random violence, of sudden annihilation, what are we all laughing about?

The answer to this question comes slowly to Bates whose formulation of the issue has been too extreme, too much an either-or proposition. We see a softening in his approach toward the end of the film when Bates imagines that he is speaking with a creature from another planet. The extraterrestrial he encounters—whose voice resembles that of a twelve-year-old Bronx High School of Science senior and who claims to have an IQ of 1600—refuses to discuss the ultimate problem of existence. When Sandy asks whether there is a God and, if so, why there is so much human suffering, the spaceman replies, "These are the wrong questions" (4:34). And when Bates asserts that "the human condition is so discouraging," the spaceman replies, "There are some nice moments too." In the end this intellectually gifted alien advises Sandy not to try to save the world: "You're a comedian. You want to do mankind a real service? Tell funnier jokes" (4:35). Although Sandy protests, saying, "Yeah, but I—I—I've gotta find meaning," we see him regaining his appreciation of humor not as an answer to philosophic questions but as a desirable experience.

We see his reviving interest in such moments in his fond recollection of a perfect spring afternoon with Dorrie, and we see it directly worked out in the resolution of Bates's on-again-off-again relationship with Isobel, a French woman who has just taken her two kids and left her husband to be with Bates. Although he has rejected her, fled from *her*, throughout the weekend, in the end he follows her onto a train and declares his love:

Sandy: I'm telling you, I was, I was, I was thinking about a lot of unusual things over the weekend, and I feel much . . . I feel lighter. Do you know what I mean? And, and, um . . . I had a very, very remarkable idea for a new ending for my movie, you know? We're, we're on a train and there are many sad people on it, you know? And, and I have no idea where it's headin' . . . could be anywhere . . . could be the same junkyard. And, uh . . . But it's not as terrible as I originally thought it was, because, because, you know, we like each . . . other, and, and, uh, you know, we have some laughs, and there's a lot of closeness, and the whole thing is a lot easier to take. (5:10–11)

Because the setting is the same, it is impossible not to compare the gloomy ending of Bates's film with the more positive resolution Allen achieves. The point is not that love, in the process of conquering all, justifies humor, but that it is possible to be outraged and depressed by pain and still laugh.

This approach to the film may help to explain a point that has troubled some critics: the way the wall-sized photographs in Bates's apartment-office keep changing. One time we see an enlarged asylum patient, another time the Saigon political murder, and then a famous Marx brothers poster. For all the apparent lack of connection between them, these pictures are as related as the moments in a day. Humor and pain are not contradictory, because they are moods not propositions, understood and arranged not by logic or argumentation but by our opacity to experience them.

SM is not the most profound or moving treatment of painful humor. It is not *King Lear* or even *The World According to Garp*. But Allen's film is revealing because it is much better than its critical and popular receptions suggest and because the hostility it received was based on Allen's refusal to do what was expected, indeed demanded, of him: to make mindlessly funny films. There is nothing narcissistic about Allen's problem as a comic writer in an age of genocide and famine; his effort to see misery and to laugh is universal. Dust to dust, indeed, but we are stardust as well, with memories that glisten and then rot.

One of the pieties of our culture is that humor is good for the soul, that a good laugh won't hurt you. But to what extent is this attitude a corollary of our determination to ignore or deny or minimize our awareness of pain? Are we, in our misery, our mortality, our vulnerability, pathetic second bananas, providing with our blood the occasion for a last laugh we will never get? These questions are the starting points for the exploration of the limits of humor in *SM*, a film that, refusing to settle for either humor or, pain, twists, combines, some would say mangles, the two. But this mangled laughter may be all that survives of humor in the face of pain.

NOTES

1. Thomas Hobbes, *Leviathan* (Harmondsworth, Middlesex, UK: Penguin, 1968), 125.

2. For an overview of efforts to refine superiority theory through experimentation, see Lawrence Le Fave, Jay Haddad, and William Maesen, "Superiority, Enhanced Self-Esteem, and Perceived Incongruity Humour Theory," in *Humour and Laughter: Theory, Research, and Application*, ed. Anthony J. Chapman and Hugh C. Foot, 63–91 (London: Wiley, 1976).

3. Neil Schaeffer, *The Art of Laughter* (New York: Columbia University Press, 1981), 17, 159. Subsequent references to *The Art of Laughter* will appear in the text.

4. See Paul E. McGhee, *Humor: Its Origin and Development* (San Francisco: Freeman, 1979), 238–39, for a discussion of this conflict.

5. For a clear summary of this conflict transposed from affective response to literary debate, see Richard Duprey, "Whatever Happened to Comedy," in *Just off the Aisle*, 149–56 (Akron, OH: Newman Press, 1962); and Clara Claiborne Park, "No Time for Comedy," *The Hudson Review* 32 (1979): 191–200. Both Park and Duprey note the collapse of our ability to participate in the good will and redemptive self-criticism of traditional comedy, but for Duprey this is a natural, if unfortunate, result of "the ever present fear of contemporary life," while for Park it is a sign of our wallowing in unrealistic and compulsive pain.

6. All references to *Stardust Memories* are to the continuity prepared by Gelula & Co., September 24, 1980. I am grateful to Mr. Allen for his assistance in obtaining this continuity. Reference to *SM*, including reel and page numbers, will appear henceforth in the text; quotations will omit camera descriptions.

7. The following reviews, quoted here, reflect the dominant response to *SM*: Robert Hatch, *The Nation*, October 25, 1980, 418–19; Pauline Kael, *The New Yorker*, October 27, 1980, 183–90; Stanley Kauffmann, "Intimation Through Imitation," *The New Republic*, October 11, 1980, 20–21; Judith Crist, *Saturday Review*, December 1980, 85. See Jack Kroll, "Woody's Identity Crisis," *Newsweek*, October 8, 1980, 71, for a review that appreciates the fusion of humor and pain in the film.

8. Allen has been protesting the biographical interpretation of *SM* since the film was released. A protestation appears in the *Boston Globe*, July 11, 1982, p. 69, cols. 2–5, and p. 76, cols. 1–2.

9. Robert Asahina, *New Leader*, October 25, 1980, 19–20.

16

Mysterious Illnesses of Human Commodities in Woody Allen and Franz Kafka

Zelig

Iris Bruce

> The thought of helping me is an illness that has to be cured by taking to one's bed.
>
> —Franz Kafka, "The Hunter Gracchus"

> The good walk in step. Without knowing anything of them, the others dance around them, dancing the dances of the age.
>
> —Franz Kafka, *Wedding Preparations in the Country*

Woody Allen's *Zelig*[1] (1983) satirizes the social and political movements of early twentieth-century society, in which the protagonist Leonard Zelig and everyone around him dance along. Leonard Zelig makes headlines in the late 1920s when he is out of step with his world and becomes famous as the human chameleon who takes on the personal and physical characteristics of

I would like to thank the students in my "Kafka after Kafka" class, WLC 392 (1996), at the University of Western Ontario for their stimulating discussions about Kafka and Woody Allen. Many thanks also go to Ehud Ben Zvi, Don Bruce, Michael Greenstein, and Stanley Corngold for their inspiration, criticism, and encouragement.

individuals whom he encounters. Various attempts are undertaken to cure
Zelig's deviant behavior and to reintegrate him into society, but there is little
success. Instead of being cured, Zelig becomes a performing freak and is exploited by a sensation-hungry public and profit-seeking individuals. During
the various stages of his struggle to both fit in and resist, there are echoes and
correspondences with the work of Franz Kafka, many of whose protagonists
attempt to retain a sense of selfhood in a commodified world. *The Metamorphosis* (1912) in particular serves as an intertext for *Zelig*, but links can also
be established between Zelig and Karl Rossmann (*Amerika* [1913]), the performing ape Rotpeter ("A Report to an Academy" [1917]), and the hunger
artist ("A Hunger Artist" [1922]). All these protagonists are involved in a
similar struggle for personal integrity that is time and again frustrated by
repressive and exploitative societal norms and presuppositions. A major difference between the two artists, however, is that Woody Allen is re-creating
an earlier period from a late twentieth-century point of view, whereas Kafka
is writing from within the social and racial discourses of his time. In addition, the very different social realities for each artist, as well as their use of
different media (film and fiction), significantly affect the types of narratives
they construct to deal with the problematic. Another fundamental distinction is the absence of a cure for Kafka's protagonists. Zelig, on the other
hand, is eventually cured of his malady and finds happiness until the end of
his days.

MYSTERIOUS PATIENTS

Zelig is the story of an exceptional human being, Leonard Zelig, who suffers
from a "unique malady" (Z, 65). This is first noted in 1928 when a few individuals recall having seen the same man in entirely different social and ethnic
environments and each time, they claim, he looked and spoke like the people
around him. Zelig does not attract general attention at this point, but those
who know him describe him as "an odd little man who kept to himself (Z,
13). "Suddenly," however, there is "increasingly strange behavior" (Z, 21),
which reaches a climax a year later when Zelig disappears from his home and
is absent from work: "Police are investigating the disappearance of a clerk
named Leonard Zelig. Both his landlady and his employer have reported him
missing" (Z, 13). Zelig is not only literally missing in person but has also lost
his identity. He is found in Chinatown as a "strange-looking Oriental" and
is immediately taken to Manhattan Hospital: "In the ambulance he rants and
curses in what sounds like authentic Chinese. He is restrained with a
straitjacket. . . . When he emerges from the car twenty minutes later, incredibly, he is no longer Chinese but Caucasian" (Z, 15–16). The doctors are bewildered, "no two can agree on a diagnosis" (Z, 25), and this bewilderment

still characterizes people's responses after Zelig is dead. In hindsight everyone keeps saying that this whole case was "quite astonishing" (Z, 4), "very strange" (Z, 4), "a very bizarre story" (Z, 5).

Gregor Samsa's story in *The Metamorphosis* is just as exceptional and equally bizarre. There are many correspondences between the two texts, but the transformations they depict manifest themselves in different ways. Gregor's metamorphosis is more sudden: it is simply a fact "one morning" (M, 3) that he wakes up as a "monstrous vermin" (M, 3). Gregor transforms only once and for good. Zelig, on the other hand, takes on various identities and physical characteristics of other people and afterward always regains his original shape. In terms of signification, Gregor, who retains his new form, seems to have acquired a solid signifier, whereas Zelig's continual metamorphoses suggest that he is a signifier that is constantly changing, a sign constantly in search of a signified. Unlike Gregor, who throughout his transformation retains his "human" soul, Zelig's transformation encompasses both body and soul as he is searching for a container to hold his slippery, continually shifting self. In view of this, Gregor and Zelig can be said to represent two different poles of Jewish identity: Gregor, golem-like, is a body in search of his soul, whereas Zelig, dybbuk-like, is a soul in search of a body, trying to find a solid frame for his unstable self.[2] Zelig's dybbuk-like attributes are also suggested by one of the signs displayed when Zelig is exhibited: "See Zelig turn into you" (Z, 44). What both protagonists share again is that they belong to the lower middle class and have similar professions: Zelig is a clerk and Gregor a traveling salesman. Their employers start looking for them when they do not appear for work, and their first "abnormal" behavior that calls for public action is job related. Signs of "illness" are perceived only after this fact: in both cases there is an immediate call for the doctor.

When Gregor's mother hears the "insistent, distressed chirping" (M, 5) in his voice, she immediately thinks that her son is "seriously ill" (M, 10) and calls for a doctor. Strangely enough, even after they see his vermin shape, the family still acts around him as if he were ill: in the living room "now there wasn't a sound" (M, 16); they go to bed "on tiptoe" (M, 17); the next morning his sister Grete again comes "in on tiptoe, as if she were visiting someone seriously ill or perhaps even a stranger" (M, 17). Later the parents wait in front of Gregor's room for the sister's report about his condition, inquiring "whether he had perhaps shown a little improvement" (M, 23). And when Grete is busy removing Gregor's furniture, the mother tries to stop her because otherwise "it looks as if we had given up all hope of his getting better" (M, 24). Ironically, though, Gregor is never helped by a doctor, and possible help in the form of medicine is not only out of reach but harmful; when a medicine bottle breaks, we hear that "a splinter of glass wounded Gregor in the face, some kind of corrosive medicine flowed around him" (M, 27). The "corrosive medicine" symbolizes the beginning of Gregor's bodily disinte-gration; immediately after this scene we see the father bombard Gregor with apples, one of which "literally force[s] itself into [his] back" (*M*, 29), causes "unbelievable pain" (*M*, 29), and later brings about his total bodily disinte-gration and death. As for Zelig, the first round of medical experiments in the hospital ends with him walking on the walls of his room—a clear intertextual allusion to Kafka's *Metamorphosis*: "He undergoes severe mood changes, and for several days, will not come off the wall" (*Z*, 42). The pun on "off the wall" suggests Zelig's corrosive state of mind and also sums up Gregor Sam-sa's whole existence after his metamorphosis, because "Ever since [Gregor's] change, except for his two excursions into the living room, he has gone no-where except up and down the floor, walls, and ceiling of his room" (*M*, 55). For Zelig, as for Gregor, medicine is equally harmful, since it is the "experi-mental drug Somadril Hydrate" (*Z*, 41) in particular which is responsible for his reduction to this subhuman level.

THE INDECIPHERABLE SIGN

Susan Sontag establishes a useful link between the act of interpreting illnesses and the many functions these can have if they are seen as metaphors: "It is diseases thought to be multi-determined (that is, mysterious) that have the widest possibilities as metaphors for what is felt to be socially or morally wrong" (*Metaphor*, 61). Zelig's "illness" is certainly perceived as "multi-de-termined" and "mysterious" by the world around him. In the eyes of the people who remember him, he was as much an enigma in his lifetime as he is now. Indeed, the many divergent interpretations in the movie can be lik-ened to the many scholarly commentaries on Gregor Samsa's metamorpho-sis. In Susan Sontag's words, Kafka is one of those authors who has "attracted interpreters like leeches" ("Interpretation," 18), and Stanley Corn-gold uses the title *The Commentators' Despair* for his collection of articles on *The Metamorphosis*. In 1937, Hans-Joachim Schoeps saw in these com-mentaries a type of modern midrash and wished for a new complete Kafka edition "in the form of old Talmud folios: the Kafka text in the middle—above, beneath, and on the sides framed by exegetical commentaries and in-terpretations" (419; my translation). Similarly, in the film we hear many commentaries on Zelig's peculiar illness, from average persons to well-known authorities and intellectual luminaries such as Susan Sontag, Irving Howe, Saul Bellow, and Bruno Bettelheim, beginning with Susan Sontag's remark that Zelig was "*the* phenomenon of the . . . twenties" (*Z*, 3–4). Zelig's impact on contemporaries was felt in all areas of society, as testified to by Professor Blum, author of the fictive study *Interpreting* Zelig:

To the Marxists, he was one thing. The Catholic Church never forgave him. . . .
The American people, in the throes of the Depression as they were, found in
him a symbol of possibility, of, of self-improvement and self-fulfillment. And,
of course, the Freudians had a ball. (*Gesturing*) They could, they could interpret
him in any way they pleased. It was all symbolism—but there were no two intellectuals who agreed about what it meant. (Z, 97)

As with Gregor Samsa, everyone is busy defining Zelig, commodifying him,
fitting him into categories, appropriating him either as their enemy or friend,
devil or saint, or using him as an object for intellectual speculation. The
many interpretations of Zelig's illness can be seen as another midrashic commentary of a secular sort that is playing serious games with Zelig's liminal
existence, while he himself regresses and progresses, trying to find his identity.[3]

The fact that Gregor never sees a doctor (his window even faces a hospital
[*M*, 12]—so close and yet so far) and that Zelig becomes worse and worse
while in the hospital does suggest that Gregor's and Zelig's metamorphoses
are not physical diseases that require medical attention, but rather that they
are illnesses whose causes are manifold. The very description of Gregor's
shape as that of a "monstrous vermin" (*M*, 3) is an inherently contradictory,
oxymoronic construction. In this light Corngold stresses that "Gregor's
opaque body is thus to maintain him in a solitude without speech or intelligible gesture, in the solitude of an indecipherable sign" ("Metaphor," 89).
Indeed, Kafka expressly asked that the insect not be depicted when he wrote
to the Kurt Wolff Publishing Company in October 1915:

Dear Sir, You recently wrote that Ottomar Starke is going to do an illustration
for the title page of *The Metamorphosis*. Now I have had a slight . . . probably
wholly unnecessary shock. It occurred to me that Starke . . . might want, let us
say, to draw the insect itself. Not that, please, not that! I don't want to restrict
his authority but only to make this request from my own naturally better
knowledge of the story. The insect itself cannot be drawn. It cannot even be
shown at a distance. (*M*, 70)

Gregor's metamorphosis is final, and as a result he is read differently by
those around him. The reader, though, knows that Gregor still has a human
consciousness. But his family is uncertain about this, and the fact that they
literally cannot understand him (*M*, 11) suggests that they cannot read him.
Still, it is as hard for them as for the reader to reduce Gregor to one signified
only. Even though the very first sentence says that he was transformed into
a "monstrous vermin," it is only toward the end of the story that he is referred to as an "it," like an animal, and only by his sister Grete: "We have to
get rid of it" (*M*, 37). Even the cleaning woman, in her great mistrust of Gregor, credits him with "unlimited intelligence" (*M*, 39), and when at one

point she calls him "old dung beetle" (*M*, 36), the narrator comments, "To forms of address like these Gregor would not respond." (*M*, 36).[4] Significantly, after Grete calls Gregor "it," her father still hesitates and uses "he" (*M*, 38), and then Grete herself seems torn again between the two pronouns: "Look father," she suddenly shrieked, "*he's* starting in again" (*M*, 38; my emphasis). Gregor, then, seems neither insect nor human, existing as he does in a liminal space between human and animal signifiers. His metamorphosis is therefore best described figuratively as a "metaphor representing a state of dehumanization" (Fingerhut, 97).

With Gregor the first signs of illness are *heard* (when his voice changes), whereas with Zelig they are *seen* (change in physical appearance). One might ask, is Woody Allen not making visible what Kafka did not want to be depicted? After all, Zelig, like any other film, is "both a visual text and a literary text, an integrated cinetext of visual and verbal images and signs" (Girgus, 6) whose aim is to make Zelig's illness visible. Thus, Dr. Fletcher decides to record her sessions with Zelig on film; "When a man changes his physical appearance, you want to *see* it. You can't read about it" (*Z*, 65). David Cronenberg's movies, *The Fly* and *Naked Lunch*, are good examples of an art form that makes visible what Kafka did not want to be depicted: both films exploit the grossness of the insect metaphor for the thrill and horror that accompanies the shock effects on the viewer. Here, Walter Benjamin's remarks about modern film are particularly appropriate: "The film is the art form that is in keeping with the increased threat to his life that modern man has to face. Man's need to expose himself to shock effects is his adjustment to the dangers threatening him" ("Work of Art" 250). In contrast, Woody Allen's film emphasizes Zelig's dehumanization and his struggle to retain his humanity. When Zelig is reduced to Gregor Samsa's state, for instance, we literally *see* him in a standing (horizontal) position, upright, as he is walking up and down the wall nonstop (*Z*, 41). The fact that he is not crawling on all fours like an animal indicates his struggle to cling to his humanity. In addition, Woody Allen, too, is concerned about retaining the mystery behind Zelig's illness. One of the commentators in *Zelig*, Susan Sontag, is identified as the author of *Against Interpretation*. In her essay by the same name, Sontag talks about interpretation as "this curious project for transforming a text" ("Interpretation," 15), where "the interpreter, without actually erasing or rewriting the text, *is* altering it" ("Interpretation," 16). She warns that this "makes art into an article for use, for arrangement into a mental scheme of categories" ("Interpretation," 19) and asks, "What would criticism look like that would serve the work of art, not usurp its place?" ("Interpretation," 22). The secular midrashic commentary in *Zelig* with its multiple perspectives prevents this usurpation of art for the purpose of popular consumption.

Both Woody Allen and Kafka want to make visible the dehumanizing commodification of life in twentieth-century society. For Kafka, working with an exclusively literary rather than a combined visual and literary medium, this visibility is achieved largely through visual and figurative language, such as animal metaphors (from vermin to ape, mice, dogs, etc.) and "animal gesture[s]" (Benjamin, "Franz Kafka," 122), which represent various states of non-well-being. These metaphors for the most part exist in a "solitude of the indecipherable sign" (Corngold, "Metaphor," 89) because Kafka "divests the human gesture of its traditional supports and then has a subject for reflection without end" (Benjamin, "Franz Kafka," 122). The attempt to retain the ambiguity of the indecipherable sign is a conscious narrative strategy in many of Kafka's narratives[5]; however, one could argue that Gregor's increasing bodily disintegration in *The Metamorphosis* indicates that Kafka is divesting "the human gesture" of so much "of its traditional supports" that the originally ambiguous signifier is gradually shifting toward an increasingly identifiable signified—the vermin.

As a matter of fact, retaining the ambiguity of the sign is necessary for Gregor to stay alive. When the ambiguity is abandoned, this amounts to a death sentence for him. Gregor's continual physical degeneration increases the family's willingness to make the sign "decipherable." Moreover, their readiness in the end to identify Gregor as vermin has serious consequences for the protagonist's reading of himself because Gregor's death occurs when he accepts the signified they impose on him. But the family's extinction of Gregor's human soul is possible only because Gregor accepts their verdict. For the reader, therefore, Gregor and his family remain "a subject for reflection without end" (Benjamin, "Franz Kafka," 122), and some of the questions that need to be asked are Who is this "family" and who is this "son"? Who is really "ill," the family or the son? Why does the son's metamorphosis take place in this particular social environment? In the following we will see that these questions are equally important for an understanding of Zelig's illness.

TWENTIETH-CENTURY STEREOTYPES
AND PRESUPPOSITIONS

Susan Sontag argues that "the modern metaphors suggest a profound disequilibrium between individual and society, with society conceived as the individual's adversary. Disease metaphors are used to judge society not as out of balance but as repressive" (*Metaphor*, 73). The representations of illness in both Kafka and Woody Allen can be seen as social critiques that expose the repressive nature of stereotypes and presuppositions in the social environment. Zelig's family background, for instance, is described as a breeding ground for his later ailment. Common public opinion perceives his illness as grounded in the social-racial stereotype of the dysfunctional, lower-class Jewish immigrant family: Zelig is a New York Jew, son of a mediocre Yiddish actor—a descendant therefore of someone whose very profession involves multiple role playing. In addition, he shares the stereotypical lax morality associated with the acting profession since he is married for the second time. He also suffers at the hands of his stereotypical cantankerous Yiddish wife: his home life consists of so much "violent quarreling that even though the family lives over a bowling alley, it is the bowling alley that complains of the noise" (Z, 19–20). Even though the ironic reversal here is used for comedy and deflects the racial stereotypes, the presuppositions in society are nonetheless that this type of family breeds illness and criminality: Zelig's brother Jack has a "nervous breakdown" (Z, 20), while his "sister Ruth becomes a shoplifter and alcoholic" (Z, 21) and associates with her "dubious-looking lover, Martin Geist" (Z, 42), who is a criminal, having been "in jail for real estate fraud" (Z, 43). Allen here humorously deflects presuppositions about social-racial origins for disease and criminality, which surprisingly have had no effect on Zelig for a long time: "Leonard Zelig appears to have adjusted to life. Somehow, he seems to have coped. And then, suddenly, increasingly strange behavior" (Z, 21). Suddenly the "human chameleon," the "lizard" (Z, 33) is coming out in him, as if something were finally catching up with him, as if he were racially or socially predisposed "to become that which he must become" (Gilman, *Patient*, 168).

Gregor, on the other hand, is not Jewish: his family is Christian. Like Zelig, he seems well adjusted before his metamorphosis: he manages to cope after the bankruptcy of his father's business and becomes the sole supporter of the family until the fateful morning of his metamorphosis puts an end to this. The cause for his illness is seen as largely work related: Gregor's mother believes that overwork made him sick (M, 8), and Gregor himself immediately identifies his "grueling job" (M, 3) as responsible for his present condition. But just as Zelig cannot escape from the stereotyping engrained in the social environment, nor can Gregor. He describes how easy it is for a traveling salesman to become the victim of "prejudice . . . gossip, contingencies, and unfounded accusations" (M, 13). And as with Zelig, some kind of stereotype eventually seems to be catching up with Gregor when he changes into vermin.

What is never mentioned in the movie or in Kafka's text is the link between the reptile and lizard or vermin metaphor and contemporary anti-Semitic discourses. Gregor's increasing filthiness, when he "drag[s] around with him on his back and along his sides fluff and hairs and scraps of food" (M, 35), intimates that there is no escaping from his fate either: in the end he literally becomes the stereotypical expression "dirty Jew." His metamorphosis from human to vermin, at least on one level of meaning, appears to be a regressive, backward metamorphosis, a return to an essentialist original state. Similarly, read within the discourses of the period of the late 1920s, the rise of fascism, and the fascist discourse on the Jew, Zelig's statement, "I used to be a member of the reptile family, but I'm not anymore" (Z, 94), alludes to the common anti-Semitic stereotype of the Jew as reptile, lizard. Leroy Beaulieu writes,

> There seems to be something of the reptile in him [the Eastern Jew], something sinuous and crawling, something slimy and clammy, of which not even the educated Israelite has always been able to rid himself. This is a quality that transforms him again . . . into an Oriental; it is a racial feature, an inherited vice, not always to be washed away by the water and salt of baptism. (quoted in Gilman, *Patient*, 17)

The Jew as Oriental is another stereotype mentioned, and it is no accident that Zelig's first "serious" transformation, which draws the public's attention, is into a Chinese person.

Kafka lived in a period when this anti-Semitic rhetoric was common and widespread. We see him employ this vocabulary in 1911 when he likens the Jews to lizards:

> The convulsive starting up of a lizard under our feet on a footpath in Italy delights us greatly, again and again we are moved to bow down, but if we see them at a dealer's by hundreds crawling over one another in confusion in the large bottles in which otherwise pickles are usually packed, then we don't know what to do. (*Diaries, 1910–1913*, 55)

This anecdote was written in response to a Zionist critique of his friend Max Brod's novel *The Jewesses*. Hugo Herrmann, the Zionist reviewer, rejected the novel out of hand because there was no ethnic specificity, not even one Jewish hero, and all Jews in it were therefore equally nondescript (2–3). Kafka is ridiculing here the reviewer's objection that we do not know who or what we are dealing with. More than that, by employing anti-Semitic rhetoric Kafka is parodying the racial Zionist discourse, thus giving a scathing commentary on the reviewer's dogmatic position.[6] Given Kafka's dislike of racial stereotyping, it comes as no surprise that he avoided specific Jewish markers in his own work.

At the same time, though, Kafka remarks enigmatically that "vermin is born of the void" (*Wedding Preparations*, 113)—which again seems to underline his insistence on the indecipherable signifier—and yet he then continues relating this statement to the negativity of his age, which he says he has internalized and thus has a right to represent:

> I have vigorously absorbed the negative element of the age in which I live, an age that is, of course, very close to me, which I have no right ever to fight

against, but as it were a right to represent. . . . I have not been guided into life by
the hand of Christianity . . . and have not caught the hem of the Jewish prayer-
mantle—now flying away from us—as the Zionists have. I am an end or a beginning. (*Wedding Preparations*, 114)

Surely, then, the vermin metaphor can be seen as a metaphor *representing* the
"negative element of the age," as a form shaped by anti-Jewish stereotypes, a
sign that is both beginning and end.

Stanley Corngold argues that "the continual alteration of Gregor's body
suggests ongoing metamorphosis, the *process* of literalization in various directions and not its end state" ("Metaphor," 86). But the continual deterioration of Gregor's body can be read through the racial stereotypes of the
period because Gregor regresses over time and becomes ever more the "dirty
Jew." It is significant to point out in this context that he is not "born" into
the Christian family as vermin, but that he "transforms" into vermin in a
Christian family. Gregor's family therefore represents more than his "real"
family: they could be seen as the Christian family in a larger sense, an extension of Christian society, which of course created and propagated anti-Semitic stereotypes. Indeed, the family's inhuman treatment of Gregor
illustrates a wounding of the Other, both physically and psychologically.

JEWISH MARKERS OF DIFFERENCE
AND THE CHRISTIAN FAMILY

Despite his transformation, Gregor at the outset is certainly not "ill." His
desperate attempts to be with his family are tragic since he hurts himself
when he falls out of his bed (*M*, 8) and when he turns the key to open the
door (*M*, 11). The first sign of illness that is perceived by his environment is
the change in Gregor's voice, his "insistent, distressed chirping" (*M*, 5). Eric
Santner has related Gregor's voice to the "obsession with the Jewish voice"
(207) in the anti-Semitic discourses of the period and argues at the same time
that Kafka's discourse is "more than a literary version of a kind of Jewish
self-hatred, more than the narrative and poetic elaboration of a series of internalized anti-Semitic prejudices" (209). In view of Kafka's earlier parody
of Zionist and anti-Semitic discourse in the lizard analogy, are we here not
dealing with another parody as well, particularly when we consider that the
"chirping" comes, after all, out of the mouth of an insect? Kafka's parody
of this "Jewish marker of difference" (Gilman, *Patient*, 150) still underlines
the fact that Gregor's inability to communicate with his environment may
have a racial cause: the narrator emphasizes that Gregor himself has no problem understanding his family, but that they cannot understand him—indeed,
they do not even try, since "it did not occur to any of them . . . that he could

understand what they said" (*M*, 19). Similarly, Kafka can be said to parody Gregor's acceptance of his vermin shape by exploiting its ironic, humorous, and liberating potential. Initially, Gregor simply ignores his transformation, and it is ironic that he blames only his job for the pain he feels (*M*, 3–4) and that he ignores "the pains in his abdomen" (*M*, 10) that he feels when he is standing upright. Moreover, we have a very humorous scene when Gregor lands on his feet again and for the first time has "a feeling of physical well-being" (*M*, 14). This initiates a "chain of comic reactions that . . . suggest[s] a Chaplinesque tragicomedy" (Bruce, 116) and ends with Gregor's involuntary expulsion of his adversary, the manager of his company. This is a reversal of Gregor's initial submissive position in the firm and at the same time a revenge and an attack on formerly repressive structures of authority that his new form now allows him to challenge, albeit inadvertently.

Ironically, Gregor's newly found feeling of well-being is of very short duration because as soon as the manager is gone, Gregor's family begins to wound him. After his father attacks him for the first time, Gregor is "bleeding profusely" (*M*, 14). He then passes out, awakens only in the evening from "his deep, comalike sleep" (*M*, 15), and discovers that he has "to limp on his two rows of legs" (*M*, 16). As Bluma Goldstein points out, these wounds close and have completely healed by the next day (209). In contrast, the father's second attack with apples causes a "serious wound" that never heals: the rotting apple that is from now on firmly lodged in Gregor's back leads to a further "deterioration of [Gregor's] situation" (*M*, 29) and eventually to his death. It is striking here that the father's punishment of Gregor is associated with religion. The apples he uses to bombard Gregor with (and the one rotting apple in particular that remains stuck in his back as a reminder) most obviously point to original sin in the Old Testament. However, from the perspective of Christian anti-Semitism the most widespread "original" sin committed by the Jews was the killing of Christ: from the Middle Ages on, "to the masses, the Jew was the worst infidel of all—the Christ killer in person" (Trachtenberg, 167). The Christ imagery when the apple leaves Gregor paralyzed as if he were "nailed to the spot" (*M*, 29) suggests that this association is relevant for *The Metamorphosis* as well. Moreover, in the family's reaction to Gregor we can see an allusion to another most common and tenacious stereotype in Christianity: the Jew as devil, demon, Antichrist (Trachtenberg, 32–43).

From the very beginning the family's encounter with Gregor's vermin shape is accompanied by religious gestures that are so exaggerated that this must be a parody: Gregor's mother has her hands "clasped" (*M*, 12) when she sees him for the first time, as if he were some kind of Antichrist, and we hear about his sister's "sighs and appeals to the saints" (*M*, 19) when she is taking care of him. As a result of the family's inhuman treatment of Gregor, his life in exile amid this Christian family, like the jackals' life among the

Arabs in Kafka's story "Jackals and Arabs," increasingly brings out "all the Jewish markers of difference" (Gilman, *Patient*, 150). The jackals have a peculiar smell, they whine, and they are "unable to truly alter their instincts" (Gilman, *Patient*, 150). Gregor, too, becomes smelly, considering that his room in the end is a dumping ground for garbage (*M*, 33), that he is covered with dirt (35), and that he has a rotting apple stuck in his back. In addition, his instincts burst out in the form of unnatural, sexual-incestuous desire: for the lady in the picture on his wall (*M*, 3) against which he later presses his "hot belly" (*M*, 26), and in his lust for his sister when she plays the violin (*M*, 36). We can see that Gregor increasingly comes to embody common anti-Jewish stereotypes of the day. When he has been reduced to this "reading," Gregor is emptied of all other signification and dies.

From time to time, his family seems to be reminded that "Gregor was a member of the family . . . who could not be treated as an enemy; that, on the contrary, it was the commandment of family duty to swallow their disgust and endure him, endure him and nothing more" (*M*, 29). But generally they do not pay too much attention to this "commandment of family duty," which can be seen as an ironic reminder of the Christian commandment to love one's neighbor. The "Christian" father's interpretation of Gregor's death as a sign from heaven is not without a touch of irony when he exclaims, "'now we can thank God!' He crossed himself, and the three women followed his example" (*M*, 40). Here, Gregor's loathsome nature is paralleled with the family's even higher loathsomeness, since their religious convictions are no more than an empty shell. Within this context, it is particularly ironic that Gregor's death should allude to the death of Christ: "He remained in this state of empty and peaceful reflection until the tower clock struck three in the morning. He still saw that outside the window everything was beginning to grow light. Then, without his consent, his head sank down to the floor, and from his nostrils streamed his last weak breath" (*M*, 39). Here we have a parody of Christ's death, the irony being that Gregor is suffering a similar fate at the hands of the Christian family. By depicting the fates of Gregor and Christ as interchangeable, Kafka underlines the common human denominator rather than racial distinctions. Furthermore, since Christ was Jewish and Gregor is supposedly Christian, the final irony is that in both cases the "family" is killing one of their own.

Given the differences in Woody Allen's and Kafka's respective sociocultural and historical environments, it is not surprising that they use different narrative strategies for depicting common racial stereotypes. Kafka's European alienation must be contrasted with Allen's Americanization where a Jew is not nearly as much of an outsider. Both artists parody cultural realities, but unlike Kafka, who mostly alludes to racial discourses, Woody Allen makes them quite explicit, manipulates them, and more obviously deflects them humorously or ironically. Allen, too, like Kafka, neutralizes anti-Semitic discourse by replacing it with Fletcher's nonracial medical theory: "Like the lizard that is endowed by nature with a marvelous protective device that enables it to change color and blend in with its immediate surrounding, Zelig, too, protects himself by becoming whoever he is around" (Z, 33). But Allen goes further than Kafka when he exploits the possibilities that his visual medium, the film, offers him. For one, he highlights the humorous side of the reptile stereotype by making it "visible" in the new dance the Chameleon, and "doin' the Chameleon . . . sweeps the nation" (Z, 35), thereby projecting the stereotype onto society: we see couples "clasping hands, looking pop-eyed at each other, and sticking out their tongues lizard-style" (Z, 35). The original racial connotations have not entirely disappeared but now reemerge in different form by including black racial problems. There is a clever juxtaposition between the "Chameleon Song" and a picture of "a Harlem street corner. Four black children . . . dance to the song, to the delight of several watching adults. . . . They are in perfect form: hands clasped, eyes open wide, and tongues flicking out" (Z, 36). The words to the song that accompanies this picture are nicely ironic: "If you hold your breath till you turn blue / You'll be changing colors like they do / And you're doin' the Chameleon. Vo-do-do-de-o" (Z, 36). There are also many records made that become extremely popular, such as "Chameleon Days" (Z, 49), "You May Be Six People, But I Love You" (Z, 49–50), and "Leonard the Lizard" (Z, 50). Another one of these songs, "Reptile Eyes" (Z, 50), is juxtaposed with a picture of Zelig looking into the screen wistfully, "trim but intensely sad" (Z, 50). Gregor Samsa, too, with his head "cocked to one side and peeping out at the others" (M, 12) may have similar wistful eyes, and his transformation is certainly not devoid of humor (Bruce, 114–16), but one cannot imagine a song called "Vermin Eyes" accompanying his first appearance in public, nor can one imagine Gregor and his family dancing a vermin version of the chameleon dance! Finally, in *Zelig*, the Chameleon dance soon becomes popular all over Europe: in France, for instance, "Josephine Baker does her version of the Chameleon dance" (Z, 54). By moving not only beyond racial boundaries but also beyond the North American continent, the joke is not on Zelig anymore but rather on the whole world.

Woody Allen even humorously manipulates the stereotype of the Jew as demon, devil, Antichrist when Zelig suddenly appears out of nowhere, like a demon, and interrupts Pope Pius XI's blessing of the congregation in St. Peter's Square. The pope literally hits him over the head with his "sacred decree" (Z, 64), physically punishing him. In addition, there is an even more important subtext to this scene. We hear about the pope's blessing that "this is the first time this ritual has been performed . . . in sixty-three years, and brings to a climax on Easter Sunday the religious ceremonies of Holy Week" (Z, 63). The historical context is that in 1929 the Pope blessed the crowds from a balcony in St. Peter's Square after discussions between Mussolini and

the Church had come to a successful and mutually beneficial end and resulted in the Concordat between the Church and the fascist state: this is "the
first time that a pontiff had shown himself in public since 1870" (Cheetham,
279–280). Allen has consciously stretched the fifty-nine-year period of the
pope's absence to sixty-three years, so that we would be in the year 1933, the
year of the Nazi rise to power. Zelig's disruption of the blessing, as well as
the pope punishing the Antichrist figure with the papal bull containing the
agreement between the Church and the fascist state, points to the continuity
of Christian anti-Semitism, foreshadowing the Church's abandonment of
the Jews during the Nazi period.

SOCIAL AND POLITICAL ILLNESSES

Zelig's illness, then, is quite specifically placed at the heart of the rise of fascism, manifesting itself at the end of the 1920s and becoming full-blown in
the fascist movement. The various stages of his illness parallel the cultural
trends and political movements of the early twentieth century and represent,
as Irving Howe puts it, "the nature of our civilization, the character of our
times" (Z, 4). Ironically, as a Jew who lacks a personal identity, Zelig is a
perfect case study for an individual drawn to fascism. In a reading of Paul
Celan's poetry, Jacques Derrida refers to the Jew "who has nothing of his
own, nothing that is not borrowed, so that . . . what is proper to the Jew is
to have no property or essence. Jewish is not Jewish" (328). Similarly, Kafka
identified this same perplexing situation for his own generation as the
"frightful inner predicament of these generations" (Letters, 288). Kafka and
his friends saw the loss of a cultural identity as a consequence of the previous
generation's assimilation into the dominant culture. Zelig clearly lacks a
sense of self: when his doctor, Eudora Fletcher, asks him if he is Leonard
Zelig, he replies, "Yes. Definitely. Who is he?" (Z, 76). We also learn that
Zelig more than anything else in the world wants to belong to a community:
he wants to be "safe," which to him means "to be like the others," "to be
liked" (Z, 32). Irving Howe rightly perceives that he "wanted to assimilate
like crazy!" (Z, 97), and this makes Zelig a perfect vessel for holding the
norms, values, and presuppositions of Western culture that produced fascism. Kafka obviously could not benefit from the postwar hindsight of
Woody Allen and his many commentators. However, Kafka's representation
of what turns human beings into commodities with no identity of their own
complements Woody Allen's.

Before they show the first symptoms of illness, Gregor Samsa and Leonard Zelig find it difficult to feel comfortable in early twentieth-century capitalist society. Modernity is mostly preoccupied with the functioning of the
system and expresses an overall indifference to personal fates.[7] In The Meta-

morphosis, it is telling that Gregor hears his mother call for the "doctor" and his father for the "locksmith" (*M*, 10). The mother-father dichotomy reveals the tension in twentieth-century society between the principle of nurturing and caring and the hegemonic patriarchal discourse, which has no room for this. Gregor himself cannot tell the difference: he feels "integrated into human society once again and hope[s] for marvelous, amazing feats from both the doctor and the locksmith, without really distinguishing between them" (*M*, 11). But the doctor never appears, and Gregor never learns "what excuses had been made to get rid of the doctor" (*M*, 19). The tension between the medical and spiritual and practical needs of twentieth-century society remains unresolved and no cure can ever be found unless this split is overcome. As it is, Gregor's crawling up and down the walls of his room is symbolic of the "crawling" that characterizes his life. He would love to rebel at his workplace but cannot because he has to pay off his family's debt:

> If I didn't hold back for my parents' sake, I would have quit long ago, I would have marched up to the boss and spoken my piece from the bottom of my heart. He would have fallen off the desk! It is funny, too, the way he sits on the desk and talks down from the heights to the employees, especially when they have to come right up close on account of the boss's being hard of hearing. (*M*, 4)

Gregor has absolutely no spiritual fulfillment in his life, having "nothing on his mind but the business" (*M*, 8). Given the demands of his job and his constant traveling, he does not have time to build up personal relationships: he complains about "constantly seeing new faces, [possessing] no relationships that last or get more intimate" (*M*, 4). He has also never had a lasting relationship with a woman: he remembers "a chambermaid in a provincial hotel—a happy fleeting memory—and a cashier in a millinery store, whom he had courted earnestly but too slowly" (*M*, 31–32). The one time he is serious about a woman he is too slow and misses his chance. Similarly, in Zelig's world there is no spiritual fulfillment. Under hypnosis Zelig identifies the lacking spiritual, family, and social support as a contemporary social disease:

> My brother beat me. . . . My sister beat my brother. . . . My father beat my sister and my brother and me. . . . My mother beat my father and my sister and me and my brother. . . . The neighbors beat our family. . . . People down the block beat the neighbors and our family. (*Z*, 77)

The link between family and society is thus established: the system punishes individuals who deviate from its norm, the neighbors punish those who deviate from their norm, and a pattern is established that reaches right down to the family unit.

One would think that at least the medical institution should have the inter-

ests of the patient at heart and help individuals fit back into "normal" life.
But the medical world is a microcosm of the world outside: both Kafka and
Woody Allen caricature doctors because they are out only for their own self-
interest. In *The Metamorphosis* Gregor reveals that the company doctor
cares only about the interests of the company that employs him. In his last
five years as a traveling salesman, for instance, Gregor has never been sick,
because he knows full well what would happen if he were: "The boss would
be sure to come with the health-insurance doctor, blame his parents for their
lazy son, and cut off all excuses by quoting the health-insurance doctor, for
whom the world consisted of people who were completely healthy but afraid
to work" (*M*, 5). This is indeed what happens on the morning of his metamorphosis when the office manager appears on his doorstep and insists that
"we businessmen . . . very often simply have to overcome a slight indisposi-
tion for business reasons" (*M*, 9). In the past Gregor had internalized this
work ethic so much that he did not even want to be reminded of illness by
the sight of the hospital right across from his room: he "used to curse [it]
because he saw so much of it" (*M*, 21). His metamorphosis finally gives him
some breathing space: "hanging from the ceiling . . . one could breathe more
freely" (*M*, 23). Gregor's transformation, then, is not only the result of but
also an escape from the commodification of life at the workplace. When Saul
Bellow says of Zelig that "his sickness was also at the root of his salvation"
(Z, 126), this applies to Gregor at this moment as well.

Gregor's feelings of elation are only momentary and his metamorphosis
in the end is fatal. In contrast to Zelig, who receives medical attention, no
one ever attempts to cure Gregor. However, since all attempts to cure Zelig
fail equally, one must ask whether his illness runs its course despite or precisely because of the various attempts that are undertaken to cure him. The
"cures" offered by the medical establishment are anything but cures. Initially, the doctors "claim to have the situation in hand" (Z, 24) but do not
take Zelig very seriously as a patient. One of them arrogantly dismisses his
illness as "something he picked up from eating Mexican food" (Z, 25), immediately resorting to stereotypes and presuppositions when he cannot explain the nature of his illness. The medical establishment does not
understand, as psychologist Bruno Bettelheim does in hindsight, that Zelig's
"feelings were really not all that different from the normal, maybe, what one
would call the well-adjusted normal person, only carried to an extreme degree, to an extreme extent. I myself felt that one could really think of him as
the ultimate conformist" (Z, 67). The doctors cannot see this because they
are themselves caught up in a life of utter conformity, "dancing the dances
of the age" (Kafka, *Wedding Preparations*, 85), thoroughly aware that their
medical careers are dependent on the whims of the market. When the newspapers "want [Zelig's] story on page one every day" (Z, 34) and news about
Zelig's condition spreads like wildfire, "Dr. Allan Sindell is forced to issue a

statement: '. . . we're just beginning to realize the dimensions of what could be the scientific medical phenomenon of the age, and possibly of all time'" (Z, 24). Now they desperately need to put a label on Zelig and must quickly construct an image of the patient to keep up an appearance of competence in the eyes of the public. Woody Allen caricatures their search for physiological causes and the certainty with which they pronounce their purely speculative diagnoses. Dr. Birsky is the most hilarious caricature when he insists there must be a brain tumor even though he has not found any evidence of one: "Ironically, within two weeks' time, it is Dr. Birsky who dies of a brain tumor. Leonard Zelig is fine" (Z, 26). This reversal of the doctor-patient role indicates clearly that it is not the patient who is ill but rather the whole medical establishment.

This is further accentuated in the "series of experiments" (Z, 22) organized by Dr. Fletcher; here one can see how "the ostensible cure proceeds today by means of further commodification" (Corngold, "Melancholy," 33). Zelig is put on display and performs on command, turning into a psychiatrist in the company of psychiatrists, into a Frenchman in the company of Frenchmen, and "begins to develop Oriental features" when talking to a Chinese person (Z, 22–23). These experiments have no scientific basis but are intended to feed the "thrill-hungry public" (Z, 61). Soon the media describe him as "the strange creature at Manhattan Hospital" (Z, 28), and the doctors willingly participate in the "myth-making about the disease" (Gilman, *Disease*, 7) that "plays to the stereotypical perception of the public and has its desired effect" (Gilman, *Disease*, 16). The doctors themselves believe the myth they have helped create because they treat Zelig ever more like a "creature" they can experiment on and are not overly concerned when their treatment makes him ill. For instance, they decide that his "malady can be traced to poor alignment of the vertebrae. Tests prove them wrong and cause a . . . temporary problem for the patient" (Z, 27). In the film we see Zelig sitting up on a bed with outstretched legs but with toes pointing down to the floor. Other tests serve only sensationalist purposes and are humiliating, as when they make him perform with "a midget and a chicken" (Z, 29), or put him into a room with two overweight men and wait for Zelig to puff himself up, or show how "in the . . . presence of two Negro men, Zelig rapidly becomes one himself (Z, 30). Even the reporter seems to suggest that this is a little too much: "What *will* they think of next?" (Z, 30).

The film deliberately juxtaposes the discrepancy between the public's frenzy and Zelig's suffering and thereby emphasizes Zelig's humanity. While endless tests continue to be performed on Zelig, the public is going Zelig-crazy: he becomes "the main topic of conversation everywhere" (Z, 34); everyone is dancing the new Chameleon dance; and they are buying photos of him as "Chinese, Intellectual, Overweight" (Z, 37). In the midst of the hilarious hype, a scene is interjected where Zelig is enduring electroshock treatment that makes him look "like one of Dr. Frankenstein's creations" (Z, 36). Like Frankenstein creating the monster, the doctors are literally molding him into a new personality: first they take his body apart by re-aligning his vertebrae, and then they put him back together in such a way that he looks like a monstrosity; finally, they deprive him of his senses through electroshock. The last torture they inflict on him in the hospital is to treat him with the "experimental drug Somadril Hydrate" (Z, 41), which turns Zelig into a golem-like Gregor Samsa figure who, deprived of his soul, mechanically continues his bodily movements as he is walking up and down the wall.

MELANCHOLY: NO CURE FOR
HUMAN COMMODITIES

The eagerness with which the sensation-hungry public appropriates Zelig, exploits his "unique malady" (Z, 65), and turns him into a celebrity under-lines the "power of the media itself, especially as it can be used for propa-ganda" (Girgus, 74). The power of the media affects everyone, including Zelig's immediate family. When they see the sensation Zelig is causing, Zel-ig's sister Ruth and her lover Martin Geist, "a businessman and ex-carnival promoter" (Z, 42), take him out of the hospital, where the doctors "are re-lieved to be rid of this frustrating case" (Z, 42). Motivated by self-interest, Zelig's sister and husband proceed to exhibit him alive as "the phenomenon of the ages" (Z, 43). For consumer society, Zelig is a "lucky find of capitalist raw material in the body of a distressed creature" (Corngold, "Melancholy," 24), and Zelig "does not disappoint, changing appearance over and over upon demand" (Z, 44). Business is flourishing since "overnight, [Zelig] has become an attraction, a novelty, a freak" (Z, 45). Even Hollywood makes a film about him in 1935, "called *The Changing Man*, in which the atmosphere is best summed up" (Z, 46) thus:

> They don't care about him. They'll exploit him—all they see in him is a chance to make money. . . . There were not only Leonard Zelig pens and lucky charms but clocks and toys. There were Leonard Zelig watches and books and a famous Leonard Zelig doll. There were aprons, chameleon-shaped earmuffs, and a pop-ular Leonard Zelig game. (Z, 47–48)

Ironically, the Hollywood film is an example of "how a certain 'antimaterial-ist' pathos . . . has itself in turn been commodified and marketed with a view to luring torpid clients onto the carnival grounds of consumption" (Corn-gold, "Melancholy," 23). And it is indeed "the goal of capitalism," "to foster ever stronger forms of need" (Corngold, "Melancholy," 23): in *Zelig* this takes the form of endless exhibitions" (Z, 51), many popular songs that sweep the nation (Z, 50), and all of this in the end leads to a tremendously successful European tour. The result is that Zelig becomes a real commodity, "a curiosity with no life of his own" (Z, 64), exploited, humiliated, and in the end forgotten by modern consumer society like Kafka's hunger artist.

The similarities between Zelig and the hunger artist are striking. The hunger artist is exhibited in a cage; Zelig is exhibited behind a fence (Z, 44). The hunger artist's constant feeling is one of melancholy (CS, 272), which is the "malady of depreciated soul-treasure, of the empty (coffered) subject"—the malady of commodities who are "without specific character, without aim, individuality, or aura" (Corngold, "Melancholy," 25). The hunger artist suffers from melancholy because there is no true art anymore: art has become a commodity because everything is geared to the attention span of modern consumer society. He is told to limit his fasting to forty days, because this is the longest period during which "the public could be stimulated by a steadily increasing pressure of advertisement, but after that the town began to lose interest" (CS, 270). For a time, the hunger artist, like Zelig, is "honored by the world, yet in spite of that troubled in spirit, and all the more troubled because no one would take his trouble seriously" (CS, 272). Also like Zelig, he suffers from a "change in public interest" and "suddenly [finds] himself deserted one fine day by the amusement-seekers" (CS, 273). In the end the hunger artist and Zelig are both forgotten. The hunger artist is literally passed by, as the circus visitors stream past his cage on their way to the menagerie without even looking at him (CS, 274–75), and so is Zelig: "A man walks by, ignoring him. Other people scurry past the camera" (Z, 56):

> Zelig's own existence is a nonexistence. Devoid of personality, his human qualities long since lost in the shuffle of life, he sits alone quietly staring into space, a cipher, a nonperson, a performing freak. He who wanted only to fit in—to belong, to go unseen by his enemies and be loved—neither fits in nor belongs, is supervised by enemies, and remains uncared for. (Z, 56)

Saul Bellow remarks that "it is ironic . . . to see how quickly he has faded from memory, considering what an astounding record he made" (Z, 5); however, considering the fast pace of modern consumer society, this state of affairs is not so surprising, since "a population glutted with distractions is quick to forget" (Z, 61).

The way the doctors, the media, as well as Zelig's family exploit the sensation-hungry public and their "thirst for thrills and novelty" (Z, 24) reveals how several "discourse[s] of power use (or generate) images of illness for many ends, drawing on this wide repertoire of images to isolate, stigmatize, and control" (Gilman, *Disease*, 9). In fact all these false and "misapplied scientific remedies of society" (Pogel, 176) are contrasted with Dr. Eudora

Fletcher's personal approach. Susan Sontag remarks that Fletcher "sensed what was needed and she provided it, and that was, in its way, a remarkable creative accomplishment" (Z, 97). As a woman, Eudora Fletcher knows what it is like to be excluded. She is in fact the only doctor who believes that "Zelig's unstable makeup . . . accounts for his metamorphoses. The governing board of doctors is hostile to her notion" (Z, 26). When she presents her theory about Zelig's chameleon-like protection device, the camera patently focuses on each one of the male doctors individually, all dressed in suits, skepticism written all over their rigid faces (Z, 33). Despite her initial success with Zelig, they dismiss her ideas as "pipe dreams" (Z, 41). Fletcher has as little a place in the medical profession as Zelig has in the world. In terms of marginalization, his fate parallels hers. It is no wonder that Fletcher feels that "here was this unique case that I could make my reputation on—not that I knew how to cure him. But if I could have him alone and, uh, feel my way, and be innovative and creative, I felt that I could change his life if I only had the chance" (Z, 63).

Fletcher and Zelig are both given this chance, and the story of Zelig's cure is reminiscent of Kafka's "A Report to an Academy," where an ape transforms into a human being.[8] In his early days Rotpeter, like Zelig, was "more or less accompanied by excellent mentors, good applause, advice, and orchestral music, and yet essentially alone" (CS, 250). He then made a living as a performing freak on a "variety stage" (CS, 258), just like Zelig when he was in his hunger artist stage. Moreover, in both Zelig and "Report" a reversal of the patient and doctor-teacher roles characterizes the beginning of their transformation into a human being. In Zelig, Dr. Fletcher becomes more and more irritated (Z, 71), whereas Zelig, according to Fletcher's nephew Paul Deghuee, "was fine . . . napping, sitting in his chair reading. He used to refer to himself as Dr. Zelig. He was reading books on psychiatry" (Z, 72). Fletcher's nephew in the end suggests that she "better get away for a day and relax. The strain is becoming too much for you" (Z, 72). In Kafka's tale, the "first teacher was almost himself turned into an ape by it, had soon to give up teaching and was taken away to a mental hospital" (CS, 258). And Rotpeter remarks ironically that he "used up many teachers, indeed, several teachers at once" (CS, 258), Rotpeter never finds any fulfillment but is sarcastic and resentful about his experience. Zelig, on the other hand, finds love. Fletcher cures Zelig precisely because she falls in love with him and gives him the personal attention he needs: "Her love for Leonard . . . crosses over professional boundaries so that, in a sense, she ultimately shares his sickness with him. This serves to sustain the visual and thematic point about psychic illness and reality. Sickness and cure tend to fuse, especially in a society of explosive fluidity and volatility" (Girgus, 75). After she cures him, she is granted the public recognition she never received before, and Zelig willingly participates in her glory. Neither Fletcher nor Zelig realize, though, that just like Zelig's illness earlier it is now his "cure" that is marketed for popular consumption.

Unlike Fletcher and Zelig, Kafka's ape Rotpeter is very aware of being put on display when he is asked to report to the learned academy. He describes his assimilation as "my forced career" (*CS*, 250) and knows that he did "his best to meet this strange universe on *its* terms rather than on his own" (Weinstein, 78). Herein lies precisely the problem, for Zelig as well as for Rotpeter. Not only is Rotpeter aping, i.e., copying, his environment (compare with the German *nachäffen*), but he pushes himself to internalize the values of the dominant society, which includes the stereotypes society projects on his kind. In Woody Allen's film, too, Zelig's own family is so assimilated that they have internalized the anti-Semitic prejudices of the day: "his parents, who never take his part and blame him for everything, side with the anti-Semites" (Z, 20). And like Rotpeter, Zelig also distances himself from his origins:

> Kids, you gotta be yourself. Ya know you can't act like anybody else just because you think that they have all the answers and you don't. . . . You have to be your own man and learn to speak up and say what's on your mind. Now maybe they are not free to do that in foreign countries but that's the American way. You can take it from me because I used to be a member of the reptile family, but I'm not anymore. (Z, 94)

By saying he once belonged to the reptile family Zelig reveals that he "actively seek[s] to accept society's sense of [his] own difference in order to create [his] sense of oneness with the world" (Gilman, *Disease*, 5). The fact that he is adopting "the American way" unquestioningly also indicates that he has so fully internalized the values of the dominant culture that he is ironically not himself or his own man at all. He is simply reproducing the patriarchal hegemonic discourse of the period. In comparison, Kafka's satire is much more bitter: this text is not a "masked or effaced discourse" (Gilman, *Patient*, 9) but the very opposite in its desire to expose and unmask the existing psychological predicament of a whole generation. Indeed, Kafka feared that Max Brod's wife, Elsa, who was scheduled to read the story in public, might want to leave some parts out and urged her to keep everything: "And should the text contain something dirty, don't leave it out. If you really tried to clean up the text, there would be no end to it" (*Letters*, 168). In sarcasm Kafka's satire is similar to Mendele Moykher-Sforim's nineteenth-century Yiddish novel *The Mare*, a satire of assimilation and the Enlightenment, with which Kafka was familiar.[9] Here the mare characterizes the process of assimilation as "pure theatre!" (*Mare*, 617): she resents this "monkey business," which means being taught "some trick or other" and asks, "What's the use of lovely harnesses, expensive decorations . . . all these rewards for clever performance?" (*Mare*, 618–19). Unlike Zelig, who enjoys the attention lavished upon him, the mare sneers, "Dance, little animals, dance!" (*Mare*, 606). Zelig does not realize that he has learned to dance the dances of the age, that instead of being cured he has become hollow at the core. This is why, when the public turns against him, he has nothing to fall back on, no sense of self that allows him to retain his equilibrium.

Zelig's "cure" is only on the surface and cannot last in this type of society. He may seem more stable, may even consider himself cured, but the deeper cause for his illness was always located in societal values and presuppositions, and society certainly has not changed. Public opinion still reflects the stereotypes of the day: Dr. Fletcher is still perceived as "a little girl from the backwoods" (Z, 89) by the press; the newspapers write, "SHE'S PRETTY TOO!" (Z, 85); and from the newsreel announcer we hear, "Who says women are just good for sewing?" (Z, 87). The end of this brief harmonious interlude for Zelig and Fletcher comes suddenly, after the public finds out that Zelig was married to several women while under different personalities. The most threatening social disease that now appears on the horizon is Christian fundamentalism. The film mocks the very narrow and rigid Christian morality when a spinsterlike Christian fundamentalist pronounces, "We don't condone scandals. Scandals of fraud, and polygamy. In keeping with a pure society, I say, lynch the little Hebe" (Z, 109). For the first time in the film do we see a connection between the playfully employed lizard motif and its original racial connotations: "Oh you lizard!" (Z, 103). For Zelig there is no escaping from Christian morality; it is proclaimed on posters everywhere, "One wife—even for reptiles" (Z, 104), or "Zelig's bigamy makes a mockery of the sacrament of matrimony. . . . polygamy attacks the heart of a Christian society. Leonard Zelig must be tried and convicted" (Z, 108). This is only the beginning of a witch hunt directed against Zelig, a hunt that ends with his disappearance.

When the tide shifts in public opinion and society turns against Zelig, the only solution he sees for himself is Gregor Samsa's solution, and he disappears. However, Zelig does not die but finds a home in Nazi Germany. Saul Bellow comments;

> Yes, but then it really made sense, it made all the sense in the world, because, although he wanted to be loved . . . craved to be loved, there was also something in him . . . that desired . . . (*Pauses*) immersion in the mass and . . . anonymity, and Fascism offered Zelig that kind of opportunity, so that he could make something anonymous of himself by belonging to this vast movement. (Z, 115)

This last stage in Zelig's illness must be considered a narrative necessity. Initially, Zelig tries to define himself by becoming like individual people. Then he identifies with a whole cultural set of values, the American Way. Now he is defining himself by becoming one with a collective identity, by identifying with a large political movement. All the time, he is still identifying with everyone by identifying with the mass. It is a small step from his beginnings to his drowning in a fascist collective identity. Trained to be a commodity with no soul of his own, he is following the next historical movement, the emergence of fascism, as if it were the newest fad society had to offer.

Zelig's desire to lose himself in the mass resembles Karl Rossmann's longing, at the end of *Amerika* (significantly, the literal translation of the German title *Der Verschollene* is *The Boy Who Sank Out of Sight*), to enter the theater of Oklahoma where "everyone is welcome!" (*A*, 272). Karl Rossmann, after having been tossed about in the New World, has also tried unsuccessfully to escape from his liminal existence. When he needs to identify himself to be admitted to the theater, he Zelig-like adopts a new identity by giving himself "the nickname he had had in his last post: 'Negro'" (*A*, 286). In Kafka's letters to Milena, Kafka uses the name "Negro" as a name for the Jew: "Naturally for your father there's no difference between your husband and myself; there's no doubt about it, to the European we both have the same Negro face" (*Milena*, 136; Gilman, *Patient*, 108). Like Gregor Samsa accepting the vermin label that is projected on him by the discourses of society, Karl Rossmann here takes the nickname that was earlier projected on him and makes it his own: it becomes his new identity. He enters the theater of Oklahoma with no illusions and under no pretexts: quite fittingly he is never seen again. Like Zelig, Rossmann at this point cannot go any farther: the dissolution of his personality is a narrative necessity, and it is not surprising that the novel remained a fragment.

Zelig returns despite himself, but only because Dr. Fletcher keeps rescuing him, even out of the clutches of the Nazis. Eudora Fletcher remains true to her name, the *eu* in "Eudora" being associated with health and her full name referring to the "seat of honour," abode "of the gods" (thereby endowing her with godlike powers), "sanctuary," and also signifying "stability" (Liddell and Scott, 478). In accordance with this, the ending in *Zelig* is blissful and sentimental: "In the end, it was, after all, not the approbation of many but the love of one woman that changed his life" (*Z*, 129). However, the representation of Zelig's marriage to Eudora Fletcher is also ambiguous. As Nancy Pogel points out, "Zelig's entire narrative is fictional and unreliable. . . . Moreover, the last images of Zelig and his bride, even as (and because) they are portrayed in the amateurish and artless manner of old-fashioned flickering, grainy black-and-white home movies, are fading figures, receding memories" (185). Nonetheless, we have also seen that during the course of Zelig's illness, Woody Allen has time and again broken the rules of logical narrative necessity by allowing his hero to be rescued. Unlike Kafka's protagonists, Zelig is allowed to live out his modest existence outside the limelight, giving talks from time to time about his experience (similar to

Kafka's ape, but without the latter's sarcasm and resentment). And like Eudora, Zelig also lives up to his name and becomes what he is supposed to become: *selig* in the sense of finding harmony and satisfaction with himself and the world. Yet *selig* also refers to the "deceased," and Zelig is indeed long dead and forgotten when the movie begins. Why then is he resurrected for us?

One answer lies in the connection Irving Howe establishes between the 1920s and contemporary capitalist society: "For a time everyone loved him, and then people stopped loving him, . . . and then everybody loved him again and that was what the twenties were like and you know when you think about it, has America changed so much? (*Shaking his head*) I don't think so" (Z, 127). In the same vein, Stanley Corngold more specifically talks about the melancholy that accompanies the commodification of contemporary life and calls for "an exercise of radical political thinking" ("Melancholy," 33), "an attempt to think a way out of a capitalist melancholy only as 'universal' as our dependency on commodity cures" ("Melancholy," 34). For Kafka, though, no such cure is possible. His country doctor is frustrated because his patients want him to be "omnipotent" (CS, 224), to be their physical and spiritual healer alike. Not only can the country doctor not cure his young patient's wound, he cannot even understand the nature of his illness. In the end, the doctor is left naked, exposed to "the frost of this most unhappy of ages" (CS, 225). Ultimately, the message in *Zelig* for our own time is no different. Girgus rightly calls the ending a "parody of the American dream" (128). It is a parody because a cure can be envisioned only in the realm of fantasy. Kafka, too, at times leaves open a window to "faery lands forlorn," as in his "Imperial Message" where the dream remains hovering on the darkling threshold: "Nobody could fight his way through here even with a message from a dead man. But you sit at your window when evening falls and dream it to yourself (CS, 5).

NOTES

1. Abbreviations will be used for the following texts by Woody Allen and Franz Kafka: *Zelig* (Z), *The Metamorphosis* (M), *The Complete Stories* (CS), *Amerika* (A).

2. I owe this insight to Michael Greenstein.

3. My thanks to Michael Greenstein for this commentary.

4. Corngold notes in this respect that Kafka had originally written here, "Did he have a bad day today, our old dung beetle," and then replaced this phrase with "Look at that old dung beetle!" (M, 53). He suggests that Kafka changed the chattier former phrase to rule out "the muddled effect of the cleaning woman's trivial, everyday attribution to the animal of a human soul, like a pet owner's to his pet, when Gregor does in fact have a human soul" (M, 53).

5. In *The Trial*, for instance, we see Kafka "parodying the aporia between door-

keeper and visitor as well as talmudic commentaries on the Law" (Greenstein, 91), and in *The Metamorphosis* he highlights and problematizes the aporia that accompanies Gregor's environment's confused readings of the vermin signifier.

6. I disagree with Hartmut Binder when he argues that Kafka's critique "in its tendentiousness is identical with that of the reviews in 'Selbstwehr'" (288; my translation). Binder ignores the ironic tone of Kafka's review. To my mind, Giuliano Baioni rightly stresses that Kafka's review reveals his "disagreement with the Zionist position" ("Zionism," 95).

7. For a discussion of Gregor's alienation see Walter Sokel, "Von Marx zum Mythos."

8. "A Report to an Academy" was published in Martin Buber's journal *Der Jude* (*The Jew*) in 1917 and immediately perceived by his contemporaries as a satire on assimilation. Max Brod wrote in the Zionist paper *Selbstwehr* (*Self-Defense*): "Is it not the most marvellous satire of assimilation that has ever been written? One should read it again in the last issue of *The Jew*. The assimilationist who does not want freedom, only a way out" (Max Brod, "Literarischer Abend" [my translation]).

9. *The Mare* is discussed in great detail in Meyer I. Pinès's Yiddish literary history, *L'histoire de la littérature judéo-allemande*, which Kafka read in January 1912 (*Diaries*, 223).

WORKS CITED

Allen, Woody. *Zelig*. In *Three Films of Woody Allen: Zelig, Broadway Danny Rose, The Purple Rose of Cairo*. New York: Orion Pictures, 1987.

Baioni, Giuliano. "Zionism, Literature, and the Yiddish Theater." In *Reading Kafka: Prague, Politics, and the Fin-de-Siècle*, ed. Mark Anderson, 95–115. New York: Schocken, 1989.

Benjamin, Walter. "Franz Kafka: On the Tenth Anniversary of His Death." In *Illuminations*, ed. Hannah Arendt, trans. Harry Zohn, 111–40. New York: Schocken, 1968.

———. "The Work of Art in the Age of Mechanical Reproduction." In *Illuminations*, ed. Hannah Arendt, trans. Harry Zohn, 217–52. New York: Schocken, 1968.

Binder, Hartmut. "Franz Kafka und die Wochenschrift *Selbstwehr*." *Deutsche Vierteljahrsschrift für Literaturwissenschaft und Geistesge-schichte* 41 (1967): 28–304.

Brod, Max. "Literarischer Abend des Klubsjtidischer Frauen und Madchen (December 19, 1917)." *Selbstwehr* Prag 12.1 (January 4, 1918): 4–5. Repr. in *Franz Kafka: Kritik und Rezeption zu seinen Lebzeiten, 1912–1924*. Ed. Jürgen Born et al. Frankfurt: Fischer, 1979. 128, 196.

Bruce, Iris. "Elements of Jewish Folklore in Kafka's *Metamorphosis*." In *The Metamorphosis* by Franz Kafka. Norton Critical Edition, ed. S. Corngold, 107–25. New York: Norton, 1996.

Cheetham, Nicolas. *A History of the Popes*. New York: Dorset, 1982.

Corngold, Stanley. *The Commentators' Despair*. Port Washington, NY: Kennikat, 1973.

———. "Kafka's *The Metamorphosis*: Metamorphosis of the Metaphor." In *The*

Metamorphosis by Franz Kafka. Norton Critical Edition, ed. S. Corngold, 79–107. New York: Norton, 1996.

———. "The Melancholy Object of Consumption." *Violence and Mediation in Contemporary Culture*, ed. R. Bogue and M. Comis-Pope. Albany: State University of New York Press, 1996.

Derrida, Jacques. "Shibboleth." In *Midrash and Literature*, ed. G. Hartman and S. Budick, 307–47. New Haven: Yale University Press, 1986.

Fingerhut, Karl-Heinz. *Die Funktion der Tierfiguren im Werke Franz Kafkas*. Bonn: H. Bouvier, 1969.

Gilman, Sander L. *Disease and Representation: Images of Illness from Madness to AIDS*. Ithaca, NY: Cornell University Press, 1988.

———. *Franz Kafka, The Jewish Patient*. New York: Routledge, 1995.

Girgus, Sam B. *The Films of Woody Allen*. Cambridge: Cambridge University Press, 1993.

Goldstein, Bluma. "A Study of the Wound in Stories by Franz Kafka." *The Germanic Review* 14, no. 3 (1966): 202–17.

Greenstein, Michael. "Breaking the Mosaic Code: Jewish Literature vs. the Law." *Mosaic* 27, no. 3 (1994): 87–106.

Herrmann, Hugo. "*Jüdinnen* [*The Jewesses*]. Ein Roman von Max Brod." *Selbstwehr* (May 19, 1911): 2–3.

Kafka, Franz. *Amerika*. Trans. Willa and Edwin Muir. New York: Schocken, 1946.

———. *The Complete Stories*. Ed. N. Glatzer. New York: Schocken, 1971.

———. *The Diaries of Franz Kafka, 1910–1913*. New York: Schocken, 1948.

———. *Letters to Friends, Family, and Editors*. Trans. R. and C. Winston. New York: Schocken, 1958.

———. *Letters to Milena*. Trans. Philip Boehm. New York: Schocken, 1990.

———. *The Metamorphosis*. Norton Critical Edition, ed. S. Corngold. New York: Norton, 1996.

———. *Wedding Preparations in the Country and Other Posthumous Prose Writings*. London: Seeker & Warburg, 1954.

Liddell, Henry George, and Robert Scott, eds. *A Greek-English Lexicon*. Oxford: Clarendon, 1996.

Moykher-Sforim, Mendele. *The Mare*. *Yenne Velt: The Great Works of Jewish Fantasy and Occult*. Ed. and trans. Joachim Neugroschel, 545–663. New York: Pocket, 1976.

Pogel, Nancy. *Woody Allen*. Boston: Twayne, 1987.

Santner, Eric. "Kafka's *Metamorphosis* and the Writing of Abjection." *The Metamorphosis* by Franz Kafka. Norton Critical Edition, ed. S. Corngold, 195–210. New York: Norton, 1996.

Schoeps, Hans-Joachim. "Franz Kafka: 'Gesarrunelte Werke' Band V und VI." *Franz Kafka: Kritik und Rezeption, 1924–1938*. Ed. Jürgen Born et al., 418–20. Frankfurt: Fischer, 1983.

Sokel, Walter. "Von Marx zum Mythos: Das Problem der Selbstentfremdung in Kafkas *Verwandlung*." *Monatshefte* 73, no. 1 (1981): 6–22.

Sontag, Susan. "Against Interpretation." In *Against Interpretation and Other Essays*, 13–23. New York: Dell, 1961.

————. *Illness as Metaphor*. New York: Farrar 1977.

Trachtenberg, Joshua. *The Devil and the Jew. The Medieval Conception of the Jew and Its Relation to Modern Anti-Semitism*. 1943. Philadelphia: The Jewish Publication Society of America, 1983.

Weinstein, Leo. "Kafka's Ape: Heel or Hero." *Modern Fiction Studies* 8 (1962–63): 75–79.

17

Zelig and Contemporary Theory
Meditation on the Chameleon Text

Robert Stam and Ella Shohat

The possession of originality cannot make an artist unconventional; it drives him further into convention, obeying the law of the art itself, which seeks constantly to reshape itself from its own depths, and which works through geniuses for its metamorphoses, as it works through minor talents for mutation.

—Northrop Frye, *Anatomy of Criticism*

In the theatre, one becomes a plebean, a flock, woman, Pharisee, parish churchwarden, imbecile, Wagnerian; in the theatre, even the most personal consciousness succumbs to the levelling magic of the greatest number; in the theatre, the neighbor is king; indeed, one becomes oneself one's neighbor.

—Friedrich Nietzsche, *Nietzsche Against Wagner*

History adds that before or after dying he found himself in the presence of God and told him: "I who have been so many men in vain want to be one and myself." The voice of the Lord answered from a whirlwind: "Neither am I anyone; I have dreamt the world as you dreamt your work, my Shakespeare, and among the forms in my dream are you, who like myself are many and no one.

—Jorge Luis Borges, "Everything and Nothing"

[For Houston Stewart Chamberlain] the Jews are the least pure race, the inferior product of a "crossing of absolutely different types."

—Sander Gilman, *Jewish Self-Hatred*

When first released, Woody Allen's *Zelig* (1983) was regarded in terms more appropriate to its protagonist than to the film, as a kind of brilliant "freak" or well-executed "gimmick." Overwhelmed by the audacity of its premise, critics ignored the film's deep rootedness in a dense cinematic and literary intertext and downplayed the multileveled suggestiveness of the film's chameleon parable. What follows is a kind of playful meditation on *Zelig*, one informed by contemporary theory (and especially by the categories of Mikhail Bakhtin), a meditation that attempts to disengage the film's generic intertext and explore the strata of its allegorical palimpsest: film as chameleon, the artist as chameleon, the Jewish experience as chameleon, the self as chameleon.

Zelig not only thematizes chameleonism through its protagonist's "uncanny" ability to take on the accent, profession, and ethnicity of his interlocutors, it also practices chameleonism on a discursive level.[1] In *Zelig*, chameleonism comes to make a metaphor of intertextuality itself, as the film, like its protagonist, assumes the coloration of its interlocutory texts. Through intertextual mimicry, fiction and documentary, the two genres subtending the film, come to resemble each other in a kind of specular mimesis. Allen's generic hybrid, the "fictive documentary," breaks down the customarily inviolate boundaries separating the two orders of discourse, replacing the usual wall with a permeable membrane. It transcends the traditional separation between the two not by merely juxtaposing them (à la Makavejev's *WR*) but rather by enlisting documentary's habitual procedures of enunciation and narration to serve what is clearly a sham and parabolic tale, pointing to the truth of Metz's *boutade* that "all films are fiction films," as well as to its obverse, that all films, even fiction films, are documentaries.

An invented story masquerading as true history, *Zelig* constitutes, to paraphrase Hayden White, "pseudo-historical text as filmic artifact." Indeed, *Zelig* can be regarded as a witty gloss on the thesis of White's *Metahistory*, that it matters little whether the world conveyed to the reader or spectator is conceived to be real or imagined; the manner of making discursive sense of it is identical.[2] By breaking down conventional frontiers between history and fiction, *Zelig* reminds us of the common roots of historical and fictive *écriture* in the tropological patterns of language and the modes of employment of narrative. Both documentary and fiction film are tailored to the ideological norms of storytelling; both orchestrate enigmas and deploy information within a specific cinematic organization of time and space aimed at the reconstruction of a world characterized by internal coherence, all mediated by the formal molds made available by the intertext.

Zelig presents the surface appearance, however, of a conventional documentary, in which the portrait of a historical figure is set against the backdrop of the portrait of an age (here the fads of the 1920s and 1930s), buttressed by the testimony of "witnesses" who recount their memories or advance their interpretations in direct-to-camera interviews. *Zelig* designates itself as documentary, furthermore, not through the "architext" of its title, which could refer equally well to a documentary or a fiction film, but rather through a facetious dedicatory intertitle that mimics the documentary etiquette of expressing appreciation to donors and collaborators ("The following documentary would like to give special thanks to Dr. Eudora Fletcher, Paul Deghuee, and Mrs. Meryl Fletcher Varney") but here addressed to *imaginary* collaborators.

Throughout, the film speaks in the double-voiced discourse of parody, which represents for Bakhtin the privileged mode of artistic carnivalization. The film lampoons all the hackneyed rhetorical procedures of the "canonical" documentary: its ponderously knowing male narrators; its ritualistic talking heads; its quasi-comic redundancy (the image of Eudora writing in her diary is accompanied by the comment "Eudora writes in her diary"); its frequent implausibilities (through what legerdemain did the documentarist manage to witness such an eminently private act as "writing in one's diary?"); its suspect manipulation of stock footage (the commentary "Eudora goes to Europe" is superimposed on a stock shot of an ocean liner—her liner? that trip?); and finally, its penchant for synecdochic music ("Horst Wessel" stands in for the Nazis, the "Internationale" evokes the Communist movement, and "America the Beautiful" substitutes for the United States.) The film subjects all these formulaic procedures to corrosive laughter, to the point that it becomes retrospectively difficult to take them seriously again.

Roughly half of *Zelig* is composed of archival footage, drawn from what was originally 150 hours of material. The filmmakers raid the archive, the available simulacrum of the past, to place the spectator in palpable reach of the aural and visual texture of the period. Here the notions of "prior textualization" (Jameson), the "already said" (Bakhtin), and "mosaics of citations" (Kristeva) take on an oddly physical connotation. We are confronted not with an abstract verbal dissemination but with material snips of celluloid drawn from stock footage, home movies, and old newsreels. Each citation of archival footage leads to a double-voiced reading: first in relation to their text, and time, of origin; and second as incorporated into the new totality of *Zelig*. Allen takes "alien words" (Bakhtin), framed in another intention, and gives them a new, ironic orientation, here exploiting the compelling immediacy of evidence to discredit the very *idea* of evidence. The film noisily activates the machinery of authentication, in sum, but within the narrative vacuum of a transparently preposterous fiction.

When *Zelig* is not archival, it is pseudoarchival. Through Gordon Willis's artful replication of the look and texture (and even the technical inadequacies) of earlier cinematography, archaic period footage and freshly staged material become virtually indistinguishable. In this sense, *Zelig* celebrates the chameleonic potentialities of the film medium itself as a multitrack, sensorial composite offering opportunities for chameleonism denied to single-track media such as literature.[3] Allen is inserted into period photographs, or is made to slither into celebrities' movies so as to carouse with William Randolph Hearst and Carole Lombard, or is simply matted into archival footage, rather like a lizard blending into a new habitat. Through the chameleonism of the laboratory, the film stock itself assumes the tonalities of another epoch. New footage is artificially aged and scratched and made to look grainy and flicker, while saccadic movement simulates actual footage. Mimetic lighting matches new shots to old material, while the dialogue, registered by 1920s-style microphones, imitates the low-fidelity recording of a bygone era. The chameleonism of montage, meanwhile, melds historical footage of Fanny Brice to staged shots of Zelig attending her performance, and the chameleonism of postsynchronization weds Hitler's recorded voice to the lip movements of a contemporary double made up to look like Hitler.[4]

This promiscuous mingling of recorded historical "truth" with staged fictive "lies" constitutes a crucial strategy in *Zelig*. The initial interview, for example, superimposes Susan Sontag's voice on images of a ticker-tape parade. Titles reassure us that it is indeed Susan Sontag we are seeing, and the style and drift of her discourse closely conform to our expectations concerning the cultural figure named "Susan Sontag." Yet her persuasive sincerity is here enlisted in the service of a "lie," that there was a man named Zelig and that she knew of him. A more striking instance of this same procedure occurs later, in an interview with the putative editors of the defunct *Daily Mirror*—Mike Geibell and Ted Birbauer. They speak convincingly of the journalistic appeal of the Zelig phenomenon, but their words, like those of the Cretan liar, paradoxically raise suspicions about their own credibility: "In those days, you got a story, you jazzed it up a little bit, you exaggerated, and you even played with the truth, to sell more papers. But with him, the truth was enough—it never happened before!" The technique is reminiscent of Cervantes's calling into question the veracity of his sources in *Don Quixote;* the spectator is teased into cognitive antinomies and a dizzying feeling of epistemological vertigo.

The figures interviewed in *Zelig* vary substantially in their fictive status. Susan Sontag, Irving Howe, Bruno Bettelheim, and Saul Bellow, for example, enact their own personae under their own names, making plausible comments reflecting what we know to be their real-life preoccupations. Howe, the author of *The World of Our Fathers*, a book about the Jewish immigrant experience at the turn of the last century, predictably interprets Zelig as a quintessential exemplum of the transformations involved in assimilation. Susan Sontag, again quite plausibly, emphasizes Zelig's "aesthetic instincts" as well as the assertive role of the woman psychoanalyst, seen as a rebel and maverick within psychoanalytic discourse much as Sontag herself once represented the rebel within art and literary criticism. (The author of *Against Interpretation*, ironically, is entirely willing to interpret). Saul Bellow, with similar predictability, stresses two motifs common in his fiction: ambiguity (that Zelig's own cowardly chameleonisin made him a hero) and individuality versus conformism (that Zelig's flirtation with fascism had to do with a desire to merge into the mass). Elsewhere, however, the coefficient of fiction is higher: Professor Morton Blum plays himself yet is credited, in a Borges-like "erroneous attribution," as the author of a clearly fraudulent book— *Interpreting Zelig*. The interviews steadily escalate into implausibility, meanwhile, just as the narrative becomes more improbable and hallucinatory. The relative veracity of the initial interviews, in which the intellectuals do at least play themselves, prods us into the illusory expectation that the other interviewees are also playing themselves, that Eudora's older sister (played by Elizabeth Rothchild) is in some sense authentic, or even that the interviewed Nazi, whose name, Oswald Pohl, refers to one of Himmler's deputies condemned to death at Nuremberg, is in fact a former SS Obergruppenführer.[5]

Zelig's voice-over narration also fictionalizes archival material. Images are highjacked, as it were, and taken to an unexpected destination.[6] Sontag calls Zelig the "phenomenon of the century" over shots of a massive parade (which we presume to be in Zelig's honor) and compares him to Charles Lindbergh, fostering an illusory sense of a historical continuum, as if the reality of both figures were of a piece. (The allusion becomes even more ironic when Zelig, following what Bakhtin calls the "logic of the turnabout," performs Lindbergh's feat in a doubly reverse sense—in the opposite direction across the Atlantic and upside down.) Another segment shows the historical F. Scott Fitzgerald engaged in his typical activity of writing at parties; here again the voice-over fictionalizes the material by claiming that the subject of Fitzgerald's writing is a "little curious man named Leonard Selwyn or Zeiman." (It is typical of the film's Borgesian procedures that it is Fitzgerald, a writer of fiction, who first notes the existence of Zelig). Thus Allen points out the "kidnappability" of the film image, the ease with which it can be cut off from the intentions of its original framers and made to lie. Central in this process is what Barthes, in another context, called "anchorage." Through verbal commentary, the polysemy of the image is tied down; an ordinary traffic jam becomes a "traffic jam for Zelig" and a 1920s dance craze becomes "doin' the Chameleon." Thus the film mocks our naive belief that seeing is believing, that what we hear is what we see, and what we see is what we hear. The narration's constant attempt to validate itself with dates, names, citations, and archival footage is an immense joke on the suspect authenticating procedures of documentary itself and on our own implicit faith that narrators will not abuse our credulity.[7]

To point out that Zelig mixes documentary and fiction is to remain somewhat schematic, however, for in fact the film intertwines *diverse* strands of documentary and *diverse* strands of fiction. Quite apart from mixed-mode antecedents such as Welles's *F for Fake* or the found-footage films of Bruce Conner, *Zelig*'s documentary intertext includes (1) television compilation films, such as those forming part of *Twentieth Century* and *Victory at Sea*, that portrayed historical figures against a period backdrop (*Twentieth Century*, interestingly, at one point considered using a *Zelig*-like technique called "blue-backing" to insert Walter Cronkite into preexisting actual footage); (2) newsreels (the venerable "Voice of God" narration underlined by bombastic music, for example, recalls the "March of Time" newsreels already parodied in *Citizen Kane*); (3) the contemporary "witness" film in which aging interviewees reminisce about their involvement in left causes of an earlier period; (4) the contemporary traditions of television reportage and cinema verité; and (5) the television news quickie portraits of unknowns, for example, anonymous assassins, who suddenly emerge into public notoriety, for which producers rely on hastily gathered materials such as family albums and group photos of the newly minted celebrity. In sum, the film calls on precisely those rhetorical formulas most associated with mass media veracity as ironic authenticating devices for a transparent fiction; the heavy artillery of verisimilitude, again, explodes into a void.

Within the general intertextual framework of ersatz documentary, Allen renders ironic homage to the traditional Hollywood black-and-white melodrama. Conjured from the same narrative materials—the life of Zelig—the melodrama offers a metalinguistic gloss on *Zelig*'s documentary facade. The voice-over identifies the quoted melodrama as *The Changing Man* (1935, Warner Brothers), reproducing the common documentary practice of incorporating clips of fiction films. Diverse stylistic stratagems re-create the ambiance of a 1930s melodrama: a mise-en-scène replicating a low-budget Warner Brothers production (*Zelig* itself is a Warner production as well), a stylized performance by glamorous "stars," and melodramatic music and dialogue highlighting Eudora's passion and self-abnegation in curing Zelig. In the first quotation, Dr. Eudora (Marianne Talum) excoriates the greed of entertainment moguls: "They'll exploit him," she cries out to her colleague, as Zelig (Garret Brown) stares vacantly. Her denunciation, ironically, forms part of what is posited as an exploitative Hollywood film, a typical product of the very industry denounced. The second citation appears in the Nazi Germany sequence. A long shot of Zelig (Allen) seated behind the haranguing führer is accompanied by an omniscient voice-over: "Like a man emerging from a dream, Zelig notices her." Zelig waves to Eudora (Farrow) in recognition, followed by a shot–reaction shot of the Dr. Eudora of *The Changing Man*, happily whispering, "Leonard," and Zelig (Brown). The alternating syntagma of fiction film and documentary, stitched together by an impossible eyeline match, underlines the moment of mutual recognition, culminates with the formulaic finale of the fiction—a close shot of the couple's prolonged kiss accompanied by romantic music swelling to a climax.

The Changing Man exposes the textual mechanisms of Hollywood dramatic representation and specifically the process by which Hollywood biographies bring to the surface a story's latent emotional appeal while editing out its historical contextualization. At the same time, it casts comic light on the central premise of all illusionistic narrative—the presupposition of a preexisting anecdotal substratum from which key blocks have been extracted—by having Zelig complain that Hollywood, when it bought the rights to his life story, took all the best parts and left him only with his sleeping hours. *Zelig* also mocks the ethnic idealizations typical of Hollywood by foiling the Zelig character, played by a Woody Allen whose charm has little to do with beauty in the conventional sense, with the more handsome appearance of his Waspish-looking avatar in *The Changing Man.*

Zelig takes advantage of documentary's presumed higher coefficient of veracity to undermine the truth claims of documentary as well as fiction. After the first citation, the narrator claims that *The Changing Man* told the truth, while after the second citation, the elderly Dr. Eudora objects that the real story was "nothing like the movie." The film then gives us the "true" portrayal of the flight from Germany, as recorded by a German newsreel. As a shaky camera records Zelig's escape, a hysterical German narrator denounces him in a string of epithets: "judische, amerikanische, dumkopf." The choice of guarantor of truth is doubly ironic, since Third Reich newsreels were notoriously mendacious and never would have emphasized an incident that turned a traitor into a hero and the Nazis into schlemiels. With evaluations of *The Changing Man*, more significantly, the documentary self of *Zelig* places itself above fiction within the generic hierarchy, reserving for itself the right to judge the truthfulness of the fiction film. The documentary portion, then, posits itself as having a privileged relation to the truth, when in fact *Zelig*'s disorienting blend of fact and fiction and its parodic representation of documentary processes undermine the cognitive pretensions of *both* modes.

Like its protagonist, *Zelig* forms a shifting mosaic of creative borrowings. (Plagiarizing, symptomatically, is one of the crimes our hero is accused of.) Within this mosaic, *Zelig* evokes the multiple narrators and investigative style of *Citizen Kane*,[8] while also spoofing Warren Beatty's *Reds*, the reconstruction of the life and loves of John Reed. Set in the same historical period, *Zelig* pilfers a key device from *Reds*—interviews with contemporaries about the events portrayed—but with what Bakhtin would call a "sideways glance." The Allen version mocks the use of witnesses to buttress illusionism by transferring their comments to a chimerical and ludicrous figure, an elusive protean entity in constant metamorphosis, a "hero without any character," a personality perpetually *sous rature*.

Zelig's lack of substance, his there's-no-there-there essencelessness, implicitly questions classical notions of character and even suggests an approximation with contemporary reconceptualizations of the literary personage. The analyses performed by Vladimir Propp and Julien Greimas posit a hero without psychological depth or biographical density, as opposed to the traditional view of character as a kind of replica or facsimile of the human being, a rounded figure endowed with personal singularity and psychological coherence. Zelig, in this sense, lacks the old-fashioned repertory of attributes associated with the stable ego. He resembles, rather, Todorov's "agent of narrative" whose significance is purely virtual, who is little more than a textual marker, a blank form awaiting "predication." The very emptiness of Zelig's expression, even in close-up, suggests a kind of cipher, a tabula rasa awaiting inscription. And although the film ultimately retreats from the wider implications of its fable, the decentered character of its protagonist does implicitly, at least, cast suspicion on the classical humanist view of character.

On still another intertextual level, *Zelig* both mocks and renovates the genre of the psychological case study—encapsulated by films like *Spellbound* and *Marnie*—in which the central enigma revolves around the traumatic origins of adult neurosis. Eudora searches for the trauma at the root of Zelig's chameleonism, much as Mark, in *Marnie*, searches for the cause of Marnie's frigidity, or as Constance, in *Spellbound*, explores the etiology of John Ballantine's amnesia. In all three cases, psychoanalytically inclined investigators become erotically involved with the objects of their investigation. As in *Spellbound*, the woman psychoanalyst, initially portrayed as coolly rational, pursues her fascination with an identity-less patient (later lover) despite the hostility of a patriarchal psychoanalytic establishment and sheds her pose of dispassionate scientific rationality in favor of passionate romance. In both cases, it is the analyst's love, as much as her professional competence, that catalyzes the recovery of the man's true self.[9] Despite the close intermingling of therapy and eros common to both *Spellbound* and *Zelig*, however, they are marked by a major structural difference. While the Hitchcockian resolution of the psychological mystery coincides with the narrative resolution, the explanation of the origin of Zelig's neurosis—chameleonism as protective device—is revealed in midfilm. When Zelig is haunted by the media concerning actions performed while still in his amnesia-like state, he disappears; the initial psychological enigma transforms itself, through a shift in genre, into a detective enigma: "Where is Zelig?" But while detective films often involve a search for a person in hiding or in disguise, rarely do they revolve around a search for a person who "embodies" his own disguise in the form of a physiological capacity for metamorphosis.

Like Allen's earlier *Stardust Memories* (1980), *Zelig* incorporates its own hermeneutic mechanism within the text itself. The intellectuals' interpretive glosses shuttle us between diegetic event and extradiegetic interpretation. These critical interludes, the equivalent of literary "pauses" (Genette), in which narrative discursive time is greater than story time, are employed not in the nineteenth-century mode of particularizing space and action (Balzac) but rather in the reflexive dialogic manner of the eighteenth-century novel (Fielding). The pauses call attention to the diverse discourses—aesthetic, philosophical, psychological, analytical, sociological—that might inflect our reading. The film *Zelig*, like the Zelig phenomenon, becomes an object-text of critical discourse and of cultural and psychoanalytic speculation. Within a kind of hermeneutic Luddism, both film and character become a text open to diverse interpretive grids. Zelig himself, Morton Blum points out, was all things to all people: a figure of infamy to Catholics, the symbol of self-improvement to Americans, and for the Freudians absolutely anything and everything. The commentaries both encourage and channel the free play of interpretation, while provoking laughter at the disparity between the comic image of the human chameleon and the seriousness of his intellectualized presentation.

Zelig's intertext is not merely mimic: it is literary and philosophical as well. Far from being a freak or a gimmick, as a provincial film-critical discourse would have it, *Zelig* can be seen as renovating a perennial literary mode, to wit, the Menippean satire anatomized by Bakhtin as a seriocomic genre intimately linked to the carnivalesque perception of the world.[10] Bakhtin posits a number of distinctive traits of the genre, encountered in Dostoyevsky but easily extended to *Zelig*: "freedom from historical limits," "total liberty of thematic and philosophical invention," "philosophical universalism," "the posing of ultimate questions," "overt and hidden polemics with various philosophical, religious and ideological schools," "encounters with contemporary or recently deceased public figures and masters of thought," and a "fondness for inserted genres." Even the chameleon-like transmutations of the protagonist recall the frequent metamorphoses of the Menippea, the transformation of human characters, for example, into pumpkins and donkeys. The Menippean hero, according to Bakhtin, has a "dialogical relationship with himself," and his "being is fraught with the possibility of split personality." As a one-man polyphony of human possibilities, Zelig literally embodies the "oxymoronic protagonist" of the Menippea, incarnating what Bakhtin calls "human non-finalizability" and a person's "non-coincidence with himself."

Zelig alludes to another intertextual influence, Melville's *Moby Dick*, at four specific points: first, when the hypnotized Zelig confesses never having finished it (Zelig's first self-splitting arises from his shame in admitting, in front of "very bright people," that he had not read the novel, a token, perhaps of the powers of intimidation of literary intellectuals); second, when Eudora uses *Moby Dick* to construct a persona to which "Dr." Zelig is supposed to react; third, when Professor Blum describes Zelig as a man who "preferred baseball to reading *Moby Dick*"; and finally, when the concluding titles inform us that Zelig's only regret as he lay dying was that "he had just begun reading *Moby Dick* and wanted to know how it came out." These apparently whimsical references to the Melville novel point reflexively to certain features of the Allen film, since *Zelig's* own generic tapestry recalls the dense textual interweave of *Moby Dick* itself, which like *Zelig* also orchestrates preexisting documents: dictionary quotations (on the etymology of *Leviathan*), bona fide correspondence (Uno von Troil's letters), conversations (Eckerman with Goethe), biblical (the book of Jonah), philosophical (Plato, Hobbes), and literary (*Hamlet*) quotations, along with encyclopedic material on whaling interspersed throughout the fiction, all mobilized in the service of what is, after all, an awesomely improbable whale story.

Zelig rings the changes on a theme—chameleonism—rich in literary resonance and philosophical association. In the broader sense of intertextuality, the film might be profitably placed in relation not only with Menippean satire and Melville but also with the Renaissance cosmovision, with Romantic poetry, and with Sartrean existentialism. To linger but briefly on a few of these relations, we are reminded that the Renaissance saw the world in terms of similitude and correspondences. Zelig most nearly embodies Renaissance *simpatia*, a kind of limitless identification through which every fragment of reality is attracted to every other fragment, with all difference dissolved in an erotic play of universal attraction. (That Zelig does not ever transform himself into a woman, that the boundary of sexual difference is the *one* line that he dare not cross, suggests, perhaps, the phallocentric limits of Allen-Zelig's *simpatia*.)[11] At the same time, *Zelig* evokes the Romantic preoccupation with Self and World. "I am part of all that I have met," asserts the narrator of Tennyson's *Ulysses*, while Walt Whitman's capacious soul comes to resemble all it encounters. Keats called the poet *chameleon*, without identity; like Zelig, the poet is "everything and nothing," to return to the phrase glossed in Borges's *ficción*. As a walking miracle of neo-Kantian *einfuhlung*, Zelig offers a seriocomic demonstration of the powers of "negative capability," here in the form of a passively empathetic penchant for assimilation to other selves.

The spectator too is "everything and nothing," everywhere and nowhere, everyone and no one, "plebean," "woman," and "imbecile"—recall the Nietzsche epigraph. In this sense, Zelig's mutations recall the plural self, the "sujet mutant" (Schefer) fashioned not only by the theatrical but also, even especially, by the cinematic experience.[12] Like the "imaginary" self of Lacanian theory, the cinematic subject defines itself by identification with *l'image d'autrui* in a veritable bric-a-brac of identifications. Already doubled through primary identification with the apparatus, at once in the movie theater and with the camera-projector-screen, the spectator is further dispersed through the multiplicity of perspectives provided by even the most conventional montage. The spectator becomes mutable, occupying a plurality of subject positions; he is everywhere, to paraphrase Lacan, *à sa place*. The "polymorphous projection-identifications" (Edgar Morin) allow ephemeral identifications transcending ambient morality and social milieu.[13] In the cinema, one becomes one's neighbor, identifying with sameness and alterity, with cop and robber, with cowboy and Indian. Zelig's transformations, in this sense, can be seen as literalizing the psychic chameleonism of spectatorship, whereby ordinary social positions, as in carnival, are bracketed, and where the poor fleetingly confound themselves with the rich, the black with the white, the woman with the man, and so forth.

Zelig can also be seen as an allegory of another kind of negative capability, that of the actor, and his transmutations evoke both the acting profession and Sartre's phenomenological updating of the *theatrum mundi* trope.[14] The human personality on stage is eminently malleable; there are no longer human beings, only roles. Zelig has the polyphonic anonymity of the character actor, whose capacity for both self-negation and self-transformation, in some ways reminiscent of mediumistic trance, makes him capable of extraordinary transfigurations. Zelig is not only seen in the company of actors he also becomes a performing freak in Martin Geist's exploitative sideshow. One of Zelig's former wives, espoused during one of his metamorphoses, claims to have known him when he was pretending to be an actor (a paradoxical formulation, since pretending is what actors do), and the chameleon-actor analogy is reinforced when we learn that Zelig's father practiced the same profession in a Brooklyn theater, playing the role of Puck in what seems like an oxymoronic production—the orthodox Yiddish version of *Midsummer Night's Dream*.

The reference to Yiddish theater points to still another intertext in which *Zelig* is embedded—that of Yiddish theater and borscht belt stand-up comedy (the explicit subject of Allen's *Broadway Danny Rose* [1984]). The theater that "fathered" Zelig was a theater full of transformations and hilarious polyglossia, fond of oxymoronic protagonists such as the schlemiel-saint and the luftmensch visionary. *Zelig* exemplifies as well the comic "universe-changing," the sometimes caricatural ethnic switch abouts typical of Yiddish-derived theatricality, of Fanny Brice performing "I'm an Indian," or Al Jolson in blackface belting out "Mammy," or Mel Brooks's Yiddish-speaking Indian in *Blazing Saddles*. Even the anachronisms of *Zelig*, whereby contemporary players are made to neighbor with deceased celebrities from the 1920s, has everything to do with the anachronistic humor of Mel Brooks's "2,000 Year Old Man" or with "Getting Even," Allen's own tale about a Hassidic rabbi who applies cabalistic numerology to the Daily Double.

If all human beings, as the *theatrum mundi* trope would have it, are actors, some human beings have been more attuned to acting than others. The force of historical experience, it has been argued, has made Jews especially sensitive to the theatrical dimension of social life, George Simmel, Helmut Plessner, and Hannah Arendt (not to mention Marcel Proust) have all spoken of this heightened sensitivity to the theatrical. Hannah Arendt speaks of the "exceptional" Jews admitted into the philo-Semitic salons of fin de siècle Paris, under the tacit condition that they would not reveal their status as Jews, a situation that made each of them an experienced actor in a theater whose curtain never closed. Life became theatrical to the point that the actors themselves, not unlike Zelig, no longer knew who they were.[15] As someone who wanted to "assimilate like crazy," as Irving Howe says of him, Zelig personifies the internal contradictions of one confronted with the "theatrical" challenge of shuttling, as it were, between the performance styles of sharply contrasting social worlds.[16]

Zelig makes a number of references to anti-Semitism. One partisan of Christian purity denounces Zelig as a polygamist and recommends that they "lynch the little Hebe." In street fights with anti-Semites, Zelig complains, his parents always sided with anti-Semites. The Ku Klux Klan denounces Zelig, and in France his convincing transformation into a rabbi leads some Frenchmen to want to send him to Devil's Island. Under hypnosis, Zelig reveals that he chameleonizes because "it's safe." Historically, Jews have reacted diversely to the temptation, and at times the decree, of assimilation. Some preferred death to forced conversion, while others chose the path of a self-preserving mimetism. Maimonedes praised the Jews of Morocco who feigned conversion to Islam to escape persecution, thus obeying the religious principle of respect for the sacred character of life, while Spinoza, in his *Tractatus Theologico-Politicus*, lamented the fate of the *marranos* who fused so well with the Spaniards that soon after nothing remained of them, not even a memory.[17] Ever since Esther, Jews have often been obliged to play a convoluted game of cultural hide-and-seek to avoid being victimized by blind violence, a challenge for which Zelig, with his singular physiological talent, is especially well equipped.

Jews formed Europe's internal Other, Todorov points out in *The Conquest of America*, before the colonized peoples became its external Other.[18] The Spanish Inquisition, designed to punish Jews and Moslems whose religious metamorphoses were deemed insincere, coincided with the invasion of the New World, and we can even discern a partial congruence between the stereotypical representations projected onto the internal enemy and the external savage: blood drinkers, cannibals, sorcerers, devils.[19] The Jew, like Zelig, was seen as a mask wearer, a diabolically fascinating shape-shifter. Zelig, in this sense, can be seen as condensing a number of the favored themes of anti-Semitism. His reptilian nature, for example, recalls Constantine Schuabe, the Jewish villain of the anti-Semitic British best-selling *When It Was Dark* (1903) who displayed the "sinister and troubled regard one sees in a reptile's eyes." More important, Zelig reflects the enforced plurality of the Jewish experience, the long historical apprenticeship in cultural mimicry and the syncretic incorporation of ambient cultures. Indeed, it was often this plurality that excited the passions of anti-Semites. The notion of a suspect plurality of identities runs like a leitmotif through anti-Semitic discourse, in Houston Stewart Chamberlain's idea of the "mongrel race," for example, or in Hitler's idea that the Jews were hiding their otherness behind fluent German. "They change nationalities like skins," ran the litany, and *cosmopolitan*, with its connotations of multicultural identity, became in Stalinist jargon a code for "Jew." It is Zelig's multiple otherness that provokes the special hatred of the Ku Klux Klan: "As Jew, Black, and Indian," the voice-over tells us, the KKK saw Zelig as a "triple threat." Zelig sums up in his metamorphoses the plurality of the Jewish experience and even the reality of Jews as a transracial people who literally range in appearance from blonde Hollywood actresses to the black Falashas of Ethiopia.[20]

The psychopathology of assimilation has at times led to extremes of self-degradation, as in the case of the notorious Jewish anti-Semite Otto Weininger, whose claim that "Judaism is the radical evil" supplied ideological ammunition for the enemies of the Jews.[21] The anti-Semite, to emend Sartre, creates not the Jew but the Jewish anti-Semite, a possibility powerfully imaged by Zelig's ephemeral transformation into a Nazi.[22] In his flight from ghettoization, Zelig demonstrates a weakness for upward mobility and a fascination with the possibility of moving freely across borders and gaining access to the real centers of power. He gains a certain mobility and even wins access to the Vatican and the Third Reich, but his mimicry is incomplete, always producing what Homi Bhabha calls "its slippage, its excess, its difference."[23] As a result, Zelig is ejected from the papal balcony and from the Third Reich rostrum.

Occupying a position of maximum social exposure, open to multifarious influences, Zelig represents the outsider as quasi insider, the marginal at the center.[24] From this position, his chameleonism can take him in virtually every direction. Indeed, his extreme ideological mobility points to the *political* ambiguities of chameleonism, for one always has the choice of chameleonizing vertically to the powerful, or chameleonizing horizontally to the analogously oppressed. (In short, one can make it to the top like Norman Podhoretz or struggle sideways like Emma Goldman and Abbie Hoffman.) Zelig, for his part, plays both pariah *and* parvenu; he is the aristocrat chatting on the lawn *and* the commoner speaking with the kitchen help.

Under hypnosis, Zelig admits to dialogically chameleonizing with another group of "hyphenated Americans." When he entered a bar on St. Patrick's Day, he relates, "I told them I was Irish. My hair turned red. My nose turned up. I spoke about the great potato famine." While critics have emphasized the bizarre aspects of Zelig's transformations, they have tended to ignore the deeper social, cultural, and historical logic that structures them. It makes perfect sense, for example, that Zelig would chameleonize, more or less horizontally, to his Irish fellow swimmers in the melting pot. Zelig also repeatedly chameleonizes to more obviously oppressed minorities—Indian, black, Chinese, Mexican. Each particular transformation bears its particular burden of historical reverberation. Zelig's recurrent chameleonizing to blackness, for example, is deeply rooted in the Jewish experience in Europe. Medieval European iconography contrasted the black image of the synagogue with the white one of the Church, an iconography that transmuted itself in the nineteenth century into the image of the black Jew common in nineteenth-century racist tracts. Hermann Wegener called Jews "white negroes," and Julius Streicher, one of the most notorious anti-Semites of the Weimar Republic and the Third Reich, argued in 1928 for the identity of language between Jew and black: "The swollen lips remind us again of the close relationship between Jews and Blacks. Speech takes place with a racially determined intonation."[25]

In another sense, Zelig can be seen as exemplifying the Bakhtinian view of the self as an echo chamber of socially orchestrated voices. (Zelig's chameleonism is also linguistic: Zelig speaks a variety of languages, apparently without accent, and adopts various social intonations.) As a walking polyphony of ethnic personalities, Zelig mimics the appearance and impersonates the voices of the diverse cultural figures with whom he comes into contact. He has "lines out," to borrow a metaphor from Melville's Pequod, to everyone else in the social "ship." His metamorphoses, in this sense, simply render visible and physical what is usually invisible—the constant process of syncretism that occurs when ethnicities brush against and rub off on one another in a context of cultural heteroglossia.

Zelig would seem, at first glance, to have a happy ending. Zelig's anarchic pluralities have been exorcised and domesticated, as Zelig discovers his true self and settles into monogamous normality. On the surface, the conclusion suggests the endorsement of a complacent American version of Sartrean authenticity expressed in the anticonformist discourse of 1950s liberalism; the formerly outer-directed Zelig is now inner directed. Paradoxically, however, Zelig is never more conformist than when he starts to be himself. In the end, he acquiesces in middle-class values and speaks in the clichés of ego-psychology and the self-help manual: "Be yourself," he tells admiring young people, "You have to be your own man." (Ironically, no one would be soliciting his opinion if he hadn't dared to be a chameleon.) In short, he has become a bland all-American, an acritical parrot of the reigning ideology, with no individuating traits more striking than being a "life-long Democrat" and "loving baseball."

The inane pronouncements generated by Zelig's epiphany generates a certain skepticism, which undermines the classical harmony of the film's happy end. In fact, *Zelig* highlights the curious doubleness of chameleonism, its possession of positive and negative poles. On the one hand, the film presents Zelig's condition as pathological, a neurosis to be cured, a disease whose symptoms include passivity, conformism, and potentially, fascism. The aleatory blank-check quality of Zelig's chameleonism makes him anxious to assimilate to *any* other, even that of his enemies. His random cannibalization of the personalities of others turns him into an aggregation of pastiches, a blank postmodern collage of available styles.[26] In this sense, Zelig lives out one pole of the possibilities pointed out by Bakhtin in terms of self-other relations; acritical absorption *by* the other.

At the same time, it is possible to tease out a latent utopia stirring within the negativity of Zelig (whose name does, after all, mean "blessed" as well as "silly"), a utopia both hinted at and repressed by the text. In an anticipatory reading, *Zelig* can be seen as pointing to the positive potentialities of chameleonism; creative adaptability, artistic transformation, and a vision of a possible communitas of reciprocally empathetic selves. This inkling of a possible life beyond the monad, transcending fixed social roles and ethnic positions, this possibility of an exhilarating indeterminacy (and what is carnival if not exhilarating indeterminacy?) is hinted at (awkwardly) by a man interviewed in a barber shop: "I wish I could be Leonard Zelig, the changing man, for then I could be many different people and some day my wish might come true." (It is a man of the people and not a celebrity intellectual, significantly, who articulates this collective fantasy.) The man imagines, in short, a Bakhtinian self that is not locked in, that can cross the border to imagine the other as subject and itself as object.[27] He sees in Zelig a man who wears other selves like carnival costumes, whose experience intimates a transindividual taste of freedom.

Zelig offers intriguing glimpses of possibilities not fully realized in the text itself. It intimates a view of the text, and the self, as a partial creation of the other. Biologic life, Bakhtin points out, depends on the capacity to respond to environmental stimuli; a living organism resists total fusion, but if completely torn from its environment, it dies. Jacques Derrida, in his essay on apartheid, makes the same point on a linguistic register: "How does one learn the other's language without renouncing one's own?" What is most suggestive in *Zelig* is the implicit parallelism that links the film's view of text and its view of self. A Bakhtinian reading might discern in *Zelig* a breaking down of the frontiers of self as well as of the frontiers of genre. The somatic membrane separating self from self, like that separating text from text and genre from genre, is more permeable than was thought; there is no ontological segregation, no rigid apartness, possible. The self, in a context of cultural polyphony, is necessarily syncretic. Zelig renders this syncretism visible by offering us a figure who is at once recognizably Woody Allen *and* recognizably black, Indian, Chinese. Woody Allen does not *become* Chinese, it is important to note; he becomes a Chinese Woody Allen. One cannot become the other, but one can meet the other part way. Within the Bakhtinian in-between, the self needs the collaboration of others to author and define itself, just as the film *Zelig* literally derives its existence from preexisting texts. (Whatever does not come from the tradition, Buñuel was fond of saying, is plagiarism.) The film's originality, paradoxically, lies in the audacity of its imitation, quotation, and absorption of other texts. Its ironic hybridization of traditionally opposed discourses undermines the monologic truth of generic purity and thus implicitly subverts, perhaps even against its will, the very idea of originality and, by extension, the idea of the true autonomous self. While *Zelig* at times seems to fall back into mystification of self and romance, its chameleonist intertextual strategies point to what Bakhtin would call "the interpersonal definition and fabrication of the world's meaning."

NOTES

1. In his essay "The Uncanny," Freud comments on one of the themes of the uncanny, to wit, "the double," defined as a situation in which one "possesses knowledge, feeling and experience in common with the other, identifies himself with another person, so that his self becomes confounded, or the foreign self is substituted for his own, in other words, by doubling, dividing and interchanging the self." Art Simon in an as yet unpublished paper, titled "Tracing Zelig," has usefully explored the relevance of Freud's ideas on the "uncanny" to the "interchanges of self" in the Allen film.

2. See Hayden White, *Metahistory: The Historical Imagination in Nineteenth-Century Europe* (Baltimore: Johns Hopkins, 1973); and Hayden White, *Tropics of Discourse: Essays in Cultural Criticism* (Baltimore: Johns Hopkins, 1978). White was not the first, obviously, to stress the inseparability of history and fiction. Many cultures do not apply the concept of fiction to traditional narrations, so that what the West calls myths are from their point of view comparable to historical events. White's line of thought, as he would be the first to point out, goes back to classical antiquity (for the Greeks, Homeric epic was at once history and fiction) and, in the modern period, to Nietzsche, Becker, and Lévi-Strauss. "History," argues the historical protagonist of Sartre's *La Nausée*, "is a complete fabrication," a "work of pure imagination."

3. The filmic analog itself can be seen as "chameleonizing," through photochemical processes, to the pro-filmic phenomena recorded on celluloid.

4. For technical information on how this filmic chameleonism was achieved, see "Gordon Willis, ASC, and *Zelig*," *American Cinematographer* (April 1984).

5. In his *Commentary* (November 1983) review of *Zelig*, Richard Grenier somewhat sanctimoniously laments the fact that Woody Allen would find "hilarious" a

man who supervised the melting down of gold teeth taken from the bodies of the victims of Hitler's gas chambers. Grenier's reaction, apart from exemplifying this kind of literal mindedness mocked by the film, also misses the point on a number of levels: (1) that the real Pohl was executed for his crimes and *therefore* can be made a figure of fun; (2) that hilarity can also entail anger and critique; (3) the joke, here, as in Purim and as in Carnival, is on the tyrant. This sequence also mocks the amoral and apolitical leveling typical of many documentaries that gives equal time to progressive intellectuals and amiable Nazis, all equaled in their status as commentators.

6. Woody Allen anticipated this kind of "kidnapping" of preexisting footage in *What's Up, Tiger Lily?* a Japanese thriller whose images are anchored by ironic commentary partially dubbed by Allen.

7. Some spectators, reportedly, have issued from screenings of *Zelig* to make comments to the effect that "if that guy Zelig was so important, how come I never heard of him?" a phenomenon that points to the fact that for some viewers the authenticating procedures even of deconstructed documentaries continue to be taken as a matter of faith. *Zelig* might be compared, in this context, to literary hoaxes and fictional biographies such as *Marbol*.

8. *Zelig* also alludes to *Citizen Kane* through the "Hearst Metrotone" newsreels, through Zelig's visit to San Simeon, and through the parody of the "News on the March" manner throughout. Both films, finally, show the capacity for the mass media to both mythify and destroy public figures.

9. The portrayal of the courageous analyst is undercut, in *Zelig*, by the psychoanalytic dialogue pregnant with comic inversions. The few staged dialogues in which Zelig participates, "scenes" in Genette's sense of literally equaling story and discourse time, show the chameleon chameleonized, as Zelig loses his bearings in the face of the analyst's feigned insecurity. Then, in another reversal, a hypnotized Zelig progresses from relating traumatic childhood experiences to analyzing his psychoanalyst. The analytical "voyeuse" is herself "vue," as the unconscious Zelig makes the hyperconscious Eudora realize what has long been obvious to the spectator, that she is "all mixed up and nervous" and attracted to Zelig.

10. For Bakhtin on Menippean satire, see *Problems of Dostoevsky's Poetics* (Minneapolis: University of Minnesota Press, 1984).

11. The film offers another index of anxiety over sexual difference in "Dr." Zelig's comment concerning his alleged break with Freud concerning penis envy: "he (Freud) thought it was limited to women." This hesitancy concerning the bridging of sexual differences on the part of Zelig contrasts with the pervasive transvestism and androgyny characteristic of carnival as practiced in Brazil, for example, and with the splitting of the self-characteristic of trance and possession in African-derived religions, where a woman is often possessed by a male *orixa* and a man, by a female *orixa*.

12. See Jean-Louis Schefer, *L'Homme Ordinaire du Cinema* (Paris: Gallimard, 1980).

13. See Edgar Morin, *Le Cinema ou L'Homine Imaginaïre* (Paris: Gonthier, 1958).

14. The evolution of the *theatrum mundi* trope over the course of literary history is inventoried in Ernst Curtius, *European Literature and the Latin Middle Ages* (Princeton, NJ: University Press, 1973). According to this perennial figure, given

phenomenological shape by Sartre, Merleau-Ponty, and others, the human personality "wears" ambient lifestyles as if they were theatrical costumes. One plays roles in life, not only for others but also for oneself. Clothes are worn as disguise and facial expression constitutes a mask. The waiter in a restaurant, Sartre argues in *Being and Nothingness*, plays at being a waiter, just as Roquentin, in Sartre's *La Nausée*, plays at being a historian.

15. See Hannah Arendt, *The Origins of Totalitarianism* (New York: Harcourt Brace, 1951). See also Georg Simmel, *On Individuality and Social Forms* (Chicago: University of Chicago Press, 1971); and Helmuth Plessner, *Anthropologie der Sinne* (Frankfurt: Suhrkamp, 1980).

16. It is worth reflecting, in this context, on the relation between names and human transformations, a subject with which Woody Allen (né Allen Stewart Konigsberg) is presumably familiar. In our culture, names change for reasons of marriage, of show-business ambition, of ethnic shame or pride, or political or cultural *prise de conscience* (Freeman to Freewoman, Cassius Clay to Muhammed Ali). In other cultures, names might change when one is ill, moves to a new locale, or is initiated into religious practice. The possibility of renaming in Western culture, and the worldwide variations in conventions of naming, cast a certain suspicion on the notion of the autonomous self, suggesting that the self is a cultural artifact as well as a bounded entity.

17. Sue Leon Poliakov, *The History of Anti-Semitism: From Mohammed to the Marranos* (New York: Vanguard, 1973).

18. See Tzvetan Todorov, *The Conquest of America: The Question of the Other* (New York: Harper & Row, 1981).

19. On the medieval diabolizing of Jews, see Joshua Trachtenberg, *The Devil and the Jews: The Medieval Conception of the Jew and its Relation to Modern Anti-Semitism* (New York: Harper, 1943).

20. It is this broad spectrum in appearance that subtends the humor, one presumes, of all those it's-funny-you-don't-look-Jewish jokes, a kind of joke of which Zelig can be seen as an extended and hyperbolic variation.

21. See Otto Weininger, *Sex and Character* (New York: G. P. Putnam, 1906). Weininger's *selbst-hass* fused anti-Semitism with misogyny, since he equaled Judaism with the female principle and saw human bisexuality as the source of evil in social life. For a related example of filmic *selbst-hass*, see Samuel Fuller's *Shock Corridor*, where a black civil rights activist, now in an insane asylum, fancies himself the leader of the Ku Klux Klan.

22. The idea of a Jew-into-Nazi transformation was anticipated, on a more frankly comic register, by an early Allen stand-up monologue alluding to a rabbi who was "very Reform, in fact, a Nazi."

23. See Homi K. Bhabha, "Signs Taken for Wonders: Questions of Ambivalence and Authority under a Tree Outside Delhi, May 1817," *Critical Inquiry* 12, no. 1 (Autumn 1985).

24. The sensibility of the Jew, George Steiner argues in "The Homeland as Text," is the medium between human unity with body and environment and human estrangement from them. Zelig's metamorphoses give physical expression to this simultaneous unity and estrangement, reflecting what Steiner calls the "ontological

foreignness": of the Diaspora Jew as a person always in transit, with a permanent visa to a messianic other homeland (for Steiner a *textual* homeland), drawing a kind of anguished vitality from dispersal and from the adaptive demands made by mobility.

25. Dr. B., "Die Rassenmerkmale der Juden," *Der Sturmer* 38 (1928), p. 2, quoted in Sander L. Gilman, *Jewish Self-Hatred: Anti-Semitism and the Hidden Language of the Jews* (Baltimore: Johns Hopkins, 1986).

26. *Zelig* at first glance would appear to partake of certain characteristics of neo-conservative postmodernism: a style rooted in pastiche, the eclectic historicism of recycled texts, the view of the past as available only through stereotypical representations, a kind of blank irony. Our view, however, is that while Zelig the character, at least in his chameleon phase (and it could be argued that Zelig never leaves his chameleon phase), does represent the postmodern, *Zelig* the film cannot be so characterized. *Zelig* does not so much trivialize history, as has sometimes been charged, as shed light on the constructed, manipulable nature of history as mediated by the culture industry. While it would be an exaggeration to call *Zelig* an example of what Hal Foster calls "oppositional post-modernism," it is still possible to coax an oppositional, anticipatory reading out of what is in some ways a recalcitrant text.

27. It is this taking oneself as object that distinguishes Bakhtinian dialogism from Romantic megalomania and the egotistical sublime.

18

Woody's Mild Irish Rose

Broadway Danny Rose

Peter J. Bailey

Why do all comedians turn out to be sentimental bores?

—Viewer at Sandy Bates Film Festival after watching the
"Stardust memory" scene of Bates's movie
in *Stardust Memories*

Perhaps "bores" is an inordinately harsh term with which to describe them, but the comedians who gather at the Carnegie Delicatessen in the opening scene of *Broadway Danny Rose* (1984) to trade borscht belt jokes, kibitz about the old days on the New York stand-up comedy circuit, and compete with each other to tell "the greatest Danny Rose story" are nothing if not sentimental. The pervasiveness of that sentimentality is but one of the elements that make *Broadway Danny Rose* seem a cinematic antithesis to the prevailing jadedness of *Manhattan*'s (1979) ethos, and even more so to the relentless perspectival and affective chill of *Interiors* (1978). Although there's hardly an explicit reference to art—as Eve would define it, at any rate—anywhere in *Broadway Danny Rose*, it's nonetheless a central movie to consider in the context of a discussion of Allen's equivocal stance toward the aesthetic because it dramatizes, albeit in distinctly mediated and elliptical terms, the values Allen counterposes to the life-consecrated-to-art ethic he so conflictedly rejected in *Interiors*. If high culture, artistic aspiration aroused in Allen an ambivalence he was incapable of resolving dramatically in *Interiors*, the pop culture world of Jewish American comedy elicits his sympathies so palpably that its depiction moves Allen as close as he ever

217

comes on film to the creation of a consonantly resolved narrative founded on a remarkably sentimental affirmation of human solidarity and morality.[1] Therefore, *Broadway Danny Rose* is as well made a film as Allen has produced, in addition to being an object lesson in Allen's conception of the conditions necessary to the creation of artistic closure in film narrative.

The protagonist of the comedians' communally generated "greatest Danny Rose story" represents the contravention of everything the aesthete Eve embodies. The contrasts between Eve and Danny Rose are easy to recognize: she decorates and dresses in tasteful, monochromatically repressed earth tones, whereas his style is 1970s polyester, his polka dot shirts competing cheerfully with loud plaid jackets; she is devoted to her personally defined, individualistic conception of beauty, wanting Arthur to see the interior of a church "before it gets cluttered up with people," whereas Danny is entirely other-directed, inquiring of every female he meets, "How old are you, darling?" and offering the world pep talks full of self-help incantations borrowed from wise dead relatives such as "star, smile, strong" and "acceptance, forgiveness, and love." Eve is the "very delicate" Matisse drawing she buys for Arthur at Parke-Barnet, while Danny is completely sold on "Mr. Danny Kaye and Mr. Bob Hope and Mr. Milton Berle"; she finds her only solace in the past, being desperately committed to the restoration of the lost unity of her family, which was her greatest creation and only protection, whereas he embraces a homiletic American belief in progress and the future, insisting that the beauty of show business lies in that "overnight, you can go from a bum to a hero."[2] Validating Danny's Horatio Algeresque faith in the possibility of self-transformation from bum to hero constitutes both the movie's pivotal dramatic project as well as the basis for its central pun.

Perhaps the most significant distinction between the two film protagonists, however, exists in Eve's dedication to an ideal of humanity-ennobling artistic perfection as opposed to Danny's unequivocal commitment to artists over art. It's not merely that the performance specialties of his clients—balloon folding, water glass playing, bird and penguin acts—bear only a parodic relation to what Eve would designate fine arts; beyond that, he seems to have deliberately sought out performers whose physical incapacities *necessarily compromise* their ability to perform their art. Far from achieving anything approaching perfect art, the performances of a number of Danny's clients—his blind xylophonist, one-legged tap dancer, and one-armed juggler—must be judged primarily on the basis of their success in overcoming the disability to which their acts unerringly draw attention. Danny is, as Jonathan Baumbach's review of the film describes him, "a one-man Salvation Army for crippled performers,"[3] and apparently it is only the utter wretchedness of Barney Dunn's jokes that prevents Danny from representing this genial stuttering ventriloquist. Client or not, Barney (Herb Reynolds) is one of the guests at the patently sacramental Thanksgiving scene that closes the movie, Danny's annual gathering of his showbiz low rollers manifesting not his belief in the magnitude of their talents but his sincere affection for them as people.

Accordingly, in attempting to sell his clients to hotels, rooms, and promoters, Danny invariably invokes their human qualities—the blind xylophone player is "a beautiful man," "a fantastic individual"—rather than the virtues of their acts, Danny's intense involvement in their lives enabling him endlessly to vouch for their characters and plead their causes for them. (The trauma of the death of one of the birds in Herbie Jayson's act, Danny argues with a club manager, justifies his being paid despite his client having been too devastated to perform.) Similarly, Danny is able to value even those whose lack of talent doesn't even have the excuse of good character to recommend it. The client of Danny's that the comedians' "greatest Danny Rose story" concentrates on is perceived by the rest of the show business community as nothing but trouble: Lou Canova (Nick Apollo Forte) is, in the words of the owner of Weinstein's Majestic Bungalow Colony, "a dumb, fat, temperamental has-been with a drinkin' problem" (154). The unfolding of the plot adds "womanizer" to that catalogue of Lou's character deficits, none of which deters Danny from devoting himself unswervingly to the promotion of the Italian crooner's career, even volunteering to waive his commissions when Lou feels financially pinched. "In business," Danny's father had told him, "friendly but not familiar," but he hasn't been able to follow that advice because, "This is personal management I'm in. You know, it's the keyword, it's *personal*" (212). His emphasis on ministering to the personal lives of his clients combined with the limitations of their talents ensures that he and they remain on the outer fringes of show business. His marginality is epitomized by his most successful performers regularly abandoning him for more powerful agents and by the snapshots on his apartment wall of himself with Frank Sinatra and Tony Bennett, of himself with Judy Garland, of himself with Myron Cohen—photographs in which Danny is never quite visible. In this most sentimentally egalitarian of Woody Allen's films, it is anything but a put-down to suggest that Danny and his clients deserve each other.

"You're livin' like a loser," Tina Vitale (Mia Farrow) tells Danny when she first visits his apartment. Tina, widow of a Mafia hit man, has aspirations to a career in interior decoration and room decors as tasteful—and as unlike Eve's—as Danny's wardrobe. The two are thrown together on the day of Lou's appearance at the Waldorf, the singer insisting that he can't go on without knowing his lover is in the audience. It's the contrast of his "loser" humanist values—concern for others and "acceptance, forgiveness, and love"—with her hard-bitten "looking out for number one" ethic that provides a central thematic tension for the film. (Whereas the moralism of *Manhattan*'s Isaac Davis is self-righteous and self-serving, Danny's is generously permeated by altruistic impulses. Nothing reflects the comedian's subjective needs in recounting his story more clearly than its dramatization of Danny's betrayal by the callous, self-interested, antihumanistic values of show business.) Undergirding the main comic business of *Broadway Danny Rose*—an extended chase scene occupying much of the heart of the film in which Tina and Danny are pursued by Johnny Rispoli's brothers, who are intent upon rubbing out "Danny White Roses" for stealing Tina from Johnny—is a debate between the couple about personal responsibility to others, a debate ultimately resolved by Tina's eventual acknowledgment of the inevitability of guilt to human interaction.

Early in the film when Lou Canova reveals his adulterous relationship with Tina to Danny, Danny points to the sky and warns the singer, "Some day you're gonna have to square yourself with the big guy"; Danny later admits that he doesn't believe in God, but he's "guilty over it." Tina spends the last third of the film attempting to square herself with all that the movie offers her to square herself with—the little guy, Danny. Tina appears uninvited at Danny's annual Thanksgiving bash (he serves his performers frozen-turkey TV dinners each year) with his Uncle Sidney's trio of virtues—"acceptance, forgiveness, and love"—on her lips, having in the last weeks undergone an object lesson in the validity of Danny's philosophy of life: "It's important to have some laughs, no question about it, but you got to suffer a little, too. Because otherwise, you miss the whole point of life" (254).

No Woody Allen film ends in a more completely earned or more satisfying sense of closure than *Broadway Danny Rose*. The conciliation scene between Danny and Tina takes place with charmingly corny aptness outside the Carnegie Deli in which the comedians, some years later, would be nostalgically reconstructing the couple's adventure together.[4] To not overextend the happy ending, Allen signals only with calculated indirection the inevitable romantic resolution and Danny's postnarrative progress from "a bum to a hero." In the film's final scene, Sandy Baron reveals that the Carnegie Deli has elevated Danny to the status of Broadway luminary through introducing a sandwich intermixing Danny's Jewish and Tina's Italian heritages called the "Danny Rose Special," the offering consisting, Morty Gunty speculates, of cream cheese on bagel with marinara sauce. Whether the sandwich Danny has become is a hero or not is left to the viewer to decide. Significantly, that sandwich is all that remains of Danny Rose in the film's present—he has become inseparable from the story told about him, or as John Pym suggested, "he has faded into the mythical anecdotes of his peers."[5] It is his withdrawal into the status of the legendary that largely accounts for the film's untypical—for Allen—happy ending, *Broadway Danny Rose* reinforcing the point implicit in *Radio Days* that happy endings are possible only for fictional characters.

Inspired by this heartwarming resolution, jocularity prevails as the closing titles scroll over some good-natured banter between the comics about the length of Baron's Danny Rose story and expressions of surprise at Corbett Monica's uncharacteristically picking up the evening's check. It's clear that the telling of the "greatest Danny Rose story" has accomplished what efficacious myths effect: it has magically altered ordinary human interactions in the Carnegie Deli. Gunty affirms that the comedians will meet again tomorrow for more nostalgia, more talk of the old days, but it's evident that we've heard the story they most needed and wanted to tell. To understand how *Broadway Danny Rose* manages to reach what so few Allen films do—an unambiguously happy ending—it's necessary to recognize how completely the fable's resolution depends on the needs and agendas of its community of tellers. (In response to Will Jordan's account of how he came to impersonate James Mason, Howard Storm indirectly calls attention to the mediatory role of the comedians in *Broadway Danny Rose*, asking, "But this thing is all in like the mask, right?" [150]. Right.) At the bleakest point in Sandy Baron's narrative (Danny, fired by Lou on the night of his nostalgia act's biggest showbiz success, walks out of Roosevelt Hospital into a rainstorm after visiting Barney Dunn, for whose pulverization by Mafia thugs he's inadvertently responsible), Morty Gunty objects, "I thought this was a funny story. It's terrible!" (291). The story is destined not to end terribly because of the purpose its telling is serving the tellers and the told.

Before they embark on their communal Danny Rose narrative, the assembled comedians schmooze about the condition of the world of show business as they experience it in the film's present, the early 1980s. It's not good. The old fail-safe jokes they've traditionally stolen from each other for their routines aren't working anymore; there are far fewer rooms for comedians to play in the New York metropolitan area, obliging them to travel as far as Baltimore and Washington for jobs and to have much better tires than they previously needed; and audiences are neither as reliable nor as loyal as they once were. "They never left," Baron recalls mournfully, invoking the old crowds in the old venues devoted solely to comedy, "they never left at all" (149). It is no coincidence that to counter these present miseries and cheer themselves up the story Baron and his fellow comics enthusiastically choose is that of Danny Rose, who—at least in their nostalgic reconstruction of him—is notable primarily for his unstinting and unequivocal loyalty to his acts. "His acts were so devoted," Will Jordan comments, "They loved him . . . I mean, where you gonna find that kind of devotion today?" (154). In his *Commonweal* review, Baumbach characterizes *Broadway Danny Rose* as "a comedy about mythmaking,"[6] which I take to mean that what we're watching in the movie is the comedians' construction of the myth that is "the greatest Danny Rose story." So it's quite appropriate that the first flashback scene the comedians evoke of Danny (the first in which Allen appears in the movie) dramatizes his attempt to sell his acts to the booking agent for

Weinstein's Majestic Bungalow Colony and includes a discussion of the dis-
loyalty—foreshadowing Lou's defection—of one of Danny's recent acts
who had begun to prosper in show business. "They get a little success," Phil,
the Colony booking agent, tells Danny, "and they leave you" (155). Danny,
to the contrary, "would work his tail off for his acts . . . if he believed in
them," comedian Howard Storm insists. The comics agree that making his
clients believe in themselves constituted much of the "star, smile, strong"
strategy of "Danny Rose, Personal Management."

"I don't see you folding balloons in joints," Danny insists in a typical
client-motivation spiel, "You're gonna fold these balloons in universities and
colleges . . . you're gonna make your snail and your elephant at, at, on
Broadway" and thus become "one of the great balloon-folding acts of all
time" (154). It's in this goofily sincere belief in other people and his endless
encouragement of them that Danny Rose differs most radically from every
other Woody Allen protagonist, and if his character is the sentimental ideal-
ization of show business of an earlier decade projected by aging, demoral-
ized, and nostalgic comics,[7] he represents Allen's least Woody Allenesque
portrayal and Allen's single most accomplished job of comic acting.

Vincent Canby eloquently described *Broadway Danny Rose* as "a love letter not only to American comedy stars and to all those pushy hopefuls who
never made it to the top in show business, but also to the kind of comedy
that nourished the particular genius of Woody Allen,"[8] his characterization
effectively accounting for the unequivocality of the film's address to the
viewer's emotions. Gilbert Adair's review of the film summarizes the affective quality of Allen's performance equally elegantly: Danny recalls Chaplin's
"little man," and "reincarnated here as Danny Rose, he *is* pathetic, melancholic, droll, poignant, affecting—that whole Thesaurus of sentimental ad-
jectives covered by the outmoded but not quite obsolete critical
commonplace 'Chaplinesque.' Danny is a born loser; and the film's premise,
one of the most moving it's possible to imagine, is the ultimate triumph of
the loser over his fate."[9] Adair's eloquent description only omits that it's the
Carnegie comedians who are engaging in the communal act of wish fulfillment that is the story of this loser triumphing over his fate. Lacking the actual Danny himself for reassurance, they are creating their own elaborate
narrative version of "star, smile, strong" to buck themselves up as they prepare to schlep themselves to Baltimore and New Jersey to perform their gigs.

For Baron and his fellow comics, Danny is the epitome of a lost world in
which performers like themselves—and even those still more inferior and
small-time—were cared for, valued in a way these comedians' opening exchange proves that they no longer are. (That a couple of the comedians turn
out to have attended one of Danny's TV dinner Thanksgiving feasts affirms
their largely unacknowledged solidarity with Danny's exotic acts.) Because
there *is* no Danny Rose beyond Sandy Baron's narrative, it is impossible to

distinguish fact from myth in the film; all we have is the "landlocked He-brew" of their telling, whose message is "acceptance, forgiveness, and love" and who will arguably become more noble and self-sacrificing with every telling of his story by the comedians who ritualistically gather at the Carne-gie Deli to cheer themselves with sentimental constructions of the superior-ity of yesterday to today. David Denby's objection that "not even Damon Runyon, Broadway fabulist and designer of improbable marches, could have imagined that this girl [Tina] is for that guy [Danny]"[10] assumes that the film's conclusion is dictated by real-world probability; insofar as Danny and Tina are united in the film's close, it's only because the comedians, in their affection for their hero, believe *he deserves her.*[11] For his loyalty to his acts, for his epitomizing humanistic values in an increasingly inhumane industry, the comedians' myth weaving rewards Danny with Tina. That's the story they tell themselves; that's the story we see. It's not even certain, in fact, that the "Danny Rose Special" *does* marry Jewish and Italian cultures: although Morty Gunty asserts it's "probably a cream cheese on a bagel with marinara sauce" (309), neither he nor the other comedians seem to have the heart to check the Carnegie Deli menu board a few feet away from their table for fear, perhaps, of finding that the honorary sandwich is actually cream cheese and lox on bagel.

Only the narrative intercession of "sentimental bores" like Baron, Gunty, Corbett Monica, Jackie Gayle, Howard Storm, Will Jordan, and (perennial Allen film producer) Jack Rollins,[12] with their communal need to remember a better day in American showbiz and to provide themselves with a Danny Rosean pep talk brightening their future prospects, could transform the workings of Danny's godless, guilt-laden universe into the encouraging little fable with its lovely, morality-affirming resolution that is *Broadway Danny Rose.* Only their benevolently mediational presence and Allen's obvious af-fection for them and the world they embody can account for the generation of this most artistically consonant and happiest of Woody Allen endings.

"You're livin' like a loser," we've already heard Tina tell Danny. As we've also noticed, Gilbert Adair took her at her word, describing Allen's protago-nist's character as that of "a born loser" whose triumph is that of "a loser over his fate"; Andrew Sarris concurred, designating Danny "a pathetic loser who lives in a rat hole"[13]; Daphne Merkin took a different tack by being offended that the film evoked concern from the audience for Danny rather than "the losers who surround" him,[14] acts whom Joseph Gelmis character-ized as Danny's "'family' of show biz losers."[15] Jack Kroll in *Newsweek* was more egalitarian in conferring the status on both agent and clients, seeing Danny as "a loser selling losers,"[16] while David Denby perceived the same redemptive movement in the film Adair did, viewing *Broadway Danny Rose* as "a fable about how losers can become winners." It's interesting that these reviewers—some of whom find Tina an unconvincing character—

nonetheless so emphatically endorse her social Darwinist ethic. She knows losers when she sees them, and so do they. Given the near-unanimity of this descriptor's application to Danny and his acts, it's worthwhile to briefly consider the validity of the label "loser" so liberally conferred not only upon characters in *Broadway Danny Rose* but to Allen's nebbish protagonists in general. Although somewhat tangential to the issue of Allen's ambivalence toward art, the "loser" tag so uncritically applied to Allen's characters may have done more to blind reviewers and critics to the nuances of Allen's vision than any other misperception.

As early as 1963, William K. Zinsser described the persona projected by Allen's stand-up routine as that of "a born loser . . . who walks onto a stage and immediately makes his presence unfelt"[17]; the first critical book published on Allen's films was titled *Loser Take All*, and contains the sentence, "Despite all the failures, however, it should not be concluded that Allen's persona is always a loser,"[18] which clearly implies that he usually is one. Maurice Yacowar did point up the paradox of Allen's having rid himself of the loser persona to great personal success, but the glib characterizing of his characters as losers continued. Does categorizing Allen's characters as losers help to clarify anything about them or about the films in which they appear? More particularly, is this derogatorily fatalistic judgment consistent with the tone and spirit of *Broadway Danny Rose*?

Perhaps there's some justice in characterizing the one-dimensional hapless bunglers of *Take the Money and Run* (1969), *Bananas* (1971), and *Sleeper* (1973) as unredeemed, unreconstructed losers, though it's difficult not to think that even there the term serves primarily as an excuse for critical—not to mention humanistic—imprecision. But what makes Allan Felix of *Play It Again, Sam* a loser? He's nervous around women, he fails to deliver the appropriate insincerities when the moment and his erotic advantage demands them, and California beauties spurn his attempts to dance with them—he's not, in short, Bogart. What makes *Annie Hall*'s Alvy Singer a loser? He's obsessed with death, he's hypochondriac and hypersensitive and—like many of us in the audience—his desire to be loved exceeds his lovability. What makes Danny Rose a loser? He's dedicated himself to supporting performing acts because he cares about the performers more than he does about the quality of their performances or about the financial rewards that might accrue from his representing them, and—as his obviously delighted hosting of the Thanksgiving feast dramatizes—he derives obvious pleasure from his relationships with them. (Not coincidentally, he lives in an apartment reflective of his indifference to the money they don't make for him.) That these are comic characters, presented to us partly for laughs, suggests that their sensibilities are extreme, exaggerated for the purpose of humor. To dismiss them as losers, however, is to ignore the fact that, throughout Jewish American comic literature, the un-Waspish "deficiencies" of Jewish protagonists, in addition to being excellent material for jokes, also satirically reflect the mainstream culture from which they represent significant deviations. The obsession Nathanael West's Miss Lonelyhearts develops with the sufferings of the letter writers to his newspaper column pushes well into comic excess, even though the novella never suggests that he isn't responding to a terrible American reality that those around him refuse to acknowledge or that they callously reduce to jokes. Moses Herzog's obsessive letter writing *is* funny, but the sensibility it expresses (one more literary than, but not unlike, Holden Caulfield's) also critiques WASP ideals of masculine reticence and expressive self-inhibition. Alexander Portnoy's incessant masturbation makes us laugh while satirizing the puritan abjuration of the physical promptings of the body he somehow failed to internalize; Bruce Jay Friedman's Stern has so completely introjected American anti-Semitism that his ongoing struggles with it are as hilarious as the cultural bigotry with which he is contending is real.

These "losers" all have in common their recognition of—or perhaps more accurately, their obsession with—human or cultural realities the denial of whose existences is a cultural code to which those around them have conformed. The excess of their overreaction to those realities is both what makes them comic *and* the works' primary documentation of their non-American mainstream humanity. While laughing at the disparity between the conduct of these protagonists and national norms of behavior and belief, we are obliged by Jewish American literature to scrutinize the validity of those values, invited to find them wanting.

In the fictional worlds through which these protagonists move, they may be perceived as losers, but is the reader intended so uncritically to adopt the values of those worlds? After all, isn't it these characters' imperviousness to the values of mainstream American culture that constitutes the very source of their "loserness"? That would seem to place those imposing the term "loser" on them in the anomalous position of defining winning as conformity to, or the achievement of success in, mainstream American culture. Lou Canova is experiencing success in that world by singing "Agita," a song that he (actually, Nick Apollo Forte) wrote about indigestion, his exploitation of the 1970s nostalgia craze allowing him to dump Danny for the more powerful management of Sid Bacharach. Is this the point of the "parable of how losers can become winners?"[19] Bacharach, whom Tina knows through her murdered husband, the Mafia hit man, expresses agreement with her ethic of "You see what you want, go for it" and "Do it to the other guy first, 'cause if you don't he'll do it to you" (254); if Bacharach represents the film's epitome of winning, Danny Rose and his stable of performers will remain losers. What Tina's appearance at Danny's apartment at the end of the film affirms with a truly Chaplinesque sentimentality unprecedented in Allen's work is Danny's Uncle Sidney's belief in "acceptance, forgiveness, and love," a moral stance that makes no provision for discriminations between winners and losers. Surely one of the objectives of an art is to demonstrate the bankruptcy of simplistic, superficial, and essentialistic conceptions of humanity. *Broadway Danny Rose*'s touching demonstration that fellow feeling and compassion for others *are* rewarded, not in heaven but in front of—or inside—the Carnegie Deli, should have been sufficient to quash for good the loser rhetoric mindlessly applied to Allen's protagonists.

That so-called loser deficiencies may constitute a manifestation of an inverted form of personal redemption is a major point not only of *Broadway Danny Rose* but also of the Allen film that preceded it, *Zelig* (1983). Saul Bellow's assessment of the Zelig phenomenon in that movie has to be understood as a view mediated by the fact that a real author is discoursing straightfacedly on a fictional character, the ironic inversions implicit in the clip dictating that we should take his mock judgment quite seriously, both as a comment on Leonard Zelig and—arguably—as a gloss on some of Bellow's own protagonists. "The thing was paradoxical because what enabled [Zelig] to perform this astounding feat [of flying over the Atlantic Ocean upside down] was his ability to transform himself," Bellow explains. In other words, the psychic pathology of imitating the world around him for which Zelig had to be treated was what allowed him to emulate Eudora Fletcher's piloting of the plane after she had passed out and to fly them safely back from Germany. "Therefore, his sickness was at the root of his salvation," Bellow continues, "and . . . I think it's interesting to view the thing that way, that it, it was his . . . it was his very disorder that made a hero of him."[20] Just as the "sicknesses" of West's, Bellow's, Roth's, and Friedman's obsessives are "at the root of their salvation," so it is Danny Rose's eccentric loyalty to and celebration of show business rejects—the one-legged tap dancer and one-armed juggler and stammering ventriloquist, all of whom, just like the rest of us, attempt to make art out of our various impairments—which constitutes the heroism the comedians implicitly reward him for and culminates in the Broadway apotheosis of his becoming a Carnegie Deli sandwich. It is his deviation from the inhuman values of American show business that makes a hero out of Danny Rose.

In the end, the best corrective to the critical tendency to reduce Allen's protagonists to losers is to invoke his own use of the term. "Basically," Allen said as early as 1969, discoursing on his favorite topic of human mortality, "everybody is a loser, but it's only now that people are willing to admit it."[21] In making this assertion, Allen was implicitly declaring his solidarity with the Jewish American literary tradition that had for years been using the satirical portraiture of Jewish characters to backhandedly skewer the WASP values that they so hilariously failed to emulate. Their inability to accommodate themselves to those values proves, ironically, that the "disorder" Bellow attributes to Zelig is in the culture rather than in them. More than any other film of Allen's, *Broadway Danny Rose* finds in the admission that "everybody is a loser" not grounds for self-hatred or narcissistic withdrawal but, instead, an affecting rationale for human solidarity.

NOTES

1. The contrast between the highly sympathetic depiction of the world of Jewish American comedy and the much more negative vision of Hollywood in Allen's next film, *The Purple Rose of Cairo*, isn't surprising, given Allen's career choices, but it is nonetheless instructive. The Hollywood film within *Purple Rose* presents nothing but illusions belied by the actions and characters of the actors who appear in the movie, but which the hopeless economic straits of the audience compel them desperately to embrace; the comedians are aware of and sensitive to their audience, enjoying each other at the Carnegie Deli as if they *are* that audience.

2. Woody Allen, *Broadway Danny Rose*, in *Three Films of Woody Allen*, 255 (New York: Vintage, 1987). Subsequent unattributed page numbers refer to this.

3. Jonathan Baumbach, "The Comedians" (review of *Broadway Danny Rose*), *Commonweal*, March 23, 1984, p. 182.

4. Another small consonance between beginnings and endings in the Danny Rose fable: when Danny arrives at Tina's apartment to meet her for the first time, she's talking to Lou on the telephone; when she arrives at Danny's apartment on Thanksgiving to make up with him, he's talking on the telephone.

5. John Pym, review of *Broadway Danny Rose*, *Sight and Sound*, Autumn 1984, p. 300.

6. Baumbach, 182.

7. The comedians are not the only ones being nostalgic in *Broadway Danny Rose*. Weinstein's Majestic Bungalow Colony, a Catskills resort where Danny is pictured pumping his acts, is where Allen's performing career had its start, the sixteen-year-old Allen Konigsberg having performed magic tricks there. Allen biographies have also established that the Danny Rose character was inspired in part by Harvey Meltzer, the agent Allen had before signing on with Charles Joffe and Jack Rollins. Meltzer is said to have used phrases similar to Danny's signature expression, "Might I interject a concept at this juncture?"

8. Vincent Canby, "'Danny Rose': Runyonesque, but Pure Woody Allen" (review of *Broadway Danny Rose*), *New York Times*, January 29, 1984, sec. 2, 13, p. 1.

9. Gilbert Adair, review of *Broadway Danny Rose*, *Monthly Film Bulletin*, September 1984, p. 272.

10. David Denby, review of *Broadway Danny Rose*, *New York*, February 6, 1984, p. 64.

11. The union of Danny and Tina would also confirm the prediction of Tina's favorite fortune teller, Angelina, that Tina would marry a Jew. That confirmation might be said to balance somewhat the film's dramatization of Danny's ethic so clearly triumphing over her cultural beliefs. That Tina's culture is largely reduced to "fortune-tellers and meat hooks" is admittedly one of the film's less pleasing comic strategies.

12. Allen's decision to have the comedians portray themselves rather than providing them with fictional identities creates a minor fact-fiction tension in the film, reversing the juxtaposition of the fictional Leonard Zelig with actual documentary footage, which was the central rhetorical ploy of *Zelig*, his previous film.

13. Andrew Sarris, review of *Broadway Danny Rose*, *Village Voice*, February 7, 1984, p. 47.

14. Daphne Merkin, "Comedy on Three Levels" (review of *Broadway Danny Rose*), *New Leader*, March 5, 1984, p. 19.

15. Joseph Gelmis, review of *Broadway Danny Rose*, *Newsday*, January 27, 1984, sec. 2, p. 3.

16. Jack Kroll, "Woody's Bow to Broadway" (review of *Broadway Danny Rose*), *Newsweek*, January 30, 1984, p. 69.

17. William K. Zinsser, "Bright New Comic Clowns Toward Success," *Saturday Evening Post*, September 21, 1963, p. 26.

18. Maurice Yacowar, *Loser Take All: The Comic Art of Woody Allen* (New York: Ungar, 1979), 21.

19. In a very grumpy review of the film, Pauline Kael suggests, "Although Woody Allen knows how repulsive Lou Canova's act is, Danny Rose doesn't. He isn't permitted to have either taste or consciousness" (*State of the Art* [New York: E. P. Dutton, 1985], p. 124). Whether Allen's film is as insistent upon the repulsiveness of Canova's act as is Kael is highly questionable—Nick Apollo Forte's performances in the film apparently differ little from the stage show he once regularly performed. The value system of *Broadway Danny Rose* is the showbiz ethic of the Carnegie comics and cruise ship lounges and Joe Franklin's *Memory Lane* television show, and much of the viewer's pleasure in the playing out of the film's fable is immersion in that frankly and unapologetically vulgar realm in which singers perform medleys of "crooners who are now deceased." Consequently, "taste or consciousness" is expressly not what this film is about, except in that Danny has too much of either to sacrifice human beings to the showbiz winner-take-all worship of success. The question Kael might have posed to herself before dismissing the premises of *Broadway Danny Rose* was the one with which she closed her review of *Another Woman*: "How can you embrace life and leave out all the good vulgar trashiness?" (*Movie Love* [New York: E. P. Dutton, 1991], 16).

20. Woody Allen, *Zelig*, in *Three Films of Woody Allen*, 126 (New York: Vintage, 1987).

21. Yacowar, 215.

19

Stardust Memories, The Purple Rose of Cairo, and the Tradition of Metafiction

Michael Dunne

Woody Allen's *The Purple Rose of Cairo* (1985) has the same relation to romantic film comedy as radical postmodern writing such as John Barth's *Lost in the Funhouse* (1968) has to traditional prose fiction. The chief parallel stems from the fact that, faced with outmoded conventional forms, Allen—like Barth—ironically raises doubts about the effectiveness of his medium to achieve a new sort of aesthetic order. Robert Scholes has called fiction that challenges its own premises in this way "metafiction," and we may follow Scholes in calling *Purple Rose* a "metafilm." Terminology is less important, however, than a recognition that Allen has succeeded in creating romantic film comedy under cultural circumstances that would seem to make such an achievement impossible.

A passage from the title story of *Lost in the Funhouse* should serve to illustrate the technique of this and other metafiction. In the first eight paragraphs of the story Barth satisfies many requirements of the traditional short story. He introduces Ambrose, a sensitive, insecure boy; his older brother Peter; Magda, the girl they both love; the boys' parents; and their Uncle Karl. He develops these characters somewhat, establishes his setting, and initiates his plot. Then the narrator says, or writes, the following in paragraph nine:

> Plush upholstery prickles uncomfortably through gabardine slacks in the July sun. The function of the beginning of a story is to introduce the principal characters, establish their initial relationships, set the scene for the main action, expose the background of the situation if necessary, plant motifs and foreshadowings where appropriate, and initiate the first complication or what-

ever of the "rising action." Actually, if one imagines a story called "The Fun-house" or "Lost in the Funhouse," the details of the drive to Ocean City do not seem especially relevant. The *beginning* should recount the events between Ambrose's first sight of the funhouse early in the afternoon and his entering it with Magda and Peter in the evening. The *middle* would narrate all relevant events from the time he goes in to the time he loses his way; middles have a double and contradictory function of delaying the climax while at the same time preparing the reader for it and fetching him to it. Then the *ending* would tell what Ambrose does while he's lost, how he finally finds his way out, and what everybody makes of the experience. So far there's been no real dialogue, very little sensory detail, and nothing in the way of *theme.* And a long time has gone by already without anything happening; it makes a person wonder. We haven't even reached Ocean City yet; we will never get out of the funhouse. (77)

The effect of such writing is, paradoxically, to italicize all the elements—character, setting, action—that Barth's narrator seems to discount. More-over, the "reader" considered in Barth's discussion is co-opted as a result of this technique into participating in the narrative process. By deliberately treating conventions as conventions, Barth draws the reader into the role of accomplice and foists upon him or her responsibility for the sorts of tradi-tional expectations that the narrative voice ridicules as futile, most especially the expectation of coherent closure. In fact, John O. Stark argues, in his study *The Literature of Exhaustion*, that postmodern fiction is distinctly marked by its resistance not merely to happy endings but to closure of any sort (8ff.).

"Lost in the Funhouse" is exemplary of this tendency also, particularly in a passage occurring about two-thirds of the way through. Since the pre-viously quoted passage, Barth has developed his characters further and has brought his fictional Ocean City into sharper focus. He has even advanced the plot a bit. As a result, by the time the illustrative passage occurs, Barth has finally succeeded in fulfilling his title by getting Ambrose lost in the fun-house. Then we read the following:

One possible ending would be to have Ambrose come across another lost per-son in the dark. They'd match their wits together against the funhouse, struggle like Ulysses past obstacle after obstacle, help and encourage each other. Or a girl. By the time they found the exit they'd be closest friends, sweethearts if it were a girl; they'd know each other's inmost souls, be bound together by *the cement of shared adventure*; then they'd emerge into the light and it would turn out that his friend was a Negro. A blind girl. President Roosevelt's son. Am-brose's archenemy. (87)

In this passage Barth is simultaneously playing with his reader and striving to fulfill a fictional design. This bifurcation is necessary because, after so many centuries of Aristotelian plotting, Barth obviously feels that it would be aesthetically invalid, and perhaps dishonest, to resolve his story neatly with a traditional conclusion. On the other hand, Barth will not accept simply dribbling off into inconclusive insignificance. Here is where the reader's participation becomes crucial. Having read so many stories already, the reader has natural—conventional—expectations about what should eventuate from Ambrose's predicament. Barth deliberately raises expectations of this sort through suggestions such as those in the quoted passage. Then he turns to what Roland Barthes has defined as ludic writing to successively reject all these possibilities. This device does not invalidate the expectation of closure, however. The reader has still been allowed, even encouraged, to entertain his desire for a happy ending, even if only momentarily. Finally, while participating in this process, the reader may justifiably infer an air of aesthetic desperation about the whole enterprise.

Scholes has attributed the origins of such writing by Barth and other "fabulators" such as Donald Barthelme and Robert Coover to the fact that these writers must approach their craft burdened by the legacy of centuries of fiction that seems to have exploited the possibilities of their medium to the point of bankruptcy. Scholes writes,

> The history of the form he works in lies between every writer and the pure ideas of fiction. It is his legacy, his opportunity, and his problem. The fiction of forms at one level simply accepts the legacy and repeats the form bequeathed it, satisfying an audience that wants this familiarity. But the movement of time carries such derivative forms further and further from the ideas of fiction until they atrophy and decay. (108)

This last state is the condition Barth writes about in his landmark essay of 1967, "The Literature of Exhaustion." There, Barth agrees that, under the circumstances Scholes describes, the serious writer must resort to some strategy of exigency. That is, the writer must actually do with the left hand what the right hand demonstrates to be impossible or futile. Furthermore, as we have seen, the writer of metafiction requires the active complicity of the reader to succeed in all this sleight of hand.

The resemblance to the fabulators of Allen's artistic dilemma is clear first of all in his 1980 film *Stardust Memories*, in which a short, balding, bespectacled filmmaker named Sandy Bates questions, in a comic film, whether comic films are worth creating. The autobiographical parallels to Allen's own situation during the stage of his career marked by *Annie Hall* (1977), *Interiors* (1978), and *Manhattan* (1979) are apparent, and thus many of Sandy's experiences may be seen as cinematic displacements of Woody Allen's own. Most obvious among these is the delicate balance required of a filmmaker caught between his audience's demand that he continue in his early mode of antic comedy and his own feeling that there is more to art and life than easy laughs. All through *Stardust Memories*, for example, fans and studio functionaries ask Sandy when he will return to his early comic manner, just as customers and critics alike asked in the late 1970s when Allen would produce another *Bananas* (1971) or *Take the Money and Run* (1969). Such thinking about film or fiction characterizes "an audience that wants . . . familiarity," as Scholes says in the previously quoted passage. The other side of the conflict is articulated by Sandy late in the film when he asks a luminous visitor from another planet, "Should I stop making movies and do something that counts, like helping blind people, or becoming a missionary, or something?" In other words, is there any aesthetic ground between repetition and silence?

In *Stardust Memories* this question is dramatized in numerous imitations of Ingmar Bergman, beginning with an obviously symbolic train ride, perhaps heading toward hell. The studio crowd, led by spokesperson Laraine Newman, wants this film to have an upbeat ending in which all these damned souls get translated to Dixieland-jazz heaven. After all, the movie is slated to open over the Easter weekend! Sandy, on the contrary, wants to end the film in a garbage dump. Clearly, an impasse blocks the conclusion both of Sandy's unnamed film and of Allen's *Stardust Memories*. Sandy ultimately solves his aesthetic dilemma by inventing another train ride in which he finds happiness with his lover Isobel (Marie-Christine Barrault). When Isobel objects to this ending as sentimental, Sandy explains that it is "the good kind of sentimental," thereby convincing himself and perhaps his lover.

Allen is less easily satisfied. Although he seems willing to concede the wit involved in Sandy's ad hoc assertion of filmic completeness, he seems unwilling to accept mere technical virtuosity as authentic aesthetic experience. This is unsurprising in light of the fact that Allen has Sandy ironically ridicule the illusion of artistic closure earlier in the film. "Only art can give you control," Sandy says, "only art and masturbation, two areas in which I am an absolute expert." Given this equivalence of completed artistic form and masturbation, it seems unlikely that any conventional ending, even an admittedly sentimental one, will win Allen's approval. In fact, his frustrated search for a suitable ending for *Stardust Memories* is apparent throughout the latter part of the film, a testimony to the difficulty of producing romantic film comedy in our time.

An astounding series of potential endings begins when Sandy takes a realistic automobile ride with a neurotic lesbian violinist (Jessica Harper). Despite the problems sure to attend any romance between the two, they seem to be riding toward some sort of romantic resolution when the Rolls breaks down and they become lost in the country. Allen introduces them immediately into a series of surreal episodes involving UFO freaks and Felliniesque magic tricks, suggesting, at least momentarily, that some sort of symbolic resolution is coming. The film does not end here, however, because this scene evolves into Sandy's conversation with the extraterrestrial about the significance of comedy. Soon this apparently crucial scene is curtailed by flashbacks to an earlier romance and by further complications of Sandy's relations with the Jessica Harper and Marie-Christine Barrault characters. Perhaps some sort of romantic mix-up will be sorted out, we think, to create an ending for the film. But any romantic resolution is blocked when a crazed fan seems to assassinate Sandy. Surely a conclusion is suggested here, we assume, especially since Sandy seems about to discover the meaning of life while on an operating table. Moreover, since this discovery takes place while Louis Armstrong's recording of "Stardust" plays, the expectation that everything will finally draw to an appropriate close seems particularly warranted. The expectation must be abandoned when we discover that Sandy has not really been shot after all. He has merely fainted and soon emerges from the hospital to be farcically arrested by the police. Surely this cannot be the ending, we think, and we are right. On his almost immediate release from jail, Sandy catches up with an irate Isobel and conceives an appropriate conclusion for his film.

However, just as we have been presented with this coherent, if contrived, resolution, the camera pulls back to reveal an audience watching the ending of Sandy's film. Perhaps the viewer is willing to accept this as an organically appropriate resolution for Allen's *Stardust Memories* since the central character is a filmmaker. This is still not the ending, however. The members of this audience go on to comment, often negatively, about what they have seen. To the viewer's surprise, this audience turns out to include Marie-Christine Barrault, Jessica Harper, Charlotte Rampling, Tony Roberts, and all the other actors in Allen's film, not Sandy's. Furthermore, as they exit, the female members of the cast compare notes on whether "he" kept his mouth open during the kissing scenes, and the viewer is left to decide whether "he" is Sandy or Woody or both. However deciding this question, the viewer is forced to recognize that he or she has been led to accept and then reject three, four, or more conclusions to *Stardust Memories*. When Woody or Sandy walks up the theater aisle alone in the film's last scene the movie is definitely over, but there is great ambiguity in the viewer's mind about how it has turned out. He might easily complain along with Barth's narrator, "We haven't even reached Ocean City yet; we will never get out of the funhouse."

Despite his inability to resolve the issues raised in his film—perhaps because of this inability—Woody Allen has even so produced a metafilm of sorts in *Stardust Memories*. He has done this, moreover, by appropriating the artistic strategies used by writers of postmodern metafiction, most significantly their insistence to the reader that what they are producing is art, not life. In *The Purple Rose of Cairo* Allen continues to develop these strategies. Furthermore, he converts his audience's desire for coherent closure—a desire he provokes only to frustrate in his earlier film—into the method by

which he achieves the very totality of aesthetic effect that his metafilm seems
to ridicule.

Purple Rose centers on Cecilia (Mia Farrow), a mousy, Depression-era
hash-house waitress who is married to a coarse, womanizing, wife-beating
sponger named Monk (Danny Aiello). Unsurprisingly under these circumstances, Cecilia seeks escape from reality in the formulaic romantic films offered weekly at her neighborhood theater, the Jewel. The contrast between
such films and Cecilia's real life emerges clearly in the opening scene, which
shows Cecilia dreamily contemplating a poster advertising this week's offering, an obviously escapist B-movie called *The Purple Rose of Cairo.* Her
imaginative trance deepens as Fred Astaire sings on the sound track,
"Heaven, I'm in heaven. . . ." Suddenly the fantasy is shattered as a letter falls
to the pavement from the marquee overhead. Fred's voice fades. Back in real-
life New Jersey Cecilia is urged by the theater manager not to miss this
week's offering. "Cecilia, you're gonna like this one," he says. "It's better
than last week's, more romantic." Immediately Allen cuts to a hard, angry
woman sitting in a diner. "Miss, I wanted oatmeal *before* my scrambled
eggs," she says to a still dreamy-eyed Cecilia, who is now wearing her waitress's uniform. Here in the first few minutes of Allen's film, the audience is
clearly warned that the movies are only movies, not real life. Barth could
hardly make the point more explicitly.

If any doubt lingers, Monk repeatedly expresses the contrast for his wife
and for Allen's audience. When Cecilia begs Monk to accompany her to the
first night's showing of *Purple Rose,* for example, he refuses, saying, "Cecilia,
you like sitting through that junk. Me, I'm gonna shoot crap, O.K.?"
Clearly, Monk rejects the premise that art—in this case, film—can transform
and illuminate experience. Just as obviously, Cecilia has different expectations, and so she goes to the Jewel, alone, to share vicariously in the devil-
may-care highlife of beautiful people such as playboy Larry Wild, the
Countess, and "explorer-poet-adventurer" Tom Baxter, "of the Chicago
Baxters." Most of Allen's audience probably also rejects Monk's unimaginative criticism to enter this fantasy world with Cecilia. After all, if we are seeking Allen's *Purple Rose* in the first place, then we must not agree with Monk
that all movies are "junk."

And the fantasy is very appealing. Within his color film, Allen has created
a brilliant replica of a 1930s black-and-white musical, down to the lighting,
set design, and tuneful soundtrack. Fred and Ginger would feel right at home
in these art deco surroundings, and so does Cecilia, and so do we. Our absorption into the black-and-white *Purple Rose* is so easy because Allen effectively cuts from color shots of Cecilia and the other patrons of the Jewel to
shots in which the theater in color frames a screen showing the black-and-
white *Purple Rose,* to shots in which the black-and-white film fills our whole
field of vision. We thus can watch exactly the same romantic comedy that

Cecilia is watching at exactly the same moment she sees it for the first time. Allen's parody is so perfectly executed, moreover, that our experience of the black-and-white *Purple Rose* can draw on our previous experience of the genre. Surely we have seen Fred, Ginger, and Edward Everett Horton in similar circumstances. Or was it Dick Powell and Ruby Keeler? And what happened to all of them? They drank champagne, found romance, and lived happily ever after. Surely the same is in store for Tom Baxter, Copacabana chanteuse Kitty Haynes, and, by extension, for our point-of-view character, Cecilia.

Such expectations are unrealistic, Allen feels. As he says in an interview with Caryn James, "The movies are just a narcotic for [Cecilia]. The reality of life was what was going on in the United States at that time and also in her personal life" (27). What was going on in the United States was the Depression, which turned Monk into a bum and Cecilia into an ineffective and eventually unemployed waitress. What was going on in her personal life is epitomized when Cecilia comes home from her second viewing of *Purple Rose*. She and we are transported directly from the black-and-white Copacabana to the apartment in dismal color in which her gross husband is flagrantly courting the sexual favors of an even grosser neighbor named Olga. This contrast between art and life so shocks Cecilia that she packs her bags to leave an obviously failed marriage. The audience can only applaud her decision. Against this applause, Monk again articulates the unimaginative, realistic attitude. As Cecilia leaves, he shouts after her, "See how far you get. Go on, go on! You won't last. You'll see how it is in the real world." Alas, Monk is right. Cecilia has no money, no skills, no wealthy friends, no prospects, no hope. She soon returns, to further abuse and humiliation.

As in the musicals of the 1930s, however, we need not despair. Romantic salvation seems possible for Cecilia when the pith-helmeted Tom Baxter steps off the screen of the Jewel to talk to her. In the process, he is transformed from a black-and-white image into a full-color inhabitant of Cecilia's world. He has watched her watching him through five showings of *Purple Rose*, he says, and she has won his heart. His plan is to leave the film, take Cecilia away with him to Egypt, and live happily ever after. Obviously, some difficulties clutter their path to romantic fulfillment, but the audience's experience of earlier films has preconditioned us to accept the possibility that these difficulties can be overcome. After all, if a millionaire and a struggling hoofer from the chorus can find true love, why not a waitress and a fictional character?

Surely desire triumphs over reason when we indulge such hopes. Allen makes this clear repeatedly in the film but perhaps most effectively during the scene in which Tom takes Cecilia to an expensive restaurant, confident that he can pay the bill with the stage money in his pocket. While they are dancing, Cecilia tells Tom about life in the real world: "People get old and sick and die and never find true love." Tom expresses surprise at this news: "You know, where I come from, people, they don't disappoint. They're consistent. They're always reliable." Allen conceals a warning to the audience in Cecilia's reply: "You don't find that kind in real life." Tom reassures her even so by saying, "You have." Assuredly, a great deal of disbelief must be suspended to maintain our hopes for a happy ending to this affair. Yet the alternative of Cecilia's returning to her life with Monk is by this point cinematically unacceptable.

Just when the unlikelihood of the Tom-Cecilia affair begins to strain our credulity, however, Allen ingeniously quiets our anxiety by turning the romance into a triangle. Enter Gil Shepherd, the actor who played Tom Baxter in *Purple Rose*. Both parts are played in Allen's film by Jeff Daniels, but Daniels succeeds in distinguishing his two roles sufficiently to suggest that Gil might be a real-life rival to the fictional Tom for Cecilia's love. In fact, the two suitors soon confront each other, arguing their relative merits before the girl they are both pursuing. Gil first asks Cecilia in surprise, "You want to waste your time with a fictional character?" Cecilia's answer echoes the audience's absurd hopes for a happy ending when she says, "But Tom's perfect." In return, Gil seems to speak for Allen when deflating this unrealistic view: "What good is perfect if a man's not real?" Tom's only defense is to claim naively: "I can learn to be real." Gil probably wins this romantic argument, and he certainly gets the last laugh, when he responds in annoyance: "You can't learn to be real. It's like learning to be a midget. It's not a thing you can learn."

Tom is not discouraged, and so the romantic competition continues. Whichever of the two heroes wins Cecilia's hand, however, he will be a marked improvement over the repulsive Monk. Thus the audience is encouraged to think that the happy ending conventional in the genre is still possible. If viewers are rooting for the "real" man, Gil Shepherd, they will be delighted when Gil and Cecilia perform two peppy musical numbers together in a quaint little music shop operated by a twinkly, piano-playing, gray-haired lady. When the two reenact a love scene that Cecilia has memorized from Gil's earlier film *Dancing Doughboys*, these viewers will be even more encouraged at seeing how good these two young people look together, especially when they kiss. Perhaps some viewers will be disturbed when Gil explains away his on-screen kissing of Ina Beasley by saying, "We professionals, we can put that stuff on, just like that." But Gil's partisans surely will distinguish his pretended passion for Ina from his real love for Cecilia. In this light, life with Gil in Hollywood seems distinctly possible for Cecilia, an ending both happy and appropriate.

If viewers find Gil too slickly packaged and prefer the wide-eyed boyishness of Tom Baxter, they may also have reason to hope. In one of the film's most imaginative segments, Tom takes Cecilia with him into the black-and-white world of the screen for the night of her life. Dozens of similar scenes echo through Allen's brilliant night-clubbing montage of the Harlequin Club, the Hot Box, the Club Harlem, and the Latin Quarter, each with appropriate music for dancing by Tom and Cecilia. This is life as we all might hope it to be. The champagne may be ginger ale, as one customer points out to Cecilia at the Copa. Sexual encounters may terminate in a fadeout, as Tom further explains. Nothing admittedly is perfect. On the other hand, Cecilia can dance merrily in the movies. Stage champagne is better than what she gets in New Jersey. A fadeout is probably preferable to actual sex with Monk. Ending up with Tom on the silver screen is an alternative happy ending equally consistent with the film's premises and the audience's desires.

As things turn out, after raising the prospect of two such satisfying resolutions, Allen denies the audience both. First, Cecilia sends Tom back onto the screen, and we learn that he will subsequently be destroyed along with all prints of his film. Having chosen Gil and Hollywood instead, Cecilia rushes home to pack and face another confrontation with Monk. Monk's parting taunts are ominous, however, an unsettling challenge to our hopes for a happy ending. "Go, go!" he shouts at Cecilia. "See what it is out there. It ain't the movies. It's real life. It's real life and you'll be back. Just mark my words." Once again Monk is correct. Gil has run out on Cecilia after persuading her to reject Tom. Gil was only a professional actor pretending to love her after all.

Monk is, of course, the only man in Cecilia's future because, as he says, "It ain't the movies. It's real life." As we all know, in real life, waitresses from New Jersey more often end up with men like Monk than with Gil Shepherds or Tom Baxters, even though romantic film comedies have traditionally ignored such harsh realities by allowing these women to live happily ever after, as they obviously deserve. Allen's genius in this film lies in bridging the chasm between realistic experience and cinematic romanticism. This is what makes *The Purple Rose of Cairo* a metafilm. In deference to the cynical objectivity demanded by contemporary audiences, Allen allows the Depression and Monk to triumph over the Copacabana and Tom Baxter. Along the way, however, he has created a dazzling black-and-white image of perfection to shine on the screen once more and appeal to the Cecilia lurking inside all experienced filmgoers. Consequently, after he has punctured all her illusions, Allen closes his film with Cecilia seated once more in the Jewel theater, her pathetic suitcase and ukulele on the seat beside her, as she stares in rapture at Fred and Ginger dancing on the screen. The soundtrack plays "Heaven, I'm in heaven. . . ." Cecilia begins to smile.

At first, the viewers probably smile along with Cecilia, relieved that she seems to be recovering from her romantic disappointment. Cecilia's peaceful absorption in *Top Hat* thus mirrors our desire to see *Purple Rose* end happily. Since viewers of Woody Allen movies are more critically aware than Cecilia is, however, reservations soon surface. We remember that Cecilia must eventually leave the theater and return to Monk—a happy ending in no one's view. Even so, this somber reflection does not totally cancel the earlier positive impression. Unlike *Stardust Memories*, this film does not serially propose and reject such conclusions. Instead, it suspends the positive and negative, the real and the imaginary, in a purely cinematic form of ambiguity. Real life, we are aware, often demands either-or choices of us, but Allen has accorded such equivalent solidity to New Jersey and to the silver screen that we can balance the double vision of Cecilia imaginatively dancing with Fred Astaire and gloomily anticipating her return to Monk. These conclusions are therefore not discrete but simultaneous. In his interview with Caryn James, Allen says about this ending, "The ambiguity may be good luck, something that came from the healthy growth of that film" (27–28). Surely, good luck can have played a very small part in such a brilliantly conceived and crafted film. On the other hand, healthy growth of more than one kind is clearly apparent.

As he fades to black over the intimations of Cecilia's faint smile, Woody Allen affirms the vitality of his medium, romantic film comedy, even in the face of a plot that appears to repudiate it. Surely the almost universal approval accorded his next films, *Hannah and Her Sisters* (1986) and *Radio Days* (1987), testifies to the audience's desire for this affirmation. And yet, Allen's enabling act of imagination takes place first in *Purple Rose*. By rejecting both the banal happy endings of conventional film comedy and the apparent inconclusiveness beclouding *Stardust Memories*, Allen succeeds in transcending the gap between desire and actuality, art and life, form and formlessness. In this respect also he comes to resemble the creators of postmodern fiction, especially their high priest. Robert Scholes has written, "The energizing power of Earth's universe is the tension between the imagination of man and the conditions of being which actually prevail" (119). The same may now be said of Woody Allen. We may thus describe *Stardust Memories* analogously as Allen's film of "exhaustion" and *The Purple Rose of Cairo* and its successors as his films of "replenishment."

WORKS CITED

Barth, John. "The Literature of Exhaustion." In *The Friday Book: Essays and Other Nonfiction*, 62–76. New York: Putnam, 1984.

———. *Lost in the Funhouse: Fiction for Print, Tape, Live Voice*. Garden City, NY: Doubleday, 1968.

Barthes, Roland. *The Rustle of Language*. Trans. Richard Howard. New York: Hill & Wang, 1986.

James, Caryn. "Auteur! Auteur!" *New York Times Magazine*, January 19, 1986, 18–30.

Scholes, Robert. *Fabulation and Metafiction.* Urbana: University of Illinois Press, 1979.

Stark, John O. *The Literature of Exhaustion: Borges, Nabokov, and Barth.* Durham, NC: Duke University Press, 1974.

20

Woody Allen's *Interiors*
The Dark Side of *Hannah and Her Sisters*

Diane Snow

In comparing the two Woody Allen films *Hannah and Her Sisters* (1986) and *Interiors* (1978), one finds two facts that present a paradox: (1) *Hannah and Her Sisters* was nominated for and received many prestigious awards, but the reception of *Interiors* was varied; and (2) *Hannah and Her Sisters* is so similar to *Interiors* that one could consider it a remake of the earlier film. If, indeed, these films are so alike, then why would the reception be so different? One answer to this question is that *Interiors* violates the horizon of our expectations. We expect comedy from Woody Allen, not dark drama. In this paper I will examine what I believe is another important key to understanding the differing reception of such similar films—the different demands that each film makes on the viewer.

I would like to use the term *viewer* as Iser has defined the "implied viewer"—an alert, informed recipient who is aware of what the text is doing. This viewer is under a contract, so to speak, to accept the cultural codes and structural signs that the text intends. The "implied viewer" differs from the "real viewer" in that the former leaves behind his or her own values and is willing to respond in the way the text demands (27–50).

I hope to accomplish three objectives: (1) to catalog the similarities of plot, characters, and themes to firmly establish that the films are saying the same things; (2) to discuss the different demands these films make from the standpoint of the viewer; and (3) to conclude why such similar turns were received so differently.

The similarities in the plot structures are striking. In *Interiors* Arthur tells

Eve that he wants a trial separation. In *Hannah* the mom and dad reveal a stormy marriage as they argue about the mom's drinking problem and the parents' past infidelities. In *Interiors* Joey is the sister that is expected to sustain her mother, even though her support is not acknowledged and she has not felt close to her mother. Hannah is the glue that holds her family together. She mediates, loves, and succors each member of her family and their mates. Both of these figures are exploited by the other members of the family. These characters disclose how complex, tangled, and far-reaching relationships become as certain events occur. Hannah is loved, yet resented, because she is too good. Joey has a love/hate relationship with Renata. Joey needs to compete with her sister's successful artistic career and feels Renata is the one that Mother loved best. Renata, on the other hand, complains that her father always doted on Joey. Flyn in *Interiors* corresponds with Lee in *Hannah and Her Sisters* not so much in character traits but in their relationships with their brothers-in-law. Elliot falls in "lust" with Hannah's sister Lee. Renata's husband, Frederick, is sexually attracted to his sister-in-law, the sensual Flyn. The first situation results in a guilt-ridden affair, while the second manifests itself in an attempted rape of which Frederick says, "It's been such a long time since I made love to a woman I didn't feel inferior to." Both relationships reveal multifarious emotions of inferiority and of sex used to hurt or escape; furthermore, each encounter is devastating to the marital relationships. Allen seems to be using these characters and their relationships to represent more than individual personalities in specific situations: these relationships show some universal weaknesses, challenges, and self-defeating behavior patterns.

Both films are about three sisters and how they relate to each other, their mates, and their parents. The family in *Interiors* struggles to adjust to a divorce that eventually results in the suicide of the emotionally unstable, domineering mother, Eve. Hannah's family wrestles with complex relationships between the sisters, the men in their lives, and the mother and father, who have problems of their own. The circumstances offer investigation of universal themes: the meaning of life and death and the nature of relationships. In both families the complexities of relationships involve communication, sex, love/hate ambivalences, parental problems passed on to children, and sibling rivalries.

Other thematic concerns are presented when the characters do not react in logical loving patterns. Hirsch regards *Interiors* as "a sexual and emotional musical chairs in which characters pair off, withdraw, get back together again, separate, in an almost ritualistic pattern of arrival and departure, reunion and retreat" (95). Jacobs suggests, "*Interiors* questions the possibility of romantic integrity in a world indifferent to ethical standards" (116) and asks how one can deal with the "incongruities within and between individuals, . . . concept and action, art and life, person and pose" (22). Although Jacobs and Hirsch are writing about *Interiors*, their comments are equally applicable to *Hannah and Her Sisters*.

The characters in these films can be sorted and matched like pairs of socks. Artistic personalities abound. Stanley Kauffmann has classified the characters in *Interiors* as follows (I have added the suitable match from *Hannah*): the realized artist, Renata (in *Hannah*, Hannah and Frederick); the unrealized one, Frederick (in *Hannah*, Holly); the yearner after talent, Joey; and the chintzy, tiny talent, Eve (in *Hannah*, Hannah's parents) (26). Also, one can find characters similar in their desire and ability to create. Lee and Eliot do not concern themselves with creativity, Renata talks of her impotence in writing, Joey refuses to have a baby, Mickey's sterility is reversed, and Eve considers Arthur one of her creations. Again, Allen treats the characters as archetypes who personify a favorite Woody Allen theme, the role of the artist in life.

The preceding listing seems to belabor the obvious similarities of the films, but establishing the like nature of the films is necessary to an exploration of differences and the conclusions I reach. It is not so much what is said about whom, but rather how it is said and how the viewer responds. The premise that the films are very much alike is the first step to understanding how they are different.

In traditional literary and film criticism, the task of the critic is to interpret the meaning found in the text. Such critics as Stanley Fish want to change the focus from the meaning in the text to the recipient's interpretive response to the text. For meaning, according to reader response criticism, is not in the text, or film in this case, but is produced as the viewer confronts and interprets the film. Though the viewer's interpretation is controlled and directed, it is only the viewer who can provide meaning (465–85). Accordingly, by evaluating the prescribed process, I would like to compare these films, not in what they mean, but in how they mean.

In both films the viewer needs to build meaning by going beyond surface literal meaning—interpreting symbols in *Interiors* and remembering details that can be interpretive signs in *Hannah and Her Sisters*. *Interiors* is full of symbols: intercutting shots of the sea during the aftermath of Eve's suicide attempt; the intercutting of the sleeping family members who wake at the time of Eve's death but then go back to sleep; a shot of bare, tangled tree branches when Renata is talking to her psychiatrist about her inability to create. Such visual symbols invite the viewer to decipher the meaning of each shot. The symbols suggest loneness, loneliness, and the influence of interacting relationships. Vases are another prominent symbol in the film. In the exposition we see a shot of five empty vases on the mantelpiece of the family home. Pearl breaks a vase as she dances at the wedding celebration. Mike cannot afford the expensive vase that Eve wants them to buy for their apartment. If the viewer decides that the empty vases are symbolic of the empty lives of the five members of the family, then the other scenes that involve vases become more meaningful.

The cinematography itself can also be read symbolically (Jacobs, 121). The viewer could and should ask, "Why do we see Renata and Flyn walking on the beach, shot through a fence?" Or, "Why is it that Arthur has his back to the camera when he gives his introductory soliloquy?" Much of the cinematography adds to thematic and character development, just like underlining important parts of a text. Brode has noted two such symbolic cinematic techniques. In the marriage scene we hear the voice of the judge, but we do not see him or Pearl and Arthur, "instead the camera remains on the faces of the daughters, and the husbands . . . making use of the contrapuntal possibilities of sound films. We receive one sort of information on the sound track and a totally different sort of information on the screen." The camera guides the audience to understand that the important event is not the union of Arthur and Pearl but the children's reactions. Likewise, "Allen films a conversation between the two of them [Arthur and Eve] in such a way that even though they are sitting near each other in the same room, we never see them on screen together, but rather view a tight shot of one, then the other, their spiritual lack of togetherness is made visual" (Brode, 185).

All of the symbols suggest emptiness and cold except for those involving Pearl. Her life and warmth are indicated by garish colors. The film is shot completely in pale cool colors—ice gray, beige, earth tones, black, white, steel blue. But Pearl, dressed in red, does not fit with the environment. Pearl prefers sun, hot sand, and blue water. She likes blood-rare steak and primitive African art. She is not accepted by the daughters. Ironically, at the time of Eve's suicide, the real mother gives death, but Joey's life is saved by Pearl. Earlier when Joey calls out to her mother, Pearl responds. A few moments later she resuscitates the drowning girl and becomes her symbolic mother.

The *Hannah* film is much less symbolic; instead it is a puzzle with many interlocking details that the viewer fits together. When Mickey attempts to find meaning through religion, he brings home a bag of "goods." Taken from a brown paper grocery sack are a crucifix, a bible, a religious picture, a loaf of Wonder bread, and a jar of Hellmann's mayonnaise. The viewer must put together the satirical visual joke on institutionalized religion.

Toward the end of the film Mickey notices Holly shopping in a record store. He joins her, and the viewer notes that she has two opera records to buy, and Mickey migrates to the jazz section. The viewer recalls Holly's unfulfilled romance that began and ended with a date to the opera. At the same time one can remember the disastrous date Holly and Mickey had when he tried to introduce her to his kind of music. Furthermore, in view of the fact that Holly's taste in music has changed from that previous date—at that time she indulged in drugs and hard rock—the viewer can speculate that her life might have changed in other ways.

Another example of putting together visual clues is provided for the viewer after Elliot and Lee confess their love and turn to go their separate ways: as the characters leave the scene, the camera focuses on an Alcoholics Anonymous sign. The shot reminds the viewer that Lee attends those meetings, suggesting that weaknesses of the flesh (alcohol and sex) are part of the nature of man. Both films offer the viewer opportunities to put together pieces of information that can add breadth and depth to the meaning of the film. *Interiors* is full of symbolism but empty in terms of incidentals. *Hannah* is less symbolic, but is richly layered with significant detail.

Pivotal scenes in both films take place at mealtimes. Food has been a typical communal metaphor that Allen has used for art, sex, and humor (Benayoun, 158). These scenes function to contrast the two family interactional styles, but more important in our evaluation is noting the function of the viewer's identification. The structure of *Hannah and Her Sisters* is unified by three Thanksgiving family gatherings. The viewer will probably identify with the occasions of warmth and humor as the family sings around the piano, or recognize the anonymous character who, because of the holiday, lets the children drink beer, or reminisce when Hannah sets out homemade turkey place cards constructed of apples and paper, or recall sitting at an adult table or a children's table. These situations strike a familiar resonance with the viewer's nostalgic memories of family and holidays.

In *Interiors* it is at the dinner table that Arthur makes his announcement about his decision to move out of the family home. The time seems appropriate. The conversation is stilted, critical, and uncaring, just as his announcement seems to be. Later in the film, the family again gathers for dinner. The occasion is to introduce Pearl. The male partners, Mike and Frederick, are drawn to her as she entertains them with card tricks and promised fortune telling. The men seem hungry for the warmth that she brings to this family gathering. Certainly Arthur has turned to her for love, fun, and sexual fulfillment. The dearth of warm family experiences is poignantly expressed by Joey after the death of her mother; she records "the few warmer moments [they'd] known" in her diary. She says that she feels they are "very powerful." The identification in *Hannah* is pleasant, whereas the identification in *Interiors* is painful.

Both films require active viewer identification and participation. They differ somewhat in how that participation is achieved and in the response to it. *Hannah* allows the viewer to observe what is happening from a greater distance than *Interiors* does. The nature of comedy requires a more distant intellectual stance, rather than an emotional closeness. Normally an audience cannot laugh at jokes about something that is intensely valued unless somehow they can distance themselves. Another way *Hannah* distances the viewer is by inserting what Prince calls "reading interludes" into the narrative flow (225–40). Captions break up, yet organize, the episodic narration.

Such titles as "Love is the only answer," "The audition," "The big leap," "We all had a terrific time," and "Nobody, not even the rain, has such small hands" not only introduce and summarize the action but also remind the audience periodically that this is a film. In opposition to the orientation provided in *Hannah*, Robert Hatch notes that in *Interiors*, "I was moved from one handsome interior to another, I frequently lost my bearings. Then I realized that Allen meant me to do so, by way of suggesting what life is like inside the characters of his film" (156).

Interiors is shot mostly with close-ups, which should invite an emotional intimacy; ironically, there is no closeness between the characters. They are distant and isolated, often filmed looking out a window, seen through a glass door, or reflected in glass and mirrors. The closed-in isolation is evident when Eve wants windows closed because the outside noises are unnerving. We see only a few characters set against a lonely isolated beach or cold, still-life *interiors*. The decorations and appointments are all elegant and beautiful, not at all warm and inviting. In Arthur's opening dialogue he tells about Eve creating a home like "an ice palace," cold and beautiful, but one that he could no longer live in. The viewer seems to be closer to the characters than they are to each other. Also, because the viewer is addressed directly, the emotional closeness is intensified. In a sense the viewer becomes an active participant, a character in the film. The viewer is the only one to hear Arthur's opening soliloquy. Later, Renata is talking to a psychiatrist whom we never see or hear.

Renata looks directly at the camera; the viewer listens to her. Much of the film directs the dialogue solely for the benefit of the viewer; we know more about the character's inner feelings than other characters in the story do. In the scene when Joey cuttingly talks to Eve, precipitating the suicide, the viewer is not even sure if Eve is there. She does not speak. The camera does not show them together in the same shot. It is not until we see Eve walking into the ocean that the viewer verifies that there was someone other than us to talk to.

When the characters do try to communicate to each other, they often fail. We hear them say, "I don't want to talk about it" or "Could we drop this please?" The characters often veer away from a subject, react defensively, or vent their anger and frustration. In *Hannah*, on the other hand, although Mickey and Holly have many problems in getting along on their first date, they are able to communicate these feelings openly. When they do get together, their relationship begins by sharing their neurotic feelings and communicating warmth and acceptance to one another.

Although Woody Allen considers *Hannah* an intimate film (Geist, 42), it has a cast of forty-nine indicated in the credits, along with extras: guests at the dinners, a rock band, people in the theater and on the streets. On the other hand, in *Interiors* the cast is confined to the eight family members.

There is only one other person seen in the film: the judge who performs the marriage is heard offscreen and seen in one shot. The viewer is isolated, as are these characters, in a world with no one else.

Before the film begins, the titles foreshadow this emptiness—they are white block letters on a black screen seen in silence. In *Hannah* there are similar white block letters on a black screen, but the pop and jazz standards that have become a signature for a Woody Allen film fill the theater. Music by Rodgers and Hart as well as Cole Porter adds not only a romantic warm glow to the film, but also some meaningful commentary on the action. When Elliot and Lee are starting their romantic misadventures, we hear "Bewitched, Bothered, and Bewildered." When Mickey and Holly get back together, we hear "Falling in Love Again." "I've Heard This Song Before" plays in the beginning of the film and under the concluding titles. This could be interpreted as a commentary on the merry-go-round repetition of themes and characters found in all Woody Allen's films.

The most obvious difference between the two films, and probably the most important, is that *Interiors* is the first film that Allen has addressed with complete seriousness. With the comic genre, even when serious themes are present, viewers, by detaching and distancing themselves, can laugh at the unexpected twists that make the heavy questions more palatable. The interspersion of humor lightens the emotional burden. No such relief is offered in *Interiors.* Woody Allen said there was not a joke in the film, "at least no intentional ones" (quoted in Brode, 180).

In *Hannah* there is an abundance of humor. For example, when Mickey's father asks, "How do I know why there were Nazis? I don't know why the can opener works," and Mickey tells Holly, "I had a great time tonight, really. It was like the Nuremberg trials." When Mickey is pondering reincarnation, he whines, "Great, that means I'll have to sit through the Ice Capades again." The film displays humor and parody, peppered with the one-liners that are Woody Allen specialties.

Woody Allen's jokes, according to Edelstein, have generally followed the same pattern. He begins with an anxiety-laden statement and finishes with a surprising twist. His humor has always been dark, but kept in a light perspective because of the unexpected endings. Edelstein asserts that *Interiors* has just left off the end of the joke. When Joey tells her mother that a sick mind is a product of a sick psyche, we want her to continue with something like "which is only a problem when you get the dry-cleaning bills" (26). In *Hannah* the film scenario is divided between Hannah's family and Mickey. It is in Mickey's half of the film that the heavy questions underlying the action of the family scenes are stated. Mickey directly asks the same questions that are addressed in *Interiors*: What is the meaning of life? What is the nature of man? What role does art play in life? The heaviness, however, is ameliorated with humor. While *Interiors* is empty of humor, *Hannah* brims over. Allen's picture of the world and the interrelationships in families is not a simple or an optimistic one. A major difference in the two films is that in *Hannah and Her Sisters*, true to the comic tradition, situations are resolved, and the viewer is left with hope. In *Interiors* the problems are unresolved and the viewer has little hope. For Allen, courage is the ability to "act in spite of an almost paralyzing fear" (Halberstadt, 17). In this film there is little action or change. Most of what we see is single people in empty rooms. Renata does not act to overcome her creative impotence; Flyn is still addicted to cocaine; the sisters see that the ocean is calm and peaceful, yet they are still standing apart and looking out the window.

The same problems have happier resolutions in *Hannah and Her Sisters*. Holly kicks her drug habit. Mickey's infertility is reversed. Even though Holly had drifted from acting to the Stanislavski Catering Company and thence to writing, she finally succeeds. Mickey and Holly find some structure to give stability to life. Mickey realizes while seeing the Marx Brothers movie *Duck Soup* that even if life cannot be understood it can still be enjoyed. Elliot concludes that he loves Hannah more than he realized. Lee marries her English teacher and is happy. The film ties up the loose ends, and the viewer renews his faith in man's ability to cope. Ironically, Allen had hoped that the serious drama would be more emotionally fulfilling and more resolved (Lax, 72). He also admits that *Hannah and Her Sisters* turned out lighter than he had intended (Ansen, 68).

The differences between the films can be summarized by the antithetical categories: full versus empty, cold versus warm, and light versus dark and heavy. Spilling over and mixing one with another, these groupings are useful to describe the tone of the films and to understand the viewer response. I believe that these differences are the key to understanding the difference in reception mentioned earlier.

Both the critics and the public critically acclaimed and warmly received *Hannah and Her Sisters*. Although "sixteen of the thirty-one reviewers surveyed by *Variety* included *Interiors* in their lists of the ten best films of 1978," many considered it a failure (Yacowar, 186). Brode judged that *Interiors* is "one of the most ill-conceived movies of all time" (185). Jack Kroll reported in *Newsweek*,

> [*Interiors*] does not have the creative elation that triggers elation in the audience, no matter how dark the artist's vision. Henry James insisted on the sense of "fun" that was in his supersubtle novels, and Yeats reminds us that "*Hamlet* and *Lear* are gay; gaiety transfiguring all that dread." In *Interiors*, Woody gives us his dread untransfigured and it's hard to swallow. (85)

Critics decried Allen's aping Bergman. But Colin Westerberck argued that "Allen has made a film which is perhaps even better than the film Bergman might have made from the same material" (630).

Allen never concerns himself too much with pleasing an audience. In making *Interiors*, Allen was pleasing himself. He has said, "The line between the kind of solemnity I want and comedy is very, very thin" (Guthrie, 173). He considers the serious genre to be more challenging—one that corresponds with the style of Bergman, Chekhov, and Buñuel. He contends that making comedy is "sitting at the children's table," and he wants to take his turn with the adults (Brode, 180). For Allen, the film was successful and valuable because it broadened his learning experience. He acknowledges, "Even if this movie is a total disaster, I still will have grown. I will have learned more about myself, about my weaknesses, my limitations" (Guthrie, 174). "Now I know what it's like to work one year on a very 'heavy' film. Like being in the army: it may be hard on you, but you learn from it" (Benayoun, 162). In *Interiors* he can deal directly with his concerns that have been overlooked and forgotten because of the lightness that accompanies his serious comedies.

When Holly tells Mickey she is pregnant, a cynical viewer of *Hannah* could wonder if the baby is his. Or perhaps an unromantic viewer would argue that life's problems are not so easy to resolve. But here we have been talking about real viewers. These are not the implied viewers who will accept the intentions of the film. Of course, there is always the possibility that the denouement of the film is ironic. Nevertheless, there would be little hesitancy for a real viewer to accept the role of the implied viewer in *Hannah and Her Sisters*. Conversely, the real viewer could be uncomfortable in assuming the role of implied viewer in *Interiors*. He or she might become weary of interpreting symbols but delight in catching visual detail in *Hannah*. When the films demand empathic identification, the real viewer shuns the painful and enjoys the nostalgic. There is no question that, if a real viewer could choose to experience, even by proxy, a warm, intimate, funny, romantic, resolved comedy rather than an intense, austere, lonely, unresolved drama, the decision would be easy. And so it was.

WORKS CITED

Allen, Woody. *Interiors. Four Films of Woody Allen*, 113–78. New York: Random House, 1982.

Ansen, David. "Manhattan Serenade." *Newsweek*, February 2, 1986, 67–68.

Benayoun, Robert. *The Films of Woody Allen*. Trans. Alexander Walker. New York: Harmony, 1985.

Brode, Douglas. *Woody Allen: His Films and Career*. Secaucus, NJ: Citadel, 1985.

Edelstein, David. "Laughing at Life: *Hannah and Her Sisters*." *Rolling Stone*, February 13, 1986.

Fish, Stanley E. "Interpreting the Variorum." *Critical Inquiry* 1 (Spring 1976): 465–85.

Geist, William E. "The Rolling Stone Interview: Woody Allen." *Rolling Stone*, April 9, 1987, 39–42, 51, 84.

Guthrie, Lee. *Woody Allen: A Biography*. New York: Drake, 1978.

Halberstadt, Ira. "Scenes from a Mind." *Take One* (November 1978): 17.

Hatch, Robert. "Films." *The Nation*, August 19–26, 1978, 156.

Hirsch, Foster. *Love, Sex, Death, and the Meaning of Life*. New York: McGraw, 1981.

Iser, Wolfgang. *The Act of Reading: A Theory of Aesthetic Response*. Baltimore: Johns Hopkins, 1978.

Jacobs, Diane. . . . *But We Need the Eggs: The Magic of Woody Allen*. New York: St. Martin's, 1982.

Kauffmann, Stanley. "Interior Decorating." *New Republic*, September 9, 1978, pp. 24–26.

Kroll, Jack. "The Inner Woody." *Newsweek*, August 7, 1978, pp. 83–85.

Lax, Eric. *On Being Funny: Woody Allen and His Comedy*. New York: Charterhouse, 1975.

Prince, Gerald. "Notes on the Text as Reader." In *The Reader in the Text*, ed. Susan R. Suleman and Inge Crosman, 225–40. Princeton, NJ: Princeton University Press, 1980.

Westerberck, Colin, Jr. "The Screen." *Commonweal*, September 29, 1978, pp. 630–31.

Yacowar, Maurice. *Loser Take All: The Comic Art of Woody Allen*. New York: Ungar, 1979.

21

The Religion of *Radio Days*

Maurice Yacowar

The subject of Woody Allen's *Radio Days* is not so much radio as that famil-iar Allen concern, the ambivalent interfusions of art and life. In addition, he has the medium of radio serve its audience as a kind of secular religion. Be-yond the ordinary reality, it provides an idealized world, populated by gods and goddesses, providing moral guidance, offering spiritual consolation and uplift, and—most importantly—forming a bond of emotional and imagina-tive support among its nation of congregants.

Two points distinguish Allen's treatment of radio here from the conven-tional discussions of such dream factories. First, the medium does not pour out only illusions. True, it can make an Everywimp like Wallace Shawn sound like a cross between Cary Grant and Superman when he plays the Masked Avenger. But it can also cast such an honestly all-American image as Jeff Daniels as the all-American hero Biff Baxter (proving that there is life after fade-out, a character type continued from *The Purple Rose of Cairo*). The wartime radio program can literally as well as metaphorically give us saber rattling. In short, the illusions of radio can also convey truth.

In this spirit, the radio stories are not always sunny. The most dramatic event in the film is the coverage of the calamity when eight-year-old Polly Phelps is brought up dead from a well. Allen shows a wide range of tableaux, people across the social and economic spectra, frozen in thoughtful grief. That drama turns the spanking of the hero (Seth Green as young Joey) into a sentimental caress, his father's priorities recovered. Here is the power of the art to arouse humanity's deepest sense of community in the face of loss. On the other hand, the medium transcends prurience and voyeurism. The preferred alternative of Cousin Ruthie (Joy Newman) to radio is to snoop on the neighbors on the party line. This gossip breeds disharmony, in contrast to the radio harmony when she's joined by her father and uncle in a spirited mime of "The South American Way."

Allen's treatment of radio also is distinctive for its continuity with the real world. As in the technology of *Zelig* and in the plot of *The Purple Rose of Cairo*, the fantasy life here is not a remote parallel to mundane reality but a world accessible to entrance. Allen provides the conventional contrast when he intercuts the dreary after-breakfast duties of the mother (Julie Kavner) with the elegant breakfast life of the radio couple Roger Daly and Irene Draper (David Warrilow and Julie Kurnitz), so fashionably married in ratings if not in name or spirit. But the real and the fantasy worlds are not hermetically separated. Thus the hero's Aunt Bea (Dianne Wiest) competes on a radio quiz show, where she converts her family's affliction with fish into a jackpot prize. That is transcendence.

This point is established in the film's opening episode. Two men burglarizing the neighbors win the jackpot on *Guess That Tune*. The episode establishes the main motifs of the film. For one thing, the burglars function in the dark world of somber reality, barely lit by their feeble flashlights. But the phone, then the radio, connect them with the brightness of the radio show. Touched by that glorious beyond, suddenly the burglars' spirits are—the first song they identify—"Dancing in the Dark." There is also the mingling of loss and gain. Winning the jackpot, one burglar exults, "I'm rich, I'm rich." In fact, the thieves have scored only fifty dollars and some silverware. The victimizers are victimized. Their jackpot goes to the people they robbed. The Needlemans return to find their home ransacked, then awaken to find their sudden new wealth being delivered. This is a comic parable of an absurd world in which punishment and reward are distributed without logic or order. Yet a rough kind of justice, beyond mortal understanding, is done; there seems to be a reward from the heavens (or at least from the airwaves) commensurate with the inexplicable suffering. The joke about the prizewinning losers is Woody Allen's book of Job.

In such ways the faithful are rewarded throughout the film. As if to confirm the element of religion in even the most popular of the arts. Allen emphasizes the element of faith in radio listening. Thus the favorite radio show of Aunt Ceil (Renée Lippin) is that of a ventriloquist, to the skeptic's disdain: "He's on radio. How do you know he's not moving his lips?" She has faith. Rocco's mother (Gina DeAngelis) is the more naive when she thinks Sally White (Mia Farrow) to be safely dumb for forgetting that she can't use her dancing skills on radio. In fact, the film celebrates the power of radio to address all the senses through the listener's imagination. The very richness of the film's period detail in costume and setting (credit Jeffrey Kurland and Santo Loquasto) prove the power of what was merely "heard." The dense images we see are the narrator's memories of the experiences that the radio imprinted on all the senses of his imagination forty years ago.

In a more explicit example of radio faith as a pulp religion, the sports announcer (Guy Le Bow) tells the heartrending saga of the southpaw pitcher Kirby Kyle (Brian Mannain), legendary for his "heart." Deprived in order of a leg, an arm, his sight, and finally his life, he continues to pitch, ultimately "winning eighteen games in the Big League in the Sky." In his last appearance for us, Kyle stands with his glove raised expectantly as the ball sails blithely beyond. Greater faith hath no blind pitcher. The fish-tale-loving Uncle Abe (Josh Mostel) laps up this religious mush with relish (or tartar sauce).

So powerful is radio as a "faith" that it is rightly regarded to be a dangerous rival by Rabbi Baumel (one of Allen's favorite names for the olive-branch—or oily—profession of the rabbinate). The good rabbi (Kenneth Mars) warns against the radio's breeding "bad values, false dreams, and lazy habits." Instead of co-opting the secular parallel to his functions, the rabbi takes (understandable) umbrage at the boy's friendly, "You speak the truth, my faithful Indian companion." Denying community with the popular medium, the rabbi leaves his young charge a lone ranger. The boy more seriously confuses his communal allegiances when he steals from the Jewish National Fund to buy the Masked Avenger ring. That he will grow up wholly secularized is apparent from his first appearance wearing Masked Avenger goggles. The romanticized view of life for which he apologizes was shaped by the forces that freed his imagination, the secular faith and ecstasy of the radio. In contrast, the rabbi's Hebrew school is illogically dark, despite all its bright ceiling lights. In the same spirit, Rabbi Baumel initiates the boy's spanking that he then righteously stops.

The two religions again conflict when Uncle Abe goes to complain about the neighboring communists' loud playing of their radio on Yom Kippur. He returns home converted to the neighbors' secular faith, Marxism. In a parody of divine punishment, Abe's indulgence of pork chops, clams, and chocolate pudding (on the day of fasting, Yom Kippur, yet) leads to indigestion—a wholly secular (or interdenominational) affliction and penance.

Because the worlds of somber reality and sunny aspiration are continuous, the film's central character is not the young Woody Allen surrogate but the cigarette girl, Sally White. She embodies the film's moral thrust because she lives out the dream life that the ordinary listener could only imagine. In this light, both the film and the casting are a reply to the heroine's choice in *The Purple Rose of Cairo*. There Mia Farrow plays a woman who, offered a miraculous chance to escape her dreary life, chooses the wrong man and remains doomed to the merely vicarious relief of the silver screen. But in *Radio Days* Farrow's character makes the leap, despite being considerably less gifted, intelligent, and attractive a character. Sally White began in the Bronx but overcame adversity and her own multiple lacks of talent to become the radio star she craved to be. After peddling the cigarette, she enjoys her own Lucky Strike.

Sally's story provides the key points in the film's plot structure. She makes her first appearance at the film's one-quarter mark, when she is hustled by the idealized radio husband, Roger Daly (who apparently must perform as his name suggests). Both characters appear doubled through a mirrored column in the nightclub. The doubling denotes the man's two-timing both as a husband and as an amphibian dweller in both radio-land and reality. As they retreat to the rooftop to "Begin the Beguine," Sally White is a hopeless gull, so her language is literalist:

Roger: I'm exploding with desire.
Sally: We can't do it now. I'm working my shift.

Blessed as she is, however, even her deficiencies will serve to advance her cause. ("Boy, that was fast. Probably helped I had the hiccups.") Later her charming openness and appetite will save her life. Instead of offing her, the hit man (Danny Aiello, playing a variation on his abusive husband in *Purple Rose*) will help to arrange her radio debut. At the film's halfway point, the war interrupts Sally's role in Chekhov but provides her with a USO appearance. Her touching song, "I Don't Want to Walk without You," is both a romantic lyric and a disavowal of independence, which leads to her climactic success.

After the voice of God (as her biography reports) instructs her to take elocution lessons, she becomes a star gossip columnist. Her first report as star of her own show, the heaven-sent Gay White Way, comes at the film's three-quarter mark. With secrets she has kept on everyone, the would-be "singer" parlays the underworld sense of the term into stardom. Oddly, she reports Clark Gable's date with a starlet named Lolly Hays. As that name foreshadows the doomed Polly Phelps, it suggests the undiscriminating, ambivalent flood of names and news that the radio—like life itself—mindlessly and randomly pours out. Indeed, the last word on the Polly Phelps tragedy is the song that segues into the high-life New Year's Eve party: it was "Just One of Those Things." At the party Sally shares a table with—implausibly—all the other radio stars we have seen. At the peak of her career, Sally still shows her roots. In a recidivist Bronx shriek, she invites the posh to the rooftop scene of her earlier embarrassment. The Dalys are there too, seemingly detached from their own memories as well as from each other.

That rooftop scene completes the telling contrast between the radio stars' lives and those of the realistic family. The family scene is defined by exuberant warmth and love. The rooftop scene sets its characters as solitary souls, detached and alone underneath the mantle of festivity. The characters remain dwarfed and taunted by the top-hat sign that impersonally rises and falls, a glamorous icon to the pedestrian life below but a palpable fake to the high livers above. The stars slip into separate monologues about their transience, both as celebrities and as mortal beings: "Time passes so quickly. And then we're old. And we never know what it's all about." Even the scripted stars know the transience and confusion of mortality. The narrator confirms that his memories of those heroes are fading away with time. The Masked Avenger's tag line ("Beware, evil-doers, wherever you are") betrays sad lacks—of a human rather than scripted self, of someone to whom to communicate such self, and of acknowledgment of the real evil forces in the world of 1944. In contrast, the narrator's family exchanges profoundly felt and supportive emotions. As the father spots Aunt Bea playing solitaire, "No date tonight? Well, it's all right. We're all together, you know."

The narrator's family is a downstairs version of the three-sister Chekhovian families that Allen developed in *Interiors* and in *Hannah and Her Sisters*. Where Sally wins her success by compromising everything but her ambition, the hero's mother and Aunt Ceil have achieved a mixed but happy life by realistically settling for someone a good deal short of their romantic fantasies. When Tess accepted Martin (Michael Tucker), she opted for a compromised realistic life over the deadlier prospects of romance: She rejected the short-lived mortician, Sam Slotkin. Still, Martin remains so self-unaccepting that he won't admit his job as a cabbie. Aptly, a broken radio leads to his exposure. The constantly quarreling parents, Tess and Martin, obviously love each other. It's a delicate, unspoken love, so the song "Paper Doll" triggers the narrator's memory of the only time he ever saw them kiss. In his fantasy of their appearance on Thomas Abercrombie's *Court of Human Emotions* (aptly sponsored by General Spark) in the surprisingly simple romantic resolutions of *Hannah and Her Sisters*, the Woody Allen of the Mia Farrow period seems more accepting of the vagaries, compromises, and disappointments both of life and of human nature than was the unrelenting moralist of the films with Diane Keaton. We find this in the poignant interlude Allen gives Keaton here, a stationary but deeply moving song, "You'd Be So Nice to Come Home To." The imaginary world of *Radio Days* encapsulates the very plenitude of life, with its open-handed outpouring of dream and disaster, tease and torment, frustration and desire, illumination and delusion. Indeed, here radio and life itself are something like the grandmother's unharnessable mammaries: "A woman in her 70s and her bosom is still growing." In Allen's current view our cups too runneth over.

But this cheer is not bought cheaply. For all its roseate nostalgia, true to form, Woody Allen looks back in dread. The film's wartime setting preserves the shadow of Hitler across both the familial tensions and the radio trivialities. Indeed, the radio brings the frightening news from the warfront, as well as the heartening pulp fictions about the "Axis rats." In one shot the camera seems to follow the radio news as it wafts up the stairs to Joey in bed. His parents question the wisdom of bringing a child into their threatened world, a concern especially serious for a Jewish family in 1943. Yet even through the fear of an air-raid drill, the mother can marvel at the beauty of the skylit snowfall and rue the intrusions by human malevolence. The local malice— Cousin Ruthie's gossip, a bigoted snoop frozen in a stroke, a neighbor running amok in his underwear—Allen dismisses with a nervous laugh. But the global evil keeps the characters' confidence and the film's comedy well within the shadows of reality. Allen's optimism here is not blind to the dangers of the day but a resolve maintained in their face. For him the most important things are not the momentous but the momentary. So against the threat of the Holocaust Allen posits the small but compelling satisfactions of an exuberant family life and the simple cigarette girl's access to the American Dream. The big Nazi experience in this film is Joey's vision of a phantom submarine, no less chilling an experience for being based more in his radio serials than in his vision. *Radio Days* is a film of small insights and emotions, of centripetal energy, homing in on private memories and sentiments as a bolster against the larger world movements of time, death, and loss.

Allen holds forth something of a secular alternative to religion when he shows his characters seeking in their imaginative life with the radio a pattern for their lives, guidance in how to deal with their problems (marital as otherwise), and the promise (or delusion) of a higher, brighter life beyond their mundane own. When the narrator—within the frame of "September Song"—rues the fading of those voices, those memories, he expresses his loss of that sense of an other-world beyond.

In *The Purple Rose of Cairo* most of the inner-film characters are terrified at the prospect of an unscripted, unguided life. They prefer their set, familiar world, where the maker's hand keeps patterns of life secure and characters predictable. But not Tom Baxter: "The real people want their lives fictional and the fictional want their lives real." By not appearing in that film in any form, Allen represented the God or Maker as an absent, unknown deity in the contemporary cosmos. When Allen appears as a voice in *Radio Days*, the traditional faith and confidence of a guiding divinity are reaffirmed. But it's not the traditional maker nor the traditional religion. It is a wholly secular religion that finds glory in an air-drill snowfall and community in shared tragedies and dreams. This community of diversion Allen would revive to override the bloody divisions of modern mankind.

22

Hlenka Regained

Irony and Ambiguity in the Narrator of Woody Allen's *Another Woman*

Maria del Mar Asensio Arostegui

My discussion of narration and narrators in film requires the previous acceptance of the fact that current narratological theories have primarily had novels as their objects of study. This fact constitutes a serious hindrance for the narrative study of movies that, as a result, have more often than not been inappropriately measured against literary standards.

Novels are not like narrative films. It is true that both are narratives and consequently have the same capacity for telling stories. However, their modus operandi is fairly different (see Chatman 1978, esp. 146–260; and especially, Chatman 1990, 124–38). Literary storytelling and cinematic storytelling constitute two separate modes of narration because the kind of language used by each mode is also different. The former is based on the symbolic nature of any written linguistic utterance, as it is the role of the reader's imagination and competence to provide the signified of each of the existing signifiers and of the novel as a whole. The latter, on the other hand, plays with the highly iconic quality of the images it is composed of. (For a discussion of this issue, see García Mainar on focalization, 1993, 153–67.) Therefore, while the concept of narration in literature is usually represented by the necessary presence of an agent, a narrator, who utters linguistic signs thus converting the initial story into the final text with which the reader is

The research carried out for the writing of this paper has been financed by the Consejo Asesor de Investigación de la Diputación General de Aragón.

presented, the concept of narration in cinema is more complex in the sense that cinematic narration involves other textual components such as mise-en-scène, music score, sound effects, or editing, among others. Nevertheless, this does not imply that such concepts as narrator or narration should be avoided when referring to films (see Deleyto 1991, 161–66). In fact, although narrators in cinema do not enjoy the same preeminence as narrators in novels do, a similar agent to the narrator in a novel may be found in many films. In this article the use of *narrator* will accordingly be restricted to the agent that actively tells a story or part of it in linguistic signs.

Graham McCann, the author of one of the most comprehensive books on Woody Allen's life, work, and persona, states that "American movies have always been passionately devoted to story-telling, and Woody Allen has become one of the great modern story-tellers" (1991, 227). In an unusually large number of Allen's films, there is always at least one character who engages in the act of explicitly telling a story. In *Manhattan* (1979), we hear Allen's peculiar voice as that of the extradiegetic narrator (Genette 1980, 228) in the difficult process of beginning his story; in *Annie Hall* (1977), we see him as a character-narrator directly addressing the audience from inside the diegesis and establishing himself as "the master of ceremonies, the person who will summon the characters and arrange the order and duration of the scenes" (McCann 1991, 31); in *Radio Days* (1987), we hear again Allen's voice, as an autodiegetic narrator (Genette 1980, 245) who recounts the golden memories of his childhood and youth from a distance; in *Zelig* (1983), Allen parodies documentaries and thus makes use of an objective extradiegetic narrative voice; even in some of his earlier comedies, *Take the Money and Run* (1969) or some parts of *Everything You Always Wanted to Know about Sex* (1972), for instance, there is also a certain emphasis on storytelling as a reminiscence of his period as a stage comedian. This agent reappears in his films *Hannah and Her Sisters* (1986) and "Oedipus Wrecks" (1989).

Another Woman (1988) is no exception in this sense. Rather to the contrary, the story reported in this film is narrated by a main agent, a woman, Marion, whose role is quite complex and significant for the development of the story and for its meaning. What I propose in this chapter is a narratological approach to this narrator's role as a means to explain how voice-over narration generates ambiguity and irony by spreading inconsistent and incomplete clues all through the film, by transforming the process of narration itself into a source of suspense and emotion, by consistently breaking the coherent temporal order of the events, and by constantly questioning and blurring the limits between different ontological levels.

The beginning of the film is quite interesting for several reasons. The opening scene, which I will analyze in some depth because of its peculiarity and narrative importance, lasts approximately ninety seconds. It is a kind of presentation that comes immediately after the Orion logo. There is no introductory title, no credits. No preliminary clue is presented for the viewer to create framing expectations. On the other hand, what the camera shows—the objective images—is situated in a space and a time other than that of what we are told—the linguistic utterances—although it may be said that the images visualize what the voice is telling.

In this sense the scene proves to be overtly stylized. Its artificiality is in a way laid bare. On the one hand, during the whole ninety seconds, all we hear is the sound of a clock plus a female voice, a woman who in an intimate, self-confident tone overtly expresses her attitude to life, introduces herself as the narrator and mediator of the story, and gives a quick but exhaustive explanation of her present situation both at a personal and a professional level. At the same time, the camera has been focusing on a long, empty corridor until the figure of a middle-age woman getting ready to leave her house approaches it. Invited by the woman's intimacy, so to speak, the camera follows her as she turns right and looks at herself in a mirror. This shot is followed by a cut to a close-up of her face. The woman is Gena Rowlands, an actress who is not well-known by the general public and, most significant of all, who is not part of Allen's usual acting crew. Nevertheless, her relationship with the camera leads the viewer to infer that she may well be playing the main character in the story. This inference is further emphasized by the fact that she claims to be telling the story: "My name is Marion Post. I'm director of undergraduate studies in philosophy at a very fine women's college though right now I'm on leave of absence to begin writing a book," she says, and the camera immediately tracks to the woman we have seen before, thus establishing the final identification of this woman with the voice that we have been listening to for the last few seconds.

Gena Rowlands is not the only unusual actress in Allen's cast, however. The same applies to the rest of the characters the narrator progressively introduces as her close relatives and whose photographs are simultaneously scanned by the camera: her husband, Ken (Ian Holm); Ken's daughter, Laura (Martha Plimpton); her brother, Paul (Harris Yulin); her sister-in-law, Lynn (Frances Conroy); and her father (John Houseman). None of them had ever worked with Allen before—with the exception of Frances Conroy, who worked with him in *Manhattan* (Girgus 1993)—so once more the viewer's expectations, at least the ones based on previous experiences of Allen's films, are broken. For Bordwell,

> the sequential nature of narrative makes the initial portions of a text crucial for the establishment of hypotheses. Sternberg borrows a term from cognitive psychology, the "primacy effect," to describe how initial information establishes "a frame of reference to which subsequent information [is] subordinated as far as possible." (1985, 38)

It is interesting to note that, for the sake of ambiguity, the opening scene paradoxically and systematically conceals all kinds of background information from the viewer. Besides, speaking in narrative terms and this time for the sake of irony, the information provided is also scarce, superficial, and misleading because all of the hypotheses concerning Marion that the viewer may establish as a frame of reference—her security, her success, her declared fulfillment in life—will be invariably proved false by the progressive development of the film.

Ambiguity is consciously searched for in this first scene. There is at least a spatial and a temporal distance between Marion as a character and Marion as a narrator. This is precisely what Sarah Kozloff (1988, 5) names "voice-over narration," which she defines as "oral statements conveying any portion of a narrative, spoken by an unseen speaker situated in a space and time other than that simultaneously being presented by the images on the screen." It is clear that this narrator is, in Genette's terms (1980, 245), a homodiegetic narrator insofar as she places herself in the space of the *fabula* by means of the possessives she uses. She is also an extradiegetic narrator, a second-level character-narrator, telling her story in the retrospect. The implications of this type of narrator are at least twofold. First, by making the narration explicit, the text foregrounds the interplay between the story and the process of telling it, the discourse. Second, the narrating character enjoys a dual status; she is both the experiencing-I and the narrating-I. The final function of the interplay between the story and the discourse, on the one hand, and the dual status enjoyed by the narrating character, on the other, is in both cases ironic, as this analysis will attempt to demonstrate.

Spatial distance is made evident from the very moment that we hear Marion's voice, as narrating-I, significantly accompanied by the sound of a clock, but we neither see her speaking nor perceive the clock anywhere in the scene. That is to say, both the voice and the clock are extradiegetic elements, they are outside the story being told. Later in the film, however, we hear the sound of a clock for the second time as Marion-narrator is speaking. But this time we *do* see the clock, for now the events she is describing do not take place at her home (as it occurred in the opening scene) but in the flat she rents as an office to write her book, the place where her life will be completely changed. So we may deduce that the process of narration physically takes place in that flat.

The question of the temporal distance between story and discourse in the opening scene remains a little more ambiguous. The first two sentences the voice-over narrator utters are in the past tense, giving thus the impression that the narration postdates the events on the screen:

> If someone had asked me when I reached my fifties to assess my life, I would have said that I had achieved a decent virtual fulfillment both personally and

professionally. Beyond that I would say I don't choose to delve. Not that I was afraid of uncovering some dark side of my character, but I always feel if something seems to be working, leave it alone.

But then the rest of the monologue is recounted in the present tense. Little by little Marion gives each and every detail of her present situation as if to make her audience believe that the narrative action, the story, and the discourse are simultaneous in time. Yet, once the credits have been shown in their entirety, the narrator retakes her narrative and invariably uses the past tense till the end of the film.

In Genette's words, "The use of a past tense is enough to make a narrative subsequent [i.e., the story precedes the discourse], although without indicating the temporal interval which separates the moment of the narrating from the moment of the story" (1980, 220). As it is finally made clear at the end of the film, the narrating-I knows perfectly well from the very beginning how her story is going to end, something that is subtly hinted at in the opening sentence of the film. Then why does she choose the present tense for the presentation of her personal and professional situation?

In my opinion, two reasons may account for the use of this textual strategy. First, according to Genette, "A present-tense narrative which is 'behaviorist' in type and strictly of the moment can seem the height of objectivity" (1980, 219). This presentation scene fulfills a very concrete function, which can be summarized as the narrator's attempt to create a strong degree of intimacy with the audience to achieve the highest possible degree of complicity. Marion's words have to be objective enough so that the viewer may trust her and suspend disbelief. Furthermore, it is only by appearing as a reliable narrator that the ironic intention of this initial scene can be fully attained. Marion introduces herself as a woman who does not like self-analysis. Yet all the elements in the story will precipitate her precisely into self-analysis and into the surfacing and acceptance of the actual dark side of her character, a despicable moral stance that has meant the sacrifice of others and of herself for the sake of an apparent success that will prove a fake, a delusion, as the film progresses.

The second reason is a consequence of the first. Once the narrator has gained the audience's confidence, she can manipulate their response to the film. Thus the first scene in *Another Woman* shows an apparently omniscient, secure narrator who controls the story she tells and who directs the viewer's perceptions and emotions. Her controlling power as a narrator is put at a level with the apparent control she has of her own life as a character. The illusion of unmediated reality is broken. Marion is the framing narrator (as we have seen, her voice is simultaneous with the film's opening shots), and for a long while what the viewer receives and accepts is her mediated story. In short, the story's significance will be clear only at the end of the film, its correct interpretation will be possible only when the viewer has patiently gathered all the important information that has been cleverly hidden till the final moment. Meanwhile, the viewer is forced to go through the same experiences and to feel the same emotions as the experiencing-I, Marion as a character, undergoes in her unconscious mediated search for authenticity and truth. The simultaneous anagnorisis of both character and viewer allows the process of narration itself to become a textual element, a source of suspense and emotion. No doubt the final function of this strategy is ironic because, as I have already said, Marion's initial self-assurance both as a narrator and as a character is progressively eroded and proved only a mask behind which Marion's true self is hidden.

Another Woman is a rich, complex narrative and the function of its narrator is not exclusively that of providing external information. Yet, before engaging in the analysis of the story proper and of the main strategies used in its telling, a brief summary of its *fabula* (see Bal 1985, 6–9) and its structure seems to be necessary in any narratological approach. *Another Woman's fabula* is fairly simple. Marion Post, a successful philosopher, has taken a leave of absence from her job to write a book. Searching for quiet and silence, she sublets a flat downtown as an office. Instead of the expected calm, she finds that because of some acoustic problem she has direct access to the private conversations of a psychiatrist and his patients. Although at the beginning she refuses to pay any attention to them, she accidentally overhears a woman's voice. The intensity of her anguish overpowers Marion and makes her feel sympathetic toward the woman. Her initial curiosity progressively turns into an obsession: she spies on her, she follows her down the street, she even invites her to lunch. But her desire to know about the other woman's problems leads her to become aware of her own personal problems. After a series of encounters with an old friend, her father, and her brother and by listening to the anguished commentaries of the other woman, she realizes that her egotistic drives have made her unable to maintain any true relationship with people, not even with those she loves the most, not even with herself. Her life embodies all the dreads and deceptions that the other woman fears so much. Her whole world tumbles down; she even has to go through a divorce. It is then that she recognizes her past mistakes and decides to adopt a more positive attitude to life. The other woman unconsciously engages her in the search for her true self and for the real values of life.

Another Woman is a psychological melodrama. There is very little action. The most important things always happen inside the characters' minds. In fact, almost all the elements that make the narrative progress are either shared feelings provoked by common experiences between characters (for instance, Hope's and Marion's melancholic remembrances of a lost true love) or by shocking revelations about past events and unconsciously hurt feelings (Claire's withdrawal from Marion because of David; Paul's decision not to bother Marion any more). The film's symbolism benefits from this fact. Almost all the action takes place indoors. The locations may change—Ken and Marion's house, Marion's flat, her parents' house in the country, a theater, a pub, a shop, an office, even a restaurant—but they are invariably enclosed spaces, interiors.

Only a few scenes are shot outdoors, but they are most of the time mere transitional scenes (Marion and Laura in a car going to visit Marion's father; Marion going to see her brother). Nevertheless, four examples of outdoor scenes are worth commenting on for their narrative value. The first occurs very soon in the film. Marion has agreed to meet her sister-in-law, but as she does not show up in time, the protagonist decides to leave. Lynn appears just as Marion reaches the street. The encounter, although brief, takes place outdoors. Lynn tells Marion that she and Paul are going to get a divorce and she asks her for some money. Their conversation uncovers Paul's actual feelings for Marion:

Lynn: You're deluding yourself. Of course, in a way he idolizes you. He also hates you.

Marion: Sorry, I don't accept that.

Lynn: You're such a perceptive woman. How come you don't understand his feelings?

Marion: Look, I'm late and . . . and, to tell you the truth, I just make it a practice of never getting into this kind of conversation. You know, they're fruitless and people just say things they're sorry for later. Why don't you just tell me how much you need and I'll discuss it with Ken. OK?

This is the first time Marion is asked to get involved, to do away with the amount of self-deceptions that are suffocating her true self.

The next two scenes are interrelated and they develop the symbolism still further. The first one is the scene in which Marion suddenly recognizes Hope, the woman whose voice she has been listening to and, moved by her curiosity, decides to follow her. Paradoxically, she does not learn anything new about Hope but, quite by chance, she meets her old friend, Claire, and her husband. This encounter provokes the second "unpleasant" revelation, another reversal of her golden memories of youth, and her second refusal to face the truth. The second one is the scene in which Marion meets Hope in a shop, while she is searching for an anniversary present for her husband, and invites her to lunch. For the first time, the film shows Marion cheerily walking the street accompanied by someone else. Again the restaurant Hope chooses is the place where Marion discovers that her husband is having an affair with their mutual friend Lydia.

The final outdoor scene I will be commenting on is, in my opinion, the most beautiful and touching of all because, in spite of its nostalgic tone, it opens a door to hope. I am referring of course to the last-but-one scene of the film. Marion has resumed her work. Free from any distraction she makes a pause and starts reading about Hlenka, one of the characters, rumored to be based on her, in the novel by Larry Lewis (Gene Hackman). The images on the screen show Larry and Marion walking around in Central Park, taking refuge from the sudden rain and kissing. Meanwhile, she reads, "Her kiss was full of desire and I knew I couldn't share that feeling with anyone else. And then a wall went up and just as quickly I was screened out. But it was too late because I now knew that she was capable of intense passion if she would one day just allow herself to feel."

The four outdoor scenes just described constitute in themselves four moments of reversal and recognition of a failure or a lack in Marion's apparently successful life. To such an extent, these four scenes ironically contradict Marion's self-assurance and personal fulfillment overtly stated in the opening scene of the film and implicitly maintained by the narrative so far. Indeed all traditional human values such as familiar relationships, friendship, love, and even self-identity are progressively questioned in Marion's life through these scenes. Thus, far from reassuring Marion's belief in her closeness to her brother, Lynn denounces Marion's self-delusion and misunderstanding of her brother and Paul's resulting feelings of hatred toward his sister; her friend Claire resentfully announces her voluntary withdrawal from Marion to free herself from her egotistic drives; Marion's relationship to her husband proves superficial, unstable, and inevitably condemned to failure; finally, she consciously hides her true feelings toward Larry, consequently banning her own capacity for emotion and passion. Marion's recognition of failure is progressive, like the viewer's. It ranges from a merely bothering statement (Lynn's) to an unavoidable fact (Ken's deceit). Yet there is hope in Larry's final sentence in the last scene mentioned previously: "I now knew that she was capable of intense passion if she would one day just allow herself to feel." Thus only by losing her stability will Marion be able to rediscover herself and become "another woman" as the title of the film foreshadows.

Apart from the symbolic potential provided by the consciously chosen location of the events, one of the most successful strategies used by the narrative as a means to manipulate the viewer's perceptions and understanding of the film is the particular selection and temporal organization of the events themselves. The film primarily consists of a present-day recounting of a set of events that the narrator experienced in a relatively short period of her recent past. One of the functions of the narrator in *Another Woman* consists in aiding the viewer not to lose hold of a complex chronology. Marion's narration, with its past tense, has the role of establishing the necessary points of reference for the narrative. It usually provides expositional and temporal information and it also sets the pace of the narrative. Thus, while she gives a detailed account of the events that took place during the first five days of the story, her narration does not specify how many more days go by till the end of the film. Her narrative puts a special emphasis on the events that bring about Marion's quest for authenticity. Very precise temporal expressions are used: "that first morning," "all day," "by late afternoon," and "the following morning." However, the decisions she makes after her cathartic experience are frequently condensed in sentences such as "the following days" or "once on a sunny morning."

Those expository chronological sections are complemented by six flashbacks (not in chronological order). Five of them are external, that is, they precede the first event represented in the story. Such external flashbacks invariably correspond to Marion's memories, although they are motivated by several characters' recollections. For instance, the first flashback is motivated by Hope's confessions to her psychiatrist. She is questioning herself about real love and about whether she has made the right choice: "I've told you there was someone else once. The last time I saw him was several years ago, before I was married, at a party." This recollection makes Marion think of a similar episode in her own life. Her memories are shown on-screen as a flashback while the story is frozen for a while. The "other woman" also acts as a narrator in some parts of the film. She could be said to possess the typical qualities of an embedded or intradiegetic narrator (Genette 1980, 228). Her voice is offscreen and she talks to a concrete person, her psychiatrist. Nevertheless, her words have a wider audience because they are heard not only by Marion but also by the viewers of the film. She is not aware of her role as narrator but she leads Marion both physically and psychologically in her way to self-discovery.

The second flashback is motivated by the old photographs Marion sees at her father's house. This time Marion narrates offscreen and gives an extremely romanticized account of her family life and her youth:

And here I am older. I could go up to the spare room and paint for hours. The time would just fly by when I was doing a picture. And there I am with my friend Claire. You know, she became an actress. We used to be so close but I haven't seen her in years. And there's my mother. She loved strolling round the grounds. And she loved all the beautiful things. She loved nature, music, poetry. That was her whole existence.

I have quoted part of this second flashback because such a dreamlike romantic account ironically and painfully contrasts with the more down-to-earth objective revelations later made by the rest of the characters. This flashback is used as a technique to stress the commonly accepted fact that stories depend on who tells them and that there is no clear-cut distinction between reality and fiction.

The third and fourth flashbacks are both motivated by Marion herself. They recount two complementary aspects of the story of her first marriage. They are used as a device to add significant information prior to the story.

And the last external flashback, which I have already mentioned, is motivated by Larry Lewis's written narrative. Its function is double. First, it is a kind of description of Marion's true self. Second, it is the only way of providing the film with a hopeful ending.

The single internal flashback, which tells about those events that occur within the temporal bounds of the story proper, is narrated by Hope, the "other" woman. Her narrative takes us back to the moment when Marion discovers that her husband and her friend Lydia are having a love affair. This information is delayed on purpose to provoke a stronger response from the viewer.

Like the previously analyzed outdoor scenes, these flashbacks further contribute to establishing the ideology of this film, namely that real personal fulfillment lies with the recognition and the acceptance of one's identity, in this case, a woman's identity, which the film locates at the side of emotion, lack of egotism, comradeship to other women, and motherhood—a series of attitudes that Marion is shown in flashback after flashback to have purposefully rejected in her life in favor of personal, social, and professional fulfillment.

So far I have referred to the use of incomplete clues, the various functions of narration and the breaking of the chronological order of events as means of generating ambiguity and irony. Now, before ending this chapter, I would like to analyze the relationship between fiction and reality and the way this relationship is constantly questioned in the film as the last resource to create irony and ambiguity.

One way of underlining that there is no clear-cut distinction between what is real and what is fictional in this film was already pointed out when I referred to the function of external flashbacks. This metafictional aspect of the film is still more clearly symbolized by the fact that, all through the movie, Marion's life is fictionalized not only by herself but also by others in one way or another. First, we are offered Marion's own excessively romanticized account of her youth and her family, which, as the film develops, proves to be quite far from the truth. Then, three very important passages of her life are literally represented in her dreams as if they were three different scenes from a theater play. Claire and Marion are the actresses; Ken, Larry, and Sam are the actors; Claire's husband is the director; and Hope, the "other" woman, is the audience. We find all the necessary elements to consider it a play within a dream within a film, and therefore there is no doubt about its artificiality, about its metadiegetic quality as it is three times removed from reality. Ironically, it is in extreme artificiality that truth about Marion is to be found. This is a common trait of these overtly acknowledged fictional scenes that engulf three different truths that Marion keeps on denying in her deceitful but apparently more real life: the fact that her present marriage is coming apart, the fact that she feels she made the wrong choice and resents having lost the man she loved passionately, and the fact that her first husband, Sam, did not die accidentally but rather committed suicide. Finally, Marion's life is also turned into a fiction when Larry Lewis, a character in the film, transforms Marion into Hlenka, the central character in his novel. Again we find a literary narrative within a cinematic narrative and again it is the novel that is paradoxically taken as the revelation of Marion's true self, as the recognition of the other woman within, whose existence she has been systematically denying and slowly suffocating. Thus the film transcends its own fictional boundaries. It constitutes a multiple game of reflections. Woody Allen had already used this strategy in some of his films; as Graham McCann (1991, 40) has pointed out, "As with *The Purple Rose of Cairo* (1985), *Radio Days*'s movie theatre offers a sanctuary from reality, momentary yet memorable, the ever changing images seeming somehow to move to a logic more reliable than the logic of everyday life."

In *Another Woman* this multiple game of reflections, this technique of infinite regress is used in like manner to show that the fictionalization or textualization of reality can be used as a means of coming to terms with our own past and that, when trusted, it can be a good guide to the rediscovery of a hidden reality.

The opening shots of *Another Woman* show Marion looking at herself in a mirror. Being the symbol of self-consciousness par excellence, this mirror diegetically foregrounds the complex self-reflective nature of the film. Simultaneously, Marion's diegetic act of facing her own image in the mirror, while her extradiegetic voice affirms that she is not afraid of uncovering some dark side of her character, contributes to presenting the viewer with an apparently self-assured accomplished woman. Yet Marion's initial self-reliance as a character soon contrasts with the ambiguity generated by the inconsistent and incomplete pieces of information that Marion, as narrator, scatters all through the film, as well as by her breaking of conventional chronology, and by her capacity to transgress the boundaries between fiction and reality. Her self-assurance is finally destroyed when the viewer finds out that indeed Marion has a dark side to uncover. Ironically, hers is a dark side not because of its negative, potentially dangerous, features but rather because, despite its being her true self, it has unconsciously been suffocated and obscured for the sake of intellectual and social achievement. It becomes, then, noteworthy that the mechanism that first sets out the process of uncovering developed in this film is precisely the narration of similar fears and mistakes by "another woman" to her psychiatrist. Significantly, the other woman's name is Hope. Indeed, the final message of this film seems to be hopeful, for even if it is true that Marion loses her stability, it is no less true that, after her cathartic experience, she becomes "another woman," an independent, creative, emotive, new woman who consequently seems to have gained her true self and who for the first time in a long while feels at peace with herself.

WORKS CITED

Bal, Mieke. *Narratology: Introduction to the Theory of the Narrative.* Trans. Christine van Boheemen. Toronto: Toronto University Press, 1985. Translation of *De Theorie van vertellen en verhalen.* 2nd ed.

Bordwell, David. *Narration in the Fiction Film.* Madison: University of Wisconsin Press, 1985.

Chatman, Seymour. *Story and Discourse: Narrative Structure in Fiction and Film.* Ithaca, NY: Cornell University Press, 1978.

———. *Coming to Terms: The Rhetoric of Narrative in Fiction and Film.* Ithaca, NY: Cornell University Press, 1990.

Deleyto, Celestino. "Focalisation in Film Narrative." *Atlantis* 13, no. 1–2 (November 1991): 159–77.

Genette, Gerard. *Narrative Discourse: An Essay in Method.* Trans. Jane E. Lewin. New York: Cornell University Press, 1980. Translation of "Discours du récit: Essai de méthode," a portion of *Figures III,* 1972.

Girgus, Sam B. *The Films of Woody Allen.* Cambridge: Cambridge University Press, 1993.

Kozloff, Sarah. *Invisible Storytellers: Voice-over Narration in American Fiction Film.* Berkeley: University of California Press, 1988.

Mainar, García Luis Miguel. "Autofocalisation in Film Narrative." *Atlantis* 15, no. 1–2 (November 1993): 153–67.

McCann, Graham. *Woody Allen.* Cambridge: Polity Press, 1991.

23

Justice and the Withdrawal of God in Woody Allen's *Crimes and Misdemeanors*

Mark W. Roche

Woody Allen's *Crimes and Misdemeanors* (1989) interlaces two tales. In the comic narrative, Cliff (Woody Allen) is a struggling filmmaker in an unhappy marriage, who is preparing a documentary on a philosopher named Louis Levy (Martin Bergmann). His brother-in-law Lester (Alan Alda) is an arrogant, successful, and lecherous filmmaker, who charms many of those around him. As a favor to his sister, who is embarrassed by her husband's lack of success, Lester agrees to let Cliff make a documentary about him for a TV series. In the process Cliff falls in love with a producer named Halley (Mia Farrow) but finds himself competing for her with Lester, who in the end wins out over Cliff. Cliff's most meaningful relationship remains that with his niece (Jenny Nichols), whom he takes to the movies and to whom he offers bits of comic wisdom.

In the other, more serious strand, Judah (Martin Landau) is a successful ophthalmologist, who is preoccupied with religious and philosophical issues even as he remains a skeptic. He tries to end a two-year affair with Dolores (Anjelica Huston), who threatens to reveal all to his wife Miriam (Claire Bloom). Judah confides in two men, the rabbi Ben (Sam Waterson), who is going blind and who counsels Judah to confront Miriam and ask forgiveness, and Jack (Jerry Orbach), Judah's unseemly brother, who is willing to arrange Dolores's murder, a path Judah eventually chooses. While visiting his childhood home, Judah re-creates in his mind a family seder discussion: the principal conflict is between traditional faith, as embodied by Judah's father (David Howard), and moral relativism, the stance of Judah's Aunt May (Anna Berger). In one of the film's last scenes, Judah and Cliff meet at the wedding of Ben's daughter. After their conversation Judah embraces his wife and strides away, seemingly unaffected by guilt; evil appears to triumph.

This chapter interprets and evaluates the film's competing philosophies of justice: the naive, the nihilistic, and the idealistic. First, I consider the simple theodicy of reward and punishment, the idea that the eyes of God are on us always. This is the position of Judah's father and the young Judah. Second, I discuss the relativistic consequence of our having seen through this seemingly objective moral code, that is, the philosophy that might is right and history is written by the winners. Judah's Aunt May voices this position, as do the film's advocates of harsh reality: Jack, Lester, and eventually Judah. Third, I weigh the philosophy of confession, understanding, and forgiveness, which is represented by Cliff, the rabbi, and the philosopher. Concluding that the film invites both nihilistic and moral interpretations, this chapter supports as the strongest reading a half-theodicy: good people do not necessarily succeed, but evil persons do suffer. Their suffering, however, consists not in God's punishment, but in God's withdrawal.

1

One position presented in the film is a simple theodicy: an all-seeing God rewards the righteous and punishes the wicked. Despite its venerable tradition and moral dignity, the position has several overlapping weaknesses. First, it is anti-intellectual and philosophically ungrounded. The naive position derives from an emotional need for justice, rather than any theoretical arguments. Judah's father asserts that he would opt for God over truth. Second, the naive position is ineffective. Like the biblical Judas, Judah betrays (or overcomes) his religion. Because the wicked are not self-evidently punished and because the father can give no arguments for his position, Judah— like Jack—feels free to transcend it. For Judah, religiously motivated goodness is a hypothetical norm he chooses not to follow: "God is a luxury I can't afford." Third, the naive position is primitive and retributive in its lack of forgiveness, an ethical corollary to its philosophical inability to integrate negativity, that is, to base itself on a refutation of alternative views.

Judah's initial fear that his crime will be recognized has a realistic as well as religious dimension. When Judah first finds Dolores's body, he leaves the door to her apartment open, and the viewer nervously wonders whether Judah will be caught. That evening he stays awake under bathroom lights that remind us of interrogation lights, and his phone rings unexpectedly. Later a detective asks him a few questions. Just as Judah fears that the police know everything and see right through him, the viewer—recognizing in the detective's clothing and demeanor an allusion to the crafty detective of popular television, Columbo—wonders for a moment whether the detective knows more than he lets on. Judah, however, is not caught. Indeed, he not only escapes punishment, he prospers.

By way of Lester the film mockingly alludes to the Oedipus story. A genuine parallel exists, however, insofar as *Crimes and Misdemeanors* and *Oedipus Rex* undermine a naive theodicy. Only a banal reading of Sophocles' play would lead to the argument that Oedipus has committed a crime and therefore receives his just punishment. Oedipus has great moral integrity; he seeks the murderer and does not waver when the search comes back to himself. Not the justice of the gods, but the strength of the individual, keeps the moral order intact. The final choral ode in *Oedipus Rex* (864–910) addresses the central question of Allen's film: Is there a moral universe? Do the gods punish the unjust, the impious, the thieves? The answer given is that the gods have withdrawn ("Apollo is nowhere clear in honour; God's service perishes" [910]). Justice is left not to fate or divine will but to Oedipus's moral integrity, his determination to do the good even as he knows that he will suffer for it.

As Sophocles problematizes the simple theodicy, so Allen mocks the naive retribution theology of Judah's father. The significant difference in Allen's film is that the great moral individual is absent. Judah does not make real the Oedipus-like scenario Cliff proposes at the end of the film: "I would have had him turn himself in, because then, you see, then your story assumes tragic proportions, because in the absence of a God or something he is forced to assume that responsibility himself; then you have tragedy." Judah's inability to reach for tragedy, to sacrifice himself for the good whatever it might cost him, underscores his distance from Oedipus.

The seder discussion between the father and the aunt penetrates to the core of the film. In this tragedy of collision virtue and right are on each side, even as each side neglects the truth of its other. The father has moral dignity, the aunt intellectual superiority: the father is just but cannot defend himself ("If necessary I will always choose God over truth"); the aunt sees through Judah's father, but cannot transcend cynicism and nihilism (she denies the existence of any "moral structure"). Neither the father nor the aunt reaches the stature of an Oedipus with his combination of self-sacrificing virtue and intellect. In the modern world morality and intellect diverge.

2

To criticize Judah from an external perspective would be easy (he is, after all, a murderer), but from the perspective of the film itself such a critique is not so simple. The shortage of viable alternatives appears to speak for Judah. Not only is Judah's father illogical and unable to justify his stance, other seemingly moral alternatives—as represented by the rabbi, Cliff, and the philosopher—are equally undermined. The rabbi is blind to the fact that Judah has committed his crime. A representative of religion, he seems to symbolize God's lack of vision or inability to offer a strong and effective moral code. Cliff is no less ineffectual than the rabbi, and despite his depth of insight, he lacks moral rigor—as when he seeks to have an affair while he is married. The philosopher meanwhile appears to cancel his position by jumping out the window. "Leap" of faith morality appears not to function as well as its proponents might think. In the nihilistic reading none of these figures is a substantive counterforce to Judah.

In the juxtaposition of Lester and Cliff, the film encourages identification with the loser, Cliff. In the juxtaposition of Judah and Dolores, the film invites the viewer to assume Judah's position. Unlike Lester, Judah is not rendered comic. The identification with Judah is further encouraged by the presentation of his inner turmoil and most intimate reflections as well as the portrayal of Dolores as "neurotic" and at times unattractive. We see Dolores solely from the perspective of her threats to Judah. Our perception of Cliff differs from our perception of Dolores: First, the film adopts Cliff's perspective—at least in part. Second, Cliff's unattractiveness is mitigated by his wit. In this nihilistic reading the eyes are not the "windows of the soul," as Dolores once suggests; instead, as Judah says of Dolores's eyes at her death, nothing is behind them but a "black void." The void, which is mirrored back to Judah, signifies not so much the nonbeing of Dolores as the emptiness of traditional religious rhetoric about the soul and thus about predetermined categories of good and evil. In this reading the viewer is invited to identify with Judah's eventual self-overcoming, his assertion of a life beyond good and evil—even as Judah's celebration of a new life presupposes the death of Dolores.

Judah erases Dolores's disturbing voice by burning her letter in the fire; later, just after the audience sees that Dolores is to be killed, the film cuts to a close-up of the fire. Judah controls the fire and transforms what would be in his eyes a hell on earth (the revelation of his misdeeds) into ashes that give birth to new life. The film appears to fulfill Lester's insight that "comedy is tragedy plus time." Judah awakens one morning with the burden of guilt wondrously lifted. Time heals all wounds; in Judah's words, "with time it all fades." The sadness of Schubert's Quartet no. 15, which formed the background to Dolores's murder, gives way at the film's conclusion: uplifting jazz tunes accompany the credits.

For the viewer who adopts this reading, the dialogue in which Judah sketches the perfect murder becomes another example of nonrecognition and nonpersuasion; the supposedly good listener (here Cliff, rather than the rabbi) fails to see behind Judah's story, and Cliff fails to move him. Judah renders his crime a mere fiction, and this is symbolic, for a truth that does not enhance our position in life becomes an illusion for the power positivist. Judah's triumphant departure with his "beautiful" wife represents resolution on his terms. Moreover, their daughter will soon marry, suggesting, again symbolically, that the line of Judah will continue and forever compete with the rabbi's descendants; power positivism will not give way to the naive hope for future norms.

In this film the harshness of reality (Judah's success) surfaces most strongly precisely when the viewer is inclined to expect cinematic reality (an aesthetic resolution of discord). This realism mocks the unrealistic aesthetic expectations of the audience, and it implies a complexly ironic happy end, insofar as the audience clandestinely identifies with the evil figures. The villain is pardoned on film, just as such villains are frequently acquitted in real life. The audience identifies with Judah's having to trouble himself with Dolores's complaints and threats as well as his desire to rid himself of this nuisance. Judah, we could argue, is the kind of character society magnifies or secretly admires. Underlining this, Genesis 29:35 and 49:8 tell us that the name "Judah" means *praised* or *object of praise*. Also supporting this claim is America's still reigning fascination with gangster films. Characters like Cliff and Dolores, on the other hand, are secretly—or not so secretly— scorned.

Developing the nihilistic reading, we might read the film's decision not to portray the kind of tragic scenario Cliff envisages as mockery of a traditional concept that art should teach a lesson. Rather than arguing a case, the film mocks the audience's expectation that the film should, or even could, provide answers. In short, the film culminates in a self-reflexive joke on untenable audience expectations. Truth personified has jumped out the window. As Judah would have it, "If you want a happy ending, you should go see a Hollywood movie." This ironic reading encounters a significant problem: the argument that films should not or need not teach a lesson is itself a lesson; the argument is self-contradictory. In response, however, we might shift our position and argue that, rather than offering a lesson of any kind, the film wants to portray a set of moral options. It presents these options without privileging any one of them. The film's structure presupposes that moral issues cannot be resolved.

3

Crimes and Misdemeanors undermines a naive theodicy and appears to accept nihilism, but these are not the only possible readings of the film. Another reading might point toward, even as it leaves unfulfilled, a possible synthesis of morality and intellect. In this section I present such an interpretation and develop it partly as a refutation of the nihilistic reading. The idealistic interpretation privileges the positions of the rabbi, Cliff, and the philosopher. Each adopts a generally moral position, and each is an intellectual; indeed, in the filmmaker, the rabbi, and the philosopher, we see the three stages of Hegel's Absolute Spirit. Alluding to an old tradition, *Crimes and Misdemeanors* invites us to recognize Ben's blindness as symbolic of inner sight: the rabbi speaks eloquently of confession, understanding, and forgiveness. In this reading, clear and complete solutions do not exist; nonetheless, the film ends with a kernel of the philosopher's wisdom and "the hope that future generations might understand more." The film inspires further thought and action; harmony becomes a goal outside the film medium rather than a lulling artistic reality.

The audience, identifying with Cliff, is naturally disappointed to see Halley become engaged to Lester. The disappointment is magnified by three long takes of Cliff's devastated expressions as he recognizes their bond; the audience is forced to stare at his pain. When Lester states that he won her with caviar and champagne, we recall an earlier scene when Cliff, trying to court Halley, says that he has no caviar; instead, he has "oatbran, which is better for your heart." The metonymy ("caviar" and "oatbran" represent differences in wealth and status) and the homonym ("heart") render the statement both comic and poignant.

Cliff is preferable to Lester; we identify with him not only from a narrative perspective but also in terms of values. Cliff has insight into negativity (as in the satiric documentary he creates about Lester), he expresses his idealism in his documentaries and in his suggestion to Judah that we must fill the void of God's absence, and he develops a beautifully happy and loving relationship with his niece. Halley defends her position to Cliff by explaining that Lester is not so bad after all, but we wonder whether this is a rationalization—also to herself—since she does not appear convinced and since Lester, rich and successful, also serves the external purpose of helping her with her career. Halley may be using Lester for her own ends; she herself tells Cliff how ambitious she is.

Consider in this context the flower parallel. The murderer gains access to Dolores's apartment by saying that he has to make "a delivery of some flowers." Lester tries to court Halley by sending her white roses. Because of her allergy, she cannot accept the flowers; therefore, the situation differs, but the symbolism suggests that the relationship with Lester will weaken her, corrupt her, lower her. Paradoxically reinforcing this reading is the association—in Allen's works—of roses with idealism and the search for transcendence (Downing). Halley symbolically rejects any ideal dimension to her love relationship and opts for caviar (which Lester has and Cliff doesn't).

She, too, is a realist. Dolores, in contrast, has her ideal taken from her: expecting flowers from Judah, she receives death.

The name Halley and her predicament of choosing between two men (along with the prominence of the rose motif) allude to one of the greatest of American films, John Ford's *The Man Who Shot Liberty Valance.* In this film the woman, Hallie, must choose between the Western hero Tom Doniphon (John Wayne) and the less heroic but more intellectual and civilized character, Ransom Stoddard (James Stewart). Hallie eventually chooses Ransom, thus sacrificing passion and stability for intellect and progress. The choice Woody Allen's Halley makes is for the newest version of the American ideal, the phony and superficial careerist. In each film the spectator senses that the woman's choice is also a loss, but in Allen's film there is no tragic collision. Lester is a comic reduction of Ransom Stoddard. As with Oedipus, the parallel is also an inversion.

The rabbi has no insight into evil, but he does have moral fiber, and his blindness may derive less from ignorance than from the incomprehensible corruption of the world. The rabbi belongs to a separate moral realm. In a supposedly indifferent universe, human beings create or deny the morality of the world; symbolically, Judah, who subverts morality, is unable (in his role as doctor) to prevent this blindness. In the nihilistic interpretation the rabbi's blindness symbolizes weakness; in the idealistic reading we focus on Judah's inability to cure this blindness: the rabbi's failure is also Judah's. In his loving relationship with his wife and daughter the rabbi appears a noble foreigner in a land of superficiality, deceit, and error.

The philosopher presents a complex view of the world. He is both insightful (like Cliff) and moral (like the rabbi), but he cannot sustain his position in such a cold and corrupt world. The line "I went out the window" is first of all and most importantly comic. We wonder whether Allen has the philosopher commit suicide because his stance is untenable or because the gag was irresistible. Nonetheless, the gag and the message might not be so simple. If a window is a kind of lens or eye, and if it is connected to the soul and the eternal (as in the film's suggestion that the eyes are the windows of the soul), then the philosopher's departure may imply withdrawal from the world of superficiality and brutality and a longing for what is eternal and harmonious. The philosopher can no longer live in such a corrupt and unloving world, and his death—like the rabbi's blindness—may shed more light on the world than on his self. Such a philosopher leaves hidden messages, not banalities. This reading of the philosopher's death as paradoxical is reinforced by the philosopher's own embrace of paradox in his brief video sermons.

On the superficial level the evil Judah gets off scot-free. In one scene Judah's brother Jack threatens that if Judah weakens (as did Dolores) and endangers Jack's existence (by turning himself in), Jack may decide to do away with Judah. This moment, which would have exhibited the immediate self-cancellation of Judah's position, is not developed beyond this one brief segment; nonetheless, the self-cancellation of Judah's position is exhibited in more subtle ways. Though we identify with Judah from a narrative perspective, we do not identify from the perspective of his values. The film distances us from him.

Judah's elliptical confession to Cliff represents a need for intersubjectivity and absolution, even if it is not fully realized. Judah's affirmation of the "fictive" murderer's actions seems forced, a pseudotriumph. The act of confession suggests that Judah is in truth barely coping with his crime. His pains of conscience will likely return, and his future bliss is unveiled as mere emptiness and vanity. A pragmatic contradiction surfaces when he implies to Cliff that he has gotten over his guilt, that it is all behind him, that "his life is completely back to normal."

Other evidence supports this reading. When last we see Judah before the wedding he is a total wreck; no evidence of a mediating transition is given. Though Judah tries to be happy at the party, he leaves the festivities. As he tells his story, he grimaces, reliving the pain of his guilt; the effect of his facial expressions is accentuated by an exceedingly long close-up. Cliff's earlier bon mot encourages us to look at a speaker's expressions: "Don't listen to what your schoolteachers tell you," he suggests to his niece, "just see what they look like, and that's how you'll know what life is really going to be about." Judah's final references to rationalization and denial exhibit how forced and strained his triumph is. Judah is still fighting within himself.

When he returns to his wife, Miriam, he tries to will a happiness that seemingly eludes him. Is this genuine happiness or the modern compulsion to insist on our being happy—even when life is most hollow and superficial? We are reminded of Mrs. Smith in Hitchcock's *Mr. and Mrs. Smith*, a film quoted in *Crimes and Misdemeanors*, who insists that she is happy at a moment of utter dejection (during her ride on the ferris wheel). Happiness is a complex concept both psychologically and philosophically. Often those who most insist on their happiness are the least content. Moreover, is happiness more a pragmatic concept (getting what we want) or an objective concept (uncovering the deepest layers of the self, its profundity, its hidden resources, its goodness)? To take an extreme example, does Jack appear happy? If not, is Judah, who has denied the moral dimension of his self, genuinely happy either? Has his good fortune deceived him into thinking that he is happy? And is the superficial Lester, who reacts with rage when Cliff unveils the deficient aspects of his self, genuinely happy?

Judah's original religious belief is an obsession with the eyes of God, with what can be and is seen. Freeing himself from the view that God can see all, Judah moves on to an obsession with appearances. He is willing to betray his wife but not to be caught. Likewise, his financial improprieties must not be uncovered. Judah is obsessed with his good home, his financial security, the appearance of philanthropy. Dolores upsets him most strongly whenever she threatens to unveil the truth. Her death is partly the consequence of Judah's treating her as an object and a means, partly the consequence of his obsession with appearances. Even as Judah abandons the essence of his father's moral code, he remains within his childlike reception of it: he still dwells on appearances.

Judah's preoccupation with appearances illustrates a contradiction in his values. As in many other literary works, the unjust individual unwittingly reveals the superiority of justice by always acting in such a way as to want to appear just and to demand justice from others (Roche). Judah asks the rabbi in his imaginary conversation: "What good is the law if it prevents me from receiving justice? Is what she is doing to me just?" Moreover, the individual who frees himself from religious values—because they are oppressive—ends up being tormented by his confused morality, including its duplicity. The film unravels the underside of Judah's appearances, just as Cliff's biting commentary reveals what lies behind the facade of Lester's success. In forgetting Dolores, Judah also wills to forget his religious past, and this leaves him isolated—not only from other persons, but also from tradition. He has broken a temporal chain; the philosopher, in contrast, emphasizes continuity with the past and the future.

Crimes and Misdemeanors not only undermines the simple theodicy, it persists in asking the most demanding questions: Why doesn't virtue necessarily lead to happiness? Why don't categorical and hypothetical imperatives coincide? The film's answer—from the perspective of this reading—is that good people (for example, Cliff, the rabbi, and the philosopher) do sometimes suffer (such that the theodicy is not resolved) but that bad people (for example, Judah) necessarily suffer (such that the theodicy is at least half answered).

The more complex moral reading of the theodicy is not that God punishes the wicked but that God withdraws from them. This is Cliff's point when he states that Judah is left with a void, his worst beliefs realized. Like his etymological namesake Judas and unlike his brother Jack, Judah is an intellectual, thus a character spiritually troubled by his betrayal. Simple suffering appears minuscule in relation to the suffering we experience from an empty universe, from the absence of truth and a moral order. A rich message found in works from Plato to Boethius and Shakespeare is that the worst suffering is *not* to be punished. Boethius, for example, writes,

> The wicked are less happy if they achieve their desires than if they are unable to do what they want. For, if desiring something wicked brings misery, greater misery is brought by having had the power to do it, without which the unhappy desire would go unfulfilled. So, since each stage has its own degree of misery, if you see people with the desire to do something wicked, the power to do it and

the achievement, they must necessarily suffer a triple degree of misfortune. . . . When the wicked receive punishment they receive something good, the punishment itself, which is good, because of its justice. . . . The logical conclusion of this is that they are burdened with heavier punishment precisely when they are believed to escape it. (4:4)

Consider also Hegel's argument that justice is the right of the criminal, or recall the despair of Kierkegaard's father that, after he cursed God in his youth, God punished him by giving him prosperity and then withdrawing from him. The resulting guilt was more wrenching than abject poverty. The words of Shakespeare's Posthumus sum it up best:

> I'll write against them,
> Detest them, curse them. Yet 'tis greater skill,
> In a true hate to pray they have their will;
> The very devils cannot plague them better.
> (*Cymbeline*, 2.5.32–35)

The idea that God's presence or absence depends on human action is prominent in Enlightenment and post-Enlightenment eras. Lessing's parable of the rings in his famous drama *Nathan the Wise* insists that our possession of the true ring (or religion) is determined by the moral behavior associated with the bearer of the ring or the particular believer. A similar idea is expressed as the central concept of Goethe's poem "The Divine," when he writes that ethical human actions teach us to believe in gods, that human justice should act as a model for otherworldly beliefs. Where pre-Enlightenment proofs for God's existence were dominated by logic (the cosmological, teleological, and ontological proofs), Kant, the contemporary of Lessing and Goethe, offers a moral proof for God's existence. Allen's concept of God is related to this moral reading of God as well as to the idea that the departure of God is the result of human, not divine, action.

Allen's view is not the naive belief that God is always with us, nor the emotional assertion that God is dead, but the more subtle suggestion that God has withdrawn from us. We are living in a less than sacred world, but the possibility of moral and religious regeneration remains. As Hölderlin suggests in "Bread and Wine," the gods have withdrawn because we are ourselves not equal to their demands. This theme of the godless age has frequently been reasserted in this century, as Heidegger's readings of Hölderlin attest and as is evident from Max Scheler's polemics against a "divine justice of reward and punishment." Echoing Spinoza, Scheler writes, "the 'good' person directly participates in the nature of God, in the sense of *velle* in *deo* or *amare* in *deo*, and he is 'blissful' *in* this participation." Any divine reward would replace this intrinsic and deep pleasure with something superficial.

God does not directly reward or punish our actions, yet, according to Scheler, God can "abandon a person" by not forgiving that person (368–69). Allen can be associated with these thinkers in his claim that the punishment of God is not revenge but withdrawal.

Consider the dominance of pale and cool colors in the scene of Judah's departure. Most prominently, Judah's wife, Miriam, wearing a blue outfit, greets and envelops him before a stale and empty space. The cool colors could imply that Judah is triumphant; he has overcome the burning of hell, the damnation of the wicked prophesied by his father. Yet the blank space and cool colors may reveal a worse punishment, the absence of God and thus the emptiness and coldness of the modern world. We recall that Judah himself describes his story as "chilling." In Thomas Mann's *Doctor Faustus* hell is likewise described as cold; it is the specifically modern hell.

No genuine reconciliation occurs in this scene (Judah is not rehabilitated, and his marriage is so fragile as to be unable to confront negativity). Just as Judah silences Dolores by burning her letter and having her killed, he silences Miriam—if in a less drastic way—by never giving her the possibility of showing understanding. A clever symbol of Judah's lack of progress is the treadmill, a gift from his wife. While Cliff enjoys viewing Hitchcock's *Mr. and Mrs. Smith*, a substantial "comedy of remarriage" (Cavell), the film in which Cliff is a player offers a mock comedy of remarriage. Moreover, the film ends not with Judah's departure but with clips from earlier in the film. The final image we see from Judah's story, offered shortly before these concluding images, is of Dolores just before her murder. Does this suggest, symbolically, that Judah still relives the crime and suffers guilt? In this reading, the void Judah encounters in viewing Dolores is the emptiness of his new reality and apparent success. Judah substitutes this void for the content of ethics, rights, duties, and laws. He longs for a spark of Dolores's soul—the spark Ben says is in every person—but it has vanished of Judah's own doing, and its disappearance—along with that of God—continues to torment him.

In this reading the terms *crimes* and *misdemeanors* refer not only to the alternation between serious and substantial issues with their resulting tragic consequences (Judah's error, murder, and guilt) and comic foibles of little harm or consequence (the shallow exploits, superficial longings, and greed of Lester), but also the escalation that takes place from misdemeanors to crimes. If in the nihilistic reading "crimes" are reduced to "misdemeanors," that is, in Judah's consciousness murder becomes a misdemeanor, something he can forget and overcome, here we can argue that misdemeanors engender crimes: one sin leads to a deeper sin. The idea that a small indiscretion carries with it the seeds of more serious destruction is represented in the fact that Dolores's apartment is located above a shop named "Jack's." From the beginning Jack (the brutally evil brother [or side] of Judah) has been invading Dolores's world.

Though Judah stands as an isolated individual, he symbolizes a more over-arching sense of decay. He has internalized much of modernity, its consum-erist greed, its external standards of success, and its moral bankruptcy. The outside shots are all taken in late fall and winter. The dominant colors throughout the film are pale: off white, tan, yellow, beige, brown, olive green, gray. References are made to an array of social and other problems—from crack addiction and insider trading to toxic waste. Judah's and Lester's wealth and social status are effectively contrasted with that of Dolores's, Cliff's, and his sister's. The devolution of morality and social justice por-trayed in the film has been viewed by Pauline Kael as symptomatic of the "Reagan eighties" (76), but the film suggests that the disintegration of values transcends political orientation: Lester considers himself a liberal intellec-tual. The decay of relations and the coldness of society are also illustrated by the seemingly excessive number of references (at least a dozen) to phone calls, phone messages, and so on. Relations are mediated and distant; human warmth appears to have vanished.

Allen's film undermines every position—the naive, the nihilistic, and the nearly synthetic—but in a differentiated way. Though everyone is ironized, not everyone is ironized equally. In the third and most comprehensive read-ing, *Crimes and Misdemeanors* remains moral. Nevertheless, I would criti-cize the film—despite its complexity, its vitality of spirit and comic wit, its substance and self-reflexivity—for succeeding more at negating what is un-tenable than at enriching the positive paradigm. The fact that Allen ironizes the advocates of a substantive and third position, along with their attempts to transcend both naïveté and negativity, might be read as an unwitting en-dorsement of stagnant nihilism. By undermining a naive ethos and replacing it with power positivism and no strong synthetic morality, Allen only in-creases the moral decay and dissolution he wants to criticize. Movement back and forth between naïveté and negativity or between these poles and an iro-nized third position is not as much of a movement forward as may be neces-sary in an age of crisis.

The film's supernatural moments illustrate the work's moral ambiguities. First, Judah's conversation with the rabbi as Judah contemplates murder: does the rabbi's presence bespeak a genuine power or force that cannot be suppressed, or is it the subconscious baggage of Judah's religious education reduced to an ineffectual ghost? Second, the phone that rings the night of Dolores's murder: is it genuinely (or symbolically) God calling or Dolores, who must remain silent (we remember that she once called Judah at home and hung up without saying a word), or is it, as Jack might suggest, mere coincidence? Finally, the seder discussion Judah envisages at his childhood home: is Judah for good reason unable to abandon his heritage and the force of its arguments, or is he simply recollecting his aunt's wisdom and thus slowly freeing himself from the unwanted torments of religion?

The film, like Judah, appears morally confused and troubled: this is formally conveyed by the back and forth movement between the two stories. The moral confusion has resulted in a common reception of the film as simply nihilistic. In lines that differ from the most widespread reception only insofar as they replace muddledness with clarity, John Simon sums up the movie's meaning: "There is no justice, no rhyme or reason in the universe, no God" (47). Even one of the few anomalous readings that discuss the film as moral, that of Peter Minowitz, reminds us that it only hints in this direction. Extracinematic developments in Allen's personal life reinforce our sense that Allen's wisdom is extremely fragile. Because the ideals sketched in his films are ungrounded and often ironized, they are not easily transferable to life.

The goodness of individual characters remains either an ungrounded choice, that is, an act of faith, or grist for Allen's irony. Thus no firm argument is presented as to why Judah's position is untenable. Even if we side with the underdogs, above all, Cliff and the rabbi, we are not sure *why* their position is preferable or how it might stem increasing power positivism. To answer the questions, "What is the good?" and "Why do the good?" with gestures toward tradition, intuition, or a leap of faith is to fall back into the naive—and indefensible—paradigm of Judah's father. However dignified such a morality might be, it is intellectually insufficient and pragmatically weak. The argument that we must act *as if* God were watching us—as Kael interprets *Crimes and Misdemeanors* (77)—bypasses the question and can easily be reduced to either an ironization of the father's genuine faith (a choice of God over truth) or Judah's construction of a different kind of fiction to circumvent over cynicism.

The ethical consequences of Judah's power positivistic position are more than private. The film alludes to ethics with the context of the Holocaust. At the dinner table Judah's aunt speaks of Hitler. Her argument is that truth and justice are determined by power. Concerning the Nazis, she states, "Might makes right—that is, until the Americans marched in and stopped them." But the aunt conflates *is* and *ought*. Her tone makes clear that something was objectively wrong with Hitler, yet she cannot make this judgment, given her elevation of power. The aunt's suggestion that Hitler should have been punished contradicts her argument that only power exists and that norms and moral arguments are irrelevant. Despite her intellectualism, she still works within the paradigm of a naive theodicy: only those who are punished are unjust; if we are not punished, we are not unjust:

> And I say, if he [Judah] can do it and get away with it, and he chooses not to be bothered by the ethics, then he's home free. Remember, history is written by the winners, and if the Nazis had won, future generations would understand the story of World War II quite differently.

Adding to the context of the Holocaust, the jump cut from Dolores's death to the fire has symbolic resonance, and the fact that the philosopher is a Holocaust survivor also reinforces the broader framework. The film invites overarching ethical questions, and Judah, like his father and aunt, cannot answer them with any satisfaction. The film's ambiguities and unsteadiness are in tension with its call for clear philosophical answers to pressing ethical issues.

Seven acts of the film are devoted to Judah (and Dolores); the other alternating seven focus on Cliff (and Lester). The final act brings the two strands together. I have suggested that in these diverse strands we identify with Judah and Cliff. A central interpretive question becomes, with whom do we identify in the final act? From a narrative perspective we must identify with Judah: we know what Judah knows, which is more than what Cliff knows. We have been privy to Judah's actions and—thanks to the nighttime conversation with Ben, in which Judah debates his moral options, and the seder discussion, in which he reflects on the limits of traditional morality—his innermost thoughts. On the other hand, if we view Judah's summary account of his act of murder as a microcosm of the film and Cliff as its objective evaluator, the reader is to identify with Cliff—and so condemn Judah's actions. Earlier we identified with Cliff in his role as spectator (indeed our first shot of Cliff is when he is watching a movie in the theater). We identify with Cliff even further insofar as Cliff is also Woody Allen. This identification, however, is ambiguous, for we know that the Woody Allen persona—here and elsewhere—is self-undermining, self-erasing. This is further reinforced by the fact that Cliff's imagined heroic ending is not the end of Allen's film. While we may emotionally identify with Cliff (rare is the viewer who would explicitly say, "Yes, let's get away with all we can"), there is no intellectual reason—internal to the film—not to identify with Judah. No religious, philosophical, or aesthetic position is left intact.

Allen's film contains a series of self-reflexive moments: the Hollywood films of which we see segments; Lester's dictation of potential plots; Cliff's films on the philosopher and Lester; the supernatural moments, which function almost as films within the film; the self-conscious appeal to a possible tragedy; the theoretical discussions of movies vis-à-vis reality; and references to Allen's earlier work—for example, the amusingly self-reflexive and critical reference to *Another Woman* (Judah comments to Ben: "I've done a foolish thing, senseless, vain, dumb—another woman."). In this rich self-reflexion Allen exhibits his awareness of the possibility of making art that is better or truer than life, but he prefers (as he did in *The Purple Rose of Cairo*) to abandon any art that is above life. We consistently hear, in a self-reflexive voice, that heroism and reconciliation are confined to Hollywood films, the implicit suggestion being that such films fail to account for the weaknesses and harshness of reality. Thus, the art of *Crimes and Misdemeanors* becomes a mimetic, rather than an idealizing, art.

Employing a metaphor, we could say that Allen opts more for the sight of the ophthalmologist Judah (who sees superficial reality clearly) than the inner vision of the rabbi (who offers an ideal to counter reality). This is not to suggest that the film fails to negate what is untenable. Just as Cliff satirizes Lester, so Allen subtly exhibits the self-cancellation of Judah's position. But a negation of negativity is not yet an articulation of valid norms. For Allen the choice is God or truth (the tragedy of collision I spoke of earlier). The idea that God and truth might be one and that they might be portrayed in an idealizing art that is nonetheless aware of the schism between the real and the ideal is not an option. The eyes of the camera that replace the eyes of God are more Judah's than they are Ben's: we think, for example, of the sweep of the camera from Judah's eyes to Dolores's body. If the film exhibits for us the three spheres of Hegel's Absolute Spirit, it also undermines them; religion is blind, and the philosopher commits suicide, leaving us with art, but art, too, is insufficient—Lester is superficial, and Cliff lacks funds and prestige.

In each of the film's male characters we see a moment of Woody Allen. Allen is the seeker after meaning, religious wisdom, and a moral universe (Ben); the nebbish, trying to influence the world through his art, but unsure of his path (Cliff); the successful and admired filmmaker (Lester); the philosophical thinker who articulates the need for love in a cold and barren world (the philosopher); and the guilt-ridden and troubled thinker obsessed with his Jewish tradition (Judah). Ben—as the figure who provides the resolution between the two tales—and Cliff—as the character played by the film's writer and director—are symbolically the most significant. But the lack of any organic unity among the characters, any synthesis of their individual strengths, suggests a world of disintegration and harshness, a world in which the newly resolute Judah and the clever, manipulative Lester seemingly triumph. We see the reality of fragmentation rather than the idealism of a norm, but the lack of an ideal answer is not necessarily the fault of the film's director. Few contemporary thinkers are willing to recognize any grounds for morality other than the nongrounds of probabilism and decisionism. Allen's film can be criticized only at the point where contemporary American society has also come to a standstill.

WORKS CITED

Boethius. *The Consolation of Philosophy*. Trans. V. E. Watts. New York: Penguin, 1969.

Cavell, Stanley. *Pursuits of Happiness: The Hollywood Comedy of Remarriage.* Cambridge, MA: Harvard University Press, 1981.

Downing, Crystal. "Broadway Roses: Woody Allen's Romantic Inheritance." *Literature/Film Quarterly* 17 (1989): 13–17.

Kael, Pauline. "Review of *Crimes and Misdemeanors.*" *New Yorker*, October 30, 1989, 76–78.

Minowitz, Peter. "Crimes and Controversies: Nihilism from Machiavelli to Woody Allen." *Literature/Film Quarterly* 19 (1991): 77–88.

Roche, Mark W. "Plato and the Structures of Injustice." In *Inquiries into Values: The Inaugural Session of the International Society for Value Inquiry*, ed. Sander H. Lee, 279–90. Lewiston, NY: Mellen, 1988.

Scheler, Max. *Formalism in Ethics and Non-Formal Ethics of Values: A New Attempt toward the Foundation of an Ethical Personalism.* Trans. Manfred S. Frings and Roger L. Funk. Evanston, IL: Northwestern University Press, 1973.

Shakespeare, William. *The Collected Works of William Shakespeare.* New York: Bantam, 1988.

Simon, John. "And Justice for None. Review of *Crimes and Misdemeanors.*" *National Review*, December 8, 1989, 46–48.

Sophocles. *Oedipus the King. Sophocles I.* Trans. David Grene. Chicago: University of Chicago Press, 1954, 9–76.

24

Between Time and Eternity
Theological Notes on *Shadows and Fog*

Paul Nathanson

For some reason, critics have ignored one of Woody Allen's best productions. *Shadows and Fog* (1992) is a cinematic commentary on the problem of how to find meaning in a modern and secular world. In that respect, of course, it is by no means unique. Almost every work of serious art over the past century has, in one way or another, explored the very same terrain. But at least two things make this one highly unusual. In the first place, I suggest, it rejects cynicism—the great temptation of our time—*without* succumbing to naïveté; on the contrary, it fosters compassion and even joy *in spite of* pervasive suffering and chaos. Then, too, it represents a specifically and characteristically (but not exclusively) Jewish way of thinking—one that is based on religious tradition, moreover, not merely on ethnic psychology or sociology. Rejecting cynicism constitutes an act of bravado. Thus it is highly reminiscent of an ancient Jewish custom. Not many Jews remember now that opening the front door on the eve of Passover, symbolically inviting Elijah to attend the seder, once implied direct exposure to a very hostile world outside. At the same time, and for that very reason, it implied a deliberate affirmation of hope over despair and joy over fear.

In some ways. *Shadows* is another version of Allen's earlier movies. Like *Manhattan* (1979), its cinematography is black and white; its music originated in the early twentieth century; and its central character is a neurotic urban Jew. In other ways, though, *Shadows* is a departure for Allen. Unlike his earlier movies, this one is stylistically abstract or even expressionistic. The cinematic world presented here is a closed but intense one. Space is confined to small rooms and narrow alleys. Time is confined to a single night. Every scene was filmed inside a studio; everything that might distract the eye, therefore, could be removed. As a result, the sets have a visual purity and perfection that renders them less realistic but also more evocative and powerful than they would otherwise have been. Nevertheless, they are not totally abstract. They strongly suggest a time and place in the recent past. The result is a world that is, paradoxically, both eternal (far removed from the distracting clutter of everyday life) and historical (overtly reminiscent of Europe in the 1920s but also, as I hope to show, covertly redolent of America in the 1990s). Before proceeding, a brief review of the story is necessary.

The protagonist is one Max Kleinman, a mild-mannered, middle-aged man intimidated by life in general but by his domineering landlady (who has marital designs on him) and his punctilious boss (who has little or no use for him) in particular. In the middle of the night, he is woken up by a gang of neighbors. These are vigilantes who have formed a posse to do what the police cannot do: capture a crazed killer at loose in the streets. Kleinman is clearly afraid of the killer, to be sure, but he is even more afraid of public opinion. While the others wait outside, therefore, he reluctantly dresses. Once on the street, though, he finds that they have gone off on their own. He has no idea of where to go, what to do, or how to act if he should actually meet the psychopath. He spends the rest of the movie wandering through the empty and eerie streets looking for, well, someone or something to give him direction. For want of anywhere else to go, he visits the coroner. This man, like Dr. Frankenstein, is preoccupied with corpses and preserves parts of them in neat jars. His ultimate aim is to dissect the monster scientifically and find the physiological origin of evil. After sharing a glass of wine with the coroner, Kleinman is glad to get away. On the circus grounds, meanwhile, a disagreement breaks out between the clown and his lover, Irmy, a sword swallower. Irmy runs away, disappointed by his unwillingness to have a baby and angered by his interest in another woman. That leaves her alone in the deserted streets. Before long, she is brought home by a kind prostitute. Though merely a nonprofessional visitor, she agrees to accept a top fee for her services by one customer, a wealthy student. Strangely enough, she enjoys the encounter. Then the brothel is raided.

At the police station, Irmy is forced to pay a fine. Kleinman turns up there too, looking for information about local plans to trap the murderer. He learns, however, that circumstantial evidence has been found that might incriminate him: after his visit, the coroner had been strangled by the psychopath and a wine glass found with fingerprints on it. Clumsily snatching the glass and stuffing it under his coat, Kleinman steps out into the street. There, he meets Irmy. The two become friends as they wander aimlessly through the menacing alleys. Passing a church, Irmy asks Kleinman to go inside and donate the money she earned at the brothel. Then they meet a distraught woman carrying her baby; she is alone and has nowhere to go. Irmy now asks Kleinman to return and ask for half the money back! The priests, who had been suspicious and contemptuous of him from the first, are now even more so. Later on, the two friends come across a voyeur peeping into a window. Assuming that this is the killer, Kleinman tries to attack him. The voyeur turns out to be his self-righteous boss, Mr. Paulsen. Paulsen immediately fires him, sputtering with outrage. Finally, the killer appears. In spite of himself, Kleinman actually stands his ground and defends Irmy. Running for their lives, they reach the circus grounds. Kleinman is overjoyed to meet the magician, whom he has always admired and to whose profession he has always aspired. He and the magician trap the killer with trick mirrors and eventually chain him to a chair. But when the good citizens arrive, the killer has escaped once more. The movie ends as Kleinman accepts the magician's invitation to leave his humdrum job and run away with the circus.

Most movies, and this one is no exception, can be interpreted at more than one level. I begin with the most obvious one. Allen evokes the atmosphere of a central European city between the wars. He does so indirectly, though, by evoking the atmosphere of German movies made at that time. Given the title, viewers should not be surprised at what they see and hear. Mist swirls past dimly lit windows, down twisting alleys, or through gothic archways hung with iron lanterns. Shadows loom menacingly against blank walls. Footsteps crack sharply against cobbled pavement. Corresponding to all this is what viewers hear: the music from Kurt Weill's *Threepenny Opera*, a musical play by Bertolt Brecht that was filmed by G. W. Pabst in 1931. Except for its anachronistic references to American dollars and English dialogue spoken with American accents, this movie might almost be mistaken for one made in the Weimar period—that is, the period immediately preceding the rise of Hitler and the Nazis. It seems clear from the foreboding mood of their movies—many of them metaphorical references to the degeneracy or even insanity of a crumbling society—that directors such as Fritz Lang, Friedrich Murnau, and Pabst himself must have known how soon the end would come. In retrospect, at any rate, it is now almost impossible not to associate those movies with the Nazi nightmare that lay just ahead. That gives another level of meaning, albeit a slightly less obvious one, to the title chosen by Allen. Not only does most of this movie take place in the fog but all of it takes place at night. At least some viewers will recall what came to be known as the "night and fog laws," under which people were mysteriously scooped up by the Gestapo, spirited away to concentration camps, and never seen again. Actually, the movie refers directly to this. Kleinman, a Jew, is told by the vigilantes (which is to say, the storm troopers) that an obviously Jewish family—the name is Mintz—has been arrested on suspicion. When he protests that no one in this family could possibly be involved with anything evil, they tell him that actual guilt or innocence is entirely irrelevant since scapegoats are wanted by a public on the verge of panic and thus required by the state. And when Kleinman complains to a police official, he is told the same thing.

Allen has not produced a documentary on European history. At this level of interpretation, it could be said that he has used European history as a way of saying something about our own society. The Nazis themselves are gone, to be sure, but not the moral, spiritual, and intellectual abyss they represented. Like Kleinman, we would all prefer to stay home in our warm beds at night, dreaming of happier times. But like Kleinman, we are sometimes woken up to find ourselves terrified in a world where evil (personified by the psychopath) runs rampant, and confused in a world where those said to be evil (prostitutes and outsiders) turn out to be good and those said to be good (clergymen, respectable community leaders, police officers, and businessmen) turn out to be evil. Not surprisingly, therefore, a well or fountain outside the police station is boarded up: the life-giving source that once sustained society has either dried up or been contaminated. The implication is that modern America is not so very different from Weimar Germany.

But *Shadows* lends itself to interpretation at much deeper levels. Most critics use art—avant-garde art—as their paradigm. To be avant-garde, art must be (1) original, innovative, or just new; (2) intensely personal; (3) shocking, challenging, or subversive; and for some critics, (4) autonomous, an end in itself rather than a means to some moral or social end. This definition is highly idiosyncratic in both historical and cross-cultural terms. In effect, it excludes almost every form of visual (or other) expression except for what was produced in the West since Expressionism, say, or Dadaism. And all movies except for art films (accessible only to elite viewers who are conversant with the theoretical discussions of academics). Other movies are dismissed as bad art, partly because they are considered aesthetically unsophisticated but mainly because they are considered ideologically sinister (intended by a ruling class to dupe the masses). Woody Allen clearly considers himself an artist in the avant-garde sense. And most critics would agree with this auteur. Some of his productions, nevertheless, cannot be examined adequately on this basis alone. To understand *Shadows* adequately, we must replace the paradigm of art with that of religion.

Religion itself begins, at both the individual and the collective levels, with an *experience* of the other, the spirit, the god, the cosmos, the infinite, the eternal, and in a word, the sacred (or holiness). By definition, this experience is ineffable. But the need to communicate something of its essence, so that other individuals and later generations can share the experience to some degree, is intense. Not surprisingly, ways are always found. Among the universal and primary *expressions* of religion are myth and ritual. These two are very closely related, in fact, because myth is always enacted through ritual, usually in connection with festivals. Another common expression of religion, though, is parable. In many ways, it is the opposite of myth.

My understanding of *parable* and its relation to *myth* is based on the work of John Dominic Crossan.[1] He identified a whole range of oral or literary genres that express religion. The two of interest here, though, are myth and parable. The former genre includes *traditional* stories that *establish* or *support* a commonly held worldview. They set the stage, as it were, for the drama of human existence. In symbolic terms, they describe a cosmos to which everyone is connected. They provide the community with its sense of origin and destiny, its sense of meaning and purpose in the larger scheme of things. The latter genre, parable, includes *innovative* stories that *challenge* or *subvert* the commonly held worldview. Crossan had biblical myths and parables in mind when he made this distinction.[2] The parables of Jesus, he wrote, were intended to make people question conventional wisdom, to jolt them into thinking about reality in new ways. (In this way, clearly, a parable is like a Zen koan.) Both myth and parable have theological content. And both are necessary, no matter what form they might take, in every society. Myth is primary, of course, because without an established worldview to question there could be no parables. More important here, though, is the fact that each approaches what Westerners call "theology" from the opposite point of view.

The connection between all this and film is very simple: some movies come to function in a modern, secular society very much (though not completely) the way either myth or parable function in traditional, religious societies. They are what I call secular myths and secular parables. These movies cannot be understood adequately in terms of art. Although parable can be identified with the avant-garde notion of art to some extent, the link is not strong enough to be of much use. It is true that both are associated with subversion of the established order. But avant-garde art is seldom associated, as parable always is, with an *alternative* order. Jesus did not want merely to destroy; he wanted to rebuild. Even when avant-garde art is associated with an alternative order, though, it is a different kind of alternative order. Jesus did not want to replace the culture he had inherited with some alien one; he wanted to purify it. Some people would argue that the proper analogy is between film and art understood in terms of *deconstruction*. I disagree. Deconstruction is not what it purports to be: an attempt to destroy the whole idea of cultural order. On the contrary, it is an attempt to clear the public square of a "dominant" cultural order and replace it with another. But those who use deconstruction for ideological purposes make it clear that the new order must be *radically different* from the old one; virtually nothing of the bourgeois or patriarchal order is to escape deconstruction (or destruction). My point is this: parable, no matter how surprising or even shocking any story might seem at first, functions (as myth does) *within a traditional worldview.* There is nothing cynical or opportunistic about traditional parables.

Shadows is highly unusual in that it seems to combine features of both parable *and* myth. Like a parable, it has been created by someone who speaks primarily as an individual (with his own distinctive and innovative style). And one thing he does is challenge conventional wisdom or, at the very least, make people think again about the way things are. Like a myth, on the other hand, it has been created by someone who speaks to and for those nourished by a tradition. And one thing he does is support traditional ways of perceiving reality or, at the very least, think again before discarding them. I suggest, however, that this movie is *primarily* mythic rather than parabolic. Its atmosphere alone evokes the wonder associated with both childhood and myth. And its archetypal characters are associated with those of dreams, both individual and collective. Of greatest importance here are the latter.

The protagonist himself is an archetypal figure in several ways. *Kleinman* means "little one," or "everyone." Most of us, like him, respond to the humdrum quality of everyday life by protecting ourselves whenever possible from conflict or disturbance. What happens, though, when the routine is suddenly interrupted? Security and complacency are shattered. Confronted directly with danger, hidden anxiety and confusion come to the surface. Why is this happening? What are we to do? What does it all mean? And so it is with Kleinman. Ostensibly referring to his lack of instruction by the vigilantes, he asks, "What's the plan? How do I participate in it? What role has been assigned to me?" But Kleinman is also the archetypal Jew. This is made clear on several occasions. At the police station, for example, an officer tells him that the murders have been linked somehow to the poisoning of wells. Allen alludes here to the fact that mass hysteria brought on by eruptions of the black death often led to accusations that Jews had contaminated the water supply. It was with this in mind, no doubt, that he placed that well or fountain just outside the police station. Having received no acceptable response, Kleinman moves on, roaming the streets. In doing so, he becomes the legendary Wandering Jew. According to the folklore of many European countries, a Jew mocked or struck Jesus on the road to Calvary. For this crime, he was cursed by God. His punishment was to wander from place to place, always the hated outsider, until the end of time—that is, until the Second Coming and the subsequent inauguration of God's Kingdom. Only then, as a witness to the truth of Christianity, would he be forgiven. By implication, of course, the entire Jewish people has been cursed to wander throughout Europe living at the mercy or pity of Christians. The Jews themselves have traditionally understood their "dispersion" theologically as a divine punishment (though not for rejecting Jesus). For traditional Jews, nevertheless, this has not meant separation from God; on the contrary, God is believed to share the exile—in the joys of everyday life no less than its sorrows—with his people. But for secular Jews, Jewish history for the past two thousand years is usually seen as a kind of waking nightmare. Maybe this is one reason why the entire movie takes place at night. But this movie is not intended only for Jews. As the archetypal outsiders, they symbolically represent all outsiders. And given the fragmentation of society in our time, almost everyone is an outsider in one way or another.

To the extent that this movie can be called a myth, it would have to be called a "secular myth," because, as I have pointed out elsewhere,[3] it does for an ostensibly modern and secular society what religious myths do for traditional and religious societies. In this case, it brings viewers face to face with a mystery that lies at the core of human existence at all times and in all places: death. It is in this connection that the killer becomes an archetypal figure. He is not just a run-of-the-mill hood. He has no name. He has no family. He has no accomplices. He is a mystery. The coroner asks him, "How did you get in?" And he answers, "Did you think you could keep me out?" Shackled in heavy iron chains at the end of the movie, he nevertheless escapes. More specifically, he disappears. These are the only clues by which viewers can identify him. Given the cinematic evidence, they must conclude that he is a metaphysical being, a cosmic force—that he is Lord Death. As such a figure, he is found in the religious myths of virtually every traditional society. Unlike traditional myths, though, this movie offers only the faintest hint of a context that would confer meaning on death and thus purpose on life. Remember that death is far more than a medical term. Throughout history, it has been symbolically associated with both evil (living in a malevolent universe dominated by sinister forces) and chaos (living in a meaningless universe at the mercy of random forces). And in both cases, it has distinctly metaphysical connotations. Unlike Ingmar Bergman's personification of death in *The Seventh Seal*, Allen's is also a personification of evil; his victims die as a result of violence, after all, not of disease or old age.

Unlike many tales of Satan or the Devil, though, this movie does not portray him as a simple externalization of evil. He is that, to be sure, but he is also part of every viewer or, to put it differently, every viewer is part of him. The vigilantes have supposedly united to capture him. Within a few hours, though, they fragment into hostile factions. In fact, they begin killing each other. They thus exemplify the very thing they claim to oppose. Also related to death are the anti-Semitic police officials who condone or even instigate the attack on innocent citizens. But the killer represents far more than the evil in all of us (just as Kleinman represents far more than the innocence in all of us). He functions primarily as a personification of chaos in general rather than of evil in particular. Though evil could be considered a form of order (as in the case of totalitarianism), it is more appropriately classified as a form of chaos because it contradicts the order of justice without which human existence is ultimately impossible.

Now consider the killer more carefully. He is a psychopath, someone who is oblivious to reason and thus to order. The coroner asks, "What makes you kill?" But there is no answer. His behavior is entirely irrational; because he strikes at random, viewers must conclude that his motivation has nothing to do with greed, rebellion, notoriety, drugs, personal animosity, or anything else commonly associated with criminal behavior. For him, killing is an end in itself. He cannot be stopped by appealing to shame, guilt, or even fear. Unlike angelic or holy beings, commonly believed to promote whatever society considers good or true, this demonic being lives beyond not only the natural order but beyond the cultural order as well. In literal or cinematic terms, he stalks individuals; in metaphorical or allegorical terms, though, he stalks the human race itself. Unless it is set within a larger context, death mocks whatever we make of ourselves in this world—no matter how wise, beautiful, or noble. In other words, the threat of personal extinction threatens to negate the meaning and purpose of life. Think of it this way: (1) neither life nor death is intelligible except in terms of the other; (2) to make sense, therefore, life must be seen in relation to death; (3) consequently, some meaning must be ascribed to death. In our time, unfortunately, the meaning of death—and thus of life as well—is often trivialized. If death is understood merely as the termination of life, if there is nothing more, then how can we ascribe any ultimate meaning or purpose to life? It is not enough to argue that biologic continuity through reproduction is enough to mitigate the problem of death. If that were so, after all, why has virtually every human society since our ancestors came down from the trees felt a need to address it? Death has always been the primary symbol of everything that threatens order, whether at the individual, collective, or cosmic level. Although the ways of understanding death vary enormously from one culture to another, one thing never varies: a universal and fundamental human need to solve the problem it creates. Nor is it enough to argue that we can metaphorically bypass death by passing on some beneficial legacy to our children. Although this solution is morally edifying and might even be emotionally comforting for a while, it is nevertheless intellectually inadequate because all those who inherit what we leave behind must also die. And if everyone and everything disappears eventually into the void—if not in the immediate future then in the remote future of civilizational collapse or planetary destruction—then what is the point of doing anything at all? Why not just enjoy whatever material or sensual pleasure we can and let the Devil, as it were, take the hindmost? And if we cannot do that, why not just die quickly and get it over with?

This last possibility has not been nearly as uncommon as many people assume. Sometimes, life can seem even more problematic than death. This happened at one particularly troubled period in the history of India. Because life, with both its sorrows and its joys, was often seen as an illusion generated by the play of the gods (*maya*), and because the ultimate goal was release (*moksha*) from the cycle of rebirth (*samsara*), many began to think that ending this life quickly was a small price to pay for release from despair. Self-willed death became so prevalent, in fact, that philosophers had to take it seriously as an urgent social problem. India pulled away from the brink of chaos by restoring a sense of meaning and purpose to life.[4] Not every society manages to do so. Emile Durkheim coined the term *anomie* to describe a state of social disintegration that leads to collective suicide. He might well have used it in connection with the collapse of aboriginal societies in North America; under such circumstances, drinking on a massive scale dulls what would be the otherwise unbearable pain of a futile existence in a meaningless world. Durkheim might also have used this term in connection with the collapse of social order among blacks in urban ghettoes. Few are surprised, nowadays, when teenage boys accept the likelihood of not living long enough to make education or even the use of condoms seem worthwhile; under the hopeless and meaningless circumstances they call "normal," gang warfare might be just another form of collective suicide.

Most people experience both joy and suffering. It is the suffering, however, that creates a problem and calls for a solution. Even the rich and powerful, after all, experience too much suffering—they fail to achieve goals, endure shame and guilt, encounter malice and grief, get sick and grow old— for life to be self-legitimating. If it has a meaning or purpose beyond mere physical existence, then no amount of suffering will be too much to bear; but if it does not, then no amount of pleasure will be enough to assuage the pain. That is why death—personal mortality—is always the most difficult and most important problem that every society must address. Traditionally, Jews and Christians have ascribed cosmic importance to death and thus placed it in a context that makes continued human existence dignified and worthwhile. (Even so, when death strikes suddenly and on a massive scale—as it did after the outbreak of plague in the fourteenth century, for example, or after attempts at genocide in our own century—even they are often forced to rethink or even reject what might otherwise have been taken for granted.) Secular people, on the other hand, must always either deny or trivialize death; consequently, they try to hide from it as long as possible. Nothing illustrates this trend more clearly than contemporary funeral rites. But death remains with us.

Still, Allen tells us, we can live reasonably happy lives even in the shadow of death. How? He suggests not one but two answers. In the first place, there is always art. Both the clown and the magician are called "artists." What they have in common with painters, say, or sculptors is creative imagination. Through carefully designed illusions—that is, through artifice—they enable people to leave the chaotic world of everyday life and enter an orderly world of their own. There, they can still live *as if* there were some inherent meaning or purpose. Then, too, the artistic world, like the circus, is a community of like-minded people. It is the required "haven in a heartless world." In the circus, Kleinman discovers other people who have rebelled against the meaninglessness of everyday life. With them, he is free from domestic tyranny (his nagging landlady), peer pressure (the vigilantes), corporate hierarchy (the pompous windbag who gets his job), and hypocritical respectability (his boss). The problem has not really been solved, of course, because Lord Death has not been defeated. Even now, he has triumphed over the city—both those he has killed and those who live in constant fear of him. Moreover, he will eventually triumph even over those who find temporary comfort under the big top.

It is in this connection that the meaning of an important visual motif becomes clear. The movie opens with a crescent moon reflected on a pool of water; it concludes with a crescent moon used by the circus as a prop. Both images of the moon are associated with illusion: the former with a mirror image, the latter with artifice. Together, they provide not only a visual frame of reference but also a temporal one. The entire story takes place during a single night: between the waxing and waning of the moon. It is thus linked symbolically to dreams—which are illusions—and, more specifically, to nightmares. By extension, this metaphor indicates that life itself—all we know of this cinematic world, after all, is what occurs on-screen—is a dream, or nightmare, from which we either can or will awaken. But the process of waking up—a term used in many religions, both Eastern and Western, as a metaphor indicating enlightenment or grace—is not as easy as it sounds. Immediately following the moon's appearance, Kleinman is woken up *physically* by pounding on the front door; it is only immediately preceding the moon's final appearance, however, that he is woken up *spiritually*.

These lunar crescents form metaphorical parentheses. By implication, the entire story is parenthetical.[5] This, too, is of theological significance. According to traditional forms of both Judaism and Christianity, life itself is a parenthetical experience. Both the individual and the community (or the human race itself) are understood within a larger, cosmic, context. The individual soul is said to be immortal. At one level, that simply means beyond mortality. At a deeper level, though, it means beyond *time* (change, contingency, finitude, decay, and so forth). The soul exists both before birth and after death. In Judaism, for example, each soul has existed in Eden since creation. At birth, it goes into a kind of exile from paradise (eternity). But its destiny is to *return* after a brief pilgrimage on earth (in time). Something very similar is characteristic of Christianity. The same is true on a collective level. History—that is, the story of Israel, the Church, or the human race itself—is surrounded, as it were, by eternity. What begins in paradise concludes in paradise. Some traditions describe eschatological destiny in agrarian terms. The once and future paradise is a garden. In fact, it is Eden, the primeval garden. Other traditions describe eschatological destiny in urban terms. It is a supernal city. In fact, it is the heavenly Jerusalem. The book of Revelation, however, makes it clear that the two are identical: growing within the heavenly city, after all, is the very tree of life known to Adam and Eve.

It is worth noting here that the parenthetical or dreamlike nature of human existence does not deny or even diminish its value. On the contrary, it is precisely because of its larger context that human existence takes on value in the first place. Whether for individuals or communities, living is understood in terms of preparation for the return. Only by going through the life cycle can individuals *learn* what it means to be with God. Only by going through history can the community *learn* what it means to serve God. Life is both an end in itself (as a divine creation) and the means to a greater end (as the vehicle by which a divine plan is worked out). The significance of every act can be measured not only in terms of its immediate effect in everyday life, therefore, but also in terms of its ultimate effect on cosmic destiny.

All of this is suggested by two lunar crescents. It is in the nature of sophisticated art to suggest eternity or infinity so economically. But do we know that Allen had any of this in mind? In this case, we can be almost certain. Very few movies in the past five or six decades have been as carefully and totally controlled by their directors. Nothing in it, after all, appears by chance (as it might have in a movie shot on location); everything viewers see on the screen was produced specifically for this production and filmed inside the studio.

In *Shadows*, unlike many of his other movies. Allen alludes briefly to another type of response, one that is characteristic of religion. Still on the run, Irmy and Kleinman stop and look up into the heavens. Irmy notices the stars through a break in the clouds. She explains that these stars might not even exist now because the light has taken so many millions of years to reach Earth. All the same, she and Kleinman look at them with a sense of wonder. As I have indicated, the cinematic world of *Shadows* is characterized primarily by closure. This particular episode, though, provides a window looking outward at a vast and open cosmos (albeit one that might be welcoming, hostile, or indifferent to mortals). What the two friends experience is not unlike what religious people call "the sacred," a sudden awareness of an underlying but often unsuspected dimension of reality. For a moment, they feel connected to a cosmos of infinite beauty, majesty, and mystery. If this is indeed a legitimate interpretation of what Allen had in mind, it deserves further comment.

Allen would probably describe himself as a secular Jew, though one who is interested in theology no less than philosophy. In this way, he is like most other Jews in America and, indeed, like all those who have either willingly or unwillingly accepted modernity. Secularity, after all, is a characteristic feature of modernity. Not all Americans have accepted modernity. Those who do often place religion in a special mental or emotional compartment, thus isolating it conveniently from other aspects of their lives. The result, though, is always some degree of ambivalence. For a quite different reason, though, this tension is a characteristic feature of American life. Most Americans by far profess at least some religious beliefs and many are members, at least nominally, of some religious community. Nevertheless, they staunchly uphold the constitutional separation of church and state. Unlike other modern societies, which maintain state churches no matter how out of touch the latter might be with the lives of most citizens, the United States is officially secular. Though by no means hostile to the religious traditions on which its way of life is based, the state is officially indifferent to any particular one. (Until recently, this theoretical separation was often overlooked. References to God—which is to say, the God of Christianity in general and Protestantism in particular—were common in public life. At the moment, though, Americans are increasingly divided by problems such as the place of prayer in the public schools or that of creation versus evolution in textbooks.) Ways have been found to bridge the gulf between personal piety and collective secularity. These include the establishment of a civil religion, for example, to celebrate the nation's history and traditions. In addition, as I have suggested, popular movies and television shows sometimes become "secular myths." Although the relation between religion and secularity is inherently problematic, in short, it is most obviously and disturbingly so in a country such as the United States. This is why *Shadows* can be described as quintessentially American despite its nod to European stylistic conventions.

To complicate matters, the ambiguous nature of secularity is matched by the ambiguous nature of Western religion itself! Allen has selected only one of the two quite different (though not incompatible) ways that Jews and Christians have traditionally understood the divine-human encounter.[6] (1) One tradition asserts that God is "out there," beyond the knowable universe, but enters it occasionally for specific purposes: creating the world; founding the holy community; rescuing the faithful collectively during history but finally bringing them out of history as well; rescuing them individually during the life cycle but finally bringing them beyond death as well. At its best, this tradition has generated hope and encouraged people to cooperate actively with God in establishing justice. At its worst, though, this same tradition has generated despair and encouraged people to wait passively for God to rescue them. (2) The other tradition asserts that God is "in here," waiting to be discovered *within* the familiar universe. In other words, holiness is built into the very fabric of everyday life; the sacred is inherent in the very structure of reality itself. Consequently, it is directly accessible at all times to those who know how to look and listen. Usually, it is mediated by ritual: the Eucharist for Christians, say, or the Sabbath for Jews. Sometimes, though, the sacred reveals itself unexpectedly (which is what happens, I suggest, to Irmy and Kleinman). At its worst, this ahistorical tradition discourages people from adapting to changing circumstances. At its best, though, it allows them to experience the joy of being connected to a cosmos of infinite beauty, harmony, and mystery. The essential difference between these two theological traditions—and Western religious traditions have affirmed not one or the other but *both*—might be summed up as follows: the former is based on the notion of divine transcendence and the latter on that of divine immanence.

Given the vicissitudes of history, the former way of thinking has always been problematic. But given the rise of secularism, one aspect of which has been the loss of belief in divine rescue operations, it has now become more problematic than ever. If God enters the finite world of time and space to save the weak and innocent, after all, then how can we explain the continuing horrors that stain the pages of every newspaper? The problem of theodicy— explaining the behavior of an allegedly all-loving *and* all-powerful deity who nevertheless permits evil—is as ancient as the book of Job. For many people, the old rationalizations no longer suffice. It is easier on intellectual grounds and even preferable on moral grounds to reject God, as Elie Wiesel has observed, than to worship a deity who permits Auschwitz for *any* reason, no matter how inscrutable. Many Americans, at any rate, are now either unwilling or unable to accept the notion of divine intervention in history—even though this tradition was the one that shaped collective identity, the sense of national origin and destiny, from the days of Puritan New England until very recently. Does this mean that, for those who reject the notion of divine providence, "God is dead"? It would if transcendence were the *only* theological resource. In fact, Western religion would have disappeared long ago— long before the modern period. But transcendence is *not* the only theological resource, as I say, and Western religion has not disappeared (although it has virtually disappeared, except for some vestigial forms, in many of the official religious institutions). This is because the question of theodicy becomes irrelevant in the context of immanence.

Where was God, ask Holocaust theologians, when Hitler was automating murder? So far, the question has generated no answer that is emotionally or even intellectually satisfying to most Jews or Christians. But the Hasidim seldom, if ever, ask this question. According to these and some other orthodox Jews—and they suffered as much as or more than any other group of Hitler's victims—the answer is self-evident: God was right *there, with them, in* the death camps. For some Christians, too, the answer is strangely simple. Their tradition is based on the notion of a god who suffered, after all, and died on a cross; Christ asked his followers to take up their own crosses, not to expect lives free of pain. But more important even than this theological framework is the simple fact that the sacred can be personally experienced at any time or place. Whatever happens after death or at the end of history, holiness, the intimacy of God's presence, is to be enjoyed here and now in the familiar context of everyday life: a colorful festival, a family meal, a flash of insight, a glance at the stars. . . . Given the rise of secularism—another aspect of which is rejection of the sacred because it cannot be verified empirically—the immanent tradition has also become problematic in our time. Even so, secular functional equivalents of the sacred are usually easier to find or create than secular functional equivalents of divine eruptions into history.[7] And they are certainly less dangerous when you consider those who use the resources of modern dictators to act out their fantasies of divine power.

Shadows and Fog can thus be considered a characteristically (though not uniquely) Jewish response to anxiety generated by "the death of God." Its power is grounded in the fact that it takes seriously the particular situation of modern, secular men and women for whom, as virtually all philosophers and theologians make perfectly clear, the central problem is precisely meaninglessness. This movie avoids condescension: death really is a problem that must be brought out of the proverbial closet. At the same time, it rejects cynicism: death does not render life meaningless and decency futile. The result is a truly compassionate view of the human condition in our time.

NOTES

1. John Dominic Crossan, *The Dark Interval: Towards a Theology of Story* (Niles, IL: Argus Communications, 1975).
2. The parabolic perspective is not necessarily expressed in the form of a short, pithy story designed to illustrate some theoretical point. Much of the moral and historical material assigned to Isaiah and some of the other prophets, for example, is parabolic in content (though not in form).
3. Paul Nathanson, *Over the Rainbow: The Wizard of Oz as a Secular Myth of America* (Albany: State University of New York Press, 1991).
4. For this insight, I am grateful to Katharine K. Young.
5. The first lunar crescent faces the same direction as an opening parenthesis; the second one faces the same direction, however, not the reverse. The "enclosed" material is thus parenthetical in the metaphorical sense, not the literal sense. Allen is being playful here and fittingly so, in view of the fact that *Shadows* is a comedy in both the modern sense (being funny) and the classical sense (having a happy ending).
6. Even though most Christians (until recently in some circles) and most Jews have preferred to emphasize the differences between Christianity and Judaism, the fact remains that *not everything* is different. Unless either one or the other is classified as something other than religion, both must have at least some characteristics in common (and not only with each other, of course, but with other religions as well).
7. One obvious exception, of course, is provided by Jewish attitudes toward the

state of Israel. The reemergence of a Jewish state provided a quasitheological and quasisecular "answer" to the Nazi experience (despite the moral problem, whether understood in either religious or secular terms, of something so good being attained at the cost of so much suffering). Given the drama of modern Jewish history, the temptation to believe that some force intervened in history is very great. This might explain, at least partially, why it is so intensely disturbing for Jews—especially Diaspora Jews—to consider the possibility of moral ambiguity in Middle Eastern politics. If Israel is the vehicle of some transcendent force, after all, then no course of action by the Israelis could possibly be questioned. Nevertheless, Jews are beginning to acknowledge moral ambiguity. This does not leave them hostile or indifferent to Israel, but it does leave them without the security of what has amounted to a kind of "secular religion."

Filmography

Note: This filmography includes only those films written or directed by Woody Allen. It lists only principal players and the major technical contributors to his movies.

What's New Pussycat (1965)

Production company: Famous Artists
Producers: Charles K. Feldman, Richard Sylbert, and John C. Shepridge (executive)
Writing credits: Woody Allen
Director: Clive Donner
Cast: Peter Sellers (Dr. Fritz Fassbender), Peter O'Toole (Michael James), Romy Schneider (Carole Werner), Capucine (Renee Lefebvre), Paula Prentiss (Liz Bien), Woody Allen (Victor Skakapopul), and Ursula Andress (Rita)
Music: Burt Bacharach; lyrics by Hal David
Director of photography: Jean Badal
Running time: 108 minutes

What's Up, Tiger Lily? (1966)

Production company: Toho (original)
Directors: Senkichi Taniguchi (original); Woody Allen (rerelease)
Producer: Tomoyuki Tanaka (original); Ben Shapiro (rerelease conception)
Writing credits: Hideo Ando (original); Woody Allen, Julie Bennett, Frank Buxton, Louise Lasser, Len Maxwell, Mickey Rose, and Bryan Wilson (rerelease)
Cast (original): Tatsuya Mihashi (Interpol agent/Phil Moscowitz), Akiko

Wakabayashi (mystery moll 1), Mie Hama (mystery moll 2), Yaki Tadao Nakamaru (drug-running gangster/Shepherd Wong), and Susumu Kurobe (smiling gangster/Wing Fat)

Cast (dubbed in rerelease): Woody Allen, Frank Buxton, Len Maxwell, Louise Lasser, Mickey Rose, Julie Bennett, and Bryan Wilson

Music: Jack Lewis and The Lovin' Spoonful (rerelease)

Director of photography: Kazuo Yamada (original)

Film editing: Richard Krown

Running time: 80 minutes

Take the Money and Run (1969)

Production company: Palomar

Producers: Charles H. Joffe, Jack Rollins, Sidney Glazier (executive), Jack Grossberg (associate)

Writing credits: Woody Allen and Mickey Rose

Cast: Woody Allen (Virgil Starkwell), Janet Margolin (Louise), Lonny Chapman (Jake), James Anderson (chain-gang warden), Jackson Beck (narrator), and Louise Lasser (Kay)

Music: Marvin Hamlisch

Director of photography: Lester Shorr

Film editors: Paul Jordan, Ron Kalish

Casting: Marvin Paige

Art director: Fred Harpman

Set decoration: Marvin March

Production managers: Fred T. Gallo and Jack Grossberg

Assistant directors: Walter Hill and Louis A. Stroller

Special effects: A. D. Flowers

Running time: 85 minutes

Bananas (1971)

Production company: Rollins-Joffe

Producers: Axel Anderson, Antonio Encarnacion, Jack Grossberg, Charles H. Joffe (executive), Ralph Rosenblum (associate), and Manolon Villamil

Writing credits: Woody Allen and Mickey Rose

Cast: Woody Allen (Fielding Mellish), Louise Lasser (Nancy), Carlos Montalbán (General Emilio M. Vargas), Natividad Abascal (Yolanda), Jacobo Morales (Esposito), Miguel Suárez (Luis), David Ortiz (Sanchez), Rene Enriquez (Diaz), Jack Axelrod (Arroyo), Howard Cosell (himself), Roger Grimsby (himself), Don Dunphy (himself), Charlotte Rae (Mrs. Mellish), and Stanley Ackerman (Dr. Mellish)

Original music: Marvin Hamlisch

Director of photography: Andrew M. Costikyan
Film editors: Ron Kalish and Ralph Rosenblum
Casting: Vicky Hernandez
Production design: Ed Wittstein
Set decoration: Herbert F. Mulligan
Costume design: Gene Coffin
Production manager: Morton Gorowitz
Assistant director: Fred T. Gallo
Special effects: Don B. Courtney
Running time: 82 minutes

Play It Again, Sam (1972)

Distributor: Paramount
Producers: Arthur P. Jacobs, Charles H. Joffe (executive), and Frank Capra
   Jr. (associate)
Direction: Herbert Ross
Writing credits: Woody Allen, based on his play
Cast: Woody Allen (Allan), Diane Keaton (Linda), Tony Roberts (Dick),
   Jerry Lacy (Bogart), Susan Anspach (Nancy), Jennifer Salt (Sharon), Joy
   Bang (Julie), and Viva (Jennifer)
Original music: Billy Goldenberg and Oscar Peterson ("Blues for Allan
   Felix"); music from "Casablanca" by Max Steiner and Herman Hupfeld
   ("As Time Goes By")
Director of photography: Owen Roizman
Film editor: Marion Rothman
Production design: Ed Wittstein
Set decoration: Doug von Koss
Costume design: Anna Hill Johnstone
Production supervisor: Roger M. Rothstein
Assistant director: William Gerrity
Running time: 85 minutes

Everything You Always Wanted to Know about Sex (1972)

Distributor: United Artists
Producers: Charles H. Joffe, Jack Brodsky (executive), and Jack Grossberg
   (associate)
Writing credits: Woody Allen, based on the book by David Reuben
Cast: Woody Allen (the fool/Fabrizio/Victor Shakapopulis/sperm 1), John
   Carradine (Dr. Bernardo), Lou Jacobi (Sam), Louise Lasser (Gina), An-
   thony Quayle (the king), Tony Randall (the operator), Lynn Redgrave (the
   queen), Burt Reynolds (sperm switchboard chief), Gene Wilder (Dr.

Doug Ross), Jack Barry (himself), Erin Fleming (the girl), Elaine Giftos (Dr. Ross), Toni Holt (herself), Robert Q. Lewis (himself), Heather Mac-Rae (Helen Lacey), Pamela Mason (herself), Sidney Miller (George), Regis Philbin (himself), Alan Caillou (the sorcerer), Jay Robinson (the priest), Ref Sanchez (Igor), and Baruch Lumet (Rabbi Chaim Baumel)
Original music: Mundell Lowe
Director of photography: David M. Walsh
Film editor: Eric Albertson
Casting: Marvin Paige
Production design: Dale Hennesy
Set decoration: Marvin March
Assistant directors: Fred T. Gallo and Terry M. Carr (second)
Visual effects: Harvey Plastrik
Running time: 87 minutes

Sleeper (1973)

Production company: Rollins-Joffe
Producers: Marshall Brickman, Jack Grossberg, Ralph Rosenblum (associate), and Charles H. Joffe (executive)
Writing credits: Woody Allen and Marshall Brickman
Cast: Woody Allen (Miles Monroe), Diane Keaton (Luna Schlosser), John Beck (Erno Windt), Mary Gregory (Dr. Melik), Don Keefer (Dr. Tryon), John McLiam (Dr. Aragon), Bartlett Robinson (Dr. Orva), Chris Forbes (Rainer Krebs), Marya Small (Dr. Nero), and Peter Hobbs (Dr. Dean)
Original music: Woody Allen
Director of photography: David M. Walsh
Film editors: O. Nicholas Brown, Ron Kalish, and Ralph Rosenblum
Casting: Lynn Stalmaster
Production design: Dale Hennesy
Set decoration: Gary Moreno
Costume design: Joel Schumacher
Assistant directors: Fred T. Gallo and Henry J. Lange Jr. (second)
Special effects: A. D. Flowers
Visual effects: Harvey Plastrik
Stunt coordinator: M. James Arnett
Running time: 89 minutes

Love and Death (1975)

Production company: Rollins-Joffe
Producers: Charles H. Joffe, Jack Rollins, Martin Poll (executive), and Fred T. Gallo (associate)

Writing credits: Woody Allen
Cast: Woody Allen (Boris Grushenko), Diane Keaton (Sonja), Georges Adet (old Nehamkin), Frank Adu (drill sergeant), Edward Ardisson (priest), Féodor Atkine (Mikhail Grushenko), Yves Barsacq (Rimsky), Olga Georges-Picot (Countess Alexandrovna), Harold Gould (Anton Inbedkov), Harry Hankin (Uncle Sasha), Jessica Harper (Natasha), C. A. R. Smith (Father Nikolai), and James Tolkan (Napoleon Bonaparte)
Music: Sergei Prokofiev
Director of photography: Ghislain Cloquet
Film editors: Ron Kalish and Ralph Rosenblum
Casting: Miriam Brickman, Juliet Taylor, and Blanche Wiesenfeld
Production design: Will Holt
Costume design: Gladys de Segonzac
Unit manager: Jean-Marie Durand
Assistant directors: Bernard Cohn and Paul Feyder (second)
Special effects: Kit West
Stunts: Gábor Piroch
Running time: 85 minutes

Annie Hall (1977)

Production company/distributor: Rollins-Joffe/United Artists
Producers: Charles H. Joffe, Jack Rollins, Robert Greenhut (executive), and Fred T. Gallo (associate)
Writing credits: Woody Allen and Marshall Brickman
Cast: Woody Allen (Alvy Singer), Diane Keaton (Annie Hall), Tony Roberts (Rob), Carol Kane (Allison Portchnik), Paul Simon (Tony Lacey), Shelley Duvall (Pam), Janet Margolin (Robin), Colleen Dewhurst (Annie's mother), Christopher Walken (Duane Hall), Donald Symington (Annie's father), and Helen Ludlam (Grammy Hall)
Director of photography: Gordon Willis
Film editors: Wendy Greene Bricmont and Ralph Rosenblum
Casting: Juliet Taylor
Art direction: Mel Bourne
Set decoration: Robert Drumheller and Justin Scoppa Jr.
Costume design: Ralph Lauren and Ruth Morley
Production manager: Robert Greenhut
Assistant directors: Fred T. Gallo and Fred Blankfein (second)
Running time: 93 minutes

Interiors (1978)

Production company/distributor: Rollins-Joffe/United Artists
Producers: Charles H. Joffe, Jack Rollins, and Robert Greenhut (executive)

Writing credits: Woody Allen
Cast: Kristin Griffith (Flyn), Mary Beth Hurt (Joey), Richard Jordan (Frederick), Diane Keaton (Renata), E. G. Marshall (Arthur), Geraldine Page (Eve), Maureen Stapleton (Pearl), and Sam Waterston (Mike)
Director of photography: Gordon Willis
Film editor: Ralph Rosenblum
Casting: Juliet Taylor
Production design: Mel Bourne
Set decoration: Mario Mazzola and Daniel Robert
Costume design: Joel Schumacher
Production manager: John Nicolella
Assistant director: Martin Berman
Running time: 93 minutes

Manhattan (1979)

Production company/distributor: Rollins-Joffe/United Artists
Producers: Robert Greenhut (executive), Charles H. Joffe (executive), and Jack Rollins (executive)
Writing credits: Woody Allen and Marshall Brickman
Cast: Woody Allen (Isaac Davis), Diane Keaton (Mary Wilkie), Michael Murphy (Yale), Mariel Hemingway (Tracy), Meryl Streep (Jill), Anne Byrne (Emily), Karen Ludwig (Connie), Michael O'Donoghue (Dennis), and Wallace Shawn (Jeremiah)
Music: George Gershwin
Conductor: Zubin Mehta
Director of photography: Gordon Willis
Film editor: Susan E. Morse
Casting: Juliet Taylor
Production design: Mel Bourne
Set decoration: Robert Drumheller
Costume design: Albert Wolsky
Production manager: Martin Danzig
Assistant director: Frederic B. Blankfein and Joan Spiegel Feinstein (second)
Running time: 96 minutes

Stardust Memories (1980)

Production company/distributor: Rollins-Joffe/United Artists
Producers: Robert Greenhut, Charles H. Joffe (executive), and Jack Rollins (executive)
Writing credits: Woody Allen

Cast: Woody Allen (Sandy Bates), Charlotte Rampling (Dorrie), Jessica Harper (Daisy), and Marie-Christine Barrault (Isobel)
Original music: Dick Hyman
Director of photography: Gordon Willis
Film editor: Susan E. Morse
Casting: Juliet Taylor
Production design: Mel Bourne
Art direction: Michael Molly
Set decoration: Steven Jordan
Costume design: Santo Loquasto
Production manager: Michael Peyser
Unit managers: Ezra Swerdlow and Charles Zalben
Assistant directors: Frederic B. Blankfein, Yudi Bennett (second), and Ed Levy (second)
Running time: 91 minutes

A Midsummer Night's Sex Comedy (1982)

Production company/distributor: Rollins-Joffe/Orion
Producers: Robert Greenhut, Charles H. Joffe (executive), Jack Rollins (executive), and Michael Peyser (associate)
Writing credits: Woody Allen
Cast: Woody Allen (Andrew), Mia Farrow (Ariel), Jose Ferrer (Leopold), Julie Hagerty (Dulcy), Tony Roberts (Maxwell), and Mary Steenburgen (Adrian)
Music: Felix Mendelssohn and Robert Schumann
Director of photography: Gordon Willis
Film editor: Susan E. Morse
Casting: Juliet Taylor
Production design: Mel Bourne
Art direction: Speed Hopkins
Set decoration: Carol Joffe
Costume design: Santo Loquasto
Assistant directors: Frederic B. Blankfein, Anthony Gittleson (second), and Thomas Reilly (second)
Running time: 88 minutes

Zelig (1983)

Production company/distributor: Rollins-Joffe/Orion
Producers: Robert Greenhut, Charles H. Joffe (executive). Jack Rollins (executive), and Michael Peyser (associate)
Writing credits: Woody Allen
Cast: Woody Allen (Leonard Zelig), and Mia Farrow (Dr. Eudora Fletcher)

Contemporary interviews: Susan Sontag, Irving Howe, Saul Bellow, Brick-
top, Dr. Bruno Bettelheim, and Prof. John Morton Blum
Original music: Dick Hyman
Director of photography: Gordon Willis
Film editor: Susan E. Morse
Casting: Juliet Taylor
Production design: Mel Bourne
Art direction: Speed Hopkins
Set decoration: Les Bloom and Janet Rosenbloom
Costume design: Santo Loquasto
Production manager: Michael Peyser
Unit manager: Ezra Swerdlow
Assistant directors: Frederic B. Blankfein, James Chory (second), and Tony
Gittleson (second)
Stunts: Pam Barber and Cole Palen
Running time: 79 minutes

Broadway Danny Rose (1984)

Production company/distributor: Rollins-Joffe/Orion
Producers: Charles H. Joffe and Michael Peyser (associate)
Writing credits: Woody Allen
Cast: Woody Allen (Danny Rose), Mia Farrow (Tina Vitale), Nick Apollo
Forte (Lou Canova), Sandy Baron (himself), Corbett Monica (himself),
Jackie Gayle (himself), Morty Gunty (himself), Will Jordan (himself),
Howard Storm (himself), Jack Rollins (himself), and Milton Berle (him-
self)
Original music: Nick Apollo Forte ("Agita" and "My Bambina")
Director of photography: Gordon Willis
Film editor: Susan E. Morse
Casting: Juliet Taylor
Production design: Mel Bourne
Set decoration: Les Bloom
Costume design: Jeffrey Kurland
Production manager: Fredric B. Blankfein
Unit production manager: Ezra Swerdlow
Assistant directors: Thomas Reilly and James Chory (second)
Music supervisor: Dick Hyman
Running time: 84 minutes

The Purple Rose of Cairo (1985)

Production company/distributor: Rollins-Joffe/Orion
Producers: Robert Greenhut, Charles H. Joffe (executive), Jack Rollins (executive), Michael Peyser (associate), and Gail Sicilia (associate)

Writing credits: Woody Allen
Cast: Mia Farrow (Cecilia), Jeff Daniels (Tom Baxter, Gil Shepherd), Danny
Aiello (Monk), Irving Metzman (theater manager), Stephanie Farrow (Ce-
cilia's sister), David Kieserman (diner boss), Edward Herrmann (Henry),
John Wood (Jason), Deborah Rush (Rita), Van Johnson (Larry), Zoe Cald-
well (the countess), Eugene Anthony (Arturo), Karen Akers (Kitty
Haynes), Annie Joe Edwards (Delilah), Milo O'Shea (Father Donnelly),
and Dianne Wiest (Emma)
Original music: Dick Hyman
Director of photography: Gordon Willis
Film editor: Susan E. Morse
Casting: Juliet Taylor
Production design: Stuart Wurtzel
Art direction: Edward Pisoni
Set decoration: Carol Joffe
Costume design: Jeffrey Kurland
Production manager: Michael Peyser
Assistant directors: Thomas Reilly and James Chory (second)
Running time: 84 minutes

Hannah and Her Sisters (1986)

Production company/distributor: Rollins-Joffe/Orion
Producers: Robert Greenhut, Charles H. Joffe (executive), Jack Rollins (ex-
ecutive), and Gail Sicilia (associate)
Writing credits: Woody Allen
Cast: Barbara Hershey (Lee), Carrie Fisher (April), Michael Caine (Elliot),
Mia Farrow (Hannah), Dianne Wiest (Holly), Maureen O'Sullivan
(Norma), Lloyd Nolan (Evan), Max von Sydow (Frederick), Woody Allen
(Mickey Sachs), Sam Waterston (David Tolcin), Daniel Stern (Dusty), Julie
Kavner (Gail), Joanna Gleason (Carol), Bobby Short (himself), Lewis
Black (Paul), Julia Louis-Dreyfus (Mary), Christian Clemenson (Larry),
J. T. Walsh (Ed Smythe), and John Turturro (writer)
Music: Johann Sebastian Bach, James V. Monaco ("You Made Me Love You"),
Giacomo Puccini ("Sola perduta, abbandonata" from *Manon Lescaut*;
overture from *Madama Butterfly*)
Director of photography: Carlo Di Palma
Film editor: Susan E. Morse
Casting: Juliet Taylor
Production design: Stuart Wurtzel
Set decoration: Carol Joffe
Costume design: Jeffrey Kurland
Production manager: Ezra Swerdlow

Assistant directors: Thomas Reilly and Ken Ornstein (second)
Running time: 103 minutes

Radio Days (1987)

Production company/distributor: Rollins-Joffe/Orion
Producers: Robert Greenhut, Charles H. Joffe (executive), Jack Rollins (executive), Gail Sicilia (associate), and Ezra Swerdlow (associate)
Writing credits: Woody Allen
Cast: Julie Kavner (mother), Julie Kurnitz (Irene), David Warrilow (Roger), Wallace Shawn (masked avenger), Michael Tucker (father), Josh Mostel (Abe), Renée Lippin (Aunt Ceil), William Magerman (grandfather), Leah Carrey (grandmother), Joy Newman (Ruthie), Hy Anzell (Mr. Waldbaum), Judith Malina (Mrs. Waldbaum), Dianne Wiest (Bea), Kenneth Mars (Rabbi Baumel), Mia Farrow (Sally White), Larry David (communist neighbor), Rebecca Schaeffer (communist's daughter), Belle Berger (Mrs. Sullivan), Guy Le Bow (Bull Kern), Brian Mannain (Kirby Kyle), Stan Burns (ventriloquist), Todd Field (crooner), Danny Aiello (Rocco), Gina DeAngelis (Rocco's mother), Dwight Weist (Pearl Harbor announcer), Jeff Daniels (Biff Baxter), Kitty Carlisle Hart (radio singer), Tony Roberts (Silver Dollar emcee), Ivan Kronenfeld (on-the-spot newsman), Yolanda Childress (Polly's mother), Diane Keaton (New Year's singer), and Woody Allen (narrator)
Music: Jimmy Eaton ("I Double Dare You") and Edward Eliscu ("The Carioca")
Music supervisor: Dick Hyman
Director of photography: Carlo Di Palma
Film editor: Susan E. Morse
Casting: Juliet Taylor
Production design: Santo Loquasto
Art direction: Speed Hopkins
Set decoration: Les Bloom and Carol Joffe
Costume design: Jeffrey Kurland
Production manager: Thomas Reilly
Assistant directors: Ezra Swerdlow and Ken Ornstein (second)
Running time: 85 minutes

September (1987)

Production company/distributor: Rollins-Joffe/Orion
Producers: Robert Greenhut, Charles H. Joffe (executive), Jack Rollins (executive), and Gail Sicilia (associate)
Writing credits: Woody Allen

Cast: Denholm Elliott (Howard), Dianne Wiest (Stephanie), Mia Farrow (Lane), Elaine Stritch (Diane), Sam Waterston (Peter), Jack Warden (Lloyd), Ira Wheeler (Mr. Raines), Jane Cecil (Mrs. Raines), and Rosemary Murphy (Mrs. Mason)
Director of photography: Carlo Di Palma
Film editor: Susan E. Morse
Casting: Juliet Taylor
Production design: Santo Loquasto
Art direction: Speed Hopkins
Set decoration: George DeTitta Jr.
Costume design: Jeffrey Kurland
Production manager: Joseph Hartwick
Assistant directors: Thomas Reilly and Ken Ornstein (second)
Running time: 82 minutes

Another Woman (1988)

Production company/distributor: Rollins-Joffe/Orion
Producers: Robert Greenhut, Charles H. Joffe (executive), Jack Rollins (executive), Thomas Reilly (associate), and Helen Robin (associate)
Writing credits: Woody Allen
Cast: Gena Rowlands (Marion), Mia Farrow (Hope), Ian Holm (Ken), Blythe Danner (Lydia), Gene Hackman (Larry Lewis), Betty Buckley (Kathy), Martha Plimpton (Laura), John Houseman (Marion's father), Sandy Dennis (Claire), David Ogden Stiers (young Marion's father), Philip Bosco (Sam), Harris Yulin (Paul), and Frances Conroy (Lynn)
Music: Johann Sebastian Bach (Unaccompanied Cello Suite in D Major and Sonata for Cello and Piano no. 2, BMV 1028), Jerome Kern ("A Fine Romance" and "Make Believe"), Gustav Mahler (Symphony no. 4), Cole Porter ("You'd Be So Nice to Come Home To"), Erik Satie (third movement from *Trois Gymnopédies*, Debussy version), Edgard Varèse ("Ecuatorial"), and Kurt Weill ("The Bilbao Song")
Director of photography: Sven Nykvist
Film editor: Susan E. Morse
Casting: Juliet Taylor
Production design: Santo Loquasto
Art direction: Speed Hopkins
Set decoration: George DeTitta Jr.
Costume design: Jeffrey Kurland
Production manager: Joseph Hartwick
Assistant directors: Thomas A. Reilly and Ken Ornstein (second)
Running time: 84 minutes

New York Stories: "Oedipus Wrecks" Segment (1989)

Production company/distributor: Rollins-Joffe/Orion and Greenhut/Touchstone Pictures
Producers: Robert Greenhut, Charles H. Joffe (executive), and Jack Rollins (executive)
Writing credits: Woody Allen
Cast: Woody Allen (Sheldon), Marvin Chatinover (psychiatrist), Mae Questel (mother), Mia Farrow (Lisa), and Julie Kavner (Treva)
Director of photography: Sven Nykvist
Film editor: Susan E. Morse
Casting: Juliet Taylor
Production design: Santo Loquasto
Art direction: Speed Hopkins
Set decoration: Susan Bode
Costume design: Jeffrey Kurland
Production manager: Joseph Hartwick
Assistant directors: Thomas Reilly and Judy Ferguson (second)
Visual effects: Nancy Bernstein, Joel Hynek, Stuart Robertson, and Joseph Iannuzzi
Running time: 42 minutes (short film)

Crimes and Misdemeanors (1989)

Production company/distributor: Rollins-Joffe/Orion
Producers: Robert Greenhut, Charles H. Joffe (executive), Jack Rollins (executive), Thomas Reilly (associate), and Helen Robin (associate)
Writing credits: Woody Allen
Cast: Martin Landau (Judah Rosenthal), Claire Bloom (Miriam Rosenthal), Anjelica Huston (Dolores Paley), Woody Allen (Cliff Stern), Jenny Nichols (Jenny), Joanna Gleason (Wendy Stern), Alan Alda (Lester), Sam Waterston (Ben), Mia Farrow (Halley Reed), Martin S. Bergmann (Prof. Louis Levy), and Jerry Orbach (Jack Rosenthal)
Director of photography: Sven Nykvist
Film editor: Susan E. Morse
Casting: Juliet Taylor
Production design: Santo Loquasto
Art direction: Speed Hopkins
Set decoration: Susan Bode
Costume design: Jeffrey Kurland
Production manager: Joseph Hartwick
Assistant directors: Thomas Reilly and Richard Patrick (second)
Running time: 107 minutes

Alice (1990)

Production company/distributor: Rollins-Joffe/Orion
Producers: Robert Greenhut, Charles H. Joffe (executive), Jack Rollins (executive), Joseph Hartwick (coproducer), Helen Robin (coproducer), Jane Read Martin (associate), and Thomas Reilly (associate)
Writing credits: Woody Allen
Cast: Mia Farrow (Alice), Joe Mantegna (Joe), William Hurt (Doug), Julie Kavner (decorator), Holland Taylor (Helen), Keye Luke (Dr. Yang), Judy Davis (Vicki), Cybill Shepherd (Nancy Brill), Alec Baldwin (Ed), Blythe Danner (Dorothy), Gwen Verdon (Alice's mother), Patrick O'Neal (Alice's father), Bernadette Peters (muse), and Elle Macpherson (model)
Director of photography: Carlo Di Palma
Film editor: Susan E. Morse
Casting: Juliet Taylor
Production design: Santo Loquasto
Art direction: Speed Hopkins
Set decoration: Susan Bode
Costume design: Jeffrey Kurland
Production manager: Joseph Hartwick
Assistant director: Thomas Reilly
Visual effects supervisor: Randall Balsmeyer
Running time: 102 minutes

Shadows and Fog (1992)

Production company/distributor: Rollins-Joffe/Orion/Columbia TriStar
Producers: Robert Greenhut, Charles H. Joffe (executive), Jack Rollins (executive), Joseph Hartwick (coproducer), Helen Robin (coproducer), and Thomas Reilly (associate)
Writing credits: Woody Allen
Cast: Woody Allen (Max Kleinman), Mia Farrow (Irmy), John Malkovich (clown), Madonna (Marie), Donald Pleasence (doctor), Lily Tomlin (prostitute), Jodie Foster (prostitute), Kathy Bates (prostitute), Anne Lange (prostitute), John Cusack (student Jack), Kate Nelligan (Eve), Philip Bosco (Mr. Paulsen), Julie Kavner (Alma), Wallace Shawn (Simon Carr), Kenneth Mars (magician), Josef Sommer (priest), David Ogden Stiers (hacker), Camille Saviola (landlady), Tim Loomis (dwarf), Katy Dierlam (fat lady), Dennis Vestunis (strongman), and Michael Kirby (killer)
Music: Kurt Weill (from *Die Dreigroschenoper*)
Director of photography: Carlo Di Palma
Film editor: Susan E. Morse

Casting: Juliet Taylor
Production design: Santo Loquasto
Art direction: Speed Hopkins
Set decoration: George DeTitta Jr. and Amy Marshall
Costume design: Jeffrey Kurland
Production manager: Joseph Hartwick
Assistant directors: Thomas Reilly and Richard Patrick (second)
Visual effects supervisor: Randall Balsmeyer
Running time: 85 minutes

Husbands and Wives (1992)

Production company: Rollins-Joffe/Columbia TriStar
Producers: Robert Greenhut, Charles H. Joffe (executive), Jack Rollins (executive), Thomas Reilly (associate), Joseph Hartwick (coproducer), and Helen Robin (coproducer)
Writing credits: Woody Allen
Cast: Woody Allen (Gabe Roth), Mia Farrow (Judy Roth), Sydney Pollack (Jack), Judy Davis (Sally), Juliette Lewis (Rain), Liam Neeson (Michael), Ron Rifkin (Rain's analyst), Blythe Danner (Rain's mother), and Brian McConnachie (Rain's father)
Director of photography: Carlo Di Palma
Film editor: Susan E. Morse
Casting: Juliet Taylor
Production design: Santo Loquasto
Art direction: Speed Hopkins
Set decoration: Susan Bode
Costume design: Jeffrey Kurland
Production manager: Joseph Hartwick
Assistant directors: Thomas Reilly and Richard Patrick (second)
Running time: 108 minutes

Manhattan Murder Mystery (1993)

Production company: Rollins-Joffe/Columbia TriStar
Producers: Robert Greenhut, Charles H. Joffe (executive), Jack Rollins (executive), Joseph Hartwick (coproducer), Helen Robin (coproducer), and Thomas Reilly (associate)
Writing credits: Woody Allen and Marshall Brickman
Cast: Woody Allen (Larry Lipton), Diane Keaton (Carol Lipton), Jerry Adler (Paul House), Lynn Cohen (Lillian House), Ron Rifkin (Sy), Joy Behar (Marilyn), William Addy (Jack, the super), Alan Alda (Ted), and Anjelica Huston (Marcia Fox)

Director of photography: Carlo Di Palma
Film editor: Susan E. Morse
Casting: Juliet Taylor
Production design: Santo Loquasto
Art direction: Speed Hopkins
Set decoration: Susan Bode
Costume design: Jeffrey Kurland
Production manager: Joseph Hartwick
Assistant directors: Thomas Reilly and Richard Patrick (second)
Running time: 104 minutes

Bullets over Broadway (1994)

Production company: Miramax
Producers: Robert Greenhut, J. E. Beaucaire (executive), Jean Doumanian (executive), Letty Aronson (coexecutive), Charles H. Joffe (coexecutive), Jack Rollins (coexecutive), Thomas Reilly (associate) and Helen Robin (co-producer)
Writing credits: Woody Allen and Douglas McGrath
Cast: John Cusack (David Shayne), Jack Warden (Julian Marx), Dianne Wiest (Helen Sinclair), Tony Sirico (Rocco), Jennifer Tilly (Olive Neal), Rob Reiner (Sheldon Flender), Chazz Palminteri (Cheech), Peter Castellotti (waterfront hood, as Pete Castellotti), Mary-Louise Parker (Ellen), Harvey Fierstein (Sid Loomis), Nina Peterson (Josette, as Nina Sonya Peterson), Edie Falco (Lorna), Jim Broadbent (Warner Purcell), and Tracey Ullman (Eden Brent)
Director of photography: Carlo Di Palma
Film editor: Susan E. Morse
Casting: Juliet Taylor
Production design: Santo Loquasto
Art direction: Tom Warren
Set decoration: Susan Bode and Amy Marshall
Costume design: Jeffrey Kurland
Production managers: Jonathan Filley and Helen Robin
Assistant directors: Thomas Reilly and Richard Patrick (second)
Running time: 98 minutes

Don't Drink the Water (television; 1994)

Production company: Daisy Productions/Magnolia Productions/Sweetland Film Corporation/BVI and Jean Doumanian Productions/ABC
Producers: Robert Greenhut, J. E. Beaucaire (executive), Jean Doumanian (executive), and Letty Aronson (coexecutive)

Writing credits: Woody Allen
Cast: Ed Herlihy (narrator), Josef Sommer (Ambassador Magee), Robert Stanton (Mr. Burns), Edward Herrmann (Mr. Kilroy), Rosemary Murphy (Miss Pritchard), Michael J. Fox (Axel Magee), Woody Allen (Walter Hollander), Julie Kavner (Marion Hollander), Mayim Bialik (Susan Hollander), Austin Pendleton (Chef Oscar), Dom DeLuise (Father Drobney), and Taina Elg (Anna Gruber)
Director of photography: Carlo Di Palma
Film editor: Susan E. Morse
Production design: Santo Loquasto
Art direction: Peter Eastman
Costume design: Suzy Benzinger
Running time: 120 minutes

Mighty Aphrodite (1995)

Production company: Jean Doumanian/Sweetland/Miramax
Producers: Robert Greenhut, J. E. Beaucaire (executive), Jean Doumanian (executive), Letty Aronson (coexecutive), Charles H. Joffe (coexecutive), Jack Rollins (coexecutive), Helen Robin (coproducer), and Thomas Reilly (associate)
Writing credits: Woody Allen
Cast: F. Murray Abraham (Greek chorus leader), Woody Allen (Lenny), Helena Bonham Carter (Amanda), J. Smith-Cameron (Bud's wife), Steven Randazzo (Bud), David Ogden Stiers (Laius), Olympia Dukakis (Jocasta), Jeffrey Kurland (Oedipus), Donald Symington (Amanda's father), Claire Bloom (Amanda's mother), Rosemary Murphy (adoption coordinator), Paul Giamatti (extra guild researcher), Danielle Ferland (Cassandra), Mira Sorvino (Linda Ash), and Jack Warden (Tiresias)
Original music: Dick Hyman
Director of photography: Carlo Di Palma
Film editor: Susan E. Morse
Casting: Juliet Taylor
Production design: Santo Loquasto
Art direction: Tom Warren
Set decoration: Susan Bode
Costume design: Jeffrey Kurland
Production manager: Helen Robin
Production supervisor (Italy): Lucia Comelli
Production managers (Italy): Paolo Pioggia and Michele Virgilio
Assistant directors: Thomas Reilly and Richard Patrick (second)
Running time: 98 minutes

Everyone Says I Love You (1996)

Production company: Jean Doumanian/Sweetland/Miramax
Producers: Robert Greenhut, J. E. Beaucaire (executive), Jean Doumanian (executive), Letty Aronson (coexecutive), Charles H. Joffe (coexecutive), Jack Rollins (coexecutive), and Helen Robin (coproducer)
Writing credits: Woody Allen
Cast: Edward Norton (Holden Spence), Drew Barrymore (Schuyler Dandridge), Alan Alda (Bob Dandridge), Gaby Hoffmann (Lane Dandridge), Natalie Portman (Laura Dandridge), Lukas Haas (Scott Dandridge), Goldie Hawn (Steffi Dandridge), Itzhak Perlman (himself), Navah Perlman (pianist), Julia Roberts (Von), and Woody Allen (Joe Berlin)
Original music: Dick Hyman
Songs: James Campbell Connelly, "If I Had You"; Gus Kahn, "I'm Through with Love"; Gus Kahn and Harry Ruby, "Makin' Whoopee"; Bert Kalmar and Harry Ruby, "Everybody Says I Love You" and "Hooray for Captain Spaulding"; Raymond Klages, "Just You, Just Me"; Matty Malneck, "I'm Through with Love"; Cole Porter, "Looking at You"; Ted Shapiro, "If I Had You"; and Harry M. Woods, "What a Little Moonlight Can Do"
Director of photography: Carlo Di Palma
Film editor: Susan E. Morse
Casting: Juliet Taylor
Production design: Santo Loquasto
Art direction: Tom Warren
Set decoration: Elaine O'Donnell
Costume design: Jeffrey Kurland
Production manager: Helen Robin
Assistant directors: Richard Patrick and Amy Lynn (second)
Special effects: Connie Brink
Visual effects: Randall Balsmeyer
Running time: 101 minutes

Deconstructing Harry (1997)

Production company: Jean Doumanian/Sweetland/Fine Line Features
Producers: Jean Doumanian, J. E. Beaucaire (executive), Letty Aronson (coexecutive), Charles H. Joffe (coexecutive), Jack Rollins (coexecutive), and Richard Brick (coproducer)
Writing credits: Woody Allen
Cast: Caroline Aaron (Doris), Woody Allen (Harry Block), Kirstie Alley (Joan), Bob Balaban (Richard), Richard Benjamin (Ken), Eric Bogosian (Burt), Billy Crystal (Larry), Judy Davis (Lucy), Hazelle Goodman

(Cookie Williams), Mariel Hemingway (Beth Kramer), Amy Irving (Jane), Julie Kavner (Grace), Eric Lloyd (Hilly), Julia Louis-Dreyfus (Leslie), Tobey Maguire (Harvey Stern), Demi Moore (Helen), Elizabeth Shue (Fay), Stanley Tucci (Paul Epstein), Robin Williams (Mel), Philip Bosco (Professor Clark), Gene Saks (Harry's father), and Stephanie Roth (Janet)
Director of photography: Carlo Di Palma
Film editor: Susan E. Morse
Casting: Juliet Taylor
Production design: Santo Loquasto
Art direction: Tom Warren
Set decoration: Susan Kaufman and Elaine O'Donnell
Costume design: Suzy Benzinger
Production manager: Charles Darby
Assistant directors: Richard Patrick and Lisa M. Rowe (second)
Special effects coordinator: John Ottesen
Running time: 96 minutes

Celebrity (1998)

Production company: Miramax
Producers: Jean Doumanian, J. E. Beaucaire (executive), Letty Aronson (coexecutive), Charles H. Joffe (coexecutive), Jack Rollins (coexecutive), and Richard Brick (coproducer)
Writing credits: Woody Allen
Cast: Kenneth Branagh (Lee Simon), Judy Davis (Robin Simon), Joe Mantegna (Tony Gardella), Famke Janssen (Bonnie), Winona Ryder (Nola), Charlize Theron (supermodel), Melanie Griffith (Nicole Oliver), Michael Lerner (Dr. Lupus), Leonardo DiCaprio (Brandon Darrow), Hank Azaria (David), Bebe Neuwirth (Nina), Isaac Mizrahi (Bruce Bishop), Gretchen Mol (Vicky), Donald Trump (himself), Mary Jo Buttafuoco (herself), Joey Buttafuoco (himself), Jeffrey Wright (off-off-broadway director), Kate Burton (Cheryl, Robin's friend), Greg Mottola (director), Dylan Baker (priest at catholic retreat), Andre Gregory (John Papadakis), Patti D'Arbanville (Iris), Allison Janney (Evelyn Isaacs), and Aida Turturro (psychic)
Director of photography: Sven Nykvist
Film editor: Susan E. Morse
Casting: Laura Rosenthal and Juliet Taylor
Production design: Santo Loquasto
Art direction: Tom Warren
Set decoration: Susan Kaufman
Costume design: Suzy Benzinger
Production manager: Charles Darby

Assistant directors: Richard Rosser, Richard Patrick, Marian G. Bostwick (second), Lisa M. Rowe (second), and Peter Lauer (second unit director)
Special effects coordinator: Russell Berg
Visual effects producer: Camille Pirolo Geier
Visual effects supervisor: Ellen Poon
Running time: 113 minutes

Sweet and Lowdown (1999)

Production company: Sweetland/Sony Pictures Classics
Producers: Letty Aronson, Jean Doumanian, J. E. Beaucaire (executive), Charles H. Joffe (coexecutive), and Jack Rollins (coexecutive)
Writing credits: Woody Allen
Cast: Sean Penn (Emmet Ray), Samantha Morton (Hattie), Uma Thurman (Blanche), Brian Markinson (Bill Shields), Anthony LaPaglia (Al Torrio), James Urbaniak (Harry), Gretchen Moll (Ellie), John Waters (Mr. Haynes), Brad Garrett (Joe Bedloe), Woody Allen (himself), Ben Duncan (himself), Daniel Okrent (A. J. Pickman), Dan Moran (boss), Tony Darrow (Ben), Constance Shulman (Hazel, hooker 1), and Kellie Overbey (Iris, hooker 2)
Original music: Dick Hyman
Director of photography: Zhao Fei
Film editor: Alisa Lepselter
Casting: Laura Rosenthal and Juliet Taylor
Production design: Santo Loquasto
Art direction: Tom Warren
Set decoration: Jessica Lanier
Costume design: Laura Cunningham Bauer
Production managers: Richard Brick and Margo Myers
Assistant directors: Richard Patrick, Lisa Janowski (second), Helen Anne Rella (DGA trainee), and Brian York (second)
Running time: 93 minutes

Small-Time Crooks (2000)

Production company: Jean Doumanian/Sweetland
Producers: Jean Doumanian, J. E. Beaucaire (executive), Letty Aronson (coexecutive), Charles H. Joffe (coexecutive), Jack Rollins (coexecutive), and Helen Robin (coproducer)
Writing credits: Woody Allen
Cast: Woody Allen (Ray Winkler), Tracey Ullman (Frances "Frenchy" Winkler), Hugh Grant (David Grant), Elaine May (May Sloan), Michael Rapa-

port (Denny Doyle), Tony Darrow (Tommy Beal), Jon Lovitz (Benny Borkowshi), and George Grizzard (George Blint)
Director of photography: Zhao Fei
Film editor: Alisa Lepselter
Casting: Laura Rosenthal and Juliet Taylor
Production design: Santo Loquasto
Art direction: Tom Warren
Set decoration: Jessica Lanier
Costume design: Suzanne McCabe
Production manager: Helen Robin
Assistant directors: Richard Patrick and Paul F. Bernard (second)
Running time: 94 minutes

The Curse of the Jade Scorpion (2001)

Production company: DreamWorks
Producers: Letty Aronson, Stephen Tenenbaum (executive), Charles H. Joffe (coexecutive), Jack Rollins (coexecutive), Datty Ruth (coexecutive), and Helen Robin (coproducer)
Writing credits: Woody Allen
Cast: John Schuck (Mize), Woody Allen (C. W. Briggs), Helen Hunt (Betty Ann Fitzgerald), Wallace Shawn (George Bond), Dan Aykroyd (Chris Magruder), Vince Giordano (Rainbow Room allstar), and David Ogden Stiers (Voltan Polgar)
Director of photography: Zhao Fei
Film editor: Alisa Lepselter
Casting: Laura Rosenthal and Juliet Taylor
Production design: Santo Loquasto
Art direction: Tom Warren
Set decoration: Jessica Lanier
Costume design: Suzanne McCabe
Production manager: Helen Robin
Production supervisor: Janice Williams
Assistant directors: Sam Hoffman and Joan G. Bostwick (second)
Special effects coordinators: John Ottesen and Ron Ottesen
Running time: 103 minutes

Hollywood Ending (2002)

Production company: DreamWorks
Producers: Letty Aronson, Stephen Tenenbaum (executive), Charles H. Joffe (coexecutive), Jack Rollins (coexecutive), and Helen Robin (coproducer)
Writing credits: Woody Allen

Cast: Woody Allen (Val Waxman), Téa Leoni (Ellie), Treat Williams (Hal Jaeger), George Hamilton (Ed), Debra Messing (Lori Fox), Isaac Mizrahi (Elio Sebastian), Marian Seldes (Alexandra), Tiffani Thiessen (Sharon Bates), Mark Webber (Tony Waxman/scumbag x), Bob Dorian (Galaxie executive), Ivan Martin (Galaxie executive), Gregg Edelman (Galaxie executive), Neal Huff (commercial a.d.), and Mark Rydell (Al Hack)
Director of photography: Wedigo von Schultzendorff
Film editor: Alisa Lepselter
Casting: Laura Rosenthal and Juliet Taylor
Production design: Santo Loquasto
Art direction: Tom Warren
Set decoration: Regina Graves
Costume design: Melissa Toth
Production manager: Helen Robin
Production supervisor: Janice Williams
Assistant directors: Richard Patrick and Danielle Rigby (second)
Running time: 114 minutes

Anything Else (2003)

Production company: DreamWorks/Gravier Productions/Perdido Productions
Producers: Letty Aronson, Benny Medina (executive), Jack Rollins (executive), Stephen Tenenbaum (executive), Charles H. Joffe (coexecutive), and Helen Robin (coexecutive)
Writing credits: Woody Allen
Cast: Jason Biggs (Jerry Faulk), Christina Ricci (Amanda), Woody Allen (David Dobel), Stockard Channing (Paula), Danny DeVito (Harvey), KaDee Strickland (Brooke), Jimmy Fallon (Bob), Fisher Stevens (manager), Anthony Arkin (Pip's comic), Diana Krall (herself), William Hill (psychiatrist), Maurice Sonnenberg (movie-theater patron), Kenneth Edelson (hotel desk clerk), and David Conrad (Dr. Reed)
Director of photography: Darius Khondji
Film editor: Alisa Lepselter
Casting: Laura Rosenthal and Juliet Taylor
Production design: Santo Loquasto
Art direction: Tom Warren
Set decoration: Regina Graves
Costume design: Laura Jean Shannon
Production managers: Helen Robin and Janice Williams
Assistant directors: Adam Howard and Richard Patrick
Running time: 109 minutes

Melinda and Melinda (2005)

Production company: Fox Searchlight Pictures/Perdido Productions
Producers: Letty Aronson, Charles H. Joffe (executive), Jack Rollins (executive), Stephen Tenenbaum (executive), and Helen Robin (coproducer)
Writing credits: Woody Allen
Cast: Will Ferrell (Hobie), Neil Pepe (Al), Stephanie Roth Haberle (Louise), Radha Mitchell (Melinda), Chloë Sevigny (Laurel), Chiwetel Ejiofor (Ellis), Michael J. Farina (man with dog), Josh Brolin (Greg), Jonny Lee Miller (Lee), Wallace Shawn (Sy), Larry Pine (Max), Matt Servitto (Jack), Arija Bareikis (Sally), Brooke Smith (Cassie), Zak Orth (Peter), Andy Borowitz (Doug), and Amanda Peet (Susan)
Director of photography: Vilmos Zsigmond
Film editor: Alisa Lepselter
Casting: Juliet Taylor
Production design: Santo Loquasto
Art direction: Tom Warren
Set decoration: Regina Graves
Costume design: Judy Raskin Howell
Production manager: Helen Robin
Assistant directors: Richard Patrick, Dean Garvin (second), and Kathleen E. Kearney (second)
Running time: 100 minutes

Match Point (2005)

Production companies: British Broadcasting Corporation (BBC), Magic Hour Video, Thema Productions, Invicta Capital Ltd., BBC Films, Jada Productions, and DreamWorks SKG
Producers: Letty Aronson, Lucy Darwin, Gareth Wiley, Jimmy de Brabant (executive), Michael Dounaev (executive), Stephen Tenenbaum (executive), Charles H. Joffe (coexecutive), and Jack Rollins (coexecutive)
Writing credits: Woody Allen.
Cast: Scarlett Johansson (Nola Rice), Jonathan Rhys Meyers (Christopher Wilton), Emily Mortimer (Chloe Wilton), Matthew Goode (Tom Hewett), Brian Cox (Alex Hewett), Penelope Wilton (Eleanor Hewett), and Margaret Tyzack (Mrs. Eastby)
Director of photography: Remi Adefarasin
Film editor: Alisa Lepselter
Casting: Patricia Kerrigan DiCerto, Gail Stevens, and Juliet Taylor
Production design: Jim Clay
Art direction: Tom Warren
Set decoration: Caroline Smith

Costume design: Jill Taylor
Production manager: Tori Perry
Assistant directors: Christopher Newman and Richard Goodwin (second)
Running time: 124 minutes

Scoop (2006)

Production companies: BBC Films, Ingenious Film Partners, Ingenious Media, and Perdido Productions
Producers: Letty Aronson, Gareth Wiley, Stephen Tenenbaum (executive), Charles H. Joffe (coexecutive), Jack Rollins (coexecutive), Helen Robbin (coproducer), and Nicky Kentish Barnes (coproducer)
Writing credits: Woody Allen
Cast: Woody Allen, Scarlett Johansson, Hugh Jackman, Ian McShane, James Nesbitt, Colin Salmon, Kevin McNally (Mike Tinsley), and Jody Halse (bouncer)
Director of photography: Remi Adefarasin
Casting: Patricia Kerrigan DiCerto, Gail Stevens, and Juliet Taylor
Production design: Maria Djurkovic
Art direction: Nick Palmer
Set decoration: Philippa Hart
Assistant director: Samar Pollitt (third)

Index

323

About the Contributors

Maria del Mar Asensio Arostegui is a lecturer in modern English literature at the University of La Rioja, Spain. She has also taught at the University of Zaragoza and is coeditor of the *Journal of English Studies*.

Peter J. Bailey is professor of English at St. Lawrence University at Canton, New York. He is author of *Reading Stanley Elkin* (1985) and *The Reluctant Film Art of Woody Allen* (2001).

Mark E. Bleiweiss, a former editor of the *Jewish Spectator Magazine*, is a rabbi, family counselor, guide, and teacher living in Israel.

Devin Brown is professor of English at Asbury College in Kentucky.

Iris Bruce teaches at McMaster University, Canada, and is an expert on Franz Kafka and Zionist theory as well as German Jewish and Israeli literature.

Bert Cardullo is NEH Distinguished Chair in the Humanities at Colgate University and visiting professor of drama at New York University. He is the author of *In Search of Cinema: Selected Writings on International Film Art*; *Vittorio De Sica: Director, Actor, Screenwriter* (2004); and other books.

Gary Commins is vicar of St. Michael's University Episcopal Church in Isla Vista, California, and Episcopal chaplain at the University of California, Santa Barbara. A graduate of the Church Divinity School of the Pacific, he has written several liturgical dramas and comedies. He also serves on the National Executive Council of the Episcopal Peace Fellowship.

Celestino Deleyto is an associate professor at the University of Zaragoza, Spain, where he teaches film studies and literature. His specialization is in U.S. cinema and film theory.

Michael Dunne is a professor of English at Middle Tennessee State University. His most recent book is *Hawthorne's Narrative Strategies* (1995).

Wes D. Gehring is professor of film at Ball State University and an associate media editor for *USA Today* magazine, for which he also writes the column "Reel World." Gehring is an award-winning author of 22 books, including *Romantic vs. Screwball Comedy*, *Irene Dunne: First Lady of Hollywood*, and *Leo McCarey: From Marx to McCarthy* (all published by Scarecrow Press). His other books include eight volumes of comedy genre criticism. Gehring's articles, comic essays, and poems have appeared in numerous journals.

Louis Giannetti is emeritus professor of English and film at Case Western Reserve University in Cleveland where he taught courses in film, literature, writing, drama, and humanities. He is the author of the best-selling textbook *Understanding Movies*, now in its sixth edition.

Christopher J. Knight is associate professor and chair of the English Department at the University of Montana. His interests are in twentieth-century American literature and critical theory. His latest book is *Uncommon Readers: Denis Donoghue, Frank Kermode, George Steiner, and the Tradition of the Common Reader* (2003).

Ronald D. LeBlanc is professor of Russian and humanities at the University of New Hampshire and center associate for the Davis Center for Russian and Eurasian Studies, Harvard University. His research interests are in history and poetics of the Russian novel and food imagery and eating metaphors in Russian fiction.

Paul Lewis is professor of English at Boston College and the author of *Comic Effects: Interdisciplinary Approaches to Humor in Literature* as well as articles on American literature and culture from 1790 to 1860. His study of post-1980 American humor is forthcoming.

Christopher Morris is professor of English at Norwich University.

Paul Nathanson, a researcher at McGill University's Faculty of Religious Studies, writes about the ambiguous relation between religion and secularity—especially their interface in popular culture. His first book was *Over the Rainbow: The Wizard of Oz as a Secular Myth of America*. Since then, he has published articles not only on other "secular myths" such as *Rebel without a Cause* but also on "secular parables" such as *The Crying Game*. More recently, he has written about a quite different venue of secular religion: political ideologies. This led to "I Feel, Therefore I Am: The Princess of Passion and the Implicit Religion of Our Time" (about public response to the death of Princess Diana) and (with Katherine K. Young) *Spreading Misandry: The Teaching of Contempt for Men in Popular Culture* (about the influence of ideological feminism on popular culture).

Sanford Pinsker is emeritus professor of humanities at Franklin and Marshall College and the author of numerous books and articles on American culture and literature. He currently lives in Ft. Lauderdale, where he continues to write about American culture.

Leonard Quart is professor emeritus of cinema studies at the College of Staten Island and the CUNY Graduate Center. He is a contributing editor to *Cineaste*, contributor to *Film Quarterly*, and coauthor of *The Films of Mike Leigh* (2000) and *American Film and Society* (2002).

Mark W. Roche is the Rev. Edmund P. Joyce, C.S.C., Professor of German Language and Literature at Notre Dame University, where he has taught courses in literature and philosophy as well as in German literature, cultural, and intellectual history and German film. His latest book is *Why Literature Matters in the 21st Century* (2004).

Thomas Schatz is professor of film studies at the University of Texas and the author of *The Genius of the System* (1988).

Ella Shohat is professor of art and public policy at the Tisch School of the Arts. Her major interests are in gender, visual culture, postcolonialism, multiculturalism, and transnationalism. Her latest book is *Talking Visions: Multicultural Feminism in a Transnational Age* (1998).

Diane Snow was a part-time instructor in the Humanities Department at Brigham Young University from 1981 to 1999, when she retired. Along with her husband, she is currently involved in teaching and missionary service in family history for the Church of Jesus Christ of Latter-day Saints.

Robert Stam is professor of cinema studies at New York University. His major interests are in third-world film, U.S. independent film, semiotics, and multiculturalism. He is the coauthor of *Unthinking Eurocentrism* (1994).

Maurice Yacowar taught for twenty-one years at Brock University, Ontario, where he helped to found Canada's first degree program in film studies and served as dean of humanities for seven years. He has published widely in film studies, edited three Criterion laser discs, and is the author of *Loser Take All: The Comic Art of Woody Allen* (1991).

About the Editor

Charles L. P. Silet teaches film in the Department of English at Iowa State University. He has written essays and reviews, conducted interviews, and edited books on a variety of subjects in literature and cultural studies as well as cinema, including *The Films of Steven Spielberg* (Scarecrow, 2002).